THE MELVILLE EFFECT

THE MELVILLE EFFECT

A Literary Afterlife Across the Arts

JOSEPH ALLEN BOONE

Columbia University Press
New York

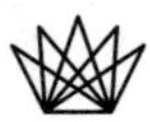

Columbia University Press
Publishers Since 1893
New York Chichester, West Sussex
cup.columbia.edu

Library of Congress Cataloging-in-Publication Data

Names: Boone, Joseph Allen author
Title: The Melville effect : a literary afterlife across the arts / Joseph Allen Boone.
Description: New York : Columbia University Press, 2026. | Includes bibliographical references and index.
Identifiers: LCCN 2025035987 (print) | LCCN 2025035988 (ebook) | ISBN 9780231222198 hardback | ISBN 9780231222204 trade paperback | ISBN 9780231564106 EPUB | 9780231566360 PDF
Subjects: LCSH: Melville, Herman, 1819–1891—Influence | LCGFT: Literary criticism
Classification: LCC PS2388.I52 B66 2026 (print) | LCC PS2388.I52 (ebook)
LC record available at https://lccn.loc.gov/2025035987
LC ebook record available at https://lccn.loc.gov/2025035988

Printed in the United States of America

Cover design: Noah Arlow
Cover image: Christopher Volpe, *Any Human Thing* (detail), 2015. Tar and oil on canvas, 36"×48". Courtesy of the artist.

GPSR Authorized Representative: Easy Access System Europe, Mustamäe tee 50, 10621 Tallinn, Estonia, gpsr.requests@easproject.com

CONTENTS

PREFACE

Sometimes the inspiration leading to our book projects is entirely straightforward; we become fascinated with a particular question or problem and begin the research that results in an argument and a book. Sometimes that path is less straightforward. In the case of *The Melville Effect*, one might say I entered this subject through the back door.

My interest in manifestations of Melville in contemporary art—innovative reenvisionings that, as I'll be arguing in the following pages, are occurring across multiple genres, media, and platforms with astonishing velocity—was spiked not by an intellectual question but by my participation in my own act of creative remediation. As a junior in college, I'd been assigned Melville's *The Confidence-Man, His Masquerade* in an advanced American literature class. Within seconds, I began imagining the potential of this proto-postmodernist puzzle of a novel as a piece of edgy theater. A small spiral notebook with a mottled green cover served as the repository for my ideas as I began sketching out possibilities for a dramatic adaptation that would be (so I dared presume) as self-reflexive, politically resonant, and seductively entertaining as I found the novel. Not only did Melville's adherence to the classical dramatic unities—one setting (a riverboat on the Mississippi), one day (from dawn to midnight), and one sustained action (a man's repeated cons)—render it eminently suited for the stage, but, so it occurred to me, it would present a golden opportunity for the actor who gets to play the title character as he transforms from unnamed deaf-mute prophet to legless Black Guinea to suave cosmopolitan. And if the novel were rendered a musical, what better setting than a riverboat to deconstruct the tradition of the modern American musical that began with *Showboat*, exposing the latter's sanitized treatment of themes such as race and sexuality?

It took three decades—and an unforeseen accident—to bring this germ of an idea to fruition. The unexpected event was the delay by several weeks of a shipment of academic books and research materials that I'd mailed to the Bellagio Foundation in Italy well ahead of a month-long residency (ironically enough, the box had been held at customs under the suspicion of being illegal contraband!). Unable to work on my scholarly project and having a copy of Melville's novel on hand, I set about writing the first draft of the book and lyrics for *CONMAN: A Musical Apocalypse*. Serendipity continued to foster the project when, after the residency, my brother Benjamin, a composer and jazz saxophonist, joined me in Paris. During a fire-alarm evacuation at our hotel, he began reading the script as we waited outside, and, sax in hand, he picked out some lyrics that grabbed his attention and composed "The Price of Vice," a song that he premiered the following day at a gig outside the Abbey Bookshop on the Left Bank. Two summers later, we were granted joint residencies at the Valparaiso Foundation in Spain to work on the musical; these efforts culminated in a workshop with the Riverside Opera Ensemble at New York University in 2005 and a production in Los Angeles in 2011.[1]

It was only when the final curtain came down that I asked myself: Who else these days is using Melville as a source of creative inspiration? That's when my eyes were opened to the world of all things Melvillean. Gradually, I became aware of the veritable explosion in contemporary artistic endeavors making Melville their fulcrum—an explosion that began in the mid-1990s and continues unabated to this day. I also learned about a much longer history of creative endeavors inspired by Melville since his reclamation from near anonymity in the 1920s. While that longer history contributes to the contemporary creative fascination with Melville, I argue that today's reenvisionings manifest an energy and effects that are unique; these remediations have created a distinctive force field that reflects, participates in, and is shaping contemporary aesthetics and their relation to the humanities and culture at large. For over roughly the past twenty-five years, an unprecedented number of artists working in multiple and mixed genres have made Melville their touchstone as they engage in often daring, form-breaking creative endeavors. This upswell reaches across the globe, involving myriad nationalities, ethnicities, and identities; they include famous and obscure artists, some at the beginning of their careers, others working collaboratively, many invested in redefining what counts as "art" and expanding its reach and reception. In illuminating the ways in which Melville's literary legacy continues to resonate, these responses suggest an alternative genealogy of literary and artistic reception and transmission, just as this book proposes an alternative critical method through which to approach this once-neglected, now canonized, ever enigmatic author.

Alongside these responses, the circulation of "Melville" as a meme in popular culture has reached new heights. Likewise, Melville scholarship is flourishing as never before as it embraces fresh approaches and brings to light archives that recast prior understandings of the author. Some of the artists investigated here are cognizant of these scholarly developments—several have participated in Melville conferences and events—but in general these creative endeavors have occurred alongside but independent of the academy, though this doesn't mean they are any the less theoretically informed. While my research has included this new scholarship, and while it has attempted to keep track of the seemingly endless proliferation of pop-cultural references to Melville, this book focuses its energies on those aesthetically stimulating, full-fledged creative remediations that have been gathering velocity since the mid-1990s, asking what they might tell us about art, the humanities, and culture today. These reenvisionings hail Melville's presence or body of work in any number of suggestive ways: as muse, as source of inspiration or instigation, as springboard to something entirely original, as coconspirator, as spur to trenchant political critique, as guide to the lower frequencies. This fervor of creativity, I suggest, forms a cultural event in itself. If the first Melville revival of the 1920s was largely the work of scholars introducing the author to a new readership, we are now experiencing a robust second Melville revival activated by the constellation of artists making up what I call "the Melville effect."

As my research made me more and more aware of the extent and depth of this phenomenon, I found myself focusing on two questions that have served as guiding principles for this book: Why *Melville*? And why Melville *now*? Those literary figures who have served as beacons for inspired adaptations in multiple genres, from Shakespeare to Charlotte Brontë, generally evince a certain porousness, a suggestiveness, a breadth of allusion that allows their writings (and often their authorial personae) to be updated, alchemized into expressions of a given epoch's cultural and aesthetic concerns, more easily than the work of their contemporaries. They are authors who, like Melville, probe "the little lower layer[s]" beneath the "pasteboard masks" of appearances,[2] the realm of the visible, and this commitment to expressing the inexpressible has a special appeal to modern artists with serious or nonmainstream artistic aspirations. To the degree that a name such as "Shakespeare" or "Brontë" or "Melville" becomes widely recognizable in the larger culture—often condensed to tags or mythemes ("to be or not to be," "the madwoman in the attic," "the white whale"), the author gains a signifying ubiquity that exceeds the general public's specific knowledge of the work at hand.[3]

That said, ever since the Melville renaissance in the early decades of the twentieth century, there has been something *especially* galvanizing about this iconoclastic writer's "way of flashing into relevance at every new cultural-political conjunction," as Daniel Hoffman-Schwartz puts it.[4] Part of the contemporaneity ensuring Melville's continuing afterlives owes to the exceptional degree to which his ponderings anticipated today's urgent social issues, including ones concerning gender, sexuality, race, class, transnationality, globalism, the environment, and the nonhuman. This troubled, complicated, contradictory author's deep dives into these equally troubling, complicated, contradictory issues have been heralded as forward-thinking or visionary by his advocates and taken to task as politically regressive by his critics, but in both cases the *prescient* quality of Melville's thinking goes unquestioned, lending an aura of "permanent contemporaneity" to our retrospective encounters with his works.[5]

And why Melville *now*? In large part, this affinity has to do not just with the relevance of the subjects he tackles but with his openness to the rapidly evolving modes of media characterizing mid-nineteenth-century culture at large. Take his polyglot mix of genres and media, his messy embrace of aesthetic hybridity, his reveling in diverse points of view: These elements may have resulted in his marginalization by the arbiters of literary taste in his day, but the same qualities make him a touchstone for contemporary artists to whom pastiche, collage, mash-ups, mixed media, and technological savvy are now the norm rather than the exception. Like Melville, these artists are keenly aware of and receptive to the technological advances that are making possible new forms of artistic expression that reflect today's global culture in its diversity and messiness.

The Melville effect, then, is expressive of a collective spirit specific to the present moment. This explosion of imaginative energy and risk-taking, as we will see, illuminates the shifting, ever-evolving horizons of the humanities and culture—indeed, sheds light on the meaning of "art" in the twenty-first century. In turn, the interplay among Melville, his legacies, his afterlives, and contemporary culture illuminates the role that literary history continues to play in imaginative work (countering the fears of those who lament the disregard of literary tradition among younger generations): These Melvillean reenvisionings and remixings bring literary history into the living, breathing, unsettled present and simultaneously make Melville's afterlives a portal through which to glimpse future directions in art and culture.

Before proceeding with more specifics, I'd like to acknowledge some debts. Whatever is original or enlightening in this book could not have been written without the indefatigable efforts of two stalwart Melville scholars—Elizabeth Schultz and Robert K. Wallace—who have dedicated their careers to tracking down, with vigor and critical generosity, artists influenced by Melville ever since his rediscovery in the early twentieth century. Schultz's landmark book *Unpainted to the Last:* Moby-Dick *and Twentieth-Century American Art* (1995), supplemented by her monograph-length essay "The New Art of *Moby-Dick*"

(2019), deftly analyzes the works of nearly every artist rendering Melvillean themes in visual form—whether realistically, as in myriad illustrations of editions of *Moby-Dick*; abstractly, as in Jackson Pollack's and Robert Motherwell's paintings; or playfully postmodern, as in Vali Myer's art and Frank Stella's sculptures. Wallace has produced equally profound commentaries on Melville and the visual arts, including *Melville and Turner* (1992) and *Frank Stella's* Moby-Dick (2002). Schultz's and Wallace's efforts have not been limited to pictorial art and sculpture; in numerous essays, both scholars have uncovered Melville's imprint in staged adaptations, songs, performance art, and opera. The thoroughness with which this duo has demonstrated Melville's century-long influence on artists has been foundational to my efforts in this book.

What differentiates the scope and thrust of *The Melville Effect* from the work of scholars such as Schultz and Wallace is, first, its focus on more contemporary remediations; second, its theorizing of the implications that make these recent endeavors a phenomenon worthy of sustained analysis; and, third, its tracking of the aesthetic, analytical, and psychological affinities with which these artists imbue Melville's afterlives. Moving across and mixing multiple platforms, overlapping and extending one another's effects, these reenvisionings collectively contribute to a zeitgeist distinct from earlier twentieth-century acts of homage, emulation, and adaptation. The effects generated by this artistic outpouring travel in multiple directions, forming—and here I draw on the vocabulary of Gilles Deleuze and Félix Guattari, taken up in more detail in chapter 1—part-objects in an assemblage that disrupts linear conceptions of time and space, of literary past and present, in telling ways. Whereas much of the Melville-influenced work produced throughout the twentieth century was understood as expressive of American culture and identity, the reenvisionings taking place now are global in their reach.

A few clarifications are in order before I outline the chapters that follow. First, despite my deep appreciation of Melville—dating back to a seminar I took with the inimitable Merton Sealts my first year in graduate school—I'm not a Melville scholar, nor, for that matter, am I a diehard enthusiast of all things Melvillean. I've always marveled at those scholars who devote their careers to a single literary figure, be it Shakespeare or Joyce, faithfully attending the annual conferences, keeping abreast of the latest scholarship, becoming intimates in the pursuit of "knowing" the object of their dedication inside and out. Perhaps because of my training as a specialist in the novel as genre, my interests have always been too widespread to focus on a single figure—there are all too many works by novelists I admire that I have yet to read. Melville is an exception in my case, thanks to Professor Sealts's tutelage: We read *everything*, from entries in *The Melville Log* to every line of *Clarel*. This intense immersion, however, occurred decades ago, and as deeply as I've tried to update myself by diving into Melville criticism while working on this book, I've only scraped the surface. For all that I have yet to learn, I beg the forbearance of those dedicated Melville scholars.

Nevertheless, I trust *The Melville Effect* offers new perspectives that will engage these scholars as well as appeal to any reader intrigued by this author, his many afterlives, and the contemporary artists who have made his creations the springboard for such exciting work. This hope ties to a second clarification worth making: *The Melville Effect* does not necessarily offer original readings of Melville's works—that isn't its intent. Rather, I hope to shed light on those Melvillean remediations engaged in creative rereadings of "Melville" that *do* offer new perspectives from which we all might learn. The quotation marks placed around Melville's name in the previous sentence signal the degree to which this "Melville" comprises both the work at hand (most often but not always *Moby-Dick*) as well as the accumulated cultural constructions of author and output that have proliferated for the past one hundred years, creating a composite entity to which these present-day creators are also responding. Learning about, appreciating, and interpreting these Melville-inflected works thus stand to enrich our ongoing encounters with Melville and his afterlives.

A third clarification has to do with my title. Why not, one of the press's readers for this manuscript asked, call your book *The Moby Dick Effect* rather than *The Melville Effect*? I resisted the suggestion for several reasons. Yes, it is certainly true that Melvillean references in popular culture continue to be almost exclusively to *Moby-Dick* the book and Moby Dick the whale.[6] But within the constellation of creative work formed by the Melville effect, the fact is that *Moby-Dick* is not the only Melvillean text serving to inspire these contemporary remediations. Hence, my fifth chapter's attention to numerous reenvisionings of *Pierre* and *Billy Budd*. Another chapter could easily have been dedicated to works inspired by *The Confidence-Man* (including two musicals, a solo performance, and an immersive enactment on a ship docked in the Hudson), and I've come across a handful of creative takes on "Bartleby" (the phrase "I prefer not" has become another cultural meme that now signifies in excess of the text itself).[7] Finally, as we will see in chapter 3, several novelists are as interested in Melville the person as in any of his specific works. In sum, the energies emanating from the force field that is the Melville effect supersede *Moby-Dick*, however central that novel remains as a gateway to this phenomenon.[8]

Among these many effects, I focus on five tropes—fictionality, gender, scale, perversity, ecology—that thread through and connect the artifacts I have chosen to analyze. To set the stage for these case-studies, chapter 1, "Sounding the Melville Effect," introduces the theoretical perspectives and methodological approaches that buttress my inquiry. Deleuze and Guattari's figure of the horizontally spreading rhizome—as opposed to a hierarchically branching structure—is particularly suggestive; the figure not only speaks to the mobile assemblage of part-objects that is the Melville effect but also has affinities with Melville's mixed or "higgledy-piggledy" aesthetics.[9] It also has affinities with the heterogeneous cultural landscape in which Melville came of age as a writer as well as with the tributaries contributing to the Melville revival of the 1920s. Another figure for this hybrid aesthetics comes from Melville: the patchwork or crazy quilt. Together these figures lend themselves to a consideration of the way in which literary history is transtemporal, past and present meshing in the remediations that grant Melville—and "Melville"—his afterlives and contemporaneity.

Chapter 2, "Multimedia Melville, Messy Culture, Contemporary Remediations," continues to introduce today's Melville effect—first, by outlining the crazy blend of genres on which Melville's prose fiction draws and, second, by finding parallels between his formal experimentation and the explosion of new media and modes of popular and highbrow entertainment rife in the nineteenth century. The chapter ends with examples of mixed-media artwork inventively riffing on Melville and repurposing for our times both his hybrid aesthetics and his openness to proliferating genres and media. The examples offered in this chapter form a primer for reading the case studies that constitute chapters 3 through 7.

The sequencing and logic of chapters 3 through 7 are straightforward. First, I begin with those remediations that have the most in common with Melville's mode of production, the written word: namely, contemporary fiction that channels Melville. Nearly three dozen such novels have appeared since the late 1990s. These texts are the subject of chapter 3, "Whence the Novel? Measuring the Melville Effect in Post-Postmodernist Fiction," which speculates on emergent trends in fiction—including the move toward what critics have dubbed "post-postmodernism"—as well as on the future of the (page-bound) novel. I focus on five examples: Sena Jeter Naslund's *Ahab's Wife*, which revives a Melville character; Frederick Busch's *The Night Inspector*, which gives fictional life to Melville himself; and novels by Mark Behr, Marianne Wiggins, and Chad Harbach that make Melvillean themes and tropes newly relevant for contemporary discussions of race, sexuality, and the American dream. The most successful of these novels offer something more important than perennial if not very productive musings about the "next" Great American Novel (a status often accorded to *Moby-Dick*), instead illuminating the ways in which literary history might be viewed as a living force that constantly reinforms and renews itself, sidestepping chronological understandings of temporality or history in its nonlinear recombinations of past, present, and future.

If chapter 3 takes up the most obvious means of channeling Melville, chapter 4 looks at the issue that seems to have galvanized the greatest number of contemporary remediations, the question of gender, despite the fact that Melville is generally associated with all-male worlds and has been taken to task for his relative neglect of women characters. Chapter 4, "Whalebone, Hoop Skirts, Corsets, and Pants Roles: Women and Melville in Contemporary Art," brings together three works in which a consideration of whalebone hoop skirts and corsets threads together nineteenth-century constructions of femininity, the brutal economies of the whaling industry, that century's gendering of material labor, and contemporary feminist aesthetics. The three vehicles for this meditation include a monumental collage series by the artist T. L. Solien in which images of Ahab's hoop-skirted wife float across ocean, land, and history, revising readings of the American quest romance and doctrines of Manifest Destiny; the dream play/movement piece *Ahab's Wife* by artist Ellen Driscoll and poet Thomas Sleigh, in which a gigantic hoop skirt serves multiple stage functions; and composer Rinde Eckert's *And God Created Great Whales*, a multimedia production in which a corseted Muse rewrites the masculinist script and score of a monomaniacal composer struggling to finish his operatic adaptation of *Moby-Dick* before dementia overwhelms him.

This focus on the material body paves the way in chapter 5, "Size Matters," for the consideration of a different mode of materiality—that of art projects in which scale and size have philosophical and aesthetic implications. Several contemporary artists sharing in the Melville effect have launched long-term projects that repeat Ahab's obsession with the White Whale, ensuing in works of expanding dimensions and volume. "Size Matters" delves into this phenomenon, first by reviewing Edmund Burke's ruminations on monumental sublimity and then by looking at recent examinations of our culture's enduring "obsession with obsession" to query the myths and aesthetic predilections that for centuries have equated size with artistic genius. Next, the chapter analyzes two midcentury artists compulsively obsessed with Melville—the impresario Orson Welles and the muralist Gilbert Wilson—to contrast their attitudes toward monumentality and artistic genius with the contemporary examples that follow. Among the multiple examples examined here, Frank Stella has spent decades creating gigantic artworks for each of *Moby-Dick*'s 135 chapters; Robert Del Tredici's hundreds of artworks illustrating specific passages have moved through several distinct phases over a half century; Matt Kish worked 552 days without stopping to create a mixed-media painting per day for every page of his edition of the novel. "Size Matters" ultimately ponders the creative freedom and ambition that artists have found in the practice of amateurism, as opposed to traditional ideas equating "genius" and "size."

In contrast to tangible art projects occupying physical space, chapter 6, "Perverse Melville and the Sub-Sub's Queer Investments," turns to the intangible realm of the psyche, pondering a variety of contemporary figures inspired by the strains of polymorphous perversity that they find haunting Melville's representations. Melville's controversial (and ridiculed) novel *Pierre, or the Ambiguities* and posthumous (and celebrated) novella *Billy Budd* become lodestones for the contemporary endeavors assembled in this chapter, ranging from critical work that amounts to a creative "rewriting" of *Pierre* to illustrations in a modern edition of *Pierre* (a controversial rewriting of the novel) that bring its unspoken sexual subtexts to the surface. The second half of the chapter turns to two highly experimental French films that bear the marks of their auteur-minded director-writers—one repositioning *Pierre* in a contemporary Paris beset by urban terrorists, the other relocating *Billy Budd* to a legionnaire base in modern-day Djibouti.

Leaving behind the realm of the human psyche for the world of the nonhuman, chapter 7, "Plastic Seas, Pasteboard Masks, Planetary Futures," investigates Melville's relevance for environmental studies, examining texts as disparate as Donovan Hohn's quest-memoir *Moby-Duck* (recounting the migration of plastic bath toys across the globe's oceans as they join the ocean's vast garbage heaps), mixed-media visual art (including Esteban Ruiz's eco-architectural whale grids, Jos Sances's gigantic scratchboard *Or, the Whale*, and Christopher Volpe's tar-and-oil paintings), installation/video/film mash-ups (mayfield brooks's *Whale Fall* and Wu Tsang's *Moby Dick; or, The Whale*), and experimental documentary film (Véréna Paravel and Lucien Castaing-Taylor's *Leviathan*). In these works, industry's waste products, species depletion, and planetary yearnings find an ally in Melville's prophetic words and work.

These chapters trace an arc that reaches from the world building of fiction to the realities of our planet in crisis. They increase incrementally in size until the final chapter, which engages artists working at the very cusp of futurity, where so much is still undetermined and evolving. From the relative comfort of the generically familiar—the novel form—to the avant-garde urgency of environmentalist artists facing grave unknowns, these remediations bestow on Melville any number of afterlives. Their diffusive effects are as significant as Melville proves prescient in the shaping of today's art and culture.

CHAPTER 1

SOUNDING THE MELVILLE EFFECT

Methods and Theory

I try all things.
—Ishmael in *Moby-Dick*

A rhizome has no beginning or end, it is always in the middle, between things, interbeing, intermezzo.
—Gilles Deleuze and Félix Guattari, *A Thousand Plateaus*

Genius is full of trash.
—Babbalanja in Herman Melville, *Mardi*

Just look around, and you'll find traces of Herman Melville anywhere and everywhere in contemporary art and culture these days. Since 2004, nearly three dozen novels have explicitly used Melville as their springboard, and the majority of them have appeared since 2010. From 2009 to 2019, major operas hailing from Germany, Poland, and the United States have used cutting-edge digital technology to breathtaking visual effects to enhance their vocal and instrumental approximations of Melville's epic ambitions.[1] In just the past decade, hundreds of paintings and sculptures have translated

Melville's words into the alternative languages of color, shape, and texture. Inventive and idiosyncratic reenvisionings abound in video installations, performance, dance, theater, orchestral pieces, musicals, and mixed-media productions. From rap songs to digital mashups to emoji translation, the nineteenth-century author's influence has been making itself felt in art forms both high and popular since the dawn of the twenty-first century and doing so at break-neck speed. On the coffee table of my living room, the party game *DICK* (2015), in which sexually suggestive questions posed by the Dick Judge are answered with cards on which appear equally suggestive phrases taken from *Moby-Dick* ("a very strange, enigmatical object"), sits beside *Moby-Dick: A Babylit Ocean Primer* (2014), a volume marked for "ages three years and under." A friendly whale beams a smile from its soft cover. If the game *DICK* might have brought a smirk to Melville's face, the kiddie-friendly primer bearing the name of his masterpiece would no doubt have left him incredulous.

In short, our twenty-first century is in the midst of a heady Melville revival that shows no signs of abating and that rivals what literary critics refer to as the first Melville revival—the recovery of the nineteenth-century author from near obscurity in the 1920s, a movement culminating in his enshrinement as one of America's greatest writers of all time. Working in various genres and media, these savvy, often cutting-edge creative artists find themselves motivated and challenged by Melville's hybrid aesthetics and authorial daring. Some have adapted Melville's work directly, rendering texts such as *Moby-Dick*, "Bartleby," *Billy Budd*, and *Pierre* into narrative genres including drama, opera, and film; some transport his plots or characters into contemporary settings and present-day idioms; some channel his spirit; others import Melvillean tropes and themes to enrich subjects as disparate as apartheid in South Africa, urban terrorism in Paris, and baseball in the heartland of America. For three decades, an overwhelming number of artists have made this presciently innovative creator a source of inspiration, a launching point, a muse, a coconspirator, a conduit, a spur for self-critique.

When considered—as I suggest in my preface—as a multifaceted cultural event, this efflorescence of creative interest forms what I call the "Melville effect," and this effect illuminates the shifting horizons of art and the humanities in a world where creative energies are increasingly shaped by the ongoing, present-day explosion in new forms of media, multimedia, and digital technology. Many of the creative interventions composing the Melville effect are examples of mixed media or multimedia; and even those works that do not explicitly incorporate multiple genres or combine media often use pastiche, collage, recombination, bricolage, or, in contemporary parlance, sampling to create richly layered and often innovative artifacts. Numbering among the effects generated by this upsurge of contemporary fascination with Melville are changing conceptions of audience and authorship as well as evolving definitions of the art object—indeed, of the object of art itself. Ultimately, I suggest that the interplay between Melville and contemporary culture invites us to reconsider how we do literary history and how twenty-first-century humanities might better engage the past to bring that history into vibrant contact with present and future horizons.

Then and Now: Transtemporal Affinities

Asking why Melville has emerged *now* as the nexus for such creative fervor, *The Melville Effect* argues that many of these contemporary artists build upon their feelings of an intuitive affinity with both the issues Melville explored and his aesthetic experimentations. Melville has always seemed ahead of his time, both as an artist and as a thinker. His texts appear prophetic in their ability to speak to contemporary concerns in ways that one might not have guessed even a decade ago. As Daniel Hoffman-Schwartz observes in his introduction to the essay collection *Handsomely Done: Aesthetics, Politics, and Media After Melville* (2019), "Melville's writings have a permanent contemporaneity." The essays in this collection illustrate this peculiar ability "to be updated," to become relevant all over again, extending from the use of *Benito Cereno* to make sense of the Attica prison uprisings to group readings of "Bartleby" during the Occupy Wall Street movement.[2] Ever since the early days of the Melville revival, of course, critics have been eager—sometimes too eager—to read *Moby-Dick* as a political allegory of their era; hence, the myriad World War II and Cold War associations of Ahab with fascism and totalitarianism and the number of newspaper editorials linking Ahab's hubris to that of U.S. presidents from the first Bush to Trump.[3] If you haven't looked at *Moby-Dick* in a while, take a moment to reread its opening chapters: You might be surprised at the novel's uncanny ability to anticipate nearly all of today's hot-button issues, from race relations, cultural diversity, and globalism (note the international range of people roaming the streets of "provincial" New Bedford and Nantucket) to disability (Ahab with his missing limb is only one of Melville's many disabled figures) to environmentalism, animal rights, and the status of the nonhuman (Ishmael makes the possible extinction of the whale species the subject of chapter 105).[4]

If these social issues underline Melville's continuing significance for today's artists, so too his evolving aesthetics and formal explorations contribute to his contemporary appeal, as noted in the preface. In an age agog with new modes of media, communication, and entertainment, Melville's facility in transgressing generic boundaries, eclectically mixing forms, and incorporating new forms of media proves to be both inspiring and timely to twenty-first-century artists working in and across multiple modes of media. Indeed, it is the "intense mediality" that is *already* present in Melville's writing, along with his engagement with "the mediality of literature itself," that renders his work so receptive an "object of translation and adaptation" by contemporary artists and thinkers.[5] Obviously, Melville's creative inventiveness was restricted to the medium of the written word, but his texts are nonetheless notoriously promiscuous assemblages that draw on innumerable literary forms as well as on an encyclopedic mix of textual sources: novel, romance, travelogue, anatomy, poetry, scripted dialogue, visual placards, Shakespearean soliloquy, scientific taxonomy, essay, satire, sermon, song lyrics. It's no wonder that the media scholar Henry Jenkins sees Melville as the top "mash-up" artist of his century and that Hoffman-Schwartz finds Melville's work striated with rich "anticipations of our media epoch."[6] This hybrid aesthetics is both a sign of Melville's inventiveness *and* the product of his resourcefulness in tapping into the spirit of his times, an age in which expanding forms of new media and multiplying forms of entertainment flooded the public sphere, creating a cultural landscape in many ways as messy, stimulating, and unpredictable as our own.

In addition to this conjunction of cultural-political relevance and forward-looking aesthetics, Melville's appeal for many contemporary artists, I suspect, lies in their identification with his ambitions, his war on convention, and his failure to gain recognition (despite his genius) when his early success as the writer of popular travel tales waned—all of which characteristics contribute to the evolving "composite entity, 'Melville,' shaped by the assumptions readers bring to the text."[7] For artists inspired by Melville's ambitions, MacArthur-winning Rinde Eckert's comment about his operatic performance piece *And God Created Great Whales* is representative: "So I suppose mine is no different than anyone else's paean to Melville for having created this extraordinary work that inspires us to our own brilliance."[8] While the Melville effect includes lauded artists such as Eckert, whose inspired remediations have only solidified their already considerable critical acclaim, less recognized or neglected artists may find a different source of kinship in Melville, one closer to commiseration: Here is an artistic genius whose best work was maligned by the general public and critics alike and who died all but forgotten—a fate many struggling artists fear awaits their own ignored efforts. Unsung though Melville might have been at the end of his life, he's had the last word, a fact that may give some of today's undervalued artists comfort as well as inspiration to continue striving despite the odds.

No doubt Melville's defiance of the expectations of the marketplace and his refusal to bend to moral or aesthetic orthodoxies also add to his luster for today's artists similarly chafing against convention or popular tastes. In a letter to his publisher in 1848, Melville expressed his frustration with those who wished him to continue "plodding along with dull common places" when all he yearned to do was stretch himself creatively, "to plume my powers for flight."[9] This author's desire to follow his own path, whatever the cost, has, as Alex Calder notes, always resonated strongly with Romantic-rebel and avant-garde artists who have felt themselves at odds with the status quo.[10] *Deviance prestige*: This is Craig Bernardini's apt term, in an analysis of the heavy-metal band Mastodon's Melville-influenced album *Leviathan* (2004), for those artists who take pride in their marginalization, seeing their difference from the mainstream as a badge of honor and sign of authenticity.[11] For a writer who—as we will see in chapter 6—gleefully and even self-destructively embraced the perverse, Melville epitomizes the "deviant prestige" of the neglected genius for many struggling artists today.

And yet: Such overidentification with Melville's "extraordinary" genius and his defiance as artist—echoed in his grandiose ambitions as he prepares to plume his "powers for flight"—is not unproblematic, especially from a post-structuralist perspective. As deconstructive philosophy has made clear, romanticized attributions of and aspirations to "genius" or artistic "originality" buttress a universalizing metaphysics that is as suspect as culture's need to identify and venerate the selected few deemed worthy of inclusion in the canon of Greats. True enough, some artists participating in the Melville effect, especially in their personal statements, seem to treat Melville with the awe bestowed on a rock star. But an equal number engage with his work critically, finding in its limitations and lacunae the inspiration for their own engagements with and transvaluations of his writings, aesthetics, and politics. As becomes apparent in the chapters that follow, the act of "identifying with" certain aspects of Melville—his sense of alienation from his culture, his angst at feeling that his talents have gone unrecognized, his daring to say "NO! in thunder" to stifling social and artistic norms—does not always translate into an authorial or artistic desire for "fame" or "immortality," those other words often linked with that of genius.[12] It sometimes translates into creatively productive affinities.

Finally, Melville's belief in art's necessary if inevitably doomed struggle to illuminate the mysteries that lie on the other side of the "pasteboard mask" of reality clouding human perception, to hint at significances that transcend language's limits, speaks to any number of artists who have inherited a postmodernist worldview grounded in the limits of representation. "Melville understood so well what we artists owe to doubt," the visual artist Claire Illouz writes of her own affinity for Melville. "The essence of things, which we try to capture by looking at them, is invisible. . . . [To] bring that essence to view . . . is a fight. It often escapes, hiding like some forbidden creature, leaving you desperate."[13] For Illouz, the elusive, "forbidden creature" forever lurking beneath the visible surface is, as for many participants in the Melville effect, her personal White Whale: that which art can never fully capture or convey.

To comprehend the degree to which the Melville effect emerging from these affinities forms a phenomenon specific to the present moment, it's helpful to recall the formation of that earlier zeitgeist, the Melville revival of the 1920s.

Recent scholarship has chiseled away at the myth of Melville's rediscovery and unprecedented rise in fame as the single-handed achievement of a group of American critics eager to promote a national literature in the 1920s.[14] Nonetheless, as Brian Yothers puts it, "there is no evading the fact that something special happened in the development of Melville's literary reputation" in the decade following World War I, beginning with the notice brought about by his centenary in 1919, swiftly followed by the advocacy of influential American cultural critics such as Carl Van Doren and Van Wyck Brooks, and punctuated by the appearance of full-scale biographies by Raymond Weaver and Lewis Mumford in 1921 and 1929, respectively. By 1926, the British biographer John Freeman's declaration that Melville was nineteenth-century America's most powerful writer was already a commonplace.[15] Oxford University Press's publication of *Moby-Dick* in its World Classics series in 1920 and of *The Complete Works of Herman Melville* in 1922 also attests to the author's meteoric rise to canonical status—again, a remarkable explosion of interest in a writer hitherto largely unknown and unread. Weaver's discovery of the manuscript of *Billy Budd* among Melville's papers and publication of the novella in 1924 generated even more excitement about this newly "rediscovered" author. F. O. Matthiessen's inclusion of Melville among the elites in his monumental work *American Renaissance* in 1941 completed this initial phase of rendering Melville an exemplar of enlightened literary nationalism. Add to this capstone the auctioning of the English first edition of *The Whale* for $1,575 in 1935 and the fact that by 1947 more than half-a-million copies of *Moby-Dick* had entered circulation in the United States, and the success of the Melville revival in making the nineteenth-century author an object of critical and popular renown is obvious.[16]

Belying this "seemingly miraculous rebound" from obscurity, however, a series of *almost* revivals predating the 1920s, indicates, as Yothers also notes, that despite popular mythology Melville was "never completely forgotten."[17] Adam Fales and Jordan Alexander Stein have pointed to the critical role that Melville's widow, Elizabeth, played in ensuring that four of the sea novels were reissued in 1892, and their sales vied with purchases made during Melville's lifetime.[18] And even before Melville's death, as Maki Sadahiro documents, a revival of interest in Melville was underway in England among the Pre-Raphaelite Brotherhood and the Christian socialist workingmen's movement, whose politics influenced those Young American critics who became Melville's greatest champions in the 1920s.[19] Likewise, a number of English writers interested in sea fiction touted their enthusiasm for the author long before the 1920s revival, as did turn-of-the-century homophiles on both sides of the Atlantic, intrigued by the homoerotic currents they perceived in his work.[20] In New England, moreover, a "regional" Melville boom had persisted from the time of his death, hailing him as a local luminary.[21] Thus, the fervor leading to Melville's elevation to the status of perhaps America's greatest novelist in the 1920s was prepared for by these multiple, sometimes interrelated, sometimes independent subcurrents keeping his reputation, however dimly, alive. Later in this chapter, I evoke the figure of the rhizome to describe the contemporary Melville effect as well as Melville's porous aesthetic practice, but the figure is also evocative of this expansive network of roots underlying and converging in the revival of the 1920s.

Once American scholars began to canonize Melville, rendering him "a kind of contemporary of 1920s modernism," the array of interests hitherto evincing a subcultural investment in Melville—from socialist working-class advocates to regionalists to protoqueer coteries—faded into the background.[22] This emergence of the author as a literary great and standard-bearer for highbrow American literary values, culture, and politics expressed specific nationalistic and disciplinary aspirations. Indeed, as Eric Aronoff notes, "No other author's canonization has paralleled so closely the development and institutionalization of American literary studies," a burgeoning new academic field.[23] Although Paul Lauter overlooks in his essay "Melville Climbs the Canon" (1994) the subsidiary streams contributing to the revival's promotion of the author, his argument nails one particularly salient factor contributing to Melville's rising reputation among university professors. For post–World War I U.S. scholars looking for ways to link modernism, high-cultural values, and national tradition in order to legitimize the study of American literature in the eyes of the larger world, to prove it of global rather than provincial significance, Melville provided the perfect answer. The "Melville" created in light of these desires was, as Lauter puts it, "distinctively masculine, Anglo-Saxon . . . [and] a lone and powerful artistic beacon against the dangers presented by the masses"—including genteel, effete, popular literature.[24] Meanwhile, what many of us now welcome as "messy" in Melville was, under the aegis of the ensuing practice of New Criticism, dismissed or ignored via the doctrine of the masterpiece, which emphasized the unitary wholeness of Melville's American mythmaking.[25]

In contrast, the creative reenvisionings and interventions occurring as part of today's Melville effect have generated a markedly different understanding of the nineteenth-century author that reflects contemporary priorities and interests. These priorities and interests, of course, are also ones raised in increasingly sophisticated Melville scholarship. At times, scholars have found in Melville's work welcome anticipations of their own progressive political beliefs—for example, what the Trinidadian historian C. L. R. James sees as Melville's celebration of collectively aligned workers and Edward Said praises as Melville's transnational cosmopolitanism. In other cases, critics have pinpointed the limitations, blind spots, and contradictions in his attitudes and stances that amount—as John Carlos Rowe and Wai Chee Dimock have argued—to forms of cultural imperialism.[26] It's not surprising that a century of lively scholarship has resulted in a powerful Melville industry in the academy; what *is* remarkable is the degree to which this "Melville"—both revered and critiqued—has become the wellspring for such an outpouring of *creative* engagement and expression. This Melville is an author whose prescient interrogation of gender, sexuality, race, and class deconstructs notions of elite Anglo-Saxon masculinity; whose global perspective trumps American exceptionalism; whose allegiance to egalitarian community overrides concepts of rugged individualism; and whose polyglot mix of genres has more in common with the contemporary aesthetics of pastiche, collage, and mashups than with modernist mythmaking.

Before proceeding further, I'd like to offer a few caveats. As I noted in the preface, drawing inspiration from Melville is not a new phenomenon in itself. Ever since the initial recovery of Melville, artists working in various genres have made his works the springboard for their creativity. A look at a few examples is instructive. Take, for instance, Jackson Pollack's ink-and-gouache painting *Blue (Moby Dick)* from 1943 (figure 1.1), a tour de force example of expressive abstraction. Yellows, blacks, and oranges mark turbulent ocean upswells, tossing aloft shapes that include what seems to be a ship cantering over the ghostly form of a white whale whose eye stares at the viewer, while bits of masts and stick-figure sailors dot the waves. Spinning globes and oneiric symbols contribute to the sense of a universe in endless motion, upheaval, and primal chaos. Benjamin Britten's acclaimed opera *Billy Budd* (1951/1965), with a libretto by E. M. Forster and Eric Crozier, is a powerful musical interpretation of Melville's novella—and rarely have subsequent productions since its Royal Opera House premiere failed to capitalize on the heady homoeroticism drawing Britten and Forster to its story, as an image from the Prague National Opera's production makes clear, showing Claggart stalked by near-naked men who represent the desires he is intent on repressing (figure 1.2).[27]

Another midcentury example is Orson Welles's stage play *Moby Dick—Rehearsed* (1955). Welles brilliantly uses its self-reflexive structure—a play about rehearsing a play that itself is an adaptation of a novel—to showcase stage magic's ability to create "reality" with minimal props. Of the handful of twentieth-century novels that channel Melville's spirit (discussed more fully in chapter 3), the most experimental, intriguingly, is the work of Melville's great-grandson Paul Metcalf, whose novel *Genoa: A Telling of Wonders* (1965) is a cut-and-paste collage composed of the present-time tale of two brothers (one with a disabled limb, like Ahab; one with a monstrous face, like Moby Dick), pages from Columbus's journals of his journeys to America, and long passages from Melville's novels and letters.

Jean-Luc Godard's short film *Le grand escroc* (The great swindler, 1964) takes its inspiration from *The Confidence-Man*, the French translation of which the

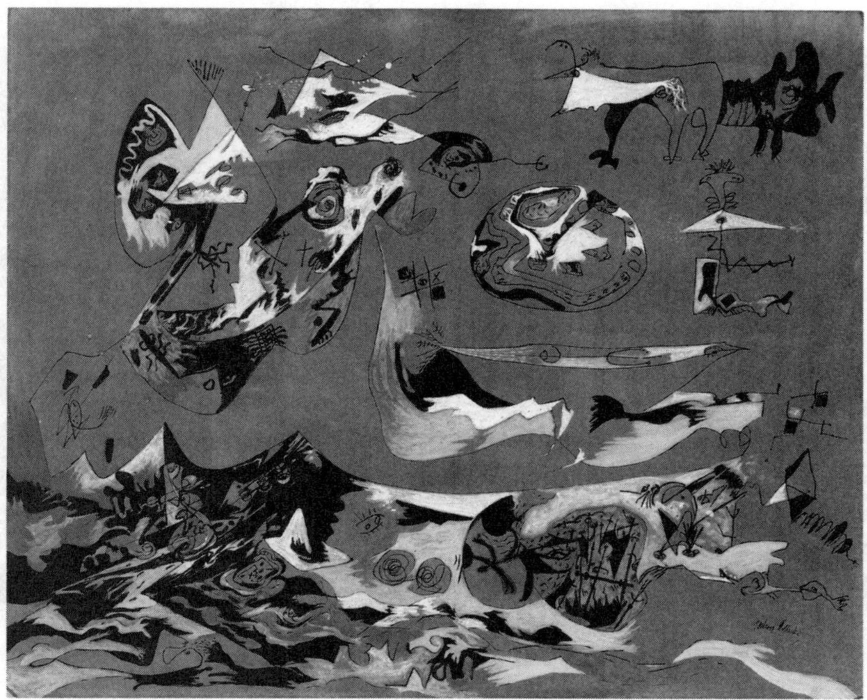

Figure 1.1. Modernist moody blues.
Jackson Pollock, *Blue (Moby Dick)*, c. 1943. Gouache and ink on composition board, 18¾" × 23⅞".

Source: Ohara Museum of Art, Kurashiki.

character Patricia Leacock (Jean Seberg) is shown reading in establishing shots before she is apprehended for passing along counterfeit money produced by a swindler every bit as garrulous a philosopher as Melville's cosmopolitan grifter. The interrogation of race and racial stereotypes in *Benito Cereno* was made newly relevant during the civil rights era by Robert Lowell's verse-drama adaptation in 1964. Similarly, Vali Myer's feminist take in her painting *Moby-Dick* (1972–1974) (figure 1.3) sends up Orientalist representations of the female odalisque by depicting a recumbent woman smoking a hookah while entertaining autoerotic daydreams of the White Whale destroying the *Pequod* (Ahab glares from the daydream bubble on the right margin, a sea-shell encrusted Queequeg looks from the left). Feminist artists reckoning with Melville's sexual politics continue to exert a dominant force in today's Melville effect, as chapter 4 illustrates.

However effective in remediating Melvillean concerns for their times, these envisionings, apart from Myers's, have largely taken the form of homages by

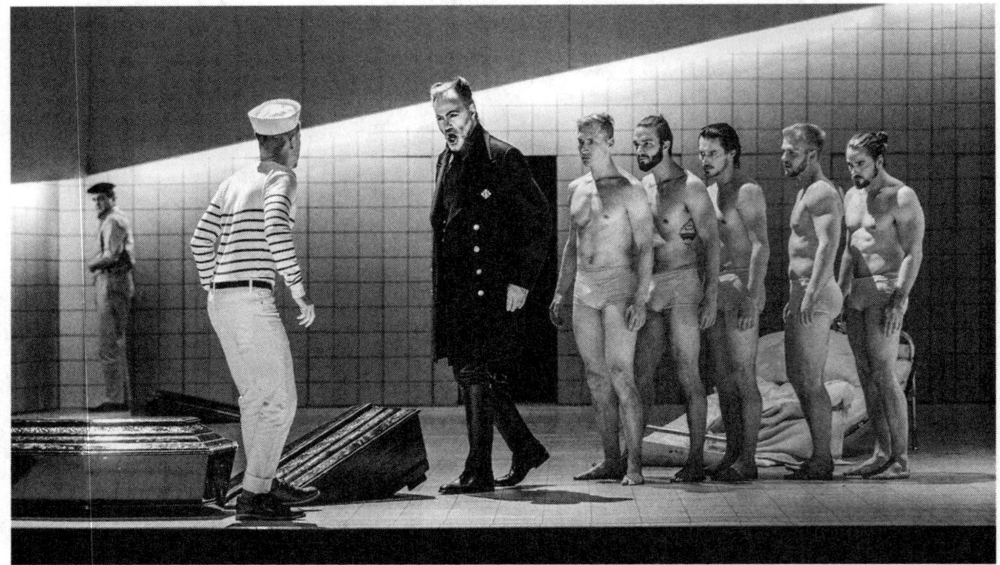

Figure 1.2. Ramping up the homoeroticism in Britten's opera.
Scene from Benjamin Britten, *Billy Budd* (1951/1965), Prague National Opera production, 2018.

Source: CTK / Alamy Stock Photo.

well-known artists whose tributes implicitly attest to their credentials, self-consciously casting themselves as worthy companions of Melville in the pantheon of masters. Missing from these responses is the cumulative force and density of today's Melville effect, which has spawned hundreds upon hundreds of creative works in a relatively short time. Since the late 1990s, one can trace an explosion of imaginative energy and risk-taking—often inaugurated by unestablished artists, including many who happily embrace their status as amateur—whose effects overlap and expand in multiple directions. Much as Melville's writings did for his era, these myriad expressions call traditional aesthetic categories into question and valorize concepts of hybridity, promiscuous mixtures, part-assemblages, multivocality, and process over finality. If some early Melville critics tended to embrace modernist mythmaking, timeless universals, and heroic defiance of the status quo, participants in today's Melville revival more often abjure the "masculine sublime" underlying such claims. Simultaneously, they reject postmodernism's trademark cynicism and contest its proclaimed "death of the author" by giving this author any number of afterlives. In the process, they bring literary history into the living present and make it a portent of the future.

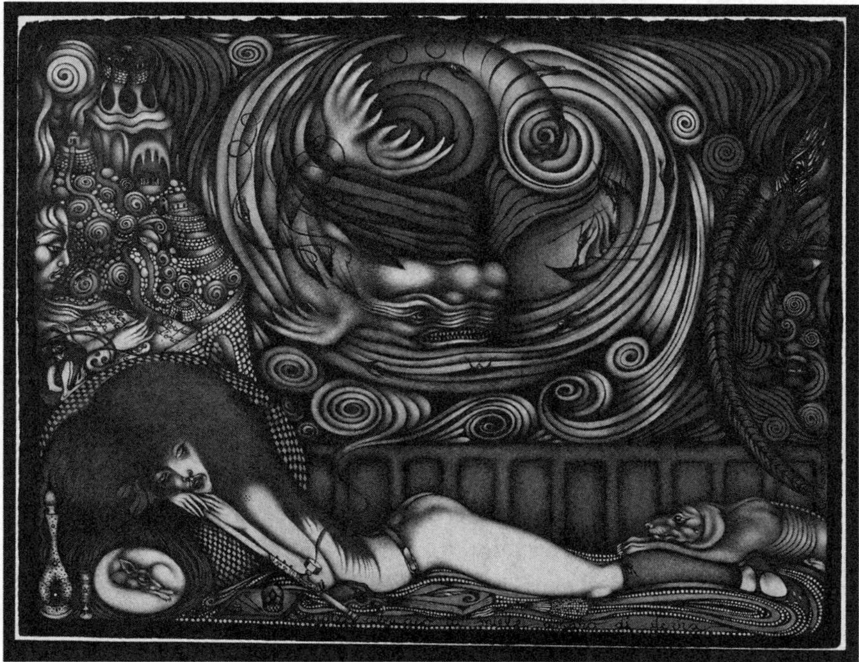

Figure 1.3. Dreams of the white whale as female revenge.
Vali Myers, *Moby-Dick*, 1972–1974. Ink, burnt sienna, watercolor, tempera on handmade paper, 11" × 16".

Source: Courtesy of the Vali Meyers Art Gallery Trust.

Two more provisos are in order. The first concerns Romantic notions of primacy or original genius, which I've already begun to address, and the second addresses contemporary theories of adaptation. Both are intrinsically tied to ways of understanding temporality—a conception at play in the title given to this section, "Then and Now," as well as in the subtitle's emphasis on "*trans*-temporal affinities." While the preceding pages have presented some of the reasons that twenty-first-century artists (creating in the "here and now") may be fascinated by a mid-nineteenth-century author (creating back "then"), the relation between past and present in these instances is not a simple, linear, or teleological one. Why? Precisely because literary history is projective as well as retrospective, existing outside a strictly chronological reckoning: It has its being in a zone or network of significations that move back and forth in and across time and space. "History," notes Dana Seitler, "in its circularity and recursivity, easily accommodates temporalities outside of non-linear ones."[28] This fluidity has important implications for the cautions I want to make about priority as well as about adaptation as a necessarily transtemporal mode of artistic expression.

Let's take the latter proviso first. Despite sophisticated theories of adaptation, popular prejudice still tends to view the source text—the "original" being adapted—as primary and hence intrinsically superior to its belated copy. Such judgments often rely on assumptions about creative "genius"—genius whose singularity or originality can only be imitated or appropriated, resulting in a *re*production that at best is a repetition. As Linda Hutcheon in *A Theory of Adaptation* (2006) has amply demonstrated, however, although adaptations inevitably exist as "doubled" works that announce their relation to an existing work, they are nonetheless autonomous, self-standing productions. As such, their value is not inevitably tethered to the source text: "A derivation . . . is not [necessarily] derivative. [It is] second without being secondary. It is its own palimpsest thing." In addition, Hutcheon emphasizes that adaptations, as doubled or palimpsestic texts, are not just products but an active *process* that involves both acts of interpretation and the creation of a new entity.[29] One result is that the interplay between reinterpretation and re-creation deconstructs "then" and "now" as fixed markers in an irreversible temporal progression leading from one to the other. Simultaneously, the interplay between source text and adaptation, like that between process and product, forms a system of transitive relationships, of diffusions across time and over space, stripping both "original" and "copy" of priority or authority over the other. The temporal and spatial implications are even more pronounced when adaptation—as is so often the case—involves movement from one medium to another; such migration across platforms is necessarily lateral rather than hierarchical, contingent rather than totalizing.

All this being said, there are degrees and then there are degrees of adaptation complicating any simplistic definition of the practice, from intertextual borrowings to intersections staged between self-standing works to the wholesale transformation of one text into an ultimately different, if uncannily similar, avatar. Hutcheon is interested primarily in what one might call straightforward or literal adaptations—texts that, like Aimé Césaire's drama *Une tempête* (1969) and Julie Taymor's film version of *The Tempest* (2010), methodically mine and echo the characters and story of a preexisting work, often a "classic," even as they radically reinterpret and imbue its plot with new meanings (by focusing on Caliban, Césaire creates a powerful anticolonialist response to Shakespeare; by transforming Prospero to Prospera, a role performed by Helen Mirren, Taymor raises questions about gender and power).[30] Scores of artworks occurring as part of the Melville effect are precisely this kind of adaptation. This is especially true of cinematic and theatrical adaptations of *Moby-Dick*, in which the basic narrative of Ahab's mad quest is reenvisioned for live audiences. But even while transformations in period, setting, or cultural context may occur in the migration from prose to performance or film in this form of adaptation, the narrative arc, primary characters, and actions closely hue to those in the novel.[31]

As interesting as these more or less literal adaptations of Melville may be, they are not my primary focus. Rather, the works to which I am repeatedly drawn are those that make looser, more freely creative use of Melville and whose "effects" are the more evocative and far-reaching for *not* being so closely tethered to the precise word and letter of the text inspiring the reenvisioning. Or, if indeed the reenvisioning is tethered to Melville's words, as is the case of the poetry that J. Martin Daughtry "finds" in Melville's chapters (his rule of composition is that each poem he creates can use only words occurring in a given chapter of *Moby-Dick*), the result is something new—in Daughtry's case, a meditation on the tension between originality and repetition, hence on the inevitable intertextuality of poetry itself:

> How is it
> that each word, each plank
> of this sea-going
> vessel was here so
> long before me?
>
> And who am I
> To set them down
> in loose-laced slabs
> like so much fresh
> cut whale flesh? Who
> am I to hear
> as poetical
> these fibers cut
> from the boundless
> pilot-cloth?[32]

Although the works considered in the following pages are indeed *inspired by* Melville, they generally use his image or work as a platform, an incitement, a stimulus, or an aggravation for transformative re-creations that I prefer to call "reenvisionings." Indeed, the link to Melville isn't necessarily obvious or overt in many of these artists' works. In some, "Melville" may exist as a thematic trace, a point of reference, a talisman, an accumulation of understandings or interpretations; in others, the fissures or lacunae in his writing—that which the fiction doesn't address or neglects or remains blind to—are precisely what become the provocations leading to the contemporary iteration; in yet others, a discovered affinity in method or aesthetics provides the connection; and almost all expand beyond Melville's imaginative worlds in creating their own, multilaminated universes.

My second caution has to do with the tendency to view Melville as the apotheosis of "American genius"—America's equivalent of England's Shakespeare, say, whose works are now often touted (rather ironically, given his prior eclipse) as "universal" in their appeal, "timeless" in the insights they shed on human nature and the truths they speak to power.[33] As previously noted, such Romantic claims of genius generally go hand in hand with proclamations of "originality," a concept that reverberates, especially in the American context, with the rhetoric of "exceptionalism," which, like that of "original genius," has bolstered self-aggrandizing and often destructive myths of American singularity, primacy, and legitimacy. (Chapter 3 notes how the perennial search to identify the "Great American Novel" operates as part of this fantasy of exceptionalism.) A risk in a project like mine that focuses on the effects that one such "great" figure has had on contemporary art is that it may seem to participate in a similar reification of Melville as the springhead or fount, the authentic source, from which all subsequent efforts flow, instead of taking into account the degree to which the "Melville" that these artists are mining is also a "concept-metaphor," an ever-changing cultural construction that both scholars and artists have participated in creating.[34] I trust that the methodology unfolded in the following section and throughout this book helps to work against such assumptions. Although some—certainly not all—of the artists examined in the following pages might seem in their pronouncements to worship Melville with an enthusiasm that borders on the uncritical, the *effects* created by their engagements with Melville are in general anything but hagiographical.

An instructive comparison can be made to the way in which an actor's performance is always a stand-in, a substitute, for an absent presence, monumentalizing what is irretrievable by giving it an afterlife. I am thinking of Joseph Roach's theory of surrogation and, by way of extension, Emily Anderson's analysis of Shakespeare's legacy for future actors such as David Garrick, whose performances of the "immortal" bard's roles is an attempt to make Shakespeare live again—to "bring the dead back to life"—and simultaneously to overcome the transience that accompanies the actor's own singular performances.[35] In contrast, throughout the following pages we will see that contemporary participants in the Melville effect, even the most famous among them (and even in this era of fetishized celebrity culture), seem profoundly *less* invested than Roach and Anderson's subjects in bringing the "great" figure—in this case Melville—"back to life" in order to place themselves in a line of succession that bridges past, present, and future. As such, they also differ from earlier twentieth-century artists whose citation of Melville is often accompanied by Bloomian anxieties of influence. Nor do these contemporary figures seem very interested in staging their reenvisionings as acts of commemoration, memorialization, or monumentality (not that aspects of monumentality aren't on full display, as chapter 5 evinces, in the Melvillean preoccupation with scale). Even those novels that literally bring Melville "back to life" as a character in a fictionalized storyline (examples of which are taken up in chapter 3) do so with a self-reflexive, postmodernist, and potentially post-postmodernist awareness from which is absent the desire to work through ephemerality and loss, "to be remembered in perpetuity," that is pertinent to performance.[36] To the contrary, these artists often wholeheartedly embrace the ephemeral, forgo quests for origins as meaningless, shrug off worries of posterity, and welcome the contingency and rootlessness to which Melville's aesthetics and metaphysics, at their most profound, also give expression. As such, they become part of the multidirectional, diffusive network of significations and affiliations that makes literary history, "then" as well as "now" and "now" as well as "then," vibrantly ever present.

Rhizomatic Effects and Patchwork Aesthetics

One of the theoretical conceptions I find most useful in describing the Melville effect is that of the rhizome. Here I draw on Gilles Deleuze and Félix Guattari's influential work *A Thousand Plateaus* (1980), where the philosophers convert the botanical term for the self-propagating, nonradial systems of root stems in certain plants into a metaphor for theorizing and mapping nonhierarchical structures of interconnection among objects that (like rhizomatic root systems) exist in contiguous, shifting, and partial relation to each other. "A rhizome has no beginning or end, it is always in the middle, between things, interbeing, intermezzo. The tree is filiation, but the rhizome is alliance, uniquely alliance." The second Melville revival, I suggest, is similarly rhizomatic in its makeup, its contours, and its effects; it exists as an assemblage of allied and part-objects in which "any point" may connect "to any other point" in ever-shifting relations and flows of energy.[37] The value of such an approach is that it avoids the overdetermined teleology implicit in viewing these artists in terms of what Deleuze and Guattari call "filiation"—that is, as progeny who are secondary copies or outgrowths of some Ur-Melville original. The latter way of thinking can too easily reduce to a traditional study of influence in which the adaptation is necessarily lesser than its source material, a belated echo of a greater predecessor.

I am more interested in the many ways these contemporary reenvisionings incorporate, reflect, and refract Melville *and* each other in a horizontal zone of play, in an arena of *af*-filiations or "alliances" that resists foreclosure even while it forms an entity that exists as a definable cultural event. Viewing the current Melville phenomenon along these more elastic lines makes room for those artists (for instance, the performance artist Laurie Anderson and the experimental New York City troupe Radiohole) who rather than "copying" Melville are discovering in his work an aesthetic sensibility that mirrors their already established practices; it makes room for those artists for whom "Melville" and "Moby Dick" exist primarily as cultural mythemes and for whom a deep knowledge of the man or his works isn't a prerequisite (not a few of these creators admit to never having read or completed *Moby-Dick*); it makes room for those artists whose Melvillean evocations exist as responses to others' evocations: The instigation for T. L. Solien's collage series *Toward the Setting Sun* (2004–2014), for example, was Sara Jeter Naslund's novel *Ahab's Wife* (1999); Kent Stephens's drama *Orson Welles Rehearses* Moby Dick (2003) responds to Welles's play *Moby-Dick—Rehearsed* (1955]).

If the figure of the rhizome provides a useful way of thinking about the Melville effect, it also underlies my methodology for organizing the chapters of this book. Rather than, say, attempting to provide a comprehensive catalog of the hundreds and perhaps thousands of artifacts that make up this phenomenon or to create a systematic taxonomy of its effects or to organize chapters around genres (an enterprise doomed to failure since so many of these examples mix forms), I focus on five different angles of approach to the material—reimaginings of fiction's potential, gender-specific interventions, obsessions with scale, perversity's overflows, environmental concerns—that allow me to gather a wide swath of examples into meaningful clusters whose Melvillean effects, when viewed alongside and intersecting with each other, offer multiple, open-ended points of entry and engagement. Such a means of organization has the potential to yield insights that might otherwise elude the purview of traditional influence studies, in which "then" and "now" become fixed markers in an overdetermined teleology. Employing the rhizome as a model of analysis and interpretation recasts literary history, art, and culture as a complex map of attractions, influences, and flows, a work in progress ("a becoming," in Deleuze and Guattari's term) rather than a stabilized entity.

In gravitating to the rhizome as one model for my enterprise, I take my cue from Melville himself, for the second page of *Moby-Dick* depicts an essentially rhizomatic sensibility at work. This occurs at the beginning of the "Extracts" section preceding the fictional narrative proper, in Melville's headnote describing the Sub-Sub-Librarian who is responsible for the ten pages of extracts that follow. Having combed the world's store of books for "whatever random allusions" he may find of all that "has been promiscuously said, thought, fancied, and sung of Leviathan," this obsessive collector has gathered his "random" bits and pieces in what Melville pointedly describes as "higgledy-piggledy" fashion. This "promiscuous" method of sampling and collecting is, I suggest, essentially rhizomatic, for the Sub-Sub is likened, in his obsessive pursuit of allusions, to a "burrower and grub-worm" haphazardly tunneling his way through "the Vaticans and street-stalls of the earth."[38] Such tunneling is of course the very essence of rhizomatic formations in nature: The paths burrowed by the grubworm mirror the nonradial root systems that give the rhizome its name. In the process, the extract's piecemeal gleanings, assembled in as "higgledy-piggledy" manner as they have been gathered, anticipate the heterogeneous mix—of styles, genres, media, high ("Vaticans") and low ("street-stalls")—that forms Melville's narrative aesthetics and his authorial signature. After all, as *Mardi*'s Babbalanja says in the proclamation forming this chapter's third epigraph, "Genius is full of trash."[39] Several examples of the contemporary Melville effect are as rhizomatic in form as the Sub-Sub is in action. Dan Beachy-Quick's *A Whaler's Dictionary* (2008) is "series of interlaced meditations" that attempt "to bring a reader near to the white squall of meaning that is *Moby-Dick*" by repeating "Ishmael's failed cetological endeavor . . . in a different guise—namely, that of a dictionary of alphabetized entries whose titles are rife with Melvillean inferences (e.g., Flame; Fool; Fossil; Freedom; Friendship.) Encouraging "the reader to thumb through the book" until a title catches the eye, Beachy-Quick notes that each entry ends with an invitation to explore a list of cross-references to *other* entries ("*See also*"), cross-references "that build upon, expand, tangentially link, or contradict the entry just read." We are essentially being emboldened to become rhizomatic readers, tunneling in multiple directions in a process will always remain unfinished.[40]

Melville provides us with a second, equally evocative metaphor for both this "higgledy-piggledy" method of assembly and *Moby-Dick*'s form in the fourth chapter, "The Counterpane," whose title refers to the patchwork design of the quilt covering Ishmael and Queequeg as they sleep together at the Spouter Inn. Known in the vernacular as "crazy quilting," patchwork consists of irregularly shaped odds and ends of fabric stitched together in no particular pattern (a contemporary reviewer used the same figure when describing *The Confidence-Man* as a "Rabelaisian piece of patchwork"[41]). Likewise, in an independent essay on "Bartleby," Deleuze uses patchwork to describe Melville's work, albeit in a more generalized sense: "The subject loses his texture in favour of an infinitely proliferating patchwork: the American patchwork becomes the law of Melville's oeuvre, devoid of a centre, of an upside down or right side up. It is as if the traits of expression escaped form, like the abstract lines of an unknown writing, or the furrows that twist from Ahab's brow to that of the Whale."[42] Or, we might add, like the way the warm bodies of Ishmael and Queequeg meld into one another in the "Counterpane" chapter. Christopher Looby argues that the "strange" sensations to which Ishmael awakens when he finds his bed companion's arm draped over him in a "matrimonial sort of style" (38) illustrates a mode of aesthetic sensibility, a sensitivity to beauty, that emerged in nineteenth-century America as a form of same-sex eroticism, hovering between earlier definitions of sodomitical acts and emergent ones of homosexual identity.[43] For the "odd little parti-colored squares and triangles" (37) of the patchwork quilt are echoed in the shape and colors of Queequeg's tattoos, ink markings that inscribe his skin with "an interminable Cretan labyrinth . . . no two parts of which were one precise shade." Thus, Ishmael declares, "this same arm of his looked for all the world like a strip of that same patchwork quilt" (37). The sensuous materiality of both patchwork quilt and the two bodies it brings together serves as a reminder that the artistic pursuit of "beauty" involves not just abstractions but also tactile objects of desire. So too with Melville's aesthetics: For all his transcendental flights of thought, it is crucial for those attempting to articulate his artistic principles to keep in view the sensuous, tactile qualities of his writing, in which text and textures (those parti-colored squares and triangles, those imprecise shades) incite aesthetic appreciation. A cannily feminist understanding of this aesthetics—*textual* in Melville's case, *textured* in hers—underlies Ann Wilson's choice of subject for her abstract *Moby-Dick* (1955): Acrylic paint has been applied to a found quilt mounted on canvas in what is the first major artwork by a woman artist in response to Melville's masterpiece (figure 1.4).

Thinking of patchwork as a metaphor for Melville's narrative design and experiments has an added benefit that the figure of the rhizome fails to capture. Deleuze clearly sees patchwork as analogous to the theoretical operations he assigns the rhizome when he describes the "American patchwork" as "infinitely proliferating . . . devoid of a centre, of an upside down or a right side up." But, in fact, a patchwork quilt—the real thing—does have finite borders. Its "crazy" irregularities, its messiness, are ultimately contained by its edges, without which it would not be functional. This is a reality to keep in mind as we ponder Melville's experiments in genre and in style. However much his texts seem an unending mishmash of proliferating elements, their elements are also contained, if only by their material embodiment in print, as bound texts, with final pages marked "Finis." This is not to say that his fiction isn't open-ended or that the effects and afterlives that his narratives set into motion don't extend beyond their borders—of course they do. Rather, it is to recognize that the crazy medley of styles, voices, genres, and forms to which his writings give play also exist as bounded systems, as zones of ordered disorder.

In this regard, I'd like to turn to another image used by Deleuze—one that is monstrously oceanic rather than cozily domestic—in his attempt to evoke the undoing of the subject in Melville's fiction. The monster at hand, however, isn't the White Whale but its oceanic counterpart, the ghastly white squid: "All referents are lost, and the formation . . . of man gives way to a new, unknown element, to the mystery of a formless, nonhuman life, a Squid."[44] True, the amorphousness of this "vast pulpy mass" (so Melville describes this sea monster in chapter 59 of *Moby-Dick*) conjures up an image of formlessness incarnate. But, in fact, the squid has a center, for as Ishmael notes, the "innumerable long arms . . . curling and twisting like a nest of anaconda" from this "unearthly,

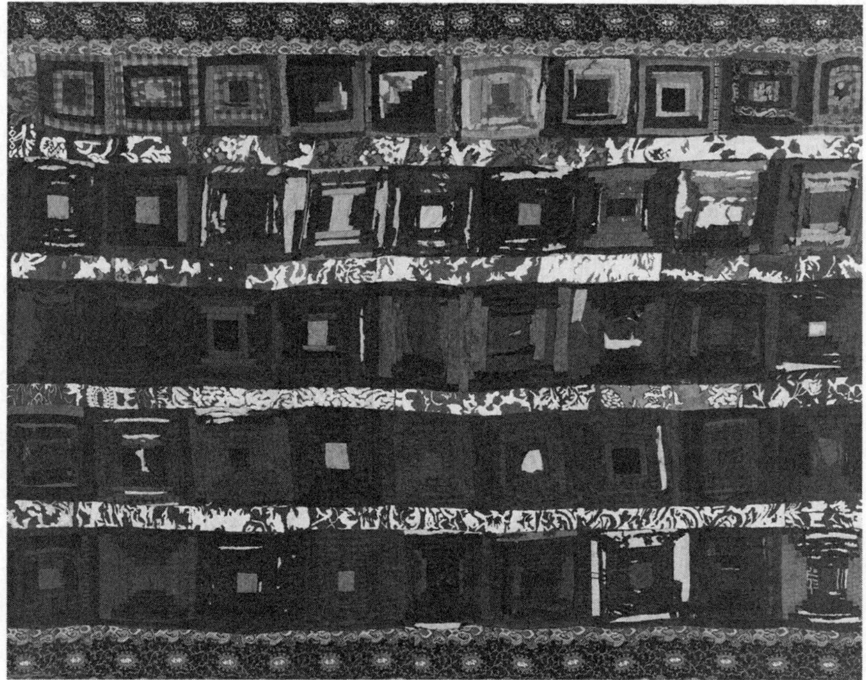

Figure 1.4. From page to painting: patchwork aesthetics and Melville.
Ann Wilson, *Moby-Dick*, 1955. Acrylic on found quilt mounted on canvas, 66¼" × 84".

Source: Digital image © Whitney American Art, New York, Inv. 71.184. Licensed by Scala / Art Resource NY.

formless, chance-like apparition of life" radiate "from its centre" (226). Again, this is not to deny Melville's persistent decentering of the quest for singular truths but to remind us that texts—even the most squidlike—contain ordering principles and frames: Melville's books unfold, for all their patchwork irregularities and seeming formlessness, *as* a form.

And form—both traditional and experimental—is a topic on which a multitude of Melville's critics have commented over the decades. As Wyn Kelley notes, Melville's writing returns the term *invention* to its nineteenth-century meaning of "the ingenuous recombining of previously existing elements."[45] Part of this recombinatory aesthetics, as Samuel Otter observes in the introduction to *Melville and Aesthetics* (2011), derives from a restlessness with traditional form that extended over the author's lifetime of writing: "From book to book Melville stylistically reinvents himself, restless with genre, experimenting with point of view and verbal line."[46] The result—which chimes with the Deleuzean emphasis on "becoming"—was long ago diagnosed by Warner Berthoff as a mode of "process" aesthetics, in which "the very occupation of writing," for Melville, "germinates its own most enriching motives and effects."[47] Discovery happens in the doing, and, thus, as Nina Baym puts it in her well-known *PMLA* essay "Melville's Quarrel with Fiction" (1979), for this author the act of "trying, instead of succeeding, becomes a badge of honor."[48] On the level of style, Melville's restless experimentation results in an unevenness—as, for example, in those moments when rhapsodic lyricism abruptly gives way to "bad" or "deliberate overwriting." The latter phrase is Calder's, and such over-the-top or "bad" moments constitute what Calder terms Melville's "metastyle," in which "modal discontinuity" proposes "its own version of [the] multivalent, multilayered, multivocal[ity]" that M. M. Bakhtin associates with the genre of the novel. In the process, the dissonance takes the reader somewhere new, communicating indirectly "that which does not bear spelling out."[49] Not only does Calder's latter phrasing call to mind the ambiguities that obsess Melville and that he teasingly flaunts on nearly every page, but the concepts of metastyle, dissonance, and multivocality also resonate powerfully with the endeavors of today's artists using mixed media and multimediated forms to channel the spirit of Melville for contemporary ends.

* * *

I'd like to conclude this overview of the methods and theories undergirding this book by turning to the concept of "the fluid text" pioneered by the notable Melville scholar and Melville biographer John Bryant, freely adapting his terms to evoke the transtemporal effects that give Melville's afterlives their special resonance today. In the world of textual editing, the focus has traditionally been that of producing an "authoritative" text, an event achieved through the meticulous comparison of manuscripts and variant editions to determine what was most likely an author's final intentions. Nowhere has this effort been more exhaustive than in the Newberry Library's undertaking to produce authoritative editions of Melville's canon—the snail pace of which, for certain volumes, has become the stuff of legend. In *The Fluid Text: A Theory of Revision for Books and Screen* (2002) and other writings, Bryant has pushed back against this model. Using Melville's *Typee* and *Moby-Dick* as examples, he argues that scholars need to focus equally on the multiple versions in which any text exists. These versions may include author's drafts, publisher's proofs, revised editions, bowdlerizations, adaptations, expurgations, and versions streamlined for children—all of which components compose "the fluid text." Thus, instead of considering books as fixed objects in space and time, we need to consider them as "fluid" works-in-progress whose emendations and changes, however minute or hidden, illuminate the cultural shifts and contexts that always surround and shape creativity.[50] We might usefully extend Bryant's concept of such spatiotemporal fluidity to illuminate the creative and cultural mobility that occurs when, as in today's Melville effect, the artistic activity spurred by a given work or figure forms a diffusive but nonetheless identifiable "event" whose presence seems especially expressive of the contemporary moment. The fluid text that composes the Melville effect, if viewed as the sum of all its reenvisionings, is thus also the text you are reading, *The Melville Effect*, as it sets out to track the varied trajectories of artistic reenvisioning in the following chapters.

CHAPTER 2

MULTIMEDIA MELVILLE, MESSY CULTURE, CONTEMPORARY REMEDIATIONS

The man made a mess of things. . . . [Melville] had to be wild or he was nothing in particular.
—Charles Olson, *Call Me Ishmael*

It's a messy culture, it's an eclectic culture, and I thought: Melville is the first one to recognize exactly how messy and grandiose and wonderful this culture is.
—Rinde Eckert, "Avoiding Melville's Vortex"

Not everyone reading this book is a devoted Melvillean scholar, and this chapter is dedicated to those general readers who may benefit from a more specific look at the degree to which Melville's fiction was so avant-garde for its time, so encyclopedic and promiscuous in its inclusion and mingling of multiple forms and modes. In addition, this chapter provides an overview of the mid-nineteenth-century explosion in modes of communication and entertainment that American culture was experiencing—an explosion that, as already suggested, is echoed in today's proliferation of new media and mixed art forms. Both these subjects—the hybridity that characterizes Melville's formal experiments and the heady multiplication of high- and popular-cultural forms during his lifetime—are integrally intertwined: Multimedia Melville reflects and borrows from his messy culture, and vice versa. The two sections dedicated to these formal elements and cultural-historical contexts are followed by a third section offering a sampling of contemporary remediations that make the most of this combination of mixed media and Melvillean aesthetics. This final section introduces the reader to important tropes, concepts, innovations, and redefinitions that recur throughout the in-depth case studies of fictionality, gender, scale, perversity, and environment that follow.

Multimedia Melville

We have already glimpsed in the previous chapter various terms that critics over the years have used to describe Melville's promiscuously inclusive, hybrid narrative style and fictional techniques. "Process aesthetics" is the phrase used by Warner Berthoff to evoke the ever-evolving, open-ended quality of Melville's writing, in which the effort is more important than the outcome. Christopher Sten writes in *The Weaver God, He Weaves* (1996) of Melville's "concerted attempt to adapt a variety of forms" constituting "a cross-section of the available literary modes" of his era. "Recombinatory aesthetics" is Samuel Otter's phrase for Melville's rowdy mix of forms and genres. More recently, Alex Calder pinpoints "modal discontinuity" as an intrinsic element of Melville's "metastyle."[1]

Although Sheila Post-Lauria provocatively suggests that nineteenth-century readers were accustomed to mixed-genre forms and didn't feel that hybridity "diminish[ed] or even negate[d] the possibility for creativity," the commentary of Melville's contemporaries suggests a less sanguine view of his penchant for muddying generic boundaries.[2] When a Paris review reprinted in Evert A. Duyckinck's journal *The Literary World* in August 1849 described *Mardi* as commencing "as a novel, turning into a fairy tale, and availing itself of allegory to reach the satirical after passing through the elegy, the drama, and the burlesque," the comment was not meant as a compliment. Nor were George Ripley's dismissal of *Mardi* as "a monstrous compound" or the *Boston Post*'s labeling it "mere *hodge-podge*"—indeed, one wonders if Melville was recalling and inverting the negative connotations of the latter colloquialism in flaunting the "*h*iggledy-*p*iggledy" collection (note the alliteration) of *Moby-Dick*'s extracts, which, as we have seen, becomes elevated to an aesthetic tenet in his hands.[3] While some mixture of romance and fact might have been acceptable to readers, per Post-Lauria's suggestion, the *London Athenaeum*'s harsh description of *Moby-Dick* as an "*ill-compounded* mixture of romance and matter-of fact" and "*so much trash* belonging to the worst school of *Bedlam* literature" makes clear its negative judgment: Melville has disdained the proper "craft of an artist."[4]

Indeed, while Brian Yothers has usefully reminded us that the critical commonplace that *Moby-Dick* was universally panned is a myth (75 of 111 reviews were basically positive), it is true that as Melville's career progressed, the increasing dismay of his reviewers and readers was tied to the eclectic, promiscuous nature of his writing, whose messy tendencies they found misguided, offensive, or, worse, downright unartistic.[5] Ironically, these critics were not entirely off-target in sensing what was different—and revolutionary—about Melville's aesthetic principles. "An ill-confounded mixture," "a singular medley . . . run mad," "wantonly eccentric," "a strange conglomeration," "hermaphroditic craft": Such pronouncements focus on the mixed ("mixture," "medley," "conglomeration") or indiscriminate ("mad," "wanton," "hermaphroditic") nature of Melville's craft and its divergence from literary norms (rendering his productions "singular," "eccentric," "strange").[6] In contrast, advocates of the first Melville revival often turned these "negatives" into a positive by using the generic category "anatomy" to legitimize those aspects of *Moby-Dick* exceeding traditional novelistic boundaries.

And now? Today's critics and artists inspired by Melville draw on an even more capacious set of adjectives and nouns to capture this dimension of the inclusive aesthetics running throughout his oeuvre: *hybrid, polyphonic, messy, multiform, heteroglossic, bricolage, pastiche, collage*. Melville's inventive pushing against traditional novelistic form is echoed, as Michael D. Snediker argues, in the nonrealistic "strangeness" or queerness adhering to his modes of characterization. Taji, Ahab, Black Guinea, the Missouri Bachelor, Pierre, Isabel, Billy the Beautiful Sailor—each is less "mimetically faithful" than "aesthetically promiscuous."[7] This aesthetic promiscuity is part and parcel of what the poet-critic Charles Olson observed in 1947 to be Melville's intrinsic wildness: "The man made a mess of things. . . . [Melville] had to be wild or he was nothing in particular."[8]

What Olson celebrated in Melville and what many earlier critics and readers found to be an unsettling violation of the laws of genre owe to the multimediated quality of Melville's prose. True, as already noted, Melville's creativity was restricted to the medium of writing, but the degree to which he makes the printed page evoke multiple genres and media is astonishing; even twenty-first-century readers accustomed to postmodernist experimentation may find themselves amazed at this inclusiveness. For those nonspecialists who might not have dipped into Melville for a decade or so, a glance at the variety of genres, forms, and modalities of artistic expression incorporated into *Moby-Dick* is eye-opening.[9] The opening page titled "Etymology" evokes the genre of the dictionary; the following section, "Extracts," is typical of the Elizabethan commonplace book, composed of handwritten quotations culled from one's reading. The "Cetology" chapter satirically mimics the scientific treatise in its divisions and subdivisions of the whale species. Moreover, in designating those divisions BOOKS, CHAPTERS, FOLIOS, OCTAVOS, and DUEDEMCIMOS, the chapter's format self-reflexively equates whales with textuality—and the epidermis of the White Whale, as readers know, is inscribed in a hieroglyphic language that defies all attempts to decipher it. Stubbs's command that Fleece "preach" to the sharks in chapter 64 inserts into the novel a sermon delivered in the cook's Black vernacular (its message a Darwinian counterpart to the Calvinistic one of Father Mapple's quoted sermon in the Whaleman's Chapel in chapter 7).[10] Chapter 24, "The Affidavit," is written in the form of the sworn legal document used as evidence in court; here Ishmael farcically argues for the veracity of the legendary White Whale as if he were testifying in a court of law.

The genre of drama marks *Moby-Dick* in myriad ways. The first chapter concludes with Ishmael's insertion into the text of a theatrical playbill, in which his life story ("WHALING VOYAGE BY ONE ISHMAEL") is satirically announced as a "brief interlude and solo" act that serves as filler material between the "more extensive performances" of international affairs (both of which are ironically prescient in regard to today's news) in "the grand programme of Providence" (22):

Grand Contested Election for the Presidency of the United States.
WHALING VOYAGE BY ONE ISHMAEL.
BLOODY BATTLE IN AFFGANISTAN.

The varied font sizes and use of italics in the playbill simultaneously call to mind newspaper headlines, another print genre on which Melville draws. The playbill format recurs in *White-Jacket*, where the advertisement for a show starring Jack Chase takes up an entire page (figure 2.1).

In *Moby-Dick*, the world of the stage is most graphically represented in chapters 39 and 40, which are written as a dramatic script, replete with stage directions and speaking parts. For these pages, the novel is quite literally no longer a novel but a play, one in which the polyglot shipboard world of the *Pequod* explodes in an externalized, surreal psychodrama of the sort that Joyce would employ in the Circe episode of *Ulysses*. This intense theatricality has been implicit since the stage direction that suddenly appears at the opening of chapter 36, "The Quarter-Deck": "*(Enter Ahab. Then, all.)*." At this moment Ahab makes his grand entrance, using the quarterdeck as the stage on which he performs to and mesmerizes his rapt audience with melodramatic, faux-Shakespearean rhetoric. In

CAPE HORN THEATRE.

Grand Celebration of the Fourth of July.

DAY PERFORMANCE.

UNCOMMON ATTRACTION.

THE OLD WAGON PAID OFF!

JACK CHASE........PERCY ROYAL-MAST.

STARS OF THE FIRST MAGNITUDE.

For this time only,

THE TRUE YANKEE SAILOR.

The managers of the Cape Horn Theatre beg leave to inform the inhabitants of the Pacific and Southern Oceans that, on the afternoon of the Fourth of July, 184–, they will have the honor to present the admired drama of

THE OLD WAGON PAID OFF!

Commodore Bougee ....*Tom Brown, of the Fore-top.*
Captain Spy-glass ....*Ned Brace, of the After-Guard.*
Commodore's Cockswain ....*Joe Bunk, of the Launch.*
Old Luff ....*Quarter-master Coffin.*
Mayor ....*Seafull, of the Forecastle.*
PERCY ROYAL-MAST ....JACK CHASE.
Mrs. Lovelorn ....*Long-locks, of the After-Guard.*
Toddy Moll ....*Frank Jones.*
Gin and Sugar Sall.................*Dick Dash.*

Sailors, Marines, Bar-keepers, Crimps, Aldermen, Police-officers, Soldiers, Landsmen generally.

Long live the Commodore! || Admission Free.

To conclude with the much-admired song by Dibdin, altered to suit all American Tars, entitled

THE TRUE YANKEE SAILOR.

True Yankee Sailor (in costume), Patrick Flinegan, Captain of the Head.

Performance to commence with "Hail Columbia," by the Brass Band. Ensign rises at three bells, P.M. No sailor permitted to enter in his shirt-sleeves. Good order is expected to be maintained. The Master-at-arms and Ship's Corporals to be in attendance to keep the peace.

Figure 2.1. Mixing genres: Jack Chase's star turn. Playbill in *White-Jacket* (1850).

Source: Public domain.

the next chapter, another inserted stage direction—"*(The cabin; by the stern windows; Ahab sitting alone, and gazing out)*" (142)—interrupts what has hitherto been Ishmael's first-person narration by opening directly into Ahab's famous soliloquy ("I leave a white and turbid wake" [142]), which in turn is followed by the carnivalesque riot of "voices" in scripted format that composes chapters 39–40. More stage directions intermittently recur throughout the narrative, as do self-standing soliloquies and monologues that signal Melville's straining at the generic confines of fiction's formal realism.[11]

The handbills reproduced here are only one example of the degree to which Melville inserts extratextual visual or graphic media into his writing. *Moby-Dick*'s reproduction of the three marble cenotaphs embedded in the walls of the Whaleman's Chapel makes us visualize these memorials as text. Likewise, note the use of special graphic devices (figures 2.2–2.4) such as "Quohog's mark" (85; Melville's joke is that Peleg mistakes Queequeg's name for the famous New England clam); the pointing finger warning of mantraps in *Redburn*; and the "round robin" design at the end of chapter 20 of *Omoo* (by means of which the sailors or "hands" sign their letter of complaint to the English consul in Tahiti, a design that "arrange[s] the signatures in such a way, that, although they are all found in a ring, no man can be picked out as the leader of it").[12]

In terms of the pictorial arts, Melville's writing presents, as an early reviewer remarked, a "unique picture gallery."[13] Most famously, *Moby-Dick* is filled with detailed descriptions of paintings, but so are other works, in particular *Pierre*. In *Moby-Dick*, they include not only the "portentous, black mass of something hovering" (26) in the oil painting that puzzles Ishmael in the bar of the Spouter Inn—whose depiction evokes Turner's impressionistic seascapes, much admired by Melville—and a ship "beating against a terrible storm" (47) in a painting hanging between cenotaphs and pulpit in the Whaleman's Chapel, but also, in metatextual fashion, the narrator's enumeration in chapter 55 of "Monstrous Pictures," then in chapter 56 of "less erroneous pictures of whales," and finally in chapter 57 "of whales in paint, in teeth, &tc."[14] In the latter, the prose soars from an appreciation of scrimshaw art to the tracery created by the constellation Cetus in the heavens.

The genre of poetry makes its way into Melville's fiction in both overt and less obvious ways. Like many nineteenth-century authors, Melville frequently inserted poetic citations into his prose narrative, reproducing lines and whole stanzas—whether from Byron's "Childe Harold" in *Moby-Dick* or from his own ballad "Billy in the Darbies" at the end of *Billy Budd*. The poetic lyricism of Melville's prose is well known, but not every reader realizes the extent to which his prose sometimes *is* poetry disguised as prose. Scan the lines of Ahab's soliloquy in chapter 37, and, as F. O. Matthiessen demonstrated some eighty years ago, one discovers why so many have intuitively felt a

Quohog.
his ✠ mark.

☞ "MAN-TRAPS AND SPRING-GUNS!"

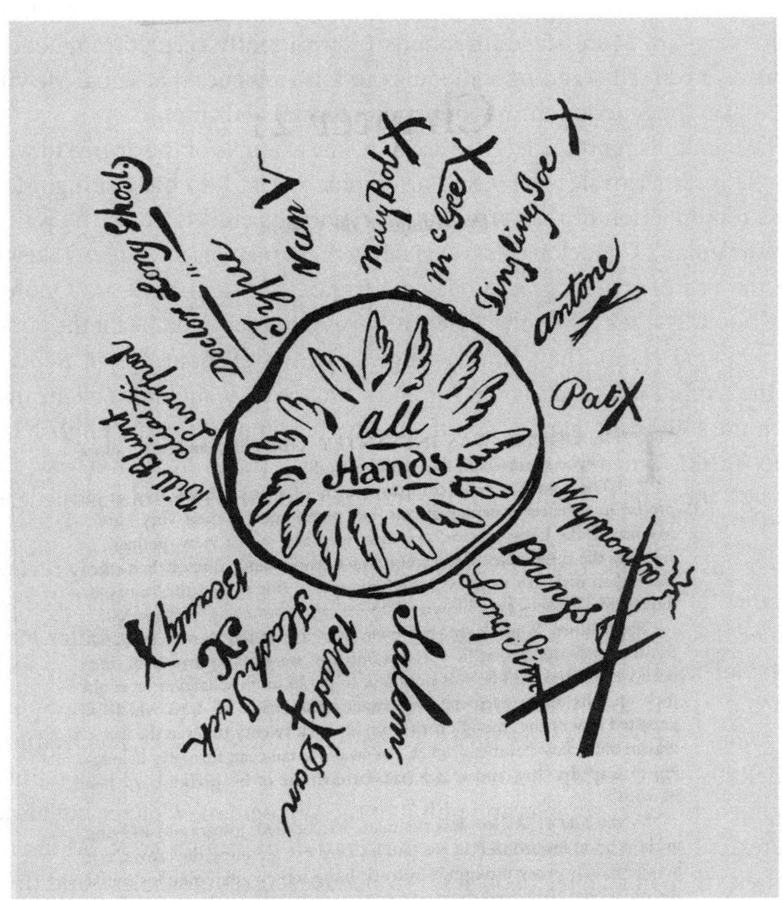

Figures 2.2., 2.3, and 2.4. Amplifying the written word with visual graphics. Queequeg's mark in *Moby-Dick* (1851); the pointing finger in *Redburn* (1849); the round-robin signatory in *Omoo* (1847).

Source: Public domain.

Shakespearean cadence in Melville.[15] In this instance, the "prose" actually *is* Shakespearean blank verse, following the rules of iambic pentameter:

> - ’ - ’ - ’ - ’
> . . . I leave a white and turbid wake;
> - ’ - ’ - ’ - ’ - ’
> Pale waters paler cheeks, where'er I sail.
> - ’ - ’ - ’ - ’ - ’
> The envious billows sidelong swell to whelm
> - ’ ’ - - ’ - ’
> My track; let them; but first I pass.
> (142)

The same is true of Ahab's words to Starbuck in the previous chapter, "The Quarter-Deck" (also marked by stage directions):

> - ’ - ’ - ’ - ’ - ’
> But look ye, Starbuck, what is said in heat,
> - ’ - ’ - ’ ’ - ’
> That thing unsays itself. There are men
> - ’ - ’ - ’ - ’ - ’
> From whom warm words are small indignity.
> - ’ ’ - - ’ - ’ - ’
> I mean not to incense thee. Let it go.
> ’ - ’ - ’ - ’ - ’ - ’
> Look! See yonder Turkish cheeks of spotted dawn . . .
> (140)

Poetry shares with the genre of music elements of rhythm and sonority, and *Moby-Dick* incorporates as many examples of song lyrics as it does poetry. A five-stanza hymn taken from Psalms 18 precedes Father Mapple's sermon in chapter 9; Stubb entertains his boatmates during an ongoing typhoon with a jaunty sea shanty ("Oh, jolly is the gale! / And a joker is the whale" [380]), and as the *Pequod* gets underway, the crew "roar[s] forth some sort of a chorus about the girls in Booble Alley," whose profanity Bildad attempts to drown out with the "psalmody" of an Isaac Watts melody (94). The sailors' mad revels in "Midnight, Forecastle" unfold to the sounds of Pip's tambourine, the sonic effects of which are evoked by the increasingly nonsensical litany of words with which the sailors command him to play: "Go it, Pip! Bang it, bell-boy! Rig it, dig it, stig it, quig it, bell-boy!" (147). In the same scene, the force of the storm that breaks up the melee between Dagoo and the Spanish Sailor is captured in sound effects that Melville embeds in Pip's dialogue: "Crash! Crash! There goes the jib-stay! Blang-whang . . . White squalls? White whale, shirr! shirr! shirr! . . . it makes me jingle all over like my tambourine" (151). The centrality of Pip and his tambourine to this midnight revelry reminds us, as Sterling Stuckey demonstrates in *African Culture and Melville's Art* (2009), that slave music and dance (especially the ring dance) were also part of Melville's hybrid aesthetics.[16] These Black cultural influences reach from the Pinkster celebrations well established in the Albany of Melville's youth to the Black marching bands parading past his New York residences to the St. Domingo melodies that the African cook in *White-Jacket* sings to motivate his cleaning staff:

> Oh! I los' my boot in a pilot-boat,
> Johnnio! Come Winum do!
> Den rub-a-dub de copper, oh!
> Oh! Copper-rub-a-dub-a-oh![17]

By incorporating these many instances of aurality ("stig it, quig it," "blang-whang," "shir! shir!" "rub-a-dub-a-oh") into the soundscape of his novels, Melville comes close to achieving the nonverbal effect of music, whose sonorities awaken feelings that exist beyond words. Perhaps the most extreme instance of this effect involves Isabel's mysteriously communicating guitar in *Pierre*, "swarm[ing] with . . . unintelligible but delicious sounds" that she claims are her only means of conveying to Pierre "the sequel of my story; for not in words can it be spoken."[18] Isabel's long description of her guitar's magic abilities, in Michael Jonik's adept analysis, "literalizes [its] dull hum. . . . [R]epeated alliterations of 's' and 'm' sounds, extended modulating assonances, on-flowing gerunds and participles create a reverb and tremolo" as words "literally echo off one another" or become "antistrophic mirrorings."[19] I quote only a bit of Isabel's narration here to make the point (with **s** in boldface, M capitalized, repeated words italicized):

> Then I *MurMured*; ***s**ung* and *MurMured* to it; very *lowly*, very ***s**oftly*; I could hardly *hear* My**s**elf. And I changed the Modulation**s** of My ***s**ingings* and My *MurMurings*; and **s**till ***s**ung* and *MurMured, lowly, **s**oftly,—More* and *More*; and presently I *heard* a ***s**udden **s**ound*; **s**weet and *low* beyond all telling was the ***s**weet* and ***s**udden **s**ound.* I clapt My hand**s**; the guitar wa**s** **s**peaking *to Me*; the dear *guitar* wa**s** ***s**inging to Me, MurMuring* and ***s**inging to Me* the *guitar.*[20]

As Jonik observes, "the passage opens" the novel to "a sonic field of reverberation" that supersedes the written word.[21] (Also relevant in this regard are the acoustics that limn the "unspeakable" plot of *Billy Budd*: first, Billy's fatal stutter leading to his striking of Claggart, then the "ominous, low . . . murmur" emanating from his unhappy shipmates as he hangs, and finally the shrill piercing sound of the boatswain's whistle that quells the potential mob violence augured by his shipmates' murmurs.)[22]

Given Melville's employment of all these generic modes in *Moby-Dick*, critics have questioned whether it is indeed a "novel" (it has been called, among other things, an anatomy, an epic, an allegory, a romance). After all, Melville's career began with writing books that we now tend to classify as novels—*Typee* and *Omoo*—but that in their time "passed" as nonfictional travel adventures or, less positively to some skeptics, prevarications passing themselves off as accounts of real events, not even autobiographical fiction. What Nina Baym has called Melville's "quarrel with fiction," however, is a quarrel with the expectations of novelistic convention that he found stultifying.[23] His sense of fiction's possibilities was, rather, much more in accord with M. M. Bakhtin's definition of the novel's multivocal qualities, its inherent plasticity, heterogeneity, and open-endedness. If there are few novels in the English-language tradition quite like *Moby-Dick*, that's because few novelists have pushed the genre to its limits to the extent that Melville was willing to attempt. Bakhtin notably argues that the novel, unlike traditional, older genres, is by definition "unfinished" in that it speaks in the (often conflicting, always dialogical) living, evolving discourses of contemporaneity: hence its open-endedness, its apparent messiness.[24] In the following section, we will see just how aptly this openness describes Melville's receptivity to the manifold, living discourses circulating in the media culture making up mid-nineteenth-century America.

Melville's Messy Culture

Melville's wide reading in the great touchstones of his literary heritage, from the Bible to Ovid and from Dante to Shakespeare, as well his copious allusions to such texts in his writing were apparent to his earliest reviewers and readers.[25] Only in the latter part of the twentieth century, however, have scholars begun to perceive the degree to which the rich intertextuality of his work includes equally copious references to the popular culture of his day. Melville was nothing if not a magpie; if *King Lear* might serve him well in one instance, that did not mean that a reform novel, a nautical melodrama, or a light opera might not also spark his imagination. David S. Reynolds's magisterial work *Beneath the American Renaissance: Subversive Imagination in the Age of Emerson and Melville* (1998) has been pivotal in refuting the myth that Melville, like the select few with whom Matthiessen grouped him in *The American Renaissance*, "was alienated from his contemporary culture." To the contrary, as Reynolds demonstrates, the rich intertextuality of a work such as *Moby-Dick* owes precisely to Melville's "openness to images from various contemporary arenas."[26] And, indeed, the sheer *range* of emergent modes of popular and middlebrow entertainment bursting onto the contemporary scene as Melville was coming of age as a writer is breathtaking. As Susan Zeiger writes in *The Mediated Mind* (2018), the nineteenth century was "the first period" in U.S. history "in which consumers began daily to consider which parts of mass-produced culture they would incorporate into their psyches and which they would reject."[27]

Heady, confusing, diverse, exhilarating, constant, messy: The bombardment of new modes of media and multiplying forms of entertainment in the first half of the nineteenth century created a carnivalesque culture that both informed and mirrored Melville's evolving hybrid aesthetics—a culture that evokes our own cultural moment of expanding media, although the historical contexts are different. Collamer M. Abbott gives fascinating glimpses of the range of cultural offerings available for Melville's attention. During Melville's Thanksgiving stay in Boston with in-laws in 1847, Armory Hall was displaying John Banvard's *Mammoth Panorama of the Mississippi River, Painted on Three Miles of Canvas*; visitors could board a Chinese junk wharfed at Charlestown bridge; a dramatic reading of Edward Bulwer's novel *The Last Days of Pompeii* was being staged; and lectures on subjects from science to art were occurring across the city. During a brief trip to Boston in 1849, Melville attended a lecture by Ralph Waldo Emerson, listened to Fanny Kemble Butler's recitations of Shakespeare, and attended a show billed as *Purrington and Russell's Original Panorama of a Whaling Voyage Round the World* (figure 2.5).[28]

A sense of this cultural diversity makes itself felt in the opening pages of Mark Beauregard's novel *The Whale: A Love Story* (2016), which takes the possibility of Melville's unrequited homosexual feelings for Hawthorne as its subject. The novel begins on August 5, 1850, the date the two authors met for the first time on a picnic excursion in the Berkshires. References to art and popular culture abound as the party rides to their picnic site. Cornelius Mathews, "Broadway playwright," talks about the plot of the new play he's writing (prompting Melville to wonder how a stage set might render a whaling ship); Oliver Wendell Holmes commends the virtues of the lecture circuit (Holmes was a popular participant in the Lyceum lecture series); Melville's friend and editor Evert Duyckinck touts the value of advertising books in journals such as his *Literary World*; James Field, Hawthorne's publisher, wears a frock coat "more suitable to the opera"; the party is joined by the nephew of the popular domestic novelist Catherine Sedgwick; Melville chafes against the publicity machine that has made him "a carnival exhibit" as the man who lived among cannibals; Jeannie Field recites Holmes's poem "The Last Leaf" from 1831; and the company composes rhyming riddles to pass the time till they reach their picnic site—all this in the space of a dozen pages.[29]

Print material, of course, afforded the most widely available form of entertainment in these decades. Central to the proliferating market in books,

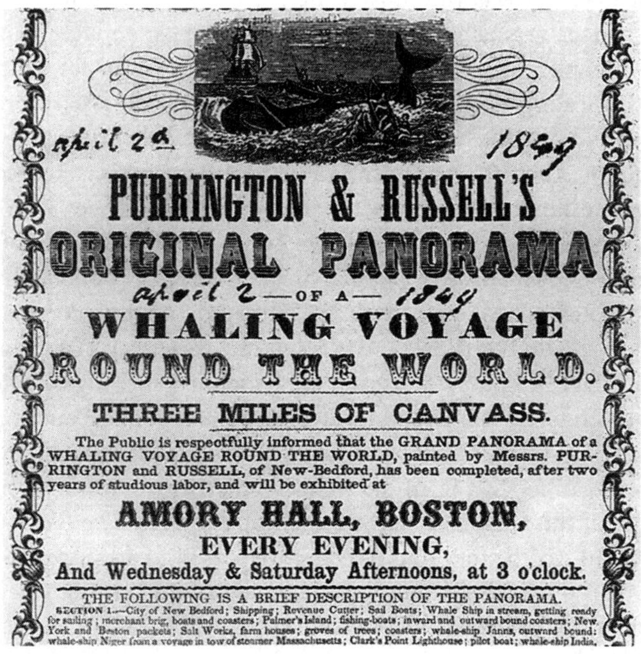

Figure 2.5. Vicarious thrills—voyaging via panorama displays.
Poster for Purrington and Russell, *The Grand Panorama of a Whaling Voyage Round the World*, Amory Hall, Boston, 1849.

Source: WikiCommons, public domain.

newspapers, journals, pamphlets, and broadsides was the development of steam power and cylinder rolls, leading in 1848 to the invention of the steam-powered rotary press: The ability to print millions of pages a day was now a reality, making reading materials more widely available than ever.[30] "Yellow-cover" literature in the form of penny or dime novels focusing on lurid crimes proliferated, providing cheap thrills at cheap prices. Reynolds demonstrates Melville's adeptness at borrowing the florid rhetoric and imagery of such pulp fiction while rejecting their themes.[31] Travel narratives trafficked (like Melville's early narratives) in the exotic and unknown; dark-reform literature focused on social vices; and city novels dramatized newcomers' bewildered encounters with urban spaces filled with types such as the crooked but likeable b'hoy (of which Ishmael is a variation) and the flimflam artist (like Melville's Confidence-Man).[32] Newspaper culture exploded as the United States shifted from a mercantile economy to a market economy, as did almanacs, literary journals, sensationalist nonfiction, guidebooks, the newspaper sketch (such as George Lippard' weekly feature "It Is a Queer World"), and the uniquely American genres of the tall tale and Southwest humor with their roots in oral culture.[33]

If print material was the most widely available medium of the day, by midcentury stage drama had become the nation's most popular form of entertainment. Melville, an off-and-on resident of Manhattan for years, was an enthusiastic theatergoer (the journal of his London trip in 1856 records outings to the Royal Lyceum, the New Strand, and Saddler's Wells). Since the early days of the republic, the major eastern seaboard cities had boasted established theaters where famous English actors entertained audiences with imported productions of Shakespeare and the like. But in the first decades of the nineteenth century, an interest in popular theater spread exponentially as more and more theaters were constructed, and homegrown acting companies began touring the states and territories. As a result, the variety and frequency of productions available for public consumption ballooned, moving beyond familiar classics to sentimental tearjerkers, lurid melodramas, political burlesques, naval dramas, farces, vaudeville acts, and pantomimes. In Manhattan, the heart of theater life began to shift from the financial district to midtown, signaled by the opening of the Forty-Second Street Theatre in 1836. *The Black Crook*, the first musical in which story and dancing were used to advance the plot, premiered in 1866 at Niblo's Garden Theatre, inaugurating one of America's original contributions to theatrical entertainment. Another homegrown theatrical offering, the minstrel show, featured white actors in blackface (Black Guinea in *The Confidence-Man* spoofs this tradition). By midcentury, touring companies regularly plied their trade across the spreading face of the nation, playing for gamblers on showboats as well as for goldminers out West.

A sense of the range of subject matters capturing the attention of the avid theatergoing public in the years that Melville was writing or living in New York is conveyed in the theatrical bills displayed in figures 2.6–2.8. Although I selected these productions randomly, they illustrate the fact that racial, interracial, ethnic, and foreign topics were a more familiar part of the mid-nineteenth-century viewer's experience than some might imagine. After all, by the Civil War, 50 percent of the inhabitants of Manhattan, the epicenter of American theater, were immigrants; diversity, as Melville saw daily upon his final move to the city, was the new norm. "We expatriate ourselves to nationalize the universe," the protagonist of *White-Jacket* proclaims.[34] While the statement may be taken as a colonization of otherness in the name of national superiority, one can also read into it another meaning, the truth that Melville's years at sea had taught him—that the transnational reaches of the ocean circling the globe far overshadowed the claims of land-based nationalities.

The tremendous success of Harriet Beecher Stowe's racially charged novel *Uncle Tom's Cabin*, published serially starting in June 1851 and then in two volumes in March 1852, guaranteed immediate adaptation to the stage. Two competing versions ran in competition with other in New York in late 1853, one being Purdy's New National Theatre production boasting, according to its flyer,

"Six Acts, Eight Tableaus, & Thirty Scenes," along with original music (figure 2.6). The bottom of the playbill announces that special arrangements have been made for "respectable colored persons desirous of witnessing this great drama" to attend by entering through "a special entrance" leading to a "neat and comfortable" seating area "entirely separate from other parts of the house." That contemporary debates about slavery commanded paying audiences is also evident in the Bowery Theatre's production in 1859 "founded on recent stirring events," *The Insurrection, or Kansas and Harper's Ferry*, featuring a Virginia Reel with fifty dancers (figure 2.7). If the latter spectacle seems to modern tastes unbefitting of the tragic arc of John Brown's life, its inclusion reminds us of the *hybrid* purposes that nineteenth-century stage entertainments regularly served; a bill of fare might offer a Molière tragedy along with a burlesque and operatic arias. So, too, the program featuring *The Insurrection* concludes with the comic spectacle *Chow-Chow, or the Mandarin's Dream*. If the characters' names are any indication, this comedy was cringingly Orientalist, but, like the Saturday matinee at the Academy of Music, *The French Spy, or, The Fall of Algiers* (n.d.) (figure 2.8), featuring a combat between a light-skinned European and a dark-skinned "Mahometan," *Chow-Chow* indicates general theatergoers' keen, if voyeuristic, curiosity about distant countries and myriad ethnicities. The attention given to intermixtures both cultural and personal in a growingly diverse society that was built on the extermination of Native populations is also evinced in Ann S. Stephens's dime novel *Malaeska, the Indian Wife of the White Hunter* (1860), its cover advertising its story of interracial romance (the child in the background intimates the sexual nature of the union), and Alfred D. Hynes's novel *The Invisible Scout, or a Romance of Early Kentucky* (1871), its cover sensationalizing and racializing an act of sexual assault (figures 2.9 and 2.10).

Operas both light and tragic were another mode of highly popular entertainment in Melville's Manhattan, and Andrew Delbanco's biography recounts that Melville became a great fan of opera as well as of theater in his New York years.[35] Imported from London and enjoying successful runs in New York, Philadelphia, and Boston in the mid-nineteenth century, the comic opera *Inkle and Yarico* (1787) (figure 2.11) by George Colman demonstrates, like the dramas and dime novels, the vicarious interest of nineteenth-century American audiences in the representation of interracial relationships. Inkle, an English sailor shipwrecked in the West Indies is saved by Yarico, an African native maiden with whom he falls in love; obstacles arise when, after his rescue, he faces social pressures to marry his very wealthy English fiancée and considers selling Yarico as a slave. A parallel dynamic is played out in the subplot, where his bumbling but faithful servant has fallen in love with Yarico's Black servant-woman and the servant's fidelity is held up as a model for the wavering Inkle. The entire plot, built on a witty comedy-of-errors format, works to demonstrate

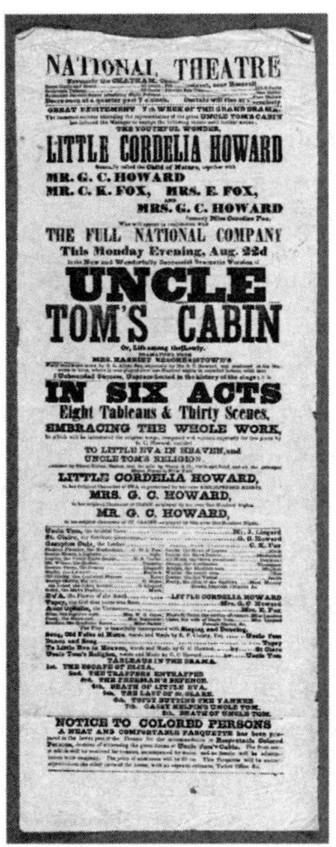

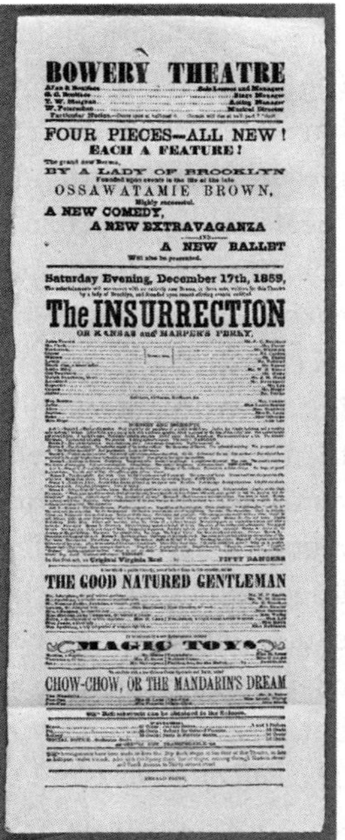

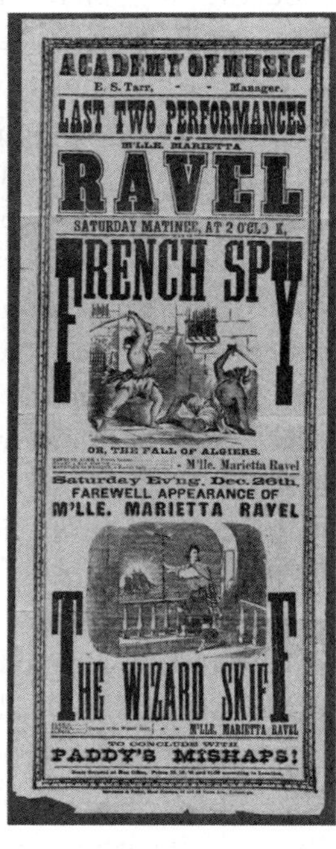

Figures 2.6, 2.7, and 2.8. Popular theater and racial themes.
Top left: Playbill for *Uncle Tom's Cabin* at the New National Theatre, 1853. *Top right*: Playbill for *The Insurrection* at the Bowery Theatre, 1859. *Bottom center*: Playbill for Ravel's *The French Spy*, Academy of Music, 1866.

Sources: 2.6: Harvard Theatre Collection, Houghton Library, Harvard University, pf TCS 65 (Chatham). Courtesy of Houghton Library. 2.7: Harvard Theatre Collection, Houghton Library, Harvard University, pf TCS 65 (Bowery). Courtesy of Houghton Library. 2.8: Courtesy of the Billy Rose Theatre Division, the New York Public Library for the Performing Arts. All in public domain.

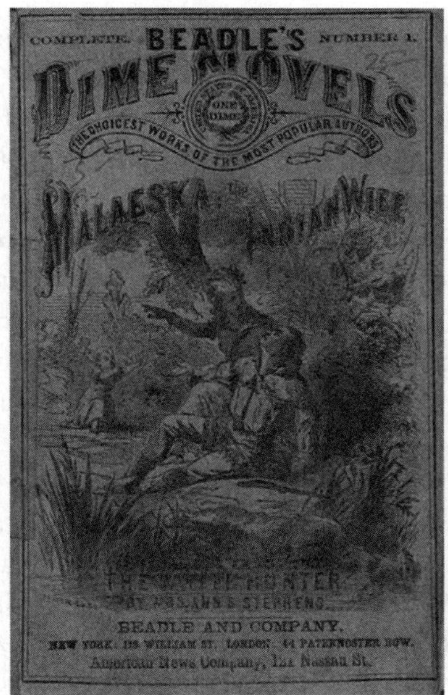

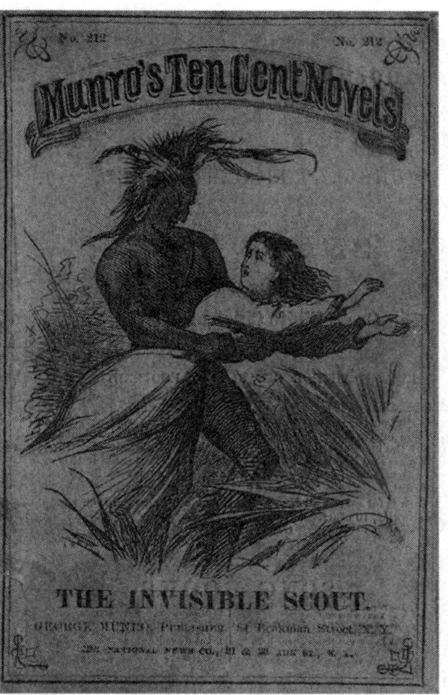

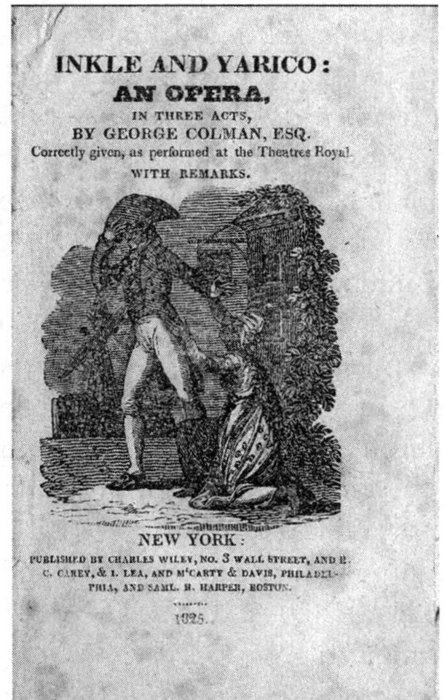

Figures 2.9, 2.10, and 2.11. Sensationalizing and sexualizing encounters with Native Americans.

Top left: Cover of Ann S. Stephens, *Malaeska, the Indian Wife of the White Hunter* (Charles Wiley and H. C. Carey and I. Lea, 1860). *Top right*: Cover of Alfred D. Hynes, *The Invisible Scout, or a Romance of Early Kentucky* (M'Carty & Davis, 1871). *Bottom center*: Cover of George Colman, *Inkle and Yarico: An Opera, in Three Acts* (1787; Saml. H. Harper, 1825).

Source: 2.9: WikiCommons, public domain. 2.10: Public domain. 2.11: Internet Archive, public domain.

that true love ought to trump both racial difference and money, and nothing in the libretto indicates the audience should find this strange.

Another prevalent mode of musical entertainment in the era were songs set to piano music for performance in the home. Some of its most popular forms—riverboat songs and sailor ballads—directly tapped into the themes and settings sparking Melville's literary imagination. But they did so with telling differences. Predictably, the romantic lyrics of sailor songs—a huge favorite—do not include the homoeroticism associated in Melville's fiction with its all-male worlds, and, likewise, sheet music cover illustrations give no hint of the racial diversity that was a reality of shipboard life (by the early 1800s, 20 percent of all American sailors were free Black men.)[36]

Three other vastly popular entertainment venues familiar to Melville were the Lyceum lecture circuit, the panorama, and Phineas T. Barnum's American Museum. Lectures featuring speakers on topics from the edifying to the fantastical became a ubiquitous feature of middle-class cultural life during the first half of the nineteenth century and quickly spread from the East Coast metropolises to midwestern towns to outposts in the western territories. By the 1850s, an estimated half-million people a week were attending such lectures in search of self-improvement, entertainment, and a glimpse of the day's celebrities.[37] As early as 1836, Emerson had declared, "My pulpit is the lyceum platform," and thirteen years later, as Collamer M. Abbott notes, Melville took in one of Emerson's lectures while on a visit to Boston. As Melville himself readied to try his luck at the lecture circuit in 1857, Oliver Wendell Holmes, a popular mainstay on the circuit, warned him that the demands of the middlebrow audience converted the lecturer into a "literary strumpet" working for barely more than a "whore's fee."[38] (Melville's attempt proved a dismal failure, reviewers bemoaning his mumbled delivery.) John Evelev argues that many of *Moby-Dick*'s cetology chapters self-consciously mime the bombastic oratory of the lecture format, poking fun at the venue's claim of providing its audiences with "useful" knowledge. Yet even as Ishmael's rhetoric undermines "the cultural authority bestowed on [the professional lecturer]," Evelev suggests the character's winking play with such oratory evinces a belief in his own "superior cultural competency" and hence his—and by proxy Melville's—enmeshment in this form of mass entertainment.[39]

The history of the panorama reaches back to late eighteenth-century England, when special rotundas were built to exhibit paintings; spectators would stroll around the rotunda's circumference as they took in the 360-degree vista. The invention in 1829 of moving panoramas, in which the painted canvas was spooled onto a roller that, when positioned upright, would wind onto a second cylinder, enabled audiences to watch the entire panorama while seated. This technological development made panorama shows easily portable, able to be shown wherever there was a stage on which the rollers might be mounted; as a result, countless people could take hitherto unimaginable virtual trips down the Mississippi, onto the open sea, or to the Holy Lands as well as relive patriotic events such as the Battle of Bunker Hill and the Mexican Campaign.[40] As an immersive visual experience in which moving images scrolled past the seated spectator's eye, this mid-nineteenth-century entertainment served as the era's equivalent of twentieth-century film and television (in fact, the cinematic term *panning* derives from *panorama*). In his journal in 1856, Melville mentioned John Banvard, one of the most prolific artists producing these miles-long canvases, and in the essay "Melville and the Panoramas" (1995) Abbott lists, as earlier mentioned, the specific panoramas to which the writer was exposed in Boston and New York City.[41] Most tantalizingly, during Melville's Boston stay in 1849, Purrington and Russell's three-mile-long *Original Panorama of a Whaling Voyage Round the World* was on display at Armory Hall (its announcement is shown in figure 2.5). The visual narrative follows a whaler's journey out of New Bedford, around Cape Horn, and into the Pacific, depicting everything from the thrills of the hunt to more mundane activities—reminiscent of Ishmael's chapters on whaling lore—such as the cutting up and boiling of whale blubber.[42] Hans Bergmann argues that, like the new journalism of the day, the perspective of the panorama shifted from the previously popular bird's-eye view of scenes of natural sublimity to a contemporary interest in representing the "continuing present," the "quotidian, the astonishing ordinary." Newspaper reviews of Purrington and Russell's panorama sound as if this particular production managed to deliver both functions successfully: scenes of natural sublimity inspiring awe alongside depictions of "the astonishing ordinary" of whaling men's lives in an immersive "continuing present."[43] As Abbott notes, Melville's grandiose writing style also overflows with sweeping vistas and vastness, expressive of "a milieu . . . conditioned to be conscious of hyperbole and gigantism[,] . . . and panoramas were part of this hyperbolic atmosphere in the 1840s and 1850s."[44]

Melville was also familiar with the wonders (and hoaxes) of the immersive experiences offered by Barnum's American Museum, located on Broadway in the financial district from 1842 to 1865, and hoaxes are intrinsic to the con games that the protagonist of *The Confidence-Man* plays on a gullible public.[45] Upon entering the museum, visitors found themselves engulfed by a panoply of media and entertainments, from museum displays to fine dining, from shooting galleries to stage performances. This temple of mixed media and popular culture included

> a combination zoo, museum, lecture hall, wax museum, theater and freak show. . . . dioramas, panoramas, "cosmoramas," scientific instruments, modern appliances, a flea circus, a loom powered by a dog, the trunk of a tree under which Jesus' disciples sat, an oyster bar, a rifle range, waxworks, glass blowers,

> taxidermists, phrenologists, pretty baby contests, Ned the learned seal, the Fiji Mermaid (a mummified monkey's torso with a fish's tail), midgets, Chang and Eng the Siamese twins, a menagerie of exotic animals that included beluga whales in an aquarium, giants, Native Americans who performed traditional songs and dances, Grizzly Adams's trained bears and performances ranging from magicians, ventriloquists and blackface minstrels to adaptations of biblical tales and *Uncle Tom's Cabin*.[46]

This kaleidoscopic array mirrors Melville's expansive inclusiveness. Both showman and writer reveal a shared sensibility when it comes to (re)presenting the "wonders" of the world and making the most of evolving modes of media and entertainment.

An apt example with which to conclude this overview of the media-saturated culture in which Melville launched his writing career is Captain E. C. Williams's panorama *South Sea Whaling Voyage*, a mash-up of multiple formats. In the same decade that Melville published *Moby-Dick*, the 1850s, Williams began touring America with his show, which in a few years evolved into a multimedia feast of the senses. Aiming to surpass the wonders of Purrington and Russell's whaling panorama, the exhibition premiered in New England in 1858 to rapturous audiences (in Fall River, Massachusetts, five thousand people, or more than half the city's population, attended its five-day run). That Melville was on Williams's mind is indisputable: A pamphlet that accompanied his panorama begins with a wholesale lifting of the "Extracts" from *Moby-Dick* and contains extracts from the novel as well as from well-known whaling authorities such as Thomas Beale and Thomas Macy.[47] Williams served as the vehicle's delineator or narrator, but from the beginning he made his presence felt, as John Marsh puts it, "as a performer with considerable histrionic ability": He was acting out, not just narrating, the show.[48] Soon enough, the panorama began to incorporate various whaling instruments as props; next, it added an on-stage whale boat with actors as crew, who enacted the chase that was simultaneously scrolling across the moving screen behind them; some months later, whaling songs and shanties were added to the spectacle, sung by the crew as chorus, as were some purely comic elements (one involved a sailor boy falling overboard, the humorous antithesis of the tragic psychosis suffered by Melville's overboard Pip). Scenes of action were punctuated, moreover, with Williams's lectures on functions such as the "cutting-in," creating "interludes" that functioned like Ishmael's narrative divagations in the whale-lore chapters. Williams capitalized on his stage success by publishing the book *Life in the South Seas* (1860), thus adding print media to his repertoire. A pamphlet version of this book sold at showings, furthermore, contained its own element of mixed media—inserted color lithographs that, if viewed sequentially, set the visual image of the whale hunt, as in "stop-motion" technology, into something close to cinematic movement.[49]

By 1861, the moving panorama, Marsh surmises, was no longer this traveling show's primary feature. Rather, it now functioned as "scenic background to the essentially dramatic activity in the foreground." The result is a full-blown example of multimedia art "smacking . . . more of the stage than of the lecture hall."[50] Originally conceived as a panorama, Williams's narration of a (painted) whaling voyage became the impetus for a hybrid stage event that exceeded generic classifications. The cultural zeitgeist that made possible Williams's extravaganza was the same one feeding Melville's ambitions earlier in the decade, when his hybrid aesthetics reached its zenith in another story of the whale hunt, *Moby-Dick*. If Williams achieved the popularity that conspicuously failed Melville, that is because Melville was no longer satisfied with simply "entertaining": He was also on his own epic quest to make great literary art and to do so by pushing fiction to places no American novelist had attempted before.

Remediations: A Repertoire

Melville's resourcefulness in tapping into the multiple media forms inundating the popular culture of his day, it is clear, goes hand in hand with the evolution of his distinctively hybrid narrative aesthetics: appropriating, incorporating, repurposing, and making something altogether new from source materials that range from revered classics to popular entertainments, from established genres to emerging modes. For some artists, such "higgledy-piggledy" borrowing may be the mark of a mind without an original idea, but in Melville's case the opposite is true: His receptivity to the possibilities offered by multiple genres, styles high and low, and varied media forms was precisely what made his fiction so radically innovative, so original, and not only "new" (in his time) but also "renewable" (in ours).

"Remediations: A Repertoire" brings together the aesthetic and historical factors recounted in the first two sections of this chapter by giving the reader a kaleidoscopic overview—a series of quick snapshots—of contemporary reenvisionings to illuminate the sheer range and global reach of the Melville effect at work today. Drawing on Deleuze and Guattari's terms, one might consider these examples as part-objects in the vaster constellation that composes the overall Melville effect. The variety, breadth, and bravado on display here introduce tropes, techniques, and themes that recur in the chapters that follow.

Let's begin with a simple but brilliant remediation, a concrete poem written under the sign of Melville by the Brazilian poet Augusto de Campos, in which sonic and visual levels blend to give a haunting presence and voice to the White Whale.[51] Published in 1994, just as contemporary interest in Melville was gaining momentum, "walfischesnachtgesang/cançãonoturnadabaleia" (The whale's night song), demands, like all concrete poetry, *to be seen* in order to be "heard" properly. As the following reproduction evinces, only by visually registering the alternation between lines filled with white *m*'s and lines in which the poem's individual words appear (separated by more *m*'s) do we begin to "hear" the

ammbrancurammdommbranco
mmmmmmmmmmmmmmmmmm
ammmnegrurammdommmmnegro
mmmmmmmmmmmmmmmmmm
ródtchenkommmmmallévltch
mmmmmmmmmmmmmmmmmm
ommmmmmmarmmmmmmesquece
mmmmmmmmmmmmmmmmmm
jónasmmmmmmemmmmmconhece
mmmmmmmmmmmmmmmmmm
sómmahabmmmnãommmsoube
mmmmmmmmmmmmmmmmmm
ammnoltemmqauemmemmcoube
mmmmmmmmmmmmmmmmmm
mmmmmmmmmmmmmmalvorece
mmmmmmmmmmmmmmmmmm
callmmmmmmemmmmmmmmmmoby

murmur of the black ocean on which these lyrics metaphorically float, as if white crests of waves rippling across the blackness of the background grid. The alliterative murmur of *m*'s anticipates the poem's final turn, when, in the last line, written in English, we learn that the speaking "me" is "moby" (more *m*'s). Here, the famous first line of Melville's text, "Call me Ishmael," recurs with a crucial difference: "**call**mmmmm**me**mmmmmmmmmm**moby**" (boldface added).

A translation of the poem, omitting the lines of *m*'s, goes:

the whiteness of white
the blackness of black
Rodtchenko Malevich
the seas forget
Jonah knows me
only Ahab isn't aware
of the night I must bear
the dawn's light
call me moby

Despite its minimalism, this short lyric is rich in allusions that support its engagement with Melville. First, as the words *night song* in the title indicate, the poem self-reflexively recalls another oceanic "night song," Christian Morgenstern's wordless "Fisches Nachtgesang" (1905), in which scansion marks create the shape and scales of a fish:

—
◡◡
— — —
◡◡◡◡
— — —
◡◡◡◡
— — —
◡◡◡◡
— — —
◡◡◡◡
— — —
◡◡
—

Second, the reference in the third line to artists Rodtchenko and Malevich calls to mind their black-on-black and white-on-white productivist paintings of 1919. These artworks, in turn, are *visual* equivalents of the *verbal* contents of the first two lines, in which the sentence structure ("the x-ness of x") is the same, but the contents are radically different ("white/ness" versus "black/ness"). These repetitions mimic the form of the poem (white letters against black background). Simultaneously, they anticipate de Campos's reinterpretation of "The Whiteness of the Whale" chapter of *Moby-Dick*, in which Ishmael expounds on the uncanny terror that "the visible absence of color" (whiteness) strikes in the human heart. As the last line of the poem reveals, de Campos replaces Ishmael's point of view with that of the whale, now revealed as the speaker of these lines. Instead of Ishmael's fear, the whale expresses a sense of oceanic mystery in which absence balances presence, sameness balances difference, and knowing ("Jonah knows") balances not knowing ("only Ahab isn't aware"). Enveloped in the darkness or "night" that he "must bear" living underwater where he is invisible to human eyes, this "moby" also looks forward to the light, the "dawn," that will come when he breaches the ocean's surface at daybreak. As Marjorie Perloff notes, *alvo*, the root of the Portuguese word *alvorece* (it dawns) also means "target"—and, as she puts it, "white light, far from being dreaded, is here the poet's goal. The cycle of nature can be accepted in all its strangeness[;] . . . black writing turns white before our very eyes."[52] The visual grid that constrains the poem within its exacting format (each letter being accorded the same weight) paradoxically liberates de Campos's words to float free and reimagine *Moby-Dick* from a posthuman perspective.

Alex Itin does more than mix sight and sound in a spellbinding, four-minute digital video titled *Orson Whales* (2007). Identifying himself as a "multimediast," the Brooklyn-based artist creates a self-reflexive dialogue among versions of Melville's afterlives by layering six distinct modes of media into a narrative that moves with breakneck speed: Itin's paintings, animation, spoken word (that of Orson Welles), music (Led Zeppelin), film (a clip from *Citizen Kane*), and text (pages of *Moby-Dick*). The voice-over derives primarily from a recording that Welles made of several chapters of *Moby-Dick* in 1971 in hopes of one day creating an avant-garde film based on the novel (which I discuss in chapter 5), but we also hear bits from Welles's infamously inebriated Paul Masson champagne commercial as well his thoughts on his last film. The rapid-fire animation consists of a montage of swiftly metamorphosing images of the whale hunt painted in broad black-and-white brush strokes onto pages of the novel (figure 2.12)—Itin reports it took two copies of the novel to produce the requisite number of animated cells. The musical soundtrack that accompanies and punctuates voice-over and animation is a mix of live and studio recordings of the Led Zeppelin classic "Moby Dick," which has gone down in the annals of rock history for Jon Bonham's fierce, monumental drum solo (in some performances lasting thirty minutes).

In light of Bonham's drumming, Itin's choice of title, *Orson Whales*, becomes all the more significant. Yes, there's the obvious pun on "Welles" and "Whales," appropriate given the actor's monomaniacal tendencies and Ahab-like obsessions, first with striving for (and most often failing to attain) artistic perfection and second with attempting to adapt *Moby-Dick* to a variety of platforms. But as John T. Hamilton notes in a terrific analysis of Itin's video, the term *whaling* has a secondary meaning: that of "beating vigorously" (possibly derived from the use of whalebone in whips). Thus, Hamilton writes, Bonham's vigorous "hand-to-hand combat" with the drums casts him as "the whaling Ahab, offering a relentless performance on an epic scale, pitting his imperious will against a mighty foe." *To whale* has another archaic meaning as well, that of haranguing through speech (as in "wailing" against the wrongs that one suffers), and Welles's oratory does tend to "whale"/"wail," most notably in the final moments of the video, where Itin cuts from the actor-director's reading of *Moby-Dick* to his ruminations on his last film, *F Is for Fake* (1974), as he laments that "everything"—all art, all monuments, all attempts at greatness—will inevitably "fall . . . into the ultimate and universal ash. A fact of life: we're going to die."[53]

Just as Welles "whales" these lines, the animation gives way to a few spliced seconds from *Citizen Kane* as Welles's aged magnate steps into a hall of reflecting mirrors, and his image is caught mise en abyme, endlessly diffusing Kane's identity to the point that it's impossible to discern the "fake" from the "real."

In contrast to the dizzying pace of the preceding animation, Itin plays this clip in exaggeratedly slow motion, and he follows the final rumination ("we're going to die") with Welles's reading of Ishmael's description of Narcissus drowning in the mirror of his reflection in the "Loomings" chapter. "The image of the ungraspable phantom of life" that Narcissus sees in the water, so Ishmael "whales," is "the key to it all" (*Moby-Dick*, 20): The quest to attain our phantom desires dooms us to defeat and failure, for inevitably the hunted becomes the hunter, and our singular identities shatter in the deceptive mirror of impossible meaning.

This existential truth is also the message self-reflexively represented in Itin's video, which insists on Ahab/Welles/Bonham as infinitely mirroring reflections of each other. In the opening sequence of animated images, flashes of the faces of the novel's characters morph into a giant eye that stares out at the viewer (figure 2.13); this eye dissolves into a tiny fish, which is then swallowed by a whale, which is then succeeded by images of a man staring in a mirror and emerging out of it. The image of the single eye returns, but now containing the faces of the novel's characters, before metamorphosing into the eye of the whale. In Itin's simultaneous wink to the rock band's name and the actor's most famous film, this whale now turns into a whale-shaped zeppelin labeled *Rosebud* (the missing "key" to meaning in *Citizen Kane*). As Ahab viciously harpoons the zeppelin, it explodes, Hindenburg-like, into annihilating flames, revealing the impermanence underlying all attempts to fix identity in the mirror of self-reflection. "Specular identification," Hamilton writes, "is but an exposure to the abyss."[54] By revisiting and updating Melville through the remediations provided by Welles and Bonham, Itin exposes the folly of those Ahabs of past and present who seek to grasp and overpower demons that are actually self-projections: You can "whale" all you like, but the end is the same—ashes. Provocatively harnessing the multimedia and digital-video technologies of the new century, Itin gives this Melvillean truth contemporary currency by refracting it through the lenses of Welles's and Bonham's earlier riffs on Melville.

In terms of size, production and distribution, Itin's intense but brief video is a far cry from the full-blown mixed-media spectacle that is Laurie Anderson's *Songs and Stories from* Moby-Dick, a nearly three-hour-long vehicle that performed to sell-out audiences across the country in 1999 and 2000. Yet, not unlike Itin, the performance artist/musician Anderson channels Melville to deliver a meditation on the existential "idea that what you look for your whole life will eventually eat you alive."[55] Like Itin's remediation, her self-conscious dive into Melville's psyche allows her, as Samuel Otter points out, to "raise questions . . . [about] the lure of immersion and the challenge of self-definition" involved in "artistic creation."[56] The responsive chords that Melville's artistic quest strikes in Anderson resound on many levels. Scott Saul perceptively notes that in Melville "Anderson has found . . . new inspiration for her ongoing bid to rewrite the American anthem"; the result is "a head-on collision between our

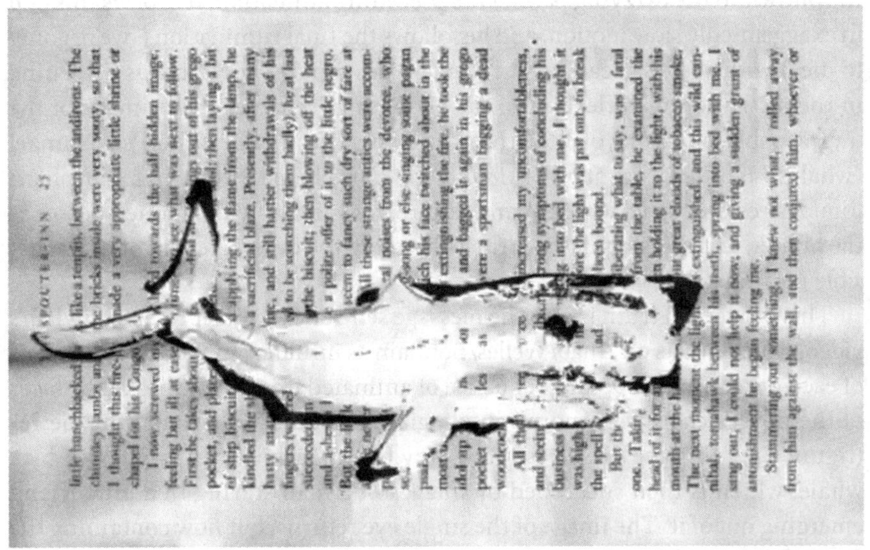

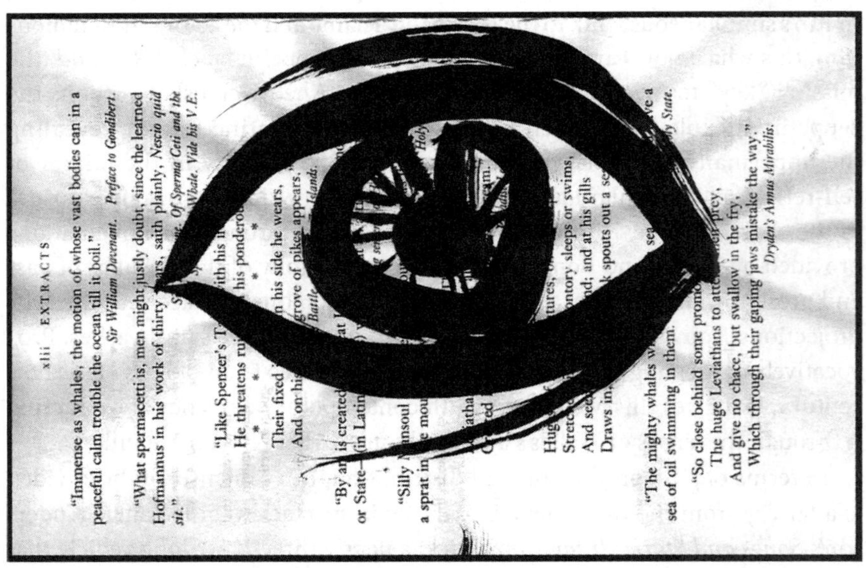

Figures 2.12 and 2.13. Images from Alex Itin's multimedia video *Orson Whales* (2007).

Source: Courtesy of the artist.

most postmodern nineteenth-century novelist and a performance artist who, since the early eighties, has been praised and skewered as a tribune of the pomo."[57]

Notably, *Songs and Stories* marked the first time in Anderson's twenty-five-year career that she based her work on another text; it is also the first time that she used a cast rather than relying on a solo performance—as if she felt the multivocality of *Moby-Dick* demanded more than one voice or presence. To call the results of Anderson's "collision" with Melville an adaptation, even a loose adaptation, is inadequate. By claiming Melville as a kindred creative spirit tackling questions and formal issues that she finds herself also exploring at the end of the twentieth century, Anderson doesn't attempt a literal reenvisioning of the novel. Rather, having deeply absorbed the text (she reread *Moby-Dick* five times in a row as part of her preparation), she transforms it into art that is uniquely her own yet simultaneously in conversation with Melville's vision and aesthetics. And she does so, as Otter perceptively notes, by "treating Melville in the same way that he treats his own sources."[58] That is, she samples various passages from *Moby-Dick*, then freely adds extratextual material and autobiographical elements as suit her themes and interests. Tellingly, there isn't that much of Ahab or the whale in *Songs and Stories*. The textual bits that most interest Anderson are the digressions, the cetology chapters, the veering into the odd or intriguing detail, which allow her, both in her storytelling riffs and in her musical renditions, to soar till her words achieve something of Melville's incantatory prose and Ishmael's enchantment as the "flood-gates of the wonder-world sw[i]ng open" (*Moby-Dick*, 22). Anderson has titled her opus *Songs and Stories*, and, indeed, that's what exactly we get—a mosaic that pieces together seemingly random items without attempting to force them into a coherent totality (as such, she channels Ishmael's lesson that "dissect him as I may," the whale can never be seen whole [296]); rather, the creative joy lies in the infinite exploration of all the "bits and pieces," as the title of the show's signature song, "Bits and Pieces," emphasizes.[59]

The multiple media used in Anderson's meditation on Melville include, in addition to those that arise from her roles as actor, storyteller, and musician, a giant split screen on which various moving images—many digitally created—appear, a round "moon" screen onto which the actors' faces are occasionally projected, dance-mime segments enacted by a cast of three actors, exaggerated stage props out of Lewis Carroll (a gigantic easy chair, three-foot stovepipe hats), text from the novel scrolling across the back screen, sound effects (including the "click" of whale songs), Anderson's famous synthesized violin, and an instrument she invented especially for this production: a six-foot-long "Talking Stick" that doubles as harpoon and, when stroked, produces a range of digitalized symphonic and percussive sounds. In terms of storytelling, what Glen Hirschberg calls Anderson's "free-roaming chatter" engages her audience with anecdotes, interpretations, and asides that reach beyond the text proper to Melville's afterlives and the performer's personal musings.[60] These monologues incorporate multiple genres as well: spoken word, poetry, and vaudeville humor. As an actor, Anderson nominally plays the roles of Pip, Whale, and Reader, but these parts are hardly inclusive and don't account for the Ishmael-like tenor of many of her ramblings.

The production's thirty-six musical numbers tap into an equally eclectic range of genres, from the experimental to the familiar. Acid jazz, funk grooves, Calypso, pop tunes, guitar punk, doo-wop, sea shanty, polyrhythms: All these musical styles are sampled. This aural diversity is heightened by the frequent digital alteration of voices and instruments to create a defamiliarizing soundscape. Sometimes the music (like Melville) fails to deliver on its potential, but the production soars, as Saul writes, in "moments of blue wonder when Melville's incantatory language rides on the swell of Anderson's music." This mélange of musical styles and stream-of-consciousness storytelling together create a nonlinear narrative structure that, as Saul puts it, gleefully "leaps and stumbles from one set piece to another, each exploring a new mood by dipping into a new musical genre."[61]

The result is a wild, messy mix of bits and pieces that, in making full use of contemporary technology, practices a patchwork aesthetics evocative of Melville's own. As such, Anderson's relation to her source material is not the case of a contemporary artist "learning" her aesthetics from Melville; rather, by engaging his spirit in the same way that he picks and chooses from all the materials his culture offered up to him, Anderson amplifies his *effects* into what becomes her unique, contemporary vision. *Songs and Stories* provides an intellectually and emotionally rich encounter between two kindred spirits separated by more than a century, and in doing so it mediates the gap between absence and presence, past and present, parts and whole, creating transtemporal resonances that allow us not only to see Melville anew but also to experience the horizons of art in a multimedia age.

Equally idiosyncratic in his borrowings is Guy Ben-Ner's highly personal *Moby Dick*, a twelve-minute video shot entirely in the artist's home in 2000 and purchased by the Museum of Modern Art in 2009. Known as one of Israel's foremost video artists, Ben-Ner has elevated the late twentieth-century tradition of the home video, documenting private family life, into an art form that, like reality television, blurs the line between art and life, public and private, spontaneous and performed.[62] Using his kitchen as setting and family members as collaborators, Ben-Ner demonstrates his penchant for taking famous works of art "that we all know, even if we haven't read them," because they are so embedded in our culture and tethering them to domestic spaces, makeshift props, and home technology. The motivating idea, he has explained, is "to bring" these classics "down to our kitchen sink, dealing with the biggest of themes with the aid of the tiniest means."[63]

Ben-Ner freely admits that he hadn't read *Moby-Dick* until he set about making this video, but that didn't stop him from finding in the novel the thematic tension that drives all his projects: the conundrum of "striving to merge the labors of fatherhood and artistic production" in a postfeminist present. As a committed stay-at-home dad equally dedicated to his career as an artist, Ben-Ner found home videos to be the perfect medium for, as Robert Wallace puts it, his "domesticat[ing] the heroic while still trying to pursue [his] own ambitions and dreams."[64] *Moby-Dick*'s "The Symphony" chapter provided the videographer with his key to reenvisioning Melville's story. If in this chapter Ahab abjures the lure of family and home to continue his mad quest, Ben-Ner chooses to embrace the domestic and make it the productive site of fantasy, adventure, and creative striving. "Is it better to go after the fantasy object and lament the family left behind or to stay at home and lament the lost object?," Ben-Ner asks.[65] Ben-Ner's transposition of Melville's whaling adventure to this domestic space reminds us as well that most of the labor on a whale ship was in fact mundane "housekeeping," or what Ishmael calls long stretches of "sublime uneventfulness" (133).[66]

When Ben-Ner speaks of bringing the big themes of culturally resonant narratives such as *Moby-Dick* "down to our kitchen sink," he's not just being metaphoric. In the home video, his kitchen sink becomes the bar at the Spouter Inn, then the *Pequod* (a huge mast rises from sink to the ceiling), and finally the vortex that sucks all but Ishmael to their deaths. Countertop, refrigerator, and other inventive props populate the scene. All roles are played by Ben-Ner and his six-year-old daughter, Elia. The word *play* is critical here: The intimate farce between father and child that we witness is an example of both playacting *and* playing, of assuming scripted roles *and* having spontaneous fun. Emulating silent-era movies, the video is filmed without words and with intertitles. The camera work also emulates the early film medium's jerky moments, and the acting self-consciously cites the slapstick antics of Buster Keaton and Charlie Chaplin. Furthermore, as father and daughter engage in a series of pranks and gags that loosely follow the story of Ishmael and Ahab, stop-motion animation is used to portray sharks' fins circling on the kitchen linoleum floor; sprinklers slipped under an area rug signify whale spouts; a mysterious hand yanks Ahab's peg leg out from under him; rungs keep collapsing on the ladder he attempts to climb (a comic version of Sisyphean striving). All these vaudeville bits and homespun elements, Jennifer Scappettone reminds us, "match the ramshackle construction of Melville's monument": Both novelist and videographer revel in an aesthetics of messiness and mayhem.[67]

Ben-Ner's response to Melville is best summed up in the two "endings" that he gives the home video. After a title card announces "The End," we see Ben-Ner as Ahab stabbing the white sink with his harpoon until (think Marx Brothers) a gush of water suddenly spouts from the drain, hits him in the face, and causes him to drop his spear; the next we see of "Ahab" is his hand, as it's sucked down the drain. The ship (the sink) has in effect become the whale that "sinks" the sink (the ship); the real enemy is not "out there" but here at hand, inside our intimate spaces and psyches. This tragicomic climax is immediately succeeded by a second, also tragicomic, ending, in which Ben-Ner, held hostage, is sliced in half with a scimitar. In a comic routine emulating Georges Méliès's classic use of trick photography in the film short *The Turkish Executioner* (1904), Ben-Ner's "legs" (his daughter in costume) run away, leaving the father's torso stranded on the kitchen floor, pitifully begging his legs to return. "They" finally do; the "magic" of cinematic editing allows a restoration of Ben-Ner's severed body to wholeness. What has been lost is found: This ending provides a concise illustration of the theory of *fort/da* that Freud posits as the basis of all narrative, and it suggests the novel's epilogue, in which we learn Ishmael has survived to tell the tale. In Ben-Ner's retelling, however, the filmmaker-father is notably reborn or resurrected by his child's agency—in the return of his "legs" to his speaking torso.[68] In the novel, the cruising ship *Rachel* in search of her captain's lost son rescues Ishmael, and, thus, Melville's "mother"–son pairing becomes Ben-Ner's father–daughter duo. The message is clear: Salvation lies in the bonds of family and in the embrace of domesticity. As Wallace notes, the "homebound quest" that "leads to the domestication and the exorcizing of the fantasy quest of the heroic captain" exposes the solipsistic quester's defiance of the universe for what it too often is: empty hypermasculine bravado.[69] A clue to this message occurs in an early visual where we catch sight of a heart that has been shaved into the artist's hairy chest. As we will see of other players in the Melville effect, Ben-Ner dares to embrace sentimentality, just like he refuses to separate his personal life from his art, as he renders his body into "text" (the shaven heart) and as he brings the public into his private home. Like other participants as well, he revels in the homespun and makeshift, finding human comedy and community rather than tragedy and solitude in his reenactment of Melville.

The three examples just reviewed involve performance, either captured on video or acted on stage. The next three remediations move us closer to the category of visual art. Reminiscent of De Campos's concrete poem, they do so by merging two genres—written text and visual art object—into a single artifact. If Ben-Nur's mingling of private and professional realms allows the subjective to bleed into the artwork, the French visual artist Claire Illouz betrays something of this tendency as well when she writes of the "passionat[e]" intensity of her desire "to pay tribute" to Melville in her *livre d'artiste* (artist's book) *The Whiteness* (2008).[70] This unabashed sentiment, as the following chapters demonstrate, recurs among contemporary artists participating in the Melville effect for whom traditional boundaries (between artist and artwork, between artist and source of inspiration, between subject and object) no longer hold.

Despite Illouz's passionate declaration, the result of her encounter with Melville—precipitated by reading *Moby-Dick* for the first time and being utterly surprised by the affinities she found in it—is as coolly immaculate an object as a marble statue on a plinth. *The Whiteness* exemplifies a hybrid genre, the artist's book or text art, in which the artist defamiliarizes the reader's conception of textuality by rendering it as an object *to be seen*. Great attention is paid to each element of the process of producing an artist's book: pagination, binding, fonts, paper texture, margins, and so forth. At its most aspirational, an artist's book makes the viewer see the revised text anew, with fresh insights.

Illouz's text-art book aims to convey a visual representation of the terrors and uncertainties of noncolor that Ishmael hauntingly articulates in the chapter "The Whiteness of the Whale." The existential and artistic concerns expressed in Melville's chapter, Illouz feels, speak deeply to the struggle of all visual artists—especially the struggle with doubt that arises when facing the blank canvas and wondering whether one can ever succeed in wrestling into representational form one's vision of the invisible "essence of things."[71] Illouz embarks on this quest, first, by deciding to emboss the passages she imports from the chapter onto her pages *without* ink. Only the shadows cast by the white letters on the white page makes them legible: We must struggle, as Melville intends his reader to do, to bring the "essence of things" to the surface of apprehension. Second, she produced her book with a concertina binding so that the pages unfold, accordion-like, in a continuous sheet nine feet long. The effect at once suggests "endless voyage and reverie" and mimics the motion of waves.[72]

The visual images created by Illouz and included in *The Whiteness* indirectly comment on the embossed words, hinting at her interpretation of the novel. The one appearing on the final pages is the most haunting: The embossed (and noninked) outline of the White Whale's tail slips below the bottom of the page (figure 2.14). This "questioning farewell" raises doubt about the ghostly whale's very existence, allowing Illouz's return to the presiding concern—"what we artists owe to doubt"—that she finds in Melville's disquisition on whiteness.[73] *The Whiteness* represents that doubt through the illusory quality of its text, in which we "see" without seeing, perceiving words and image even as their gradations of whiteness waver before our eyes.

If Illouz's Melvillean white script threatens to disappear from the page, the orthography of Justin Quinn's art-book project *Moby Dick, or EEEE EEEE* (2003–2010), demands our notice, its black lettering inducing near-hallucinatory states. Interested in exploring "the distance between reading and seeing," Quinn began experimenting in 1998 with making the letter E (in both upper and lower cases) the starting point for abstract visual compositions; he fixed on E both because it is "often found at the top of vision charts" and because it "is the most commonly used letter in the English language." Making E "a surrogate for all letters in the alphabet," he proceeded to transcribe every letter in *Moby-Dick* into a master language composed solely of his handwritten Es. By emptying written words of "their use as legible signifiers," he thus renders in their place "a vacant parallel language" that becomes the site for "visual manufacture."[74] As Alice Bailey notes, this process "abstract[s] the text away from something that is read into something that is seen."[75] Quinn's ambitious project consists of two volumes. The first follows the traditional page layout of the novel,

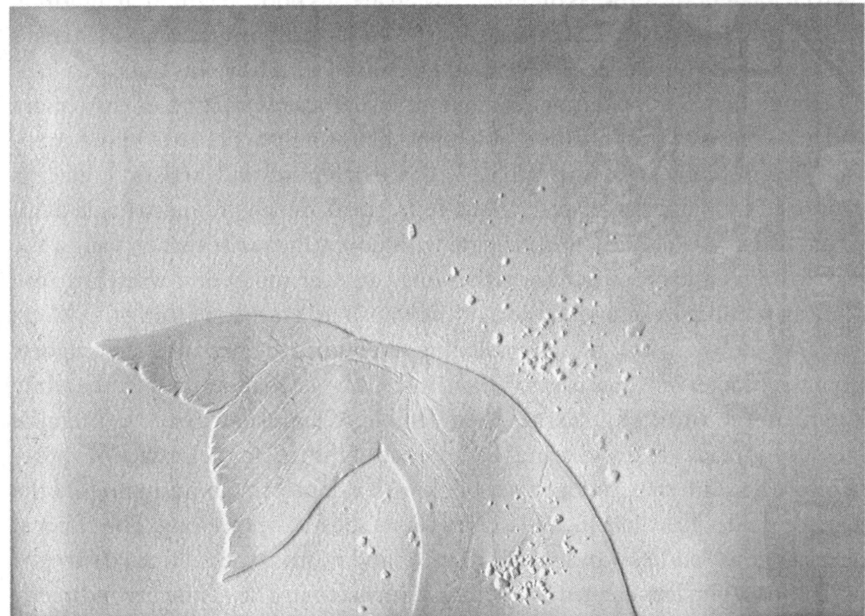

Figure 2.14. Whiteness disappearing into whiteness.
Claire Illouz, page from *The Whiteness*, artist's book, 2008. Text by Herman Melville, with two double-page etchings and three embossed images. Letterpress by Jean-Jacques Sergent. Edition of twenty-five, on BFK Rives paper, 34 × 26 × 3 cm. (13¼" × 10¼").

Source: Courtesy of the artist.

replacing its letters with E's in linear lines, replete with chapter breaks and paragraph indentations. The second volume, *177,649 Times E*, consists of abstract drawings of every chapter made of the requisite number of Es to match the chapter's letter count; thus, we have *Chapter 35 or 2,128 Times E* (2009) (figure 2.15) and *Chapter 54 or 6,618 Times E* (2004) (figure 2.16). Look hard enough, and one begins to imagine Ishmael's dizzying view from the masthead (chapter 35) and the zigzagging narrative layers in "The *Town-Ho*'s Story" (chapter 54). Again: Look hard enough, and one begins to "drown" in the knots and vortexes of an unknowable language that threatens to tug one under as surely as Ahab's harpoon rope ties him to foe and drags him to his doom. Making us feel the precariousness of language, whose arbitrary signifiers tease us with yet continually defer meaning, Quinn provocatively echoes one of Melville's most profound themes. The dedication and dogged determination it took Quinn to do the one-for-one transcription that makes up *EEEE EEEE*, demanding that he overcome the monotony and repetition of matching every letter of Melville's text with yet another E, seem both cloistered and sublimely Zen-like, inducing

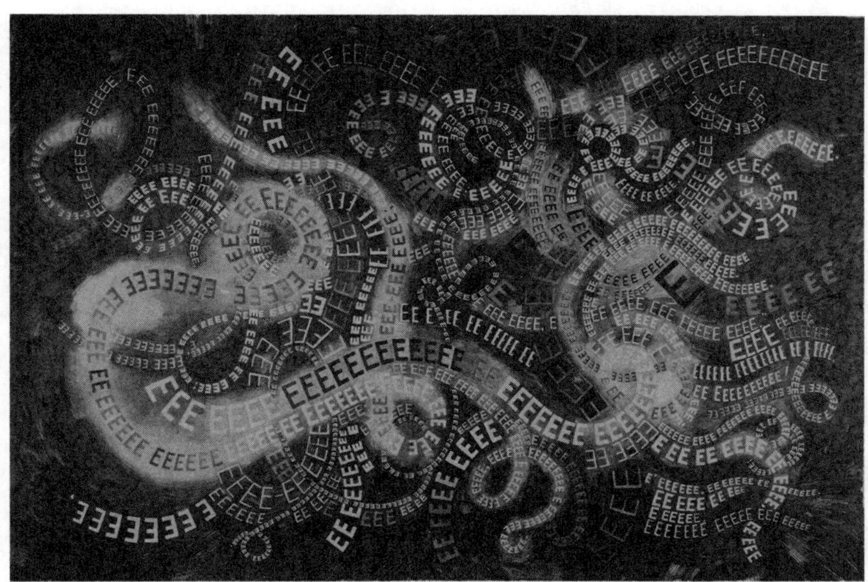

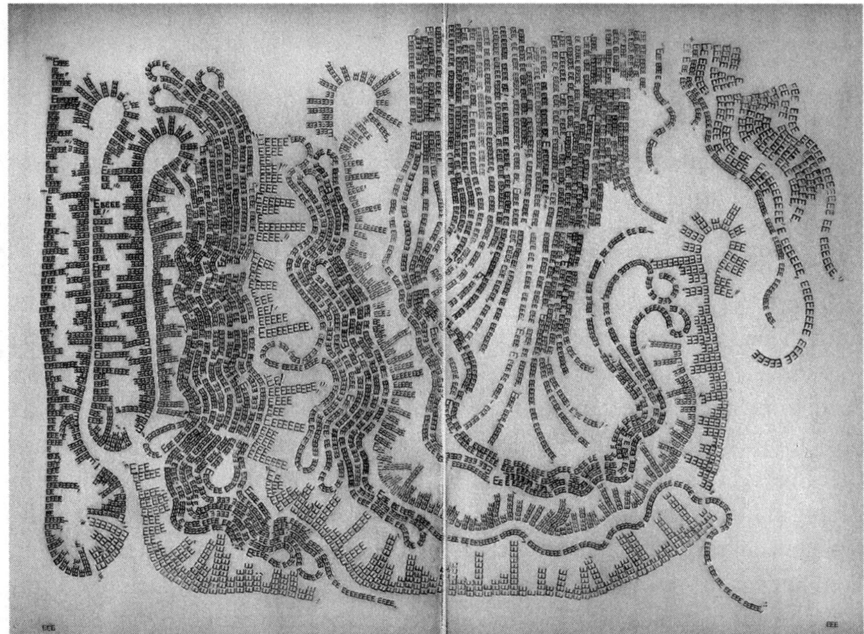

Figures 2.15 and 2.16. A swarm of swimming E's.
Top: Justin Quinn, *Chapter 35 or 2,128 Times E*, for the art book *Moby Dick, or EEEE EEEE* (2003–2008). Graphite on cotton rag, 26½" × 40". *Bottom*: Quinn, *Chapter 54 or 6,618 Times E*, 2004, for the art book *Moby Dick, or EEEE EEEE*. Drypoint intaglio, 9" × 12".

Source: 2.15: Artist's collection. Courtesy of the artist. 2.16: Private collection. Courtesy of the artist.

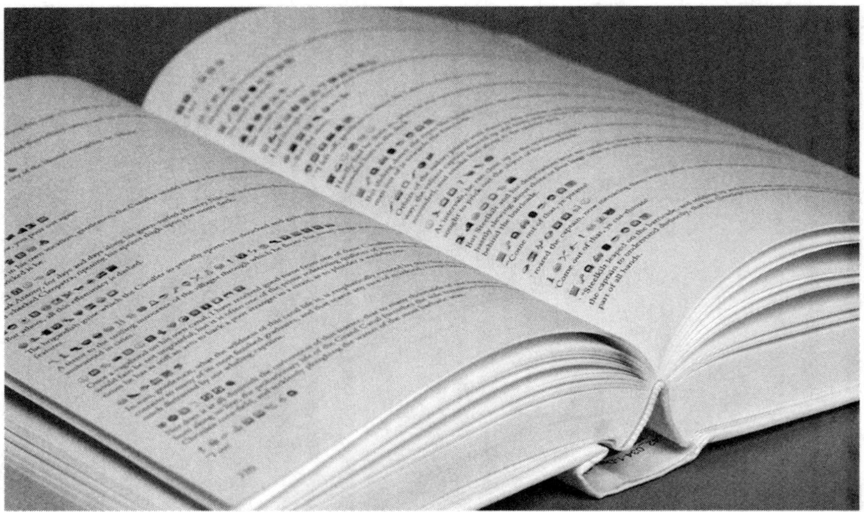

Figure 2.17. Crowdsourcing *Moby-Dick* as emoji text.
Pages from Herman Melville, *Emoji-Dick* , ed. and comp. Fred Benesen, trans. Amazon Mechanical Turk (unknown publisher, 2010).

Source: Photograph courtesy of Fred Benesen.

a state of mind that, literally in this case, exists outside language as a system of knowable signifiers. Likewise, Quinn's focus on transcribing every letter of *Moby-Dick* into E's reveals an obsessiveness that, as chapter 5 explores, is shared with many of Melville's other contemporary collaborators.[76]

The act of translating a written language into a visual text is pushed to its limit in *Emoji Dick: Or* 🐳 (2010), a communal project in which the entire novel was converted into corresponding emoji characters (figure 2.17). The result is a hardbound book (one can purchase it for $200) that is also a conceptual art object. Like Quinn's *EEEE EEEE*, it exists to be looked at—with the difference that instead of seeing a recognizable letter of the alphabet, we find ourselves gazing at ideograms and pictographs (the term *emoji* is an Anglicization of the Japanese characters for "picture-letter").[77] The creative force behind the project, Fred Benenson—an early pioneer in emoji art—explains that *Emoji Dick* originated in his fascination with "how our language, communications, and culture" are rapidly being transformed by advances in "digital technology."[78] Since some cultural commentators lament the advent of emojis as a denigration of proper language, while others see it as an invigoration, Benenson felt that creating a "juxtaposition between this really simple, constrained language and [an example of] classical literature" would allow him to "confront a lot of our shared anxieties about the future of human expression."[79] This anxiety also encompasses traditional conceptions of authorship and the nature of collaboration, conceptions interrogated by several players in the Melville effect. *Emoji-Dick* provocatively puts the former into question by embracing fullheartedly the anonymity of the latter, involving more than eight hundred unnamed participants.

Although the title page announces Berenson as the translator, his role is more specifically that of curator, setting perimeters and soliciting the project's contributors. Crowdfunding the project on Kickstart, he then crowdsourced each sentence of *Moby-Dick* on Amazon Mechanical Turk (on this server, "requesters" offer "providers" minimal compensation to complete mundane tasks too complex for automated processes and requiring human intelligence; the more tasks a provider accepts, the more income the person makes). Benenson provided this workforce with a dictionary of 471 emojis; the first three submissions of any individual sentence were then judged by another set of providers. The sentence winning the most votes secured a place in the published text. In an interview in *The Guardian*, Benenson explained his interest in "pushing the boundaries of crowd-sourcing and also [of] Emoji—to see how far you can take" either innovation.[80] While detractors picture Melville rolling in his grave at this violation of his prose, the fact is that Melville, like Benenson, was forever eager to "push[] the boundaries" of given forms as "far" as they might be taken. Benenson acknowledges this affinity in ambition: "The story behind *Moby-Dick* is about this huge seemingly insurmountable challenge, told using metaphors and stylized language, and in a way that's what translating a book into Emoji is—a weird, huge challenge told in metaphors and stylized language."[81] What Melville strives to do with language provokes Benenson's equivalent effort, "translating" Melville's novel into a conceptual art object composed of tens of thousands of individual "pictures," and the result reconfigures both the notion of authorship as well as the book. Whether one calls the result "art" or "trash," *Emoji Dick*, bursting with colors, is eerily beautiful and awesome to look at. After all, to repeat Babbalanja's observation in *Mardi*, "Genius is full of trash."

Lofty goals, as Melville well knew, are often doomed to failure, and *Emoji Dick* has its flaws. The selection of emoticons in many of the sentences seems arbitrary (which the reader can check because Melville's text is given below each emoji translation), despite the competitive selection process they went through. Nor is the limited emoji vocabulary (471 ideograms and pictographs) adequate to the metaphoric richness of Melville's prose. Authorship is multiple, but it is far from shared collaboration in the sense of minds working together. Inevitably, the pressure to perform and to outperform the competition lessened the time any individual spent attempting to create the nuances that might do justice to Melville's language; often, the chosen sentences are composed of one-to-one correspondences between word and emoticon that are the simplest solution at hand. Yet, for all these flaws, the creation of *Emoji Dick* reminds us, as

Samantha Gorman writes, that language has *always* been a "crowdsourced" event.[82] The meanings of words change over time and according to their usage by different sectors of society; new words arise; others disappear. Melville himself was very much a participant in this process, his penchant for neologisms irking some contemporary (and even more recent) critics to no end.[83] Hence, the implications of *Emoji Dick* are particularly relevant in this day and age, in which the reality of exponentially developing digital technology inevitably "speeds up the mutability of signs," creating instabilities in our conception of language, literature, communication, and the arts in general.[84]

The issues of translation across media and language raised by *Emoji Dick* take a transpacific turn in painter Eleen Lin's fascinating series of Melville-inspired canvases, *Mythopoeia*, begun in 2014 and still going strong. Describing herself as a "third culture" kid—born in Taiwan, raised in Thailand, living in the United States—Lin finds inspiration in having come of age in an era "of cultural cannibalism where everything is brought together and rearranged to form new identities."[85] This dismantling and reassembling of borrowed parts is as descriptive of Lin's themes and techniques as it is of her multiple identities. Her desire to combine Asian folklores and classical Western mythologies into "contemporized cross-cultural narratives" finds a perfect focal point in *Moby-Dick*.[86] Not having read the novel since high school, Lin was amazed upon returning to the Mandarin-language version to discover that its many errors in translation made it nearly incomprehensible to Chinese readers. The novel had been rendered into Mandarin in 1957, and because of the general ban that Chinese martial law placed on literary translations in Taiwan from 1949 to 1987, that text remained the template for subsequent editions until 2019, when a more accurate translation finally appeared.[87] Much of the original mistranslation was due, Lin hypothesizes, to "the lack of whaling culture and history in China or Taiwan" as well as to the difficulty of adapting Melville's highly figurative use of language to Mandarin's grammatical constructs while maintaining the original sentence structure. It's no wonder, Lin says, that Chinese-speaking audiences often mistake mention of *Moby-Dick* for *The Old Man and the Sea*.[88]

These mistranslations gave Lin her specific inspiration for bringing Western and Eastern mythologies into dialogue because the mistranslations so often occur when the Mandarin translator takes Melville's metaphors or metaphysics at face value or as literal events. In these moments, traces of Eastern folklore and mythology unexpectedly surface, at which point, as one reviewer puts it, "odd serendipities emerge."[89] The mistranslations are sometimes humorous, but in Lin's inventive visual evocations of these errors they also uncannily enrich and contemporize Melville's themes. If these paintings allow Lin to "showcase how our cultural background changes the way we understand parts of the story," the dialogues between cultural contexts that Lin embeds in her paintings give rise to new mythologies, ones attuned to contemporary global perspectives.[90]

The facts that the *Pequod*'s crew hails from around the world and that the search for Moby Dick occurs in the South Pacific make the novel all the more appropriate a launching point for Lin's cross-cultural, transpacific meditation.

Lin has thus far produced more than thirty large canvases (generally around five by six feet) that burst with vibrant color and activity. Each bears a title referencing a chapter or passage of *Moby-Dick*. Lin's identification as a third-culture kid is reflected in the eclectic mix of styles and techniques composing these paintings: Undercoats created from thin washes of acrylic evoke the fluidity of Chinese ink watercolors; folkloric monsters from Thai, Slavic, Hindu, and Japanese myths vie with the creatures of the deep that Melville describes; Nantucket whaling vessels bear lifeboats resembling origami and sails made of delicately patterned Asian fabrics; mundane items such as clothes pins, flip-flops, knitting needles, a student composition book, and an ad for Quaker Oats vie for visual space. The raw canvas on which the paint is applied—the same material from which ship's sails are made—signifies for Lin the materiality of nautical life. Meanwhile, abstract geometric designs derived from nature, such as the honeycomb pattern, interlace with tangled fishnets and gelatinous bodies of waste polluting the ocean. Water—blue, aquamarine, emerald—is everywhere, cresting, whirling, crashing; as the one element that transcends cultural contexts, it flows freely and without restriction, unifying Lin's aesthetic mix of realism, surrealism, and abstraction. (See chapter 7's focus on the role that the oceanic plays in recent environmentalist art.) Underlayers of color that spray in unexpected arcs are covered with clear gesso, over which oil is painted in a more controlled application; these layers give the paintings a collagelike effect that Lin likens to the experience of digital culture: "I like to flood the painting with different images to simulate what we experience in the digital world, where multiple representations and images pop on to the same screen and reproduce the feeling of an excess of information."[91] Given Lin's interest in evoking these digital sensations through a hybrid mixture of techniques, styles, and cultural inflections, it is easy to understand the appeal that Melville's aesthetics of excess holds for her. *Moby-Dick* continues to dominate Lin's imagination; she once imagined the *Mythopoeia* series to be a five-year project, but it shows no signs of flagging. "Obsession plays a big part in *Moby-Dick*," Lin says, "and I feel this book has definitely captivated me in that way."[92]

Lin's inventive and intensive remediation of Melville's novel and its Mandarin translation is humorously on view in *The Young Philosopher* (2015, figure 2.18). This painting glosses chapter 35, "The Mast-Head," in which Ishmael digresses into the history of the so-called crow's nest. The Mandarin translation takes this masthead feature literally, which inspires Lin, in the bottom right of *The Young Philosopher*, to include an egg-filled nest made of twigs on the masthead's wooden "crow's nest." The translation also takes Ishmael's fanciful meditation on the dangers that await those youthful lookouts who fall into

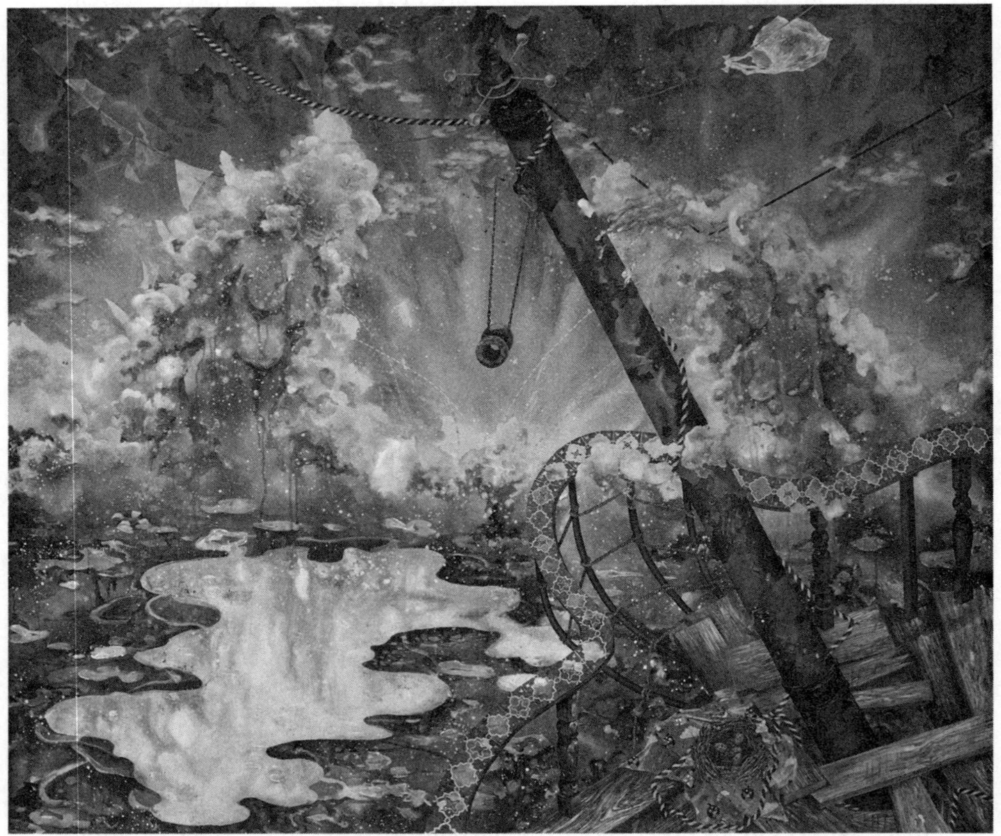

Figure 2.18. The dangers of crows' nest daydreams.
Eleen Lin, *The Young Philosopher*, 2015. Oil and acrylic on canvas, 70" × 94".

Source: Courtesy of the artist.

transcendental reveries, only to tumble to their deaths, as fact. Accordingly, the planks of the crow's nest in Lin's painting are pulling apart, and the masthead is about to tumble into the ocean. The unused lifebuoy floating in the distance intimates that this "young philosopher" has already disappeared into what Ishmael facetiously calls the ocean's "Descartean vortices" (136). The red bands of the lifebuoy are balanced by the reds of the patterned Japanese textile that unexpectedly forms the railing of the disintegrating crow's nest; along with the tattered pastel pennants hanging from the lines attached to the masthead and blowing loose in the wind, there are, at the upper right, an attached plastic bag (alluding to the plastic waste polluting modern oceans) and clothes pins. The latter adds a humorously domestic touch, in line with Ishmael's riff on how sailors often turn their crow's nest stations into cozy little homes.

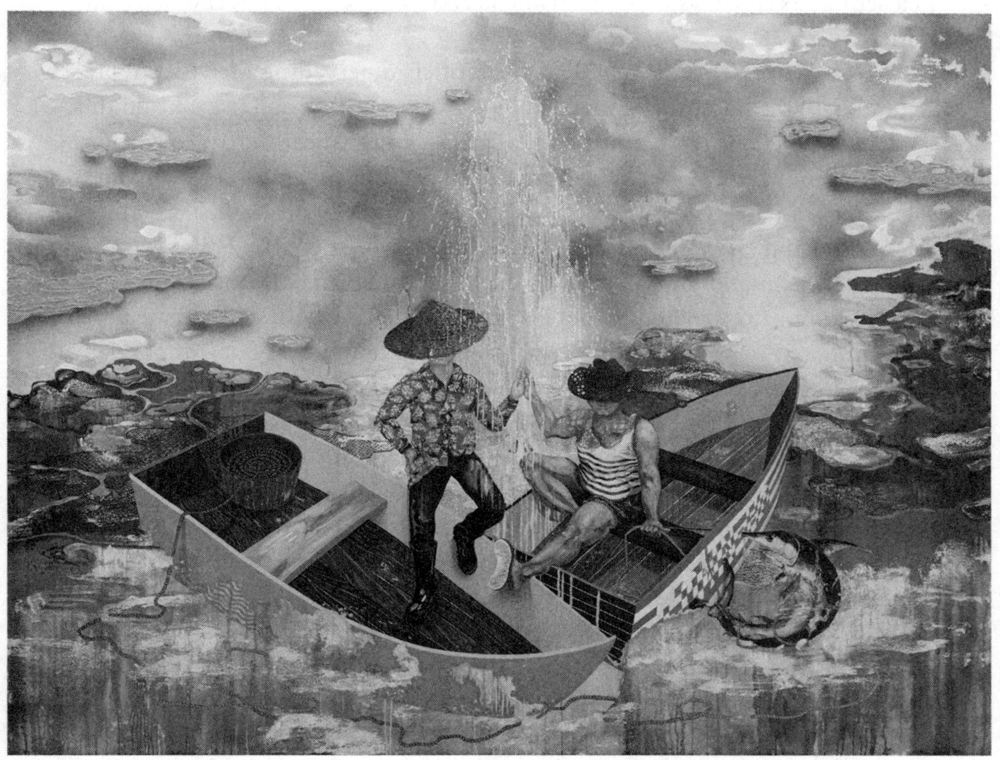

Figure 2.19. Sea gams as gay fantasia.
Eleen Lin, *Meet. Greet. Fleet*, 2018. Oil and acrylic on canvas, 72" × 96".

Source: Courtesy of the artist.

Another intersection among Melville, Eastern mythologies, and contemporaneity is staged via the politics of queer sexuality in *Meet. Greet. Fleet.* (2018, figure 2.19), Lin's representation of chapter 54, "The *Town-Ho*'s Story." In Melville's telling, this particular gam with the *Town-Ho* whaler centers on the inset story of two of its previous crew at murderous odds, and the story's "secret parts," as Ishmael calls them, include the words that Steelkit whispers to the captain that stops the latter in his tracks when about to flog the sailor. Melville's chapter takes the form of a nested tale—what happened on the *Town-Ho* is covertly told by three of its sailors to the *Pequod* harpooner Tashtego, who inadvertently discloses it as he talks in his sleep. Ishmael, thus made privy to the tale, passes it on to drinking companions in Lima in the narrative present of the chapter, years after the *Pequod*'s destruction. The story, we are told, is known only belowdecks, never by the boat's officers or mates. All this "undercover" secrecy, along with the tale's levels of nested narration, has the effect of "closeting" its core mystery—What *did* Steelkit whisper?—in impenetrable narrative layers.

This closeting effect, along with the eroticism pervading Melville's representation of the homosocial world of men at sea, occasioned Lin's take on this chapter: The "gam" represented on the canvas is an erotically charged encounter between two men, each in a separate dingy as they meet alone in the middle of the sea. This is no "virtual" hookup, as in contemporary trysts; what these men desire and experience is face-to-face, body-to-body contact.[93] The way that one leg of each sailor crosses into or touches the lifeboat of the other connotes the frisson uniting them, as does the rainbow-hued whaling line that subtly runs from one craft to the other. This gay "gam," however, is not without danger; the lowered hats hiding the faces of the two men indicate that it is a clandestine encounter. Likewise, although many Asian cultures have made major strides in gay rights, the power of family and tradition still often enforces silences to which Western gay subjects may not be as accustomed. The swordfish drilling a hole in the lifeboat on the right (symbolic of the act of penetration?) hints at the risks that attend such clandestine encounters. The latter visual detail is Lin's riff on a Mandarin mistranslation that takes the *Town-Ho* captain's reference to a swordfish endangering his boat as literal truth (the ship draws water but doesn't sink). Despite these presentiments, the meeting of the two men is euphoric, as signaled by their meeting palms and the orgasmic plumes of spray rising behind their erect fingers. The mist created by the spume, in turn, has created a glowing rainbow, a veritable gay flag, in the sky. How long will this encounter last? *Fleet*, the last word of Lin's title, perhaps intimates its evanescence. One is reminded of the way traces of homoerotic meaning in Melville's text appear like mirages before teasingly dissolving, then (as we will see in chapter 6) resurfacing elsewhere.

Dire current events also add layers of meaning to Lin's *Perils of Life* (2020, figure 2.20), which draws on "The Squid" and "The Line" chapters for its imagery. Ishmael turns the whale line in the latter into a resonant metaphor for life's perils: "So the graceful repose of the line, as it silently serpentines about the oarsmen before being brought into actual play. . . . But why say more? All men live enveloped in whale-lines. All are born with halters round their necks; but it is only when caught in the swift, sudden turn of death, that mortals realize the silent, subtle, ever-present perils of life" (21). This riff follows the usual pattern of Ishmael's thoughts; he begins with scrutiny of an object at hand, then soars to metaphysical insights or universals. Lin, however, returns her viewer to the material base of Ishmael's philosophical observation—namely, the boat's line. *Perils of Life*'s scenario, lifted from contemporary headlines, overtly alludes to today's refugee crises, depicting those who, in attempting to flee the stranglehold of famine or war, find themselves entangled in a life-or-death battle for survival in their flights by sea to reach other countries. Three crafts float in

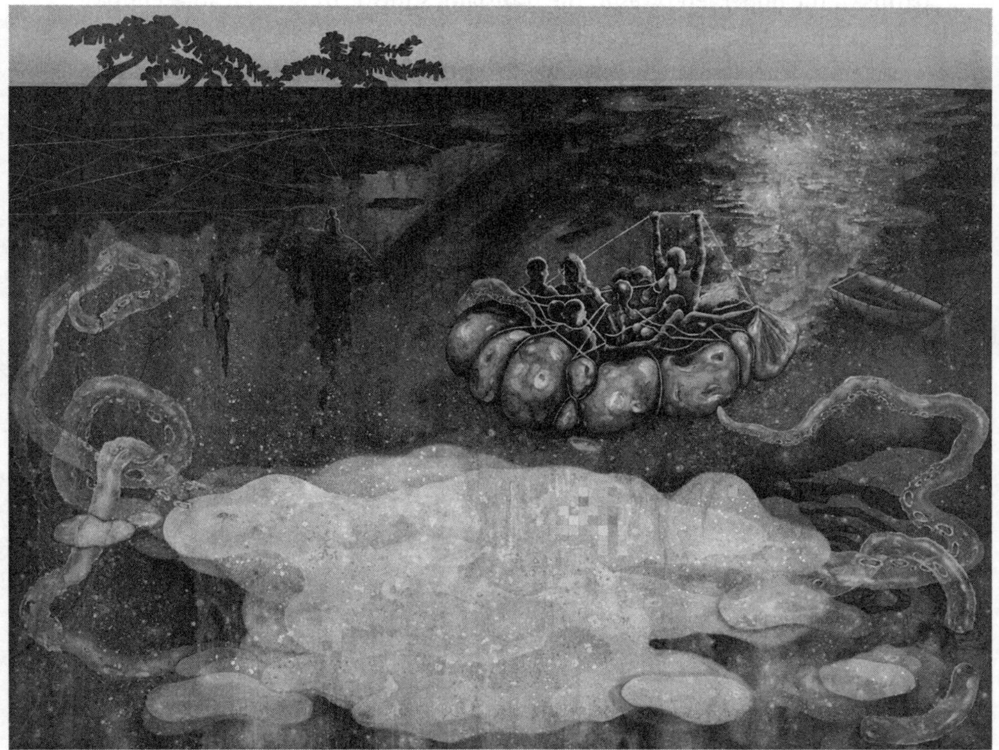

Figure 2.20. The flight and plight of refugees.
Eleen Lin, *Perils of Life* (2022). Oil and acrylic on canvas, 72" × 96".

Source: Courtesy of the artist.

the forebodingly purple water dominating Lin's painting, rendered ominous by a sickly lime-green sky. One is an empty lifeboat, entangled in rope; another has capsized, a single survivor sitting on its upturned helm; and the third, an inflatable life raft, is crowded with nine despairing passengers. An intricately twisted line of rope anchors their bodies to the boat, imprisoning them in its meshes—the one face turned to the viewer gapes in Goya-like horror.

The surreal depiction of this nightmarish situation is underlined by Lin's inclusion of a transparent golden thumb descending on the right to push the boat in the direction of the ominous squid lurking in the foreground; the sea creature has already wrapped one of its tentacles—analogous to the ropes strangling the refugees—around the raft. This golden thumb is Lin's nod to the Mandarin text's mistaking of a simile in "The Squid" for a real event: Melville likens "the long burnished sun-glade on the waters" to "a golden finger laid across them" (225). Lin's inclusion of the grid-covered plane/plain with its three palms in the upper left owes to the translator's misreading of an adjacent passage, in which Melville compares the *Pequod*'s "three tall tapering masts mildly wav[ing] to [the] languid breeze" to "three mild palms on a plain." The translator reverses the direction of the figure, describing a tropical island that looks *like* a boat. Even if the painting's refugees were able to reach this island, its grid-like surface promises no succor. And the commanding squid? In Japanese folklore, the cephalopod augurs an irreversible condition or coming calamity; in contrast, Melville's chapter informs us that squid sightings are positive because they portend the proximity of the sperm whales that feed on the creatures. Again, cultural contexts make all the difference in interpretation—and cultural misunderstanding lies at the heart of the contemporary humanitarian refugee crisis, a calamity in the making that finds vivid articulation in this meshing of Melville and Mandarin, East and West, under the aegis of Lin's "third-world" eye.

***

From a Brazilian poet's concrete verse experiment to Lin's massive canvases, one gets a sense of the global reach of the Melville effect as it crosses and recrosses geographies, genres, cultures, and media, inspiring a plethora of creative expressions that—whether an online video that lasts four minutes or a book composed of more than one hundred thousand emojis—attest to the "permanent contemporaneity" and "updatability" of this author's work. If, as Schwarz-Hoffman puts it, mention of Melville has a "way of flashing into relevance at every new cultural-political conjunction," these examples demonstrate one reason why: His hybrid, promiscuous aesthetics are particularly well suited to express those "cultural-political conjunctions" whose causes and effects are diffuse, multiple, and resistant to easy explanations.[94] For those contemporary artists making Melville a launching point for their aspirations, critiques, collaborations, and visions, what has already been written—"literary history"—is far from being irrelevant. Through the dynamic processes of remediation, the reverberations and afterlives of this history renew and inform the present and future of art and culture.

CHAPTER 3

WHENCE THE NOVEL?

Measuring the Melville Effect in Post-Postmodernist Fiction

It is not altogether agreed that the novel has anything but a past. . . . [H]ave [we] come to the end of the line [?].
—Saul Bellow, "Where Do We Go from Here? The Future of Fiction"

Today's most engaged young fiction does seem like some kind of line's end.
—David Foster Wallace, "E Unibus Pluram: Television and U.S. Fiction"

The pages are still blank, but there is a miraculous feeling of the words being there, written in invisible ink and clamoring to become visible.
—Vladimir Nabokov, "The Art of Literature and Common Sense"

In designating the Melville effect as a contemporary phenomenon, I have already made an important caveat worth repeating in the context of this chapter's focus. Throughout the twentieth century, there are notable instances of artists using Melville as a source of inspiration. In general, they reflect individual artists' responses to the various imperatives—often Americanist, elitist, masculinist—spearheading the first Melville revival in the 1920s as well as their era's construction of "Melville" as part of a political allegory of democracy. Some of these artworks serve as admiring tributes or homages; some manifest Bloomian anxieties of influence. As responses to Melville, however, they do not contribute to a collective zeitgeist; they are not participants in an unfolding dialogue about the possibilities of art in today's world.

In considering the period prior to the emergence of what I am calling the Melville effect in the 1990s, one might expect that several of the most powerful, innovative responses to Melville would occur in the genre for which he is most famous and whose conventions he most daringly challenged: the novel. To the contrary: The most well known of these twentieth-century inspirations—Benjamin Britten's opera, Orson Welles's play, Rockwell Kent's illustrations, Alan Hovhaness's symphony—occurred in media *other* than fiction. But this doesn't mean that no novelists prior to the 1990s channeled Melville in crafting their fictions. Rather, they did so in subtly allusive ways, or their works simply have not attracted the lasting attention and repeated revivals of, say, Britten's opera or Welles's play. Several of them evince investments in modernist ambitiousness that echo the values of many of the scholars initially responsible for rehabilitating Melville. I am thinking of Norman Mailer's *The Naked and the Dead* (1948), Paul Metcalf's *Genoa: A Telling of Wonders* (1965), Stefano D'Arrigo's *Horcynus Orca* (Killer Whale, 1975), and László Krasznahorkai's *The Melancholy of Resistance* (1982). Despite Mailer's declaration that "I was sure everyone would know" that *Moby-Dick* lay behind his testosterone-propelled World War II novel of an epic quest "because I had Ahab in it," its Melvillean associations are loose and not overt.[1] (I'd argue that Mailer's novel contains "Ahabs" in the plural since General Cunnings is Ahab-like in his despotism and Sergeant Croft in his monomaniacal obsession with conquering Mount Anaka.) The great-grandson of Melville, Metcalf, creates a mind-blowing "cut-up" or collage text in *Genoa*, in which he interweaves the story of two physically disabled brothers (one is a club-footed doctor, one has a distorted forehead), passages from Melville's works, and extracts from Columbus's journals. Combining stream of consciousness and surrealism, Krasznahorkai's Hungarian modernist masterpiece features a circus displaying the body of the largest whale in the world. D'Arrigo's 1,257-page epic is a lifelong work that liberally draws on the *Odyssey*, Joyce, and Melville. Monumentality marks all these novels.

Another wave of novels touting Melvillean allegiances surfaced after mid-century in science fiction, appropriating Melville's quest format and metaphysical elements for futuristic ends. In Samuel R. Delany's *Nova* (1968), the scarred Captain Von Ray obsessively quests with his crew of outcasts for a supernova; in Jose Philip Farmer's *Wind Whales of Ishmael* (1971), Ishmael falls through a fissure in time–space to a future earth devoid of oceans; in John Kessel's *Another Orphan* (1982), a contemporary financier wakes to find himself on Ahab's ship; and in Daniel Quinn's *Ishmael* (published in 1991 but written in 1976, the first volume in a trilogy that also includes *The Story of B* and *My Ishmael*), a learned gorilla named Ishmael engages in philosophical dialogues with his auditor about how to save earth from global disaster. Thomas Pynchon's *Gravity's Rainbow* (1973), which borrows from *Moby-Dick*, folds both modernist and fabulous strains into its postmodernist ambitions and sheer magnitude. Traces of Ahab inhabit the huge, white, hairless Judge Holden, the monstrous, monomaniacal leader of a gang of marauders, in Cormac McCarthy's *Blood Meridian* (1985). The masculine sublime, in all its awe and terror, dominates these sporadic fictional responses to Melville written between 1948 and 1985.

Something rather different happens in the flood of recent novels that use Melville as the springboard for their fictions; since 1995, at least thirty-one such novels (and two short stories) have appeared, with new titles cropping up by the year. Just between the writing and revising of this chapter, yet three more examples have come to my attention. One is Brett Ashley Kaplan's metatextual *Rare Stuff* (2022), in which the protagonist sets out on a quest to solve the mystery of the disappearance of her mother, a passionate whale advocate, while reading her deceased father's unpublished novel, in which Yiddish-speaking whales living in glass houses at the bottom of the ocean scheme with human allies to save the world from its self-destructive quest for new energy sources. The second, Chris Bachelder and Jennifer Habel's *Dayswork* (2023), is an autofiction (fictionalized autobiography) that takes place during the COVID pandemic. The unnamed female narrator, feeling set adrift by the immobilizing lockdown, obsessively researches Melville online; the darker truths about the author's domestic life that she feels Hershel Parker's biography elides become her metatextual means of dealing with tensions in her marriage. Xiaolu Guo's *Call Me Ishmaelle* (2025), set in the mid-nineteenth century, features an orphaned girl who disguises herself as a cabin boy on a whaleship manned by a Black captain obsessed with his tragic past. The conceptual and geographical span within which all these contemporary fictions put Melville to work is vast: They make Melville the inspiration for Leviathanic visions of everything from the horrors of apartheid in South Africa (Mark Behr) to the homosocial rites of college baseball in the American Midwest (Chad Harbach) and from the cutthroat industry of molecular biology diagnostics (abbreviated as "moby-Dx") in the Silicon Valley (Don Seligson) to a poststructuralist parody of male academic oedipal anxieties (Frank Lentricchia).[2]

Given that novelists work within the confines of the printed page, by definition they can't overtly play with disparate media forms as do many of the more daring exemplars of the current Melville effect. Nonetheless, a degree of inventiveness and experimentation does permeate the most talented of those contemporary novelists turning to, citing, and channeling Melville. Several find textual equivalents to suggest an interplay of generic modes and media; furthermore, the plasticity of novelistic form, its dialogic mesh of competing and overlapping voices, facilitates an interweaving of multiple themes, concerns, and perspectives that heighten the differences separating their work from those fictional attempts following the author's recovery earlier in the twentieth century.

The degree to which the novels that I highlight in this chapter look *backward* to Melville in order to look *forward* to the future of fiction is perhaps most evident in the degree to which they participate in a shift from high postmodernism as a marker of novelistic excellence to a revitalized deployment of realism that several critics have taken to calling the "post-postmodern turn" in contemporary fiction. Critics and reviewers have noted the increased prevalence since the 1990s of novels eschewing postmodernist irony, self-reflexivity, and affective distance. Instead, this new wave of fiction reembraces mimetic realism—dismissed by postmodernists as outmoded and naively transparent—and demonstrates a renewed belief in realism's abilities to engage social and historical reality, even while it *simultaneously* continues to be inventive, daring, experimental, and expansively inclusive. The "Melville" that these contemporary novelists activate and embrace is an exemplar of such inclusiveness and possibility, an author for whom realism exists alongside self-reflexivity, feelings, and engaged social commentary, and their contemporary takes allow these writers to straddle past and present to notably different ends than those championed by his earlier twentieth-century advocates. Turning to the literary past—particularly in the form of the now canonical but always radical Melville—becomes the means of envisioning a novelistic ethos and aesthetics for the here and now.

The novels surveyed in the following pages hail Melville in a variety of ways. A surprising number either fictionalize Melville's life or resurrect various of his characters as players in their fictional tales, notably Ahab and Ishmael, sometimes Bartleby or others. Some attempt to capture the epic sweep and encyclopedic inclusiveness of *Moby-Dick* by rewriting its epic-quest form—for instance, by reworking it as a specifically female experience or by tracing the arc of twentieth-century American technological inventions from the airplane to the A-bomb. And some adapt Melvillean tropes—the destructive will to power that reveals itself in fascistic obsession and toxic masculinity; the homosocial conundrums of male bonding; the traumatic legacies of slavery and empire; the capitalist globalization of both goods and knowledge and the threats they pose to the environment—to create politically charged allegories relevant to our age.

The first section of this chapter evaluates the values that emerge when an alternative, female-centric plot shapes itself out of the givens of *Moby-Dick*, as in Sena Jeter Naslund's *Ahab's Wife, or, The Star-Gazer* (1999). In the second section, I examine Frederick Busch's *The Night Inspector* (1999), an instance in which Melville appears as a fictionalized character and confronts in his daily life a literalization of the pasteboard mask he has already made into so potent a metaphor in his fiction. In contrast to these historical fictions, the novels examined in the third section—Mark Behr's *The Smell of Apples* (1995), Marianne Wiggins's *Evidence of Things Unseen* (2003), and Chad Harbach's *The Art of Fielding* (2011)—are set in the late twentieth century and self-reflexively channel, appropriate, and rework Melvillean concerns such as monomania, aggressive masculinity, racism, apocalyptic doom, totalitarianism, and the simultaneously homophobic and homoerotic resonances of all-male worlds. In the final section, I meditate on an evolving ethics and aesthetics found in contemporary fiction that looks backward (in this case to Melville and hence to literary history) in order to envision art's efficacy in the future.

Avatars of Ahab

Among novelistic manifestations of the Melville effect, Sena Jeter Naslund's *Ahab's Wife, or, The Star-Gazer* (1999) perhaps most daringly attempts to capture the style, voice, and textures of Melville's masterpiece, all the while creating its own original tale. As the next chapter demonstrates, women are central to the contemporary revival of interest in Melville, both as artists forging new visions of the author's work and as the subjects of any number of artworks attempting to answer the "But what about women?" question often asked in connection with Melville's male-dominated fictions.

Ahab's Wife is exemplary in this regard. As the word *wife* in the title indicates, Naslund takes her inspiration from the two brief mentions in *Moby-Dick* of the "sweet, resigned girl" (79) and "girl-wife" (406) whom seafaring Ahab has left behind. The story that results—narrated by Una, the wife and "star-gazer" of Naslund's title—is, like *Moby-Dick*, a quest-romance adventure with lofty metaphysical overtones. The voyage it traces, however, is uniquely female-centric and proleptically feminist. Of all the contemporary novels making use of Melville, *Ahab's Wife* most closely attempts to channel *Moby-Dick*'s plot and themes while echoing—sometimes in wonderfully inventive ways—its style, destabilizing shifts in point of view, and encyclopedic inclusiveness. Although Naslund doesn't succeed in all her ambitions, those ambitions are, like Melville's, monumental and fascinating to witness in their very execution.

The opening line cleverly sets Naslund's revisionary feminism into motion by relegating Ahab to a secondary place in Una's tale: "Captain Ahab was neither my first husband nor my last," the narrator-protagonist declares up front.[3] The interpretation of Ahab as a defiantly heroic if maddened quester seeking for universal truths celebrated by earlier scholars (and resurrected as fictional character in at least six other recent novels) is subtly taken down a notch. Likewise, the narrative's opening in media res signals Naslund's intention to rewrite the genre of the epic from a woman's point of view. In the dead of winter, the pregnant Una Spenser (named after the heroine of book 1 of Edmund Spenser's *The Faerie Queene*) has traveled to her mother's home in Kentucky to give birth, at which point her life collides with that of a runaway slave, Susan. From her hiding place between the feather mattresses of Una's bed, Susan experiences a metaphoric act of (re)birth as "in a smooth lunge" she slides "out onto the floor" (8). Her sudden appearance anticipates the birth of Una's child and triggers one in a series of intense female-bonding experiences that echo but revise Melville's emphasis on men's intimate bonds. As the two women cradle in the bed, kindling a sensual "friction" (8) that protects them from the freezing temperatures outside, each serving as the other's "husband, mother, sister, shadow, angel" (10), the interracial "heart's honeymoon" (*Moby-Dick*, 57) of bedmates Ishmael and Queequeg is rewritten as an embrace between two women, one Black and one white.

Such intertextuality continues. After helping Una through her pregnancy, Susan eludes bounty hunters by leaping from ice floe to ice floe across a river. Here, Naslund is channeling Eliza's famous escape scene in that *female* epic of American literature, *Uncle Tom's Cabin* (serialized in 1851, the same year of *Moby-Dick*'s publication), a passage of which is included in the self-reflexive "Extracts" with which *Ahab's Wife* begins. Thus, in just a few pages Naslund has created an innovative mash-up of Melville's novel (in the form of the occluded story of Ahab's spouse), Stowe's domestic national epic, and Spenser's verse quest romance—only *this* Una (later accompanied by a dwarf leading a white donkey, also right out of Spenser) doesn't need a Red Cross Knight to save her from the world's threatening dragons (or whales). Like Ishmael when he is reborn from the vortex created by the sinking of the *Pequod* at the end of *Moby-Dick*, Una is a survivor who—undergoing continual symbolic rebirths throughout her adventures—lives to "tell the tale" because of an unflinching ability to incorporate horrific experiences into a nonjudgmental, free-form, life-affirming, plastic mode of being that is reminiscent of Ishmael's saving openness; she converts her husband's thunderous "NO!" into a defiant "YES!"

Naslund's mix of literary forms and traditions in these opening chapters is just a sampling of the self-reflexivity that follows, which uses lyrical riffs, free association, out-of-time moments, digressions, first-person monologues that veer into other character's consciousnesses, and incursions of dramatic script in combination with the creative recasting of some of *Moby-Dick*'s most resonant images to promote contemporary concerns closely aligned with today's Melville effect. Thus, Ishmael's musings on fate inspired by loom weaving in "The Mat-Maker" chapter are repeated in Una's elevation of the female art of tatting, or lace making, into a mode of stitching back together the wounded self ("Oh, mankind, you must learn to tat if you would live content" [232]); Melville's meditations on the "dumb blankness" of "whiteness" (*Moby-Dick*, 165) are echoed in the "brightness of brightness" (89) that Una experiences when she (like Ahab) is struck by lightning; the marble cenotaphs set in the walls of the Whaleman's Chapel in New Bedford become a riverboat's wanted posters for escaped slaves (25–26); Ishmael's transcendental reveries atop the *Pequod*'s masthead are rewritten as Una's star-gazing experiences on the widow's walk of her Nantucket home—the domestic architectural equivalent of the tar's crow's nest.

This self-reflexivity and intertextuality are also apparent in Una's pre-Ahab life, when she dons a male disguise (and renames herself after another archetypal quester, Ulysses) to enlist as a cabin boy on the whaler *Sussex*—a stand-in for the historical *Essex*, whose sinking at sea by a sperm whale in 1820, recounted in Owen Chase's *Narrative of the Most Extraordinary and Distressing Shipwreck of the Whaler-ship the Essex* (1821), served as an initial inspiration for Melville. This setting allows numerous occasions for the cross-dressed Una to express Ishmaelean rhapsodies about life aboard a whaleboat and the cosmic frights and wonders of the sea. In the following passage, the furious beat of the whale hunt becomes Una's metatextual metaphor for the writer's pursuit of those words that come closest to unmasking the realities one seeks to put to paper:

> How the excitement comes upon me to tell it all! In the quest of writing, the heart can speed up with anticipation—as it does, indeed, during the chase itself of whales. I can swear it, having done both, and I will tell *you* though other writers may not. My heart is beating fast; I am in pursuit; I want my victory—that you should see and hear and above all feel the reality behind these words. For they are but a mask. Not the mask that conceals, not a mask that I would have you strike through as mere appearance, or, worse, deceitful appearance. Words need not be that kind of mask, but a mask such as the ancient Greek actors wore, a mask that expresses rather than conceals the inner drama: "But do you know me? Una? You have shipped long with me in the boat that is this book."
>
> (147–48)

Like the *Essex*, so too is the *Sussex* staved by a sperm whale, and Una is one of few who survive on a drifting rowboat and who, also like the *Essex* survivors, resort to cannibalism. Nowhere is Naslund's prose as starkly Melvillean yet as authentically her own as in a wrenching, five-sentence chapter titled "The Human Animal." Here Una, delirious with thirst and hunger, describes in hallucinatory prose her participation in these acts of cannibalism: "Someone puts a finger in my mouth. I suckle. But I know. I will always know. I am drinking blood" (225). The frenzied, bloody, inhumane slaughter of whales recounted by Ishmael has become the violence of the "human animal" turned against itself in Naslund's representation (in the maternal image of suckling, no less) of the primal will to live: For such crimes there is no atonement or any point in cursing the universe or its dark malignities. We must forgive ourselves and, like Una, tat our fragmented selves back together to rejoin the world of the living.

The audacious qualities of Naslund's novel take an ambivalent turn midtext, however, precisely when Una meets Ahab, who enters the novel stalking Nantucket's moors like a moody Brontë lover. On the one hand, this mash-up extends the play of generic modes that links Naslund's hybrid, mixed aesthetics to Melville's; one might argue that she is deliberately recuperating both the sentimental tradition of popular women's writing so scorned by Hawthorne and then dismissed by early twentieth-century scholars establishing the bona fides of an all-male, white American Renaissance as well as the subversive aspects of the female Gothic tradition. On the other hand, the open-ended narrative momentum of Naslund's novel, hitherto marked by a series of intense bonds with women that facilitate Una's continual rebirths and reinventions of self, now narrows into a more conventional male–female coupling and a more restrictive generic format, the marriage plot, whose ideological imperatives uphold an understanding of the sexes that sits uneasily with Naslund's revisionary feminist take on Melville.

How does this courtship commence? Ahab is the captain of the ship that rescues Una after the sinking of the *Sussex*; disembarking in Nantucket, Una undergoes a literal and figurative dark night of the soul. Filled with survivor's guilt, she finds herself disconsolately and directionlessly roaming the island's moors on a starless night, in which "the blackness was utterly complete." Imagining the sound of footsteps in pursuit, she breaks into a panicked run, "driven by fear of who I was and of what kind of world I lived in" (333). Yet the anonymous pursuer turns out to be a rescuer, who, leading her back to safety, shows her that she deserves compassion, that she is still human.

Who is the "dark stranger" returning Una to the world of the living? "Why, it was the hand of Captain Ahab" (334), Una reveals to the reader in the last sentence of the chapter, and thus the novel's love plot begins in earnest. If courtship diminishes Una's independence, it also converts the existential defiance of Melville's Ahab into the erotic blandishments of a Byronic paramour. Responding to Una's suggestion that she is unmarriageable, this Ahab's "eyes dart[] defiance," not of the universe but of anything that comes between him and the object of his desire; the "electric discharge" that envelops his entire body smacks, in Gothic-Romantic language, of "storm and power" (346). Ahab as Una's "dark stranger" has become an heroic amalgam of Heathcliff and Rochester—although, ironically, in *Jane Eyre* it is Jane herself who rescues Rochester, fallen from his horse on a dark night and later set afire in his bed, evincing her own quiet powers, whereas Ahab rescues the lost Una in Naslund's revision of the trope.

The narrowing down of the novel's epic-quest format to male–female romance also troubles Naslund's choice of ending. In a penultimate moment of revelation, the widowed Una, stargazing from the roof of her Nantucket home, has a transcendental vision of unity with the "glittering universe" (662), which seems a confirmation of her hard-earned wholeness: As she asserts after Ahab's death, "I marry myself" (561). This merging of the sentence's subject, "I," and object, "myself," into one entity presages the rooftop scene's climactic "in-gathering" (620) of the many facets of Una's identities, experiences, and relationships in a union of Emersonian multiplicity-in-oneness. The moment is echoed in the closing lines of the novel, as Una triumphantly declares that she has "given time a home" (666)—a declaration that might seem Naslund's attempt to reclaim sentimental fiction's valorization of the domestic space or "home," giving it a more expansive sense of Odyssean return (*nostos*).

But, in fact, Una makes this declaration when arm in arm with her *new* life partner, who turns out to be—drumrolls!—none other than Ishmael, even after she's declared she's "had enough of husbands" (598). The unlikely coincidence bringing about their meeting and courtship, occurring amid a flurry of marriages and romantic unions among secondary characters, is of a piece with Naslund's summoning forth of nearly every character who has crossed Una's path in order to tie up all loose ends. The tidy knot created by these closural moves "domesticates," in the negative rather than positive sense of the word, the wandering energies hitherto valorized in Una: the protean, unfixed, ever-questing restlessness that also makes Melville's Ishmael the symbolically appropriate survivor of the sinking of the *Pequod*, reborn into an open future as wandering "orphan" (*Moby-Dick*, 427). Even as Naslund's efforts to generate contemporary insights through an imaginative wresting with the literary past often seem presciently post-postmodernist, the creation of this final harbor for her now content and happily coupled protagonist—recall the sentence in which "time" is at last given a "home" (666)—saps the narrative of the multivocal, self-reflexive, feminist energies that inspired its attempt to tell the story of the women whom Melville's text omitted.

Fictionalizing Melville

Realism and literariness, history and contemporary concerns combine in Frederick Busch's *The Night Inspector* (1999), a re-creation of a period in Melville's life that also serves as a damning critique of issues that continue to reverberate uneasily today: American capitalistic culture gone mad (for Busch, in the years following the Civil War), the widening division between the haves and have-nots, the speculative and transactional economics that increasingly define human contact, and the literal and figurative ghosts of racial injustice that emancipation has not yet vanquished. When authors import an already-written character into their fiction, it's nearly inevitable that the new version of the character will be compared to the original, and the imitation does not always fare well in this comparison. Fictionalizing the life of an author is perhaps an even more daunting task. As in the writing of historical fiction, the imaginative re-creation of a real person's life must, whatever the novelist's original insights, cohere with known facts as well as with the historical timeline. The problem is that while this adherence to fact may enrich a novel's realistic texture, it can also overdetermine the depiction of the life at hand.

The reticences and silences that mark so much of Melville's life make him an especially tempting subject for the genre of fictionalized biography: Those blank spaces seem to beg for a storyteller's imaginative supplement. Hence, it's no surprise that Melville's private life has been re-created in a spate of novels over the past two decades. Of all these attempts, Busch's *The Night Inspector* imputes the most psychologically dense fictional afterlife to Melville. The novel envisions the friendship that develops between the aging author, now a customs inspector long forgotten by the literary world, and a former Union sniper, Billy Bartholomew. Billy's face was obliterated by return fire in one of his sorties, so now he wears a mask of painted pasteboard. This prosthetic inevitably rivets the attention of the author who had already made the "pasteboard mask" such an evocative metaphor in *Moby-Dick*. "He became enchanted . . . by my mask," Billy comments upon meeting the night inspector. "He would have to be. He had spent his squandered or cursed career in writing about men who struck through the mask or curtain or surface of things."[4]

Set in New York City in 1867, the novel features as its focalizing character and narrator not Melville but—in Busch's ingenious twist—the Union sharpshooter Billy. Now a cynical financial speculator who measures the worth of others by their use-value, Billy ventures out only by night to mitigate the shock his masked appearance creates in others. "Once I hunted; now I lurk" (31). The first-person narrative alternates between traumatic memories of the atrocities Billy committed during the war and his present-day existence, which soon involves encounters with the man he only refers to as "M."[5] The scars that Billy's mask hides are not only external. In a world where cutthroat competition and survival of the fittest form the terrain of the nation's new battlefield, Billy has hardened himself to emotion and sees every relationship in transactional terms: "It was money that won. As the credit notice . . . says, *No Trust*" (27). Billy's sardonic words echo those of the deeply cynical Confidence-Man, whose world of riverboat chicanery foreshadows the duplicitous Wall Street cons and double-crosses that Billy and M inhabit in the late 1860s.

Busch's resolve to strike through the mask, as it were, to strip back the facades papering over a postwar society gone mad with greed, is matched by his commitment—like Melville's—to "dive deep" into the darker reaches of the human mind.[6] The novel's resulting psychological density is enhanced by the degree to which Billy and M serve as each other's mirror. Both are severely traumatized souls. "I have plummeted" (55), M tells Billy. Billy, in turn, literally "plummeted"—to earth—when shot out of the tree from which he had been picking off enemy soldiers. Both lead diminished lives as recluses who seek invisibility under the cover of night. Both feel silenced by their society, Melville as a writer manqué haunted by "the awful, terrorizing whiteness of the white page" (115) and Billy as a faceless man living in the shadows. And both suffer profound survivor's guilt—Billy for his morally dubious actions as soldier-stalker, M for the lack of emotion that, as "batterer father" (178), he fears contributed to his son Malcolm's suicide.

Considerations of race run throughout Melville's work, sometimes overtly, sometimes subtly, but they are nearly always explored in morally complex ways. Busch follows in Melville's wake, bringing race to the forefront of the postbellum world eviscerated in *The Night Inspector.* The plot that eventually entangles Billy and M's lives hinges on the defaced younger man's relationship with a Creole prostitute, Jessie, whose body is tattooed with indecipherable designs and who therefore *seems* to play the role of life-giving (and tattooed) Queequeg to Billy's reluctant Ishmael. Jessie, reading beyond his mask to the wounded man hidden within, makes Billy feel whole again. This compassion, however, turns out to be a ruse. By degrees, she lures Billy into abetting what seems a noble scheme: her plot to free Southern Black children secretly being shipped north into virtual slavery despite emancipation. To help this seemingly righteous cause, Billy needs M's cooperation as customs inspector of incoming boats. This female avatar of Queequeg, however, turns out to be more a combination of the duplicitous Babu from *Benito Cereno* and the Confidence-Man: It transpires that Jessie, for ambiguous reasons that strike at the darkness underlying all human motivation in this grim novel, is part of the cartel trading in Black flesh and using both Billy and M for her own deeply ambiguous purposes.

Penetrating to the heart of this dispiriting truth ultimately propels M and Billy on one last quest, a voyage upriver to free the children: a doomed mission because they have already died of suffocation in the casks smuggling them north. But the futile effort at least gives M the momentary chance to play an active role as he gives chase, albeit in a rowboat rather than a whaler, and it allows Billy the chance to begin to repair his sundered soul and body. But a shroud of Melvillean ambiguity and despair overhangs all the players in this elaborate double cross: The contradictions that have led to Jessie's participation in the slave enterprise remain unknown to the end; the truth of these Black children's horrific fate is literally entombed underwater; and the meaninglessness of such human barbarity raises an existential and resolutely

Melvillean question that neither Billy nor M can penetrate. "And what meaning lurks in this? What cause? How dare we witness this and *live*? And yet we do, and then we do" (262, Busch's emphasis), the night inspector says in despair before hurling a pole he's holding like a harpoon "into a darkness that accepted it" (266).

Busch's success in making his Melville character seem not only real but empathetic owes greatly to his decision to have M participate in a series of actions that Busch has *imagined*—namely, the scheme in which Billy gets him involved—and thus have no historical reference. This emplotment, importantly, enables Busch to bring M to life on the *novel's* terms, freeing narrative action from the historical overdetermination that fictional biography otherwise risks. Second, Busch's success derives from choosing Billy as his protagonist-narrator and making Melville into *Billy's* doppelgänger, his kindred "inspector of the night," rather than vice versa (as a more traditional rendering might have done). This move not only enriches the psychology of both characters and creates a depth of inner despair, of darkness and silence, that echoes the reader's experience of Melville's *Moby-Dick*, *The Confidence-Man*, and "Bartleby" (which shares with Busch's novel the bleak world of Wall Street) but also means that we encounter and engage M *as Billy reads him*, which in turn heightens the novel's "reality" effect since we are more apt to accept Billy's subjective impressions of M's personality and actions as those of an outside observer.

Third, Busch's depiction of postwar capitalist America—of which Manhattan is the microcosm, a shark tank of ruthless speculation haunted by its dark shadows, ranging from the nameless poor of Five Points to the continuing oppression of freed African Americans—casts an epic net of traumatized national suffering that is worthy of Melville. Like Melville's writing at its most expansive and pessimistic, Busch's tale is a national allegory, one in which Manhattan is a ship at sea plunging after the age's latest white whale: capitalistic greed. "I am trying to say that you could feel the city coiling itself. In Manhattan, you could feel the national effort begin," Billy explains. "This polluted energy, this vastness on a small island, was the national beginning of a new lunge toward—what? I did not know" (39–40).

But contemporary readers *do* know—especially those coming of age during the unregulated financial highs of 1990s, when the same Leviathan ruled American speculators: the dream of profit without end, the biggest catch known to *Homo sapiens*. True to theories of post-postmodernism, Busch's allegiance to realism—here, historical realism combined with literary history—never forgets its fictiveness (the title of the novel is created by an intradiegetic journalist who is experimenting in writing Melville's life from Melville's point of view), producing a damning account of individual and national trauma whose ethical belief in the power of fiction to make a difference is as sincere as its depiction of a transactional culture is deeply, disturbingly ironic.

Leviathan Allegories

Making Melville the means of telling a larger story of nation also characterizes another group of contemporary novels manifesting the Melville effect: fictions set in the modern era that undergird their plots with densely thematic and imagistic substructures that advertise their debt to the author. In metatextual fashion, one or more characters in each of these novels reads a copy of *Moby-Dick*. In Mark Behr's *The Smell of Apples* (1995), set in South Africa in the early 1970s when the country was still subjected to the rule of apartheid, the boy-narrator Marnus's reading of Melville is inadequate, blinding this protogay eleven-year-old to the fact that fascistic authoritarianism latches onto his nascent sexual desires in order to bend them to his nation's masculinist and racist ideology. In Marianne Wiggins's *Evidence of Things Unseen* (2003), a copy of Melville's novel becomes the clue by which an orphan's obsessive quest to learn the fate of his parents ultimately unmasks the false optimism underlying twentieth-century America's embrace of technological "miracles" from flight to nuclear fission. And in Chad Harbach's *The Art of Fielding* (2011), a mash-up of coming-of-age, sports, campus, and coming-out fictional genres, Melville is revered on the midwestern campus of Westish College, where the baseball team is named the Harpooners, students wear T-shirts bearing the slogan "Our Dick Is Bigger Than Yours," posters of the text of the "Leeshore" chapter decorate dorm-room walls, the college president and his daughter sport identical whale tattoos, and the obsessive quest for perfection becomes the White Whale that consumes outfielder Henry Skrimshander. If the scholars who launched the Melville revival and the artists following in their wake tended to fix attention on Ahab—as a defiant quester, as a tragic hero, as a nonconforming iconoclast—these novels tend to valorize the plasticity, openness, and multivocality associated with Ishmael's perspective, values opposed to the dangers posed by Ahab's solipsistic, authoritarian point of view. Hence, in all three novels, the deadly "whiteness of whiteness" looms conspicuously, whether figured as apartheid or atomic cloud or speeding baseball.

The references to *Moby-Dick* in Behr's *The Smell of Apples* are carefully chosen for maximum effect. "You who were always so caught up in whales when you were a boy," the narrator Marnus's mother writes to him near the end of his life.[7] (The first-person narrative—as in Busch's *Night Inspector*—alternates between two present-tense time periods: 1973, when the boy is eleven, and 1988, when he leads a covert South African squad that is facing certain death in the Angolan War.) The eleven-year-old exults in watching the occasional whale swim into False Bay, which his Cape Town home overlooks, and he treasures stories of the old days when "thousands of whales" (121) swarmed the area. But as indigenous fisherman Jan Bandjies tells the boy, these "old stories" are getting harder and harder to believe now that industry has all but driven the whales away (84).[8] A vista of this bay from the top of Sir Lowries Pass is connected in the boy's mind to the smell of the apples that he and his father carry home from his uncle's nearby orchard. For author and reader, however, the Edenic connotations of such bounty are overwritten by the sins of colonialism. Marnus's major-general father, a high-ranking player in the apartheid government, reminisces about the uncle's forced expulsion from his original apple farms in Tanganika (the mainland of Tanzania), but, in attempting to re-create this lost "paradise" in South Africa, Marnus's privileged Afrikaner family only repeats its original sin through violent acts of land appropriation that official history elides. "This country was empty before *our people* arrived," Marnus's father falsely schools his son. "This is *our place*, given to us by God" (124, emphases added).[9] Myths and mythmaking, whether whale tales or stories of lost Edens ("false bays," indeed), are duplicitous in the reality in which Marnus finds himself coming of age.

Given Marnus's obsession with whales and fishing, it is no surprise that his "favourite story in the whole world" is *Moby-Dick*, even if he's read only the "revised edition for children" (36), as his older sister, Ilse, caustically likes to remind him. Later, when Ilse is asked by a visiting, rabidly anticommunist Chilean general if she reads "love stories," she parries his gendered assumption by declaring she's reading *Moby-Dick*, adding that the novel "is about much more than whaling." The general "frowns at her" as she explains "Captain Ahab and Queequeg . . . stand for different things. . . . Ishmael has to choose between them" (150). Both general and her father, Ilse pointedly notes, are definitely more "like Captain Ahab" (151) than like Ishmael or Queequeg.

These subtle references to Melville undergird and enrich Behr's stark tale of the young Marnus's inculcation into a world where the worship of phallic masculinity and a racist belief in white superiority join forces with authoritarian rule. This is a world, moreover, in which power rests in the elitist homosocial bonding enacted by military men like the general and Marnus's father. As well documented in Melville criticism, the dictatorial masculinity and fanaticism central to Ahab's hold over his crew presage the birth of twentieth-century fascist ideology and authoritarian regimes rooted in claims of racialized difference, such as South Africa's.[10] In Melville's novel, Ahab's desire to bend others to his iron will is countered by the ideal of democratic brotherhood celebrated by Ishmael in the "A Squeeze of the Hand" chapter. And that chapter's homoerotic overtones, wherein the communal act of squeezing sperm becomes a masturbatory grope-fest, are deeply relevant to Behr's coming-of-age fable, for young Marnus, who worships his handsome father and fetishizes the major-general's hypermasculinity, is overwhelmed with inchoate erotic desires for men. Behr nightmarishly illustrates how the male bonds celebrated in Melville's novel can be manipulated to make homoerotic desires an extension of—rather than a counter to—fascist ideology; under the scrim of valorized masculinity, sex between men plays itself out in acts of violence, domination, and damning secrecy.[11] Marginalized sexualities are a frequent subject of contemporary artworks participating in the contemporary Melville revival, but whereas those works, as chapter 6 evinces, tend to tease out the homoeroticism latent in Melville's writing for politically progressive ends, *The Smell of Apples* is intent on showing how even illicit sexualities can be high-jacked by ideologies of power and coercion.

The world of male power and hypervirility by which Marnus is being hailed reveals itself, on the most basic level, in the blatant phallic references punctuating the text. In the opening sentence, Marnus reveals that his father affectionately calls him "my little bull" (10).[12] When father and son shower together (a daily ritual that grows increasingly perturbing as the story unfolds), Marnus voyeuristically observes his father's "John Thomas hang[ing] out from a bushy black forest" (62). The father jestingly asks, "Does that little man of yours stand up yet sometimes in the mornings?" (63)—a comment that hovers between father–son camaraderie and pedophilic prurience. Marnus and his best friend, Frikkie, are fascinated to learn that a whale's "John Thomas" measures eight feet (10). Size also equates with masculinity during a fishing scene when Marnus feels a tremendous tug on his line. "It's a hell of a *big thing* . . . the biggest fish in the bay" (91, emphasis added), he exclaims, and the brutalizing tug-of-war that follows (he's hooked a shark) becomes a test of manhood that his father deems he's failed miserably: "He beat you" (98).

This obsession with phallicity and size is matched by young Marnus's fascination with the male body—and his father's in particular. In oedipal fashion, Marnus wants both to "be" his father and, on a subliminal level, to "have" him. He is happiest in those moments when the two of them are alone together—either fishing or swimming nude in the surf—and he's delighted when the visiting Chilean general tells him he is "a carbon-copy" of his father (35). But even Marnus subconsciously knows it is taboo to have erotic thoughts about his dad, and much of Behr's plot revolves around the way that Marnus displaces his oedipal attraction for his father onto the Chilean general, whose equally handsome and militaristic virility the boy furtively absorbs: "His arms are . . . covered in black hair and there are thick veins running up his forearms. *Almost like Dad's*" (37, emphasis added). One night he and Frikkie decide to spy on the general in the guest room through a hole in the floor of Marnus's bedroom; their voyeuristic gazes discover the man to be "completely naked," and Frikkie's awed praise of the general's pumped arms solicits a retort from Marnus that indicates his subconscious collapsing of the two men into one phallic object of awe: "But my Dad's are bigger" (99–100).

These triangulated desires come to a head in the novel's damning reveal. Not only are we mistaken in thinking that the general is sexually interested in the boy (his affection, ironically, turns out to be paternal), but Marnus is also mistaken in thinking that his sister is the desired object of the general's flirtations (when, in fact, the man is seducing their mother). Waking to find Frikkie missing from bed during a sleepover, Marnus once again spies into the guest room and sees a man he *assumes* is the general genitally fondling then forcibly sodomizing his friend. But Marnus finally realizes the assaulter is his father, whom we now intuit may have been carrying out this pedophilic abuse for some time. The psychic outcome of this shattering self-knowledge determines the rest of Marnus's life, and it retrospectively explains the "*already too late*" (187) adulthood that dooms Marnus in the italicized passages of narrative set in 1988.

Behr's last reference to *Moby-Dick*, tellingly, immediately follows the child Marnus's discovery of his father's rape of Frikkie and inculcation into his father's racist and patriarchal ideology. Marnus walks into the room where his sister is sitting, about to finish the novel, and his reaction to its cover art hints at the trauma occasioned by the sexual violence that he has just witnessed as well as at the authoritarian, masculinist drive that underlies such violence: "On the cover there's a picture of Captain Ahab throwing his harpoon, and just in front of him, in the bloody water, is Moby Dick. There's a fountain of blood spurting from the little blow-hole on Moby's head, and his jaw is open *as if he is screaming*" (180, emphasis added). Who is really screaming? we wonder. Ilse has already likened her father to Ahab, Queequeg's opposite. Marnus's wavering—to which of the two men will he pledge his being?—continues the next morning when his father invites him to join him for their usual shower. Only when both are completely naked does Marnus demur, which causes his father to look at him "in a funny way" (193). The boy's ambivalence is also revealed in his refusal to wear the epaulets the Chilean general has left him as a parting gift: "I don't want anything from the General, and I hate Dad" (194). Underlying this rebellion is not only the boy's fear of what he's learned and the psychic trauma it occasions but also, even more disturbingly, his inchoate jealousy at being replaced by Frikkie as the object of his father's desire. This "hatred," in turn, becomes terror at the consequences of filial disobedience as Marnus's father mercilessly beats him for the first time in the boy's life for refusing to wear the military insignias.

Despite this terror—or rather because of it—masculine authority and male homoerotic desire find common ground in violence and suppression, the same qualities that, as Behr's stark realism makes clear, sustain the rule of apartheid. Father and son collapse in tears, hugging each other in an embrace that seals the unspoken Faustian bargain that has just transpired. "What's up with all this crying? Bulls don't cry" (196), the father jokes, reinstating the masculine norm. The boy, relieved to have recovered his father's love—and the hope that in "being like" his father he can once again "have" him—now submits willingly as the father fastens the disputed military epaulets on his shoulders. Realizing that Frikkie will never reveal his sexual violation, Marnus feels "safe"—about both his father's love and the "secret" that is now the condition of their love's continued being. Solaced by this illusion of "safety" as he drifts to sleep, Marnus simultaneously feels "something between my legs. My John Thomas is hard" (199). He has indeed become his father's "little man"—the identical phrase that the father earlier used in the shower: "So tell Dad, does that little man of yours stand up . . . in the mornings?"

This deeply unsettling father–son bonding in eroticized virility manifests itself again the following morning as the family readies to set off on summer vacation. Marnus is anticipating the pleasure of just "the two of us going fishing every day" (200) when the father, smiling, asks, "Tell me first, *my little bull*, is there froth in the water yet in the mornings when you have a pee?" (200, emphasis added). Marnus nods affirmatively, also smiling, and the novel ends with the eleven-year-old thinking that this day is "a perfect day, just like yesterday" (200)—the very "yesterday" when the scales fell from his eyes, only to be replaced with an even greater willed blindness. Such blindness is part of the complicit bargain between men—between "big" and "little" bulls—that makes power-mad authoritarians such as Ahab possible, that makes the memory of whales in False Bay the faintest trace of an alternative manhood, and that, as the present-tense narration of 1988 reveals, ties both Marnus and apartheid rule to the death-drive that inevitably dooms both. The tropes, images, and states of mind borrowed from Melville powerfully buttress Behr's warning about the cost, in Ilse's terms, of choosing Ahab over Queequeg.

If Behr homes in on the totalitarian dangers of Ahab's control of his crew and shows how they manifest themselves in the politics of the nation-state, the final two novels examined in this chapter focus on the perils of Ahab-like monomania and obsession when it comes to twentieth-century ideals and ideologies of progress and perfection. The death-drive that Behr links to apartheid recurs in the form of the atomic bombings of Hiroshima and Nagasaki in Marianne Wiggins's *Evidence of Things Unseen* (2003), as gargantuan a novel as *The Smell of Apples* is minimalist. The *New York Times Book Review* aptly called it "a true epic," and another reviewer noted how it draws on the lineage of "American literature laid down by Melville" and amplified by successive generations of modernist American writers.[13] Melville's presence is indeed deeply felt in the sweep of this novel as it barrels forward with an epic velocity that encompasses the entire first half of the American twentieth century. It does so, moreover, in lyrical, self-reflexive, experimental prose that approaches Melville's narrative inventiveness. The spatial and temporal arc of *Evidence of Things Unseen* reaches from Kitty Hawk—the birthplace of aviation at the beginning of the century—across Tennessee, home of the Tennessee River Valley Authority (TVA) and the Manhattan Project's Oak Ridge compound in the 1930 and 1940s, to the glittering white void of melted sand left by the testing of the atomic bomb in the New Mexico desert. Three intertwined, epic quests form the backbone of the novel. The first is America's love story with modern technological innovation. The second traces the arc of the "binding energy" of love that unites the novel's two central characters, Fos and Opal—ultimately victims of radiation poisoning—in an eternal "embrace that curve[s] their bodies into one."[14] The third, overlapping macro- and microcosmic levels, forms the climactic action of the novel: the obsessive quest of Lightfoot, Fos and Opal's adoptive son, to discover the truth about their death and hence about his identity, a voyage that takes him to the westernmost rim of America in the 1950s.

Channeling Melville as her muse, Wiggins signals from the beginning that she is out to do no less than write her own epic for her contemporary moment. Every chapter bears a suggestive epigraph from *Moby-Dick*; in addition, several chapter headings evoke Melville's phraseology (the lower cases are Wiggins's postmodern emendation): "fast fish and loose fish," "the incognito," "the whiteness of the whale," "ENTER LIGHTFOOT, radiant" (*Moby-Dick*, 243, 321, 351, 205). The first mention of *Moby-Dick* occurs on a fishing expedition that Fos and Opal take with their best friend, Flash, who's obsessed with hooking a phantom carp that's escaped him the past twenty years. "Just between the two of us," Fos jokes to his wife, "it's anybody's guess the dang thing's even real. [Flash is] like Captain Ahab over it. Calls the thing his Moby" (98). This leads Opal to begin to read *Moby-Dick*, and, although she stalls midway, she intuitively "gets" that Melville's whale represents the ungraspable phantoms, the inverse side or photographic negative of visible reality, that elude human strivings.

Whales again make an uncanny appearance when Opal and Fos take over her cousin Earl's Tennessee farm and discover a spare room filled with hundreds of small "white whale[s]" (201) that the desolate Earl has carved from pine. Later, the boy Lightfoot will make two of these carved whales his special friends that he takes to bed every night to narrate to them the events of the day, veritable whale-of-a-tale stories that transform his boyhood "secrets" (296) into words and thereby give his nascent inner life shape and meaning. And when the orphaned Lightfoot inherits the "Box of Clues" that his mother has left him, it is the presence of Flash's worn copy of *Moby-Dick* inside the box that ultimately triggers Lightfoot's quest to conquer the "white whale"—the trauma and mystery of his parents' death—that has become his haunting monomania.

The potentially destructive nature of obsession comprises Wiggins's biggest thematic debt to Melville. America's fascination with technological progress in the twentieth century is one such obsession, characterized by an unqualified optimism and a belief in science's ability to tame nature's energies that spur the era's unending race for scientific innovation and invention. Progress is the burgeoning century's lifeblood, its mantra, its excitement, and its desire:

A gladness seemed to spread between them.
The lustre progress generates.
The radiant of problem solving.
Lightning bolts and job creation.
Social intercourse and calories.
Make-work in the glow of government: a New Deal.
(212)

Fos, Opal, and Flash fully inhabit this promised "brand new" world of possibility (208)—of cars (Opal is an expert under the hood and behind the steering wheel); photography (Flash runs a photographic studio, capturing reality in "flashes" of light); electricity (Fos is hired by the TVA to win farmers over to the benefits of hydroelectricity); X-ray machines (Fos, fascinated by "invisible" light, keeps a chunk of radiant phosphorus in his and Opal's bedroom); and nuclear fission (Fos and Opal end up working at Oak Ridge). "It was an age of passionate discovery for his generation, Fos would say . . . an age of general rapture with the unseen, with harnessing the unseen natural forces to man's will and his desires" (156).

Wiggins, however, intends this idea of "harnessing" nature to "man's will and his desires" to give readers pause, for this paean to the new age contains the seeds of its self-destruction, manifested in the annihilating will to power that erupts—as Ahab exemplifies—when the obsessive desire to "harness" nature leads to the unchecked imposition of "man's will" over life itself. The apogee of this drive—the goal toward which all this scientific innovation has been hurtling like a *Pequod* plunging through seismic waves—is the twentieth century's gigantic White Whale of apocalyptic destruction: the atomic cloud breaching the skies like Moby Dick in all its sublimity and terror.[15]

Wiggins makes these links explicit in a chapter called "fishin" (a pun on *fission*), when Opal and Fos begin working at the secret Oak Ridge compound. The chapter's epigraph is taken from "The Chase—Day Two," as Moby Dick's pursuers close in on their target: "Ah! how they still strove through that infinite blueness to seek out the thing that may destroy them!" (*Moby-Dick*, 415). Wiggins follows this epigraph with a lyrical sequence of phrases that illuminate the inexorable causality leading to—in Melville's words—"that fatal goal" of "seek[ing] out the thing that may destroy them" (415). Literally, that "fatal goal" encompasses the deaths of Fos and Opal; figuratively, it encompasses the demise of America's blind faith in scientific progress. Wiggins writes:

A LITANY. It goes like this:

No flood, no TVA.
No TVA, no cheap electric power.

No cheap electric power, no factories.
No factories, no aluminum.
No aluminum, no long-distance bombers.
No long-distance bombers, no atomic bomb.

No atomic bomb, no Oak Ridge, Tennessee. (261)

The metaphoric links among Fos and Opal's deaths by radiation, the exploding A-bomb, and Melville's breaching whale pervade the novel. They begin in a poetic prelude to the novel proper titled "white sands," which describes the blasted desert site of the first nuclear test. This vast blankness of silicon has melted into glass onto which (like Moby Dick's forehead) one can project anything and nothing. "A forbidden place," the "blankness" of the site inexorably compels humans to penetrate its enigmatic meaning: "Like a harpoon, this magnet, this glass desert calls our irons the way a whale's heart used to beckon a harpoon" (3).

The obsessive nature of America's quest to make the invisible visible, to reveal nature's secrets at any cost, finds a counterpart in Lightfoot's obsessive desire to fathom the mystery surrounding his parents' deaths. Nine years old when taken to a foster home, Lightfoot's only *visible* evidence that his parents ever existed is the Box of Clues that Opal left for him, with Flash's copy of *Moby-Dick* nestled inside. When Lightfoot begins to read Melville's novel seven years later, the orphan feels an electric flash of recognition as he scans the first line and identifies with Ishmael: "Call me Outcast. . . . *This book is about me*," he thinks to himself (335). Pages later, he realizes that "he could have been the character called Ahab, too—Ahab, the *light-foot*, the one-legged Captain of the ship, obsessed with searching, driven by his quest for the White Whale" (335). Uncovering the truth of his parent's deaths, he admits, is "kind of like a *white whale* with me, if you know what I mean" (337, all original emphases). Yet the more Lightfoot is obsessed by his "desire for a verifiable history" (353), the more he becomes "like Ahab on the bridge of the Pequod . . . steering only for a course in the direction of the thing he couldn't see" (352). When Lightfoot uses information inscribed in the copy of *Moby-Dick* to locate Flash, the man warns him that such quests for absolute truths or answers become monomanias that cripple rather than enable: "You think you're out here hunting for the great white whale? Trust me. You're wrong. . . . The whale is coming after you" (362).

In the final chapter, titled "the whiteness of whiteness," Lightfoot and Flash embark on a road trip out west. Flash's goal is to realize his dream of seeing the Pacific; Lightfoot's motivation is to visit the A-bomb testing site in New Mexico, the final puzzle piece in his quest to understand his parents' deaths. Only as Lightfoot enters what he perceives as New Mexico's annihilating emptiness—"a large white nothing" (380) that self-consciously evokes Ishmael's commentary on the psychological terrors occasioned by the color *white*—does he realize in an "flash" of illumination what Flash has been attempting to teach him all along: His parents' binding love is the only knowledge of the past that he needs to carry into his future. Instead of thrusting himself, like Ahab, at a blankness that he will never be able to penetrate, Lightfoot abjures the quest, heading back to Monterrey, where not only Flash but a (figuratively) radiant young woman he's met await his return.

Even though Lightfoot never reaches the blast site, in a brilliant stroke Wiggins guarantees that the reader *has already* encountered this empty void, a glassy mirror of melted silicon that is the ultimate signifier of modernity's deadly obsession, for this is the same landscape presented in the novel's prelude, which alerts us that "the end is where we start" (3). What would have been a literal and figurative end—a *dead end*—for Lightfoot thus *never occurs* in the diegetic narrative: The nonevent becomes yet more "evidence of things unseen." And this narrative "vanishing act," whereby an anticipated scene drops out of the text, makes way for a different ending to Lightfoot's quest story. In turning away from the blast site before he reaches it, he chooses life over deathly fixation, visible love over invisible mystery, Eros over Thanatos, Ishmael over Ahab.

Similar choices form the end of Chad Harbach's bestseller *The Art of Fielding* (2011), a powerful meditation on the continuing relevance of Melville for the new century that concludes on a note of optimism that is nonetheless open-ended. Stylistically and structurally, this story of a baseball fielder's monomaniacal obsession with perfection is an example of old-fashioned realism whose capaciousness has been refitted for the present. As such, it is a quintessential example of post-postmodernism—self-reflexively aware (as the title's reference to the title of a text within the text reveals) but committed to traditional storytelling and humanist values such as atonement and redemption. At its most clever, it is also a mash-up of *multiple* fictional genres: bildungsroman, sports yarn, campus novel, gay love story. It is also, in the reviewer Gregory Cowles's words, a "bromance," a "comedy of manners," and a "tragicomedy of errors" (Cowles's pun on baseball "errors" is perfect for a novel that accepts "erring" as part of the human condition).[16]

If this generic interplay forms one link between Harbach's novel and Melville's hybrid aesthetics, another tie is spelled out in Cowles's term *bromance*, for a central question raised by *The Art of Fielding*—one familiar to literary critics via Leslie Fiedler's analysis in *Love and Death in the American Novel*—concerns the vexed meaning of men's rituals, bonds, and relationships in American literature and culture.[17] We have seen how Behr's *The Smell of Apples* summons Melville to condemn the negative potential of male homosociality when yoked to ideologies of state authoritarianism, racial bigotry, and erotic domination. Harbach returns his readers to the more democratic and pluralistic—although still contentious—possibilities of male bonding in the context of Westish College's baseball team, a group whose trademark insularity and camaraderie forms a twenty-first-century analogue of the all-male shipboard world of the *Pequod.* Baseball, a traditionally male sport, is also a quintessentially American sport. Harbach thus makes this "great American pastime" an occasion to examine, on the microlevel of college athletics, America's more general reassessment of gender in the twenty-first century, an arguably postfeminist age where new masculinities are being put to the test.

The looming presence that Melville casts over this novel is apparent in the "thriving cult of Melvilleania" that has taken root at Westish, a small college located on the western shores of Lake Michigan in Wisconsin.[18] Decades before, in 1969, undergraduate Guert Affenlight has discovered in the bowels of the library the faded transcription of a speech that Melville gave at the college in 1880—a trip and lecture hitherto escaping the notice of Melville's biographers (Harbach has invented these events). The publicity generated by this discovery creates a veritable campus industry: A statue of the author faces Lake Michigan, inscribed with his description of the Great Lakes in the found lecture as "America's secret sinew of inward-collecting seas" (62); the athletic teams are rebranded the Harpooners; students revel in Melvillean references, while the school hawks whale paraphernalia. Affenlight goes on to earn a doctorate at Harvard, where his unrelenting work ethic awes his fellow students: "Monomaniacal, they called him, an Ahab joke" (55). His book *The Sperm Squeezers,* "a study of the homosocial and homoerotic in nineteenth-century American letters" (55–56), becomes an unlikely bestseller in 1987, and fifteen years later he returns to Westish to take the helm as its president.

Eight more years have passed when the novel opens. It is 2010, and the school's baseball team has recruited a sensational new fielder, Henry Skrimshander (his surname evokes the whaler's art of "scrimshaw," or carving whalebone), whose perfect throwing record may push the Harpooners into regional and even national finals for the first time ever. The Harpooners' tight-knit male camaraderie inevitably gives rise to questions of gender and sexuality, some humorous (it's no Freudian slip that the team's coach is named Cox) and some graver. As Henry approaches the weight room one midnight, he overhears dialogue—"Come on baby . . . That's it. All night long . . . You're big! You're fucking huge!" (29)—intended to mislead readers into thinking Henry is about to stumble onto a sexual tryst. But, no, it's just his baseball buddies happily pushing their bodies to the breaking point—"taking one for the team," as it were. The leader of this testosterone-charged crew of bodybuilders is Mike Schwartz ("Aye, aye, my Captain!," his teammates regale him [407]), who has been crucial in recruiting Henry and is even more critical in nurturing the fielder's growth in self-confidence. Henry and Mike are teased for sounding "like two lovebirds" (12), and, indeed, theirs is as codependent a bromance as can be. After "devot[ing]" himself to Henry's betterment for three years, Mike's greatest fear is no longer being "needed" (150), which throws him in a deep funk that occasions his girlfriend Pella's retort: "What you two need is couples counselling. Classic codependency" (241). Likewise, Henry fears no longer being needed by Mike as Mike's relationship with Pella grows. For both hetero- and homosexuals in love, Henry muses despondently, there are "plans" that can be made, possibilities one can envision, because the world "had words for what you were doing. But if you were Henry and you needed Mike you were simply screwed. There were no words for that, no ceremony" (421). Harbach tackles a cultural and psychological conundrum as insoluble as any of the "ambiguities" broached in Melville: What if you are a man and deeply, even passionately, committed to another man, where the bond is as intimate as that of a married couple, but neither of you is gay? What, exactly, is the nature of same-sex friendship when pushed to its limits?

Harbach's exploration of the liminality of such nameless affinities—affinities that trouble assumptions about sexuality even in an age of metrosexuality—has its roots in a century of speculation over the nature of Ishmael and Queequeg's relationship.[19] Harbach's exploration also spills over into questions of the gender discrimination to which all-male sports inevitably give rise. Mike's girlfriend, Pella, who is also Affenlight's rebellious, grownup daughter, is the lightning rod for these questions. In a classic instance of homosocial triangulation, the relationship between men that reinforces patriarchy, as articulated by Lévi-Strauss, depends on a female third, the woman "traded" between men to seal the relationship.[20] And in many ways Pella does find herself as the third, the intermediary, yoking Mike and Henry—even though the role of "middleman" (358), as she ironically words it, is one that she'd rather forgo. When in the second half of the novel Pella temporarily becomes Henry's sexual partner, the erotic triangulation is complete: Although the two men don't have sex together, they have sex with the same person. What makes Harbach's exploration of these dynamics compelling is his self-conscious critique of the rites of masculinity and his understanding of the outsider status befalling women like Pella in the homosocial world that is Mike and Henry's home. While patriarchy is reinforced by men's homosocial transactions over the bodies of women, the progressive world of Westish embodies a twenty-first-century, postpatriarchal optimism about gender relations. The question then becomes whether male bonds and men's intimacy have a place in a supposedly postpatriarchal world.

Within the all-male cadre of the Harpooners, both Henry and Mike stand out for harboring monomanias of Ahab-like proportions, monomanias masking the existential fear that nothingness may be all that lies on the other side of their obsessive drives to succeed. Harbach relates both young men's desires and fears to those fostered by American culture at large. Henry is the embodiment of the American dream. His is a classic story of rags to riches as he moves from small-town existence in South Dakota to the chance "to realize his dreams" (140)—making it to the pros—under Mike's tutelage. Henry's particular obsession is perfection: "Perfection is what he was going after here" (149). Such perfection, the elimination of all error, however, depends on repeatability, on sameness, an emptying out of the self to become a machine. But Henry's efforts to attain the "holy vacancy" (198) needed to throw the perfect pitch renders him, as Mike comes to realize, a cipher, a blankness—in effect, a pasteboard mask. Even when Mike first scouts out Henry, he registers Henry's "blank look" (5), a blankness that at once renders him sublime in his transcendent talent (hence the "holiness" of his "vacancy") *and* impenetrable (vacant) to others, as much a metaphysical enigma as the White Whale is to Ahab. At the same time, Henry's pursuit of perfection is Ahab-like in its relentless fixity, its sadomasochistic acceptance of unfreedom: "The only free life worth living was the unfree life . . . the life in which you were chained to your one true wish, the wish to be simple and perfect" (346). Perfection, of course, is inhuman, and when Henry throws the first error of his life, thereby ending his perfect record, he enters a downward spiral of repeated errors and self-doubts that force him to wrestle with a simple truth: "The name of the game is failure, and if you can't handle failure, you won't last long. Nobody's perfect" (172).

If the rest of Henry's coming-of-age story deals with his slow acceptance of this truth, Mike has been grappling with imperfection all along, and it accounts for his own monomaniacal efforts to keep playing the sports that are crippling his body by the day. He, too, is a classic embodiment of the American dream, having gone from living penniless in a car to becoming an admired honors student and ace athlete. All his life Mike has succeeded by telling himself that "you'll win in the end, because you'll refuse to lose" (108), but this projection of infallibility has become an albatross around his neck. Not only is he hiding the fact that, contrary to others' expectations, he has failed to gain admission to law school, but he also knows that he, unlike Henry, doesn't possess a "single transcendent talent," a mark of unique "genius" (6). In place of this lack, he has made fostering Henry's talent his compulsion, his fixed drive, and his means of redemption from feelings of inadequacy and personal fear. But the pressure of living up to Henry's belief in his teammate as a "miracle worker" throws Mike into existential freefall: "The only thing he knew how to do was motivate other people. Which amounted to nothing, in the end" (245).

Mike increasingly begins to feel that the "implacable, solitary blankness" (157) on Henry's face is a pasteboard mask that pushes him away as much as it lures him on; like Melville's whale, Henry has become a "cipher, sphinx, silent courier" (159–60) that represents the "nothingness" Mike must face within himself: "If he could crawl inside that empty head, crack open the oracle of the kid's blank face . . . maybe then he'd know what he should do" (260). In the end, Mike's monomaniacal drive toward (if not his own, then Henry's) perfection does not consume him; if he is at times an Ahab in relation to Henry's Moby Dick, he is also a selfless "captain" who successfully navigates his "crew" to the national finals despite Henry's dropping off the team: "If he was the Ahab of this operation, this tournament the target of his mania, then [the rest of the team] were Fedallah's secret crew" (454). It is the communal effort rather than the drive of one individual, Ishmael's values rather than Ahab's, that Harbach's characters, like Behr's Ilse and Wiggins's Lightfoot, learn to embrace.

These Melvillean tropes come to a conclusion that (as in Wiggins's novel) gestures toward possibility and openness. The "Now what?" ambiguities that have haunted both Henry's and Mike's thoughts of the future—What if I succeed? What if I fail? What follows for "us," for our relationship without a name, after graduation?—play out in a series of acts of sacrifice and redemption that reconcile them to immediate, grounded, realizable futures that reflect Ishmael's philosophy of life instead of Ahab's death drive. The final scene has Mike striking baseballs faster and faster for the still error-haunted Henry to field. In the process, the white spinning sphere becomes both a deadly harpoon launched at its elusive target *and* the speeding White Whale, the implacable foe that Henry must overcome. Only when Henry fields the supposedly "last" ball that Mike hits him does he finally smash it into the staked-out target: "One perfect throw. Now what?" (572). But, of course, in a nice twist, there's actually one more ball in Mike's bucket, so the effort, the quest, continues beyond the final words of the novel. However, it is no longer a quest toward a singular, monomaniacal goal; it's the movement itself, the act of journeying into whatever lies ahead, that both Henry and Mike accept as the reality of growing up and accepting life in all its errors.

The Future of Fiction: "Now What?"

In our consumer-driven culture where even moderately successful films seem destined for sequels and writers routinely recast literary classics or create novels that fictionalize the lives of famous people to cash in on their cult status, a reasonable reaction to the increase in contemporary art dialing up Melville might be to dismiss these efforts as manifestations of a similar bandwagon mentality: What better way to draw attention to your work than to associate it with a literary master? Although this is true of some authors, what I find particularly striking about the current efflorescence of Melville-influenced fiction in general is the degree to which those novelists who take their affiliation with Melville seriously are *not* parasitic imitations, secondary refractions in which a hierarchy of "original" to "copy" or "master" to "scribe" is the driving force or outcome. Rather, the writers examined in this chapter recognize in Melville an affinity that speaks to them, a quality that hails them, because his enterprise resonates so deeply with their own concerns, aesthetics, authorial self-conceptions. The "Melville" that emerges from this recognition represents values—tackling assumptions about gender and sexuality; confronting the traumatic scars of racial discrimination, impoverishment, and global-environmental catastrophe; exulting in hybridity and parts rather than wholes—that are in many ways foreign to those buttressing earlier twentieth-century resuscitations of Melville.

So what might the Melville effect that I've been exploring tell us about developments in the genre of the novel itself? When friends have asked if I've discovered a "new" Melville among these fictional reenvisionings, I reply that there is no *Moby-Dick* hiding among these texts—no single work of such originality or subversion that it explodes the form of the novel as hitherto known. For example, the potential of *Moby-Dick* as hypertext has not yet, to my knowledge, been exploited, although one can imagine a text where the cetology chapters float, sink, reemerge, breaking the textual flow like fins; where words peel back to show the reverse side of the pasteboard mask or whiteness itself; where plotlines splinter into paths that defy linearity; where multiple media exist simultaneously in a sensorium evocative of Melville's textual polyphony.[21]

In fact, I suggest, to look for a singular "new" *Moby-Dick* or Melville is to fall into the trap that Lawrence Buell diagnoses in *The Dream of the Great American Novel* (2014). As noted in chapter 1, pinpointing the singular "great" anything presumes a myth of origins and originality that grates against the aesthetics of hybridity, heterogeneity, and multiplicity fueling Melville's imagination and energizing so many of these currently creative endeavors. Taken not as individual works ("Which is *Moby-Dick*'s most worthy successor?") but rather as manifestations of a greater force field, a constellation of partial objects coexisting in a mesh of rhizomatic relays, these novels indeed shed light on contemporary directions in novelistic fiction and, as Buell puts it, on the "broader contexts of shifting artistic practice and public priorities" in twenty-first-century culture.[22]

What do the more successful of these novels—such as the five analyzed here—take from Melville that makes their efforts stand out? Melville's ability to harness the realistic minutiae of a whaling adventure and make those gritty details into allegories and critiques of a fissured nation is clearly at work in those novels whose storylines also serve as parables of nation or meditations on the condition of modernity—most notably in Behr's damning critique of apartheid in the Republic of South Africa, but also in Busch's portrait of the soulless engine of capitalist speculation masking the unresolved traumas of war, Wiggins's vision of the costs of America's love affair with technology, and Harbach's deconstruction of the American dream of perfection. These meditations on modernity also tend toward a narrative expansiveness, an inclusiveness, that echoes the epic and encyclopedic dimensions of *Moby-Dick*—Naslund's epic intentions in this regard are explicit, as is the comprehensiveness of Wiggins's novel, temporally spanning the first half of the twentieth century and geographically spanning coasts. The ways in which Melville makes individual trauma—Ishmael's "splintered heart" and Ahab's splintered body—the canvas on which to inscribe universal questions as well as socially specific conundrums are also echoed in all these Melville-inspired fictions: Una's horrific experience of cannibalism in order to survive, Billy Bartholomew's gruesomely disfigured face, Marnus's traumatic witnessing of his father's rape of his best friend, the orphaning that Lightfoot suffers upon being severed from his parents without explanation, Henry and Mike's failures to live up to their own expectations of perfection—all these individual traumas expand to encompass networks of human suffering and amelioration that create, in realistic representation, epic panoramas of life that are larger than their individual characters.

This shared investment in realism as a way of making ethical and affective demands on the reader is symptomatic of the post-postmodern turn in novels of recent years. Various labels have been proposed to describe this return to a more self-conscious realism—*post-postmodernism*, *metamodernism*, *metaffective fiction*, *affective neorealism*, the *New Sincerity movement*—but the characteristics are the same: an unashamed turn to mimetic verisimilitude, the reemergence of authenticity, the belief that fiction can engage in constructive moral engagement (rather than simply espouse postmodernist cynicism), and the recuperation of language's referential function, in which form and function work in tandem not only to critique the historical past but also to explore "the possible terms of contemporary community informed by an understanding of the past."[23] The Melvillean fictions of Naslund, Busch, Behr, Wiggins, and Harbach are noteworthy examples of this current development in the genre. Irony is not eschewed but enfolded into the realistically depicted worlds of these novels; and metafictionality, a postmodernist trademark, coexists with dominantly realistic modes of storytelling—whence the book of Zen-like aphorisms, *The Art of Fielding* by (fictional) fielder Aparicio Rodriguez, quoted throughout *The Art of Fielding*; the novel *The Star-Gazer*, which Una readies to write at the end of *Ahab's Wife; or, The Star-Gazer*; and the writings of the journalist Samuel Mordecai in the intradiegetic world of *The Night Inspector*, who pens the obituary for Melville's son, Malcolm, then attempts to capture in Melville's first-person voice the latter's despair upon Malcolm's death, and (we are led to believe) eventually writes a book titled *Inspector of the Night*, which provides the epigraph opening *The Night Inspector*. Moreover, several of these examples of post-postmodern fictionality might be said to evince the "planetary" turn in contemporary arts. Considered in this vein, Una's distinctive "star gazing" in *Ahab's Wife* is not simply a nod to nineteenth-century transcendentalism but an attempt to project a world and embrace a cosmos beyond its Americanist or human-centric framing; likewise, "the curve of binding energy" in

Wiggins's epic, stretching from the first chapter's evocation of Perseid meteor showers at Kitty Hawk to its concluding vistas of the Pacific Ocean, make its "American" story a simultaneously planetary one.

Theophilus Savvas and Christopher K. Coffman note that post-postmodern novelists writing after 2001 have turned in particular to *literary* history, not just history, to grapple seriously with the past in order to posit new modes of community and possibility. Their description is uncannily descriptive of the Melville effect at work in novels of the past two and a half or so decades. For the post-postmodernist novelist, the two critics argue, literary history as well as the myriad literary forms generated by that history have emerged as a primary "means to enact affectively powerful and authentic considerations of the present in relation to the reality of the past."[24] If we think about this proposition in terms of the Melville effect, we can posit the turn toward Melville (a fixture of literary history since his meteoric rise in status in the 1920s) in the novels examined here as their creators' affective means of responding to the interplay between past and present. In these reenvisionings, they create a heightened historical awareness of and engagement with the "real" of "reality," an engagement that is both aesthetically and ethically motivated. Further, if we consider this reinvigorated, reengaged novelistic interplay of past and present in realist form as rhizomatic rather than linear—past and present interweaving and informing the other—the Melville effect may lead us to reconsider how we engage in and conceive of literary history itself.

CHAPTER 4

WHALEBONE, HOOP SKIRTS, CORSETS, PANTS ROLES

Women and Melville in Contemporary Art

[Moby-Dick] is a masculine book in the obvious sense that it is all about men and men's activities. . . . But it is masculine too in its deepest dramatic fantasies.
—Richard Brodhead, "Trying All Things"

Could I remake me! Or set free
This sexless bound in sex . . .
. . . .
For Nature, in no shallow surge
Against thee either sex may urge,
Why hast thou madst us but in halves,
Co-relatives? This makes us slaves.
If these co-relatives never meet
Self-hood itself seems incomplete.
—Herman Melville, "After the Pleasure Party"

Captain Ahab was neither my first husband nor my last.
—Sara Jeter Naslund, *Ahab's Wife*

The paucity of female characters in Herman Melville's works is a critical commonplace, one often aligned with the sense that his most powerful writing occurs in male-dominated settings. Thus, Richard Brodhead's assessment of *Moby-Dick* in 1986 as "outrageously masculine" builds on Julian Hawthorne's observation a century earlier that *Moby-Dick* was a "man-book[]" and that the rest of the writings of his father's friend were mere "boys' books."[1] Since the early twentieth-century's resurgence of interest in Melville, the question of whether the relegation of female characters to minor roles in his fiction should be a reason for critical concern has been subject to various opinions. Scholars spearheading the Melville revival in the 1920s tended to justify the nearly all-male worlds of his oeuvre as the inevitable result of his subject matter (life at sea), and they saw the absence of women as a positive sign of his noble revolt against stultifying ("feminine") domesticity and women's sentimental ("bad") fiction. Indeed, critical opinion prior to the 1960s viewed Melville's defiance of such gender-coded conventionality as one of the qualities raising him to the ranks of those few other great (male) authors constituting the American Renaissance. A few early critics, however, acknowledged that the predominantly male slant of his imagination came at a price; as the early Melville biographer Lewis Mumford put it, the sea fiction shares "one anomaly and defect from . . . the central, human point of view: one half of the race, women, is left out."[2] In omitting this constituency, Mumford implies, Melville risked alienating half of his potential readership—for, as Hawthorne's son avers, "Melville wrote books that were certainly not for women."[3]

"Not for women"? "Outrageously masculine"? These are claims that, since the advent of feminist criticism in the 1970s, have increasingly been scrutinized in Melville scholarship. For several decades, critics have demonstrated the degree to which his writing often reveals a sensitivity to issues of gender, to the uneven power dynamics embedded in marriage, to the reclamation of attributes associated with femininity but integral to humanity at large, to questions of polymorphous desire and taboo sexuality.[4] This chapter's second epigraph , taken from Melville's poem "After the Pleasure Party," expresses both an acute understanding of and a deep yearning to break through limiting gender and sex roles to attain a more "complete" or androgynous selfhood.[5] That Melville expresses such sentiments—echoing Aristophanes's myth of the original sexes in Plato's *Symposium*—through a female speaker, Urania, demonstrates that indeed he could, on occasion, imaginatively enter a woman's point of view with psychological acuity.

But for all the insights that feminist critics and theorists of gender and sexuality have brought to bear on the sexual politics implicit in Melville's writing, they cannot do away with the overwhelming absence of women characters from his oeuvre. Nor can they erase the larger aesthetic, cultural, and ideological issues at stake for artists in general in representing worlds where women by and large have no place. However, such intransigent questions make all the more fascinating the number of contemporary artists working in various genres and media—women as well as men—who have recently made female characters central to their engagements with Melville, particularly in their reworkings of that "outrageously masculine" opus *Moby-Dick*. Some (such as Sara Jeter Naslund, quoted in the third epigraph) have done so by bringing a "Mrs. Ahab" into being, some by transforming Ishmael into a woman, some by making Pip a "pants role" (a female actor playing the male part), some by feminizing the White Whale.

These reenvisionings are occurring as part of the larger phenomenon this book is exploring: the explosion of savvy, edgy, Melville-inspired creations over the past two and a half decades. Perhaps the most persistent issue explored in these works involves questions of gender, most evidently in those creative remediations that make the literal presence of women central to their visions.[6] This chapter singles out three such cutting-edge efforts: T. L. Solien's collage series; artist-sculptor Ellen Driscoll and poet Thomas Sleigh's movement drama; and an operatic chamber piece by the actor-singer-composer Rinde Eckert. Not only do these three works give women center stage (two of them, like Naslund's novel, imagine Ahab's wife into being), but they do so by intimating the material and metaphorical overlaps of women, whales, and whaling, all of which find common ground in the historical use of whalebone in the manufacture of hoop skirts, corsets, and other items of adornment that nineteenth-century women were exhorted to wear. In so doing, these contemporary art productions illuminate a critical intersection between whaling as an international industry and the female body as a site of consumption.

As recently as 2000, the historian Lisa Norling's book *Captain Ahab Had a Wife: New England Women and the Whalefishery, 1720–1870* brought to light the integral role played by whalers' shoreside wives in maintaining the maritime economy, acting as "deputy husbands" in affairs of business and maintaining the social networks and lines of communication that sustained their male spouses, whose whaling voyages might last up to three years.[7] Likewise, scholars taking a fresh look at Melville's biography have revealed the degree to which the author was dependent on the women in his family: They provided his domestic comforts, transcribed his nearly unreadable manuscripts for publishers, and, in the case of his wife's family, made available desperately needed financial support. In monetary matters, indeed, Elizabeth Melville might well be called Herman's "deputy husband."[8] Contrary to the alleged gap between the domestic life of mariners' wives left behind on shore and the world of men at sea for years on end, male and female spheres were more densely interconnected than generally assumed: Domestic space and workplace were firmly emmeshed in one another. We catch a glimpse, somewhat comical in its censoriousness, of the collision of gender assumptions, the feminine by-products of the whaling enterprise, and the Melvilles' domestic realm in an anecdote relayed by Melville's granddaughter, Eleanor. In it, her mother (Melville's youngest daughter) is chastised for "leaving her own well-boned undergarment on the back of a chair in her own bedroom," where any male of the family might glimpse it.[9]

How upset, one wonders, would Melville have *really* been at the ungodly sight of his daughter's whalebone stays? Would they have brought to mind his White Whale?

Today, historians of fashion and laypersons alike tend to view these undergarments as evidence of the way clothing has worked to discipline and constrain women's bodies. Such undergarments function, according to Susan Bordo, "as an emblem of the power of culture to impose its designs on the female body."[10] Hooped petticoats, for example, enveloped women in cagelike structures that impeded movement through space and simultaneously rendered their wearers virtually untouchable, at arm's-length contact from would-be suitors. The facts regarding the hoop skirt, however, turn out to be more nuanced. When whalebone replaced cane as a skirt prop in the eighteenth century and then became the primary stiffener in caged crinolines at the beginning of the Victorian period, some wearers, as Elizabeth Ewing documents, found the fashion liberating. Made of whale baleen, the lightweight braces holding the bell shape of the dress eliminated the need for the multiple layers of heavy underskirts that previously added cumbersome weight to women's wardrobes; wearing hoop skirts, women felt lighter than ever before. Moreover, the pliability of whalebone versus cane braces, allowing access through narrow spaces but springing back into shape, abetted the wearer's mobility.[11] Moralists condemned the fashion for being risqué, for potentially inciting rather than constricting female desires: first, because the influx of fresh air circulating beneath the skirt might be overly stimulating; second, because the skirt's easy tipping action might encourage women to give their male admirers glimpses of their feet and ankles.[12]

Whale baleen also became the mainstay of that other female wardrobe essential of the age, the corset. In contrast to the hooped skirt, there is nothing positive (or healthy) to say about the ribbed corset: Its intention was to enhance women's sexual attributes by creating an impossibly pinched waist while pushing the breasts upward to swell the cleavage. The constriction to the lungs impeded women's capacity to inhale deeply, with deleterious effects on the wearer's energy and health. Corsets were generally fronted with a piece of solid whalebone called the "busk," which flattened the belly and accentuated breasts and hips in contrast.[13] In sum, as Sarah Frontiera postulates, the production factories aboard whaleships were intricately connected both to women's consumption of the feminine clothing items that the whaling enterprise helped produce and to women's (re)production of the male bodies whose labor manned these ships.[14] Melville was not unaware of these interfaces between women's material bodies and the material labor of a whaling crew, as is apparent in

Ishmael's winking reminder that "every one knows" the baleen from the right whale's mouth is used to "furnish the ladies their busks and other stiffening contrivances" (*Moby-Dick*, 266). Given Melville's penchant for phallic jokes, one suspects an innuendo at play: What "stiffens" are the male admirers of the pulchritude that such contrivances evoke. Whaling as an enterprise and female sexuality prove inextricably entwined.

This eroticized overlap of the gendered arenas of production and consumption also finds intriguing expression in another by-product of the whaling industry—the use of sperm whales' teeth in creating scrimshaw objects and art. Among the subject matters that sailors at sea carved onto these teeth were idealized versions of the women they hoped to find waiting for them upon their return to shore—images of women fully outfitted in enticing hoop skirts and corsets (figure 4.1). There is a circular irony embedded in these images of objectified femininity: In the process of the whale being stripped of every usable part that might turn a profit, these particular skeletal remains—teeth—became the canvas on which to depict the commercial gains to which other "leftover" whale parts—whalebone and baleen—were put in manufacturing the very garments that made these women appear desirable. Fascinatingly, sperm whale teeth also served as the medium on which sailors etched their pornographic fantasies: Carvings of acts of copulation and nude women abounded (figure 4.2). In a world of men at sea, whalebone became the repository of heterosexual men's missing objects of desire *and* a visual stimulant—or "stiffening contrivance"—for masturbatory relief. Art and erotic fantasy sutured production and consumption in the whaling industry.[15]

These links among whaling, whalebone, and women find both material and figurative expression in the three contemporary artworks analyzed in the following pages. All three move women from the margins to the center of narratives invoking *Moby-Dick* and thus focus attention on the stakes of female representation in art forms traditionally dominated by men. Notably, each is also inspired by the aesthetics of hybridity and pastiche inhering in Melville's stylistic and formal experiments. And all three explore, materially or metaphorically, the imbricated worlds of whaling and women by making whalebone's use in fashion a point of entry to their postmodern and feminist engagements with the author.

For Solien, the deployment is literally sartorial. He uses a child's drawing of a woman caged in a wide hoop skirt and corset as the template for his avatar of Mrs. Ahab, whose outlined presence floats across myriad scenes in an epic collage series that spans nineteenth-century sea exploration and American westward expansion.[16] In Ellen Driscoll's performance piece *Ahab's Wife, or The Whale*, a huge onstage hoop skirt morphs into stage prop, scenery, scrim, whale's eye, diving-bell cover, and more. Nineteenth-century undergarments also provide a hermeneutic for understanding Rinde Eckert's multimedia chamber piece *And God Created Great Whales*: Not only is the visibly corseted, Black Muse

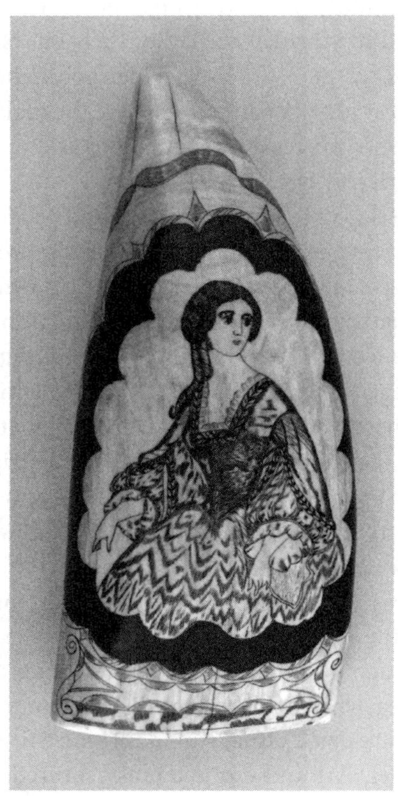

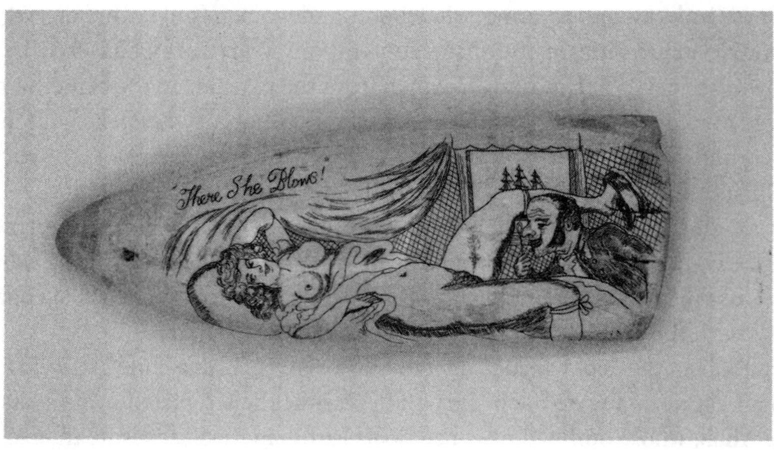

Figures 4.1 and 4.2. Women in scrimshaw, idealized and eroticized.
Top: "Onyx portrait," ca. 1860. Whale ivory. *Bottom*: "Erotic scrimshaw," n.d. Whale ivory.

Sources: 4.1: New Bedford Whaling Museum, Kendall Whaling Museum Collection Transfer, 2001.100.1466. Item 1923.6 18. Courtesy of New Bedford Whaling Museum. 4.2: Obj. No. 1991.1001.004. Courtesy of Vancouver Maritime Museum.

(imagined into being by a very white composer, Nathan) initially confined, or figuratively corseted, by existing in Nathan's mind, but Nathan too is caged, both in his monomaniacal drive to complete an opera based on *Moby-Dick* and in his violently masculinist interpretation of the novel. As long as he refuses to include the realm of the feminine in his composition, the project of "self-hood" (Urania's yearning in "After the Pleasure Party") remains "incomplete."

These manifestations of whalebone—imprisoning costume, multifaceted stage prop, crippling state of mind—form facets, or part-objects, in the assemblage of meanings circulating around women, whaling, and Melville in contemporary art.[17] By returning to Melville's field of representation the reality of women largely missing in his texts, these artists are not simply replacing a "lack" or correcting a "flaw" but also locating, unearthing, and recovering in Melville's politics and aesthetics the hints, the clues, the empathies that make their female-centric additions an oddly logical continuation of his never-ending, restless quest for deeper meanings and new forms to express them.

Leaping the Hoops Toward Liberation: Solien's Mrs. Ahab

Over ten years in the making, the fifty-eight mixed-media and collage pieces composing T. L. Solien's monumental series *Toward the Setting Sun* (2003–2011) grant the feisty protagonist of Sara Jeter Naslund's novel a fascinating alternative life, one in which wardrobe—notably Mrs. Ahab's hoop skirt—becomes a primary signifier.[18] Solien began the series by exploring the parallels between Ahab's mad quest and the drives underlying nineteenth-century American western expansionism; whether by land or by sea, both types of venturing forth into a vast unknown rely on mythologies of heroism and the natural sublime that tend to erase the brutal economic realities, heartbreaking disasters, and loss of human life undergirding these quests. It took reading Naslund's *Ahab's Wife* to give Solien the creative hook he needed to combine sea voyaging and frontier travel under one rubric.[19] As noted in the previous chapter, the two asides in Melville's text mentioning Ahab's "girl-wife" (*Moby-Dick*, 79, 406) inspired Naslund to give fictional life to this unnamed character. Written in the stylistic vein of *Moby-Dick*, Naslund's version of the heroic quest romance includes the lofty metaphysics and earthy materiality characteristic of Ishmael's narration, only now told from Una Spenser's female and ultimately feminist point of view.

Taking the idea if not the specific events of Ahab's wife from Naslund's text, Solien first envisages his character in situations suggesting the constricted existences that whalers' wives led once their husbands embarked to sea. But succeeding images, once Ahab's wife embarks on widowhood, depict an afterlife that supersedes even that of Naslund's protagonist in both geographical and temporal terms. Whereas Una Spenser makes a final home on Nantucket (settling down with none other than the shipwreck survivor Ishmael), Solien's

Mrs. Ahab leaves the island to become part of the great mass migration westward, setting up a homestead in the North Dakota Badlands and finally becoming an ageless time traveler into the automotive 1940s.

Nothing in Solien's artwork is as linear as this summary indicates. Rather, from an assembly of picture collages that are often abstract and deliberately elliptical, one learns to recognize leitmotifs relating to Ahab's wife that allow one gradually to surmise the arc of her evolution. Composed of mixed media, "cutout dollops of color," and paint, the compositions making up *Toward the Setting Sun* render their subjects in unsettlingly shallow spaces and against flattened landscapes that fracture perspective and defy visual coherence.[20] Incorporating old postcards, carpentry manuals, vintage children's activities books, historical snapshots, and cut paper, Solien blends these ephemera with art-historical references to a number of acclaimed artists, from Winslow Homer to Edgar Degas.[21] Such bricolage, Elizabeth Schultz observes, creates an "agitated vitality" filled with "nervous lines" and "spatial distortions" that compel the viewer to wrestle with meaning that—as is true of Melville—will always be ambiguous.[22] In these ways, Solien's pastiche aesthetic aligns him directly with Melville's crazy-quilt experiments in narrative form.

Mrs. Ahab floats ghostlike across this destabilized landscape in the shape of an abstracted outline. The child's drawing from the 1930s that served as the template for Solien's Mrs. Ahab shows a female figure clad in an exaggerated hoop skirt, waist pinched by her corset, and head in profile (figure 4.3). Throughout Solien's collages, the face of Ahab's wife maintains an unreadable flatness, a masklike quality that brings to mind Melville's representation of the White Whale's inscrutable pasteboard mask. Sometimes her face takes on a

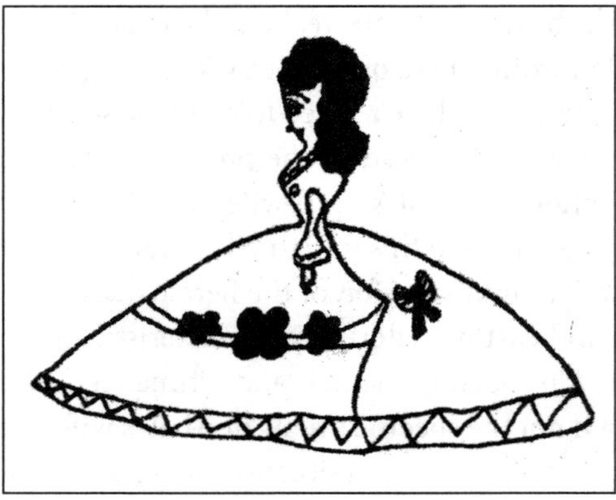

Figure 4.3. T. L. Solien's inspiration for Mrs. Ahab. Found child's drawing and source of Solien's inspiration.

Source: Artist's collection. Courtesy of the artist.

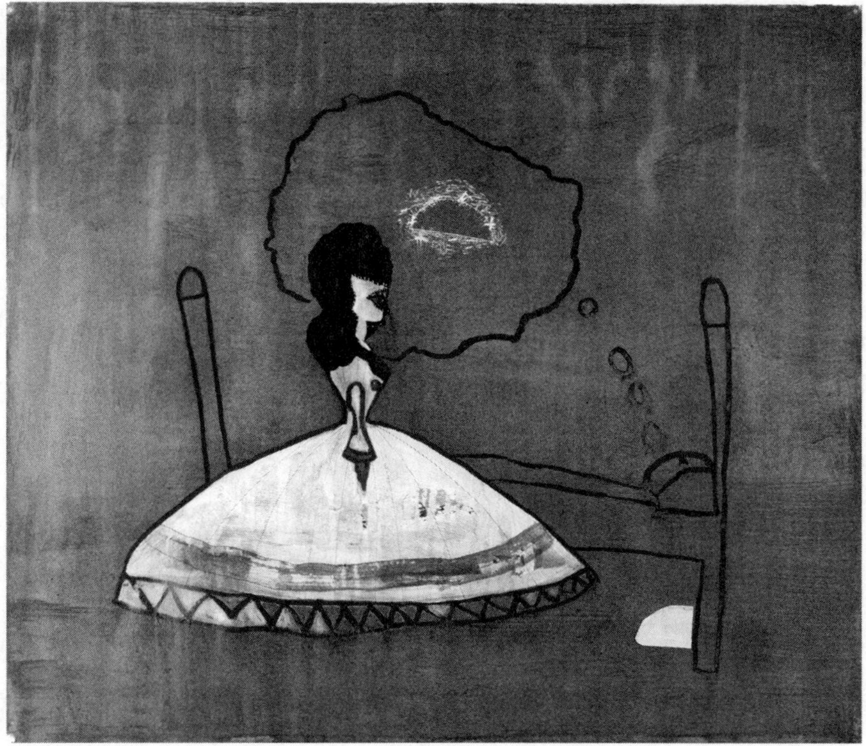

Figure 4.4. Ahab's nightmare: embodied wife, evacuated whale.
T. L. Solien, *Night Nurse*, 2005. Mixed media on paper. 30½" × 35¾".

Source: Courtesy of the artist.

white-powdered, kabuki-like semblance; sometimes it seems more like that of a circus clown; sometimes it is like a snowman with lumps of coal for eyes. But, most notably, throughout the paintings that invoke *Moby-Dick*, her hoop skirt is the ubiquitous signifier of her presence.

In *Moby-Dick*, of course, we never do see Ahab and his wife together. In contrast, Solien portrays Mrs. Ahab and her husband in the same frame three times. All occur, significantly, in their bedroom, reverberating with the unspoken tensions in their marriage. In *Night Nurse* (2005, figure 4.4), Mrs. Ahab stands by the marital bed, looking down at her sleeping husband (the description of her as "nurse" leads one to imagine that Ahab has just returned from the voyage where he suffered the loss of his leg). The image rivets the eye: Her billowing white hoop skirt jumps out against the muted background. Lying in a bed with phallic bedposts represented only by their outline, the symbolically de-manned Ahab (also an empty outline) is dreaming (as the cartoon bubbles

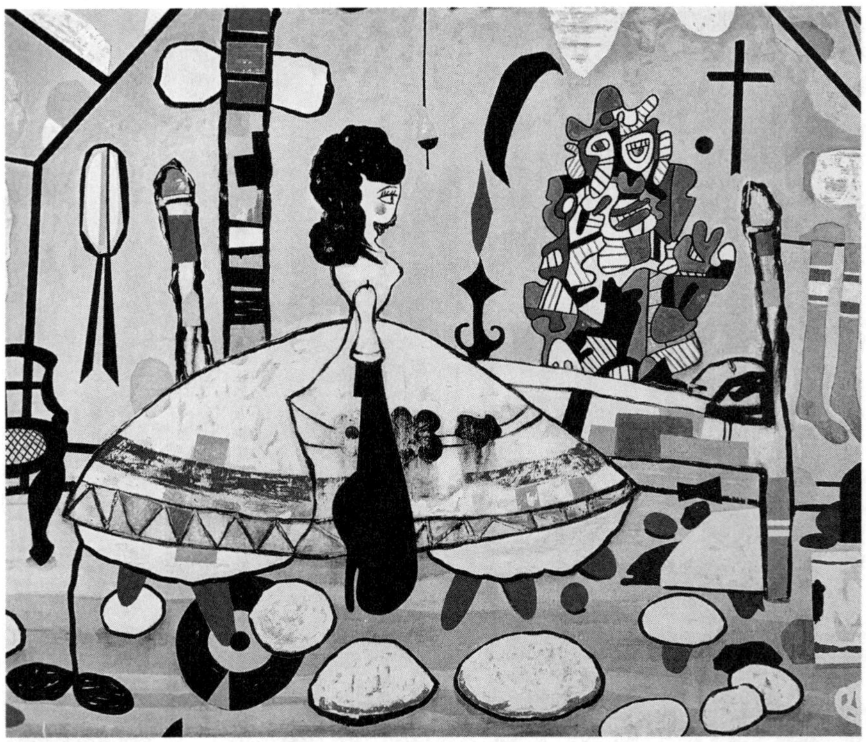

Figure 4.5. Whale of a cudgel.
T. L. Solien, *Sap*, 2006–2007. Oil and enamel on canvas, 60" × 72".

Source: Courtesy of the artist.

rising from his face indicate). That dream, moreover, is of a ghostly semispherical shape visible by its scratchy white halo—Solien's leitmotif for Moby Dick. But this shape, tellingly, is identical to that of his wife's hoop skirt. To what degree, then, is she *his* White Whale? Intriguingly, his dreamed "whale" is a void within its penumbra of white halo; the outline of Mrs. Ahab's dress, in contrast, is filled with white paint, as "present" as the hue can be. Both sublime and terrible, like the paradoxical meanings of whiteness enumerated in Ishmael's ruminations, Mrs. Ahab is the agent, the active force, in this picture, her vertical posture domineering over the horizontal line created by her sleeping husband. Solien's characterization thus emphasizes the emptiness at the heart of Ahab's dreaming desire—it is only vacancy, like the emptily erect phallic posts of his bed that signify his own lack. In vivid contrast, Mrs. Ahab is the one fleshed-out and upright presence in the scenario.

A female erotics of revenge becomes manifest in *Sap* (2006–2007), a second Solien bedroom scene (figure 4.5). The composition forms a palimpsest of *Night*

Nurse: Bed and figures occupy identical places within the frame, and Mrs. Ahab again looms over a sleeping Ahab. He, however, is even less visible here. Our attention is drawn to her right hand, which has transformed into "the kind of club used by gangsters," a surreally large sap with which she appears smilingly ready to bash her husband.[23] The sap also curiously resembles a whale: Is she about to do violence to her husband with the very object he hunts to kill? The now unrestrained resentment that Mrs. Ahab feels against her lot is indicated by the bursts of color that dot the image; the erotic vitality of her potential agency vibrates in the multicolored phallic bedposts. This agency vibrates as well in the number of feet—at least four—that appear to be whirling in motion beneath her hooped skirt.[24]

The third bedroom scene, *Reading with Laundry* (2006), glosses the dynamics of this marriage from a different tack.[25] A smiling Mrs. Ahab is in bed, propped up against its headboard and happily reading. A stack of unfolded laundry (including a pair of ribbed stays) separates her from the diminutive stick-figure representation of Ahab gesturing from the foot of the bed. Clearly, "feminine" domestic duties such as folding laundry are not going to stand in the way of the freedom the corsetless Mrs. Ahab experiences with book in hand. Along with pillows and undergarments on the floor, there's an oblong black object within Mrs. Ahab's reach that looks suspiciously like a dildo (Una's discovery of this self-pleasuring device forms a memorable scene in Naslund's novel). Given that quilting has always been considered a female form of art, it is telling that the patchwork covering under which Mrs. Ahab nestles is dotted with coffins of various sizes juxtaposed with star shapes. Do the black coffins betoken her wish for her husband or his inevitable fate? Are they nods at Queequeg's lifesaving coffin, on top of which Ishmael is reborn at the end of *Moby-Dick*? Are the stars a reference to Naslund's liberated, star-gazing Una? Does the quilt, like the book Ahab's wife is reading, signal her authorship of her own story?

Mrs. Ahab's own rebirth is imminent, as subsequent images limn the metaphoric and literal "voyage out" that her life begins to take once she sheds her husband's influence after his death (an image of Mrs. Ahab in mourning evokes her pent-up energy and eagerness to move by depicting a number of mobile feet visible beneath her elevated hooped skirts). The most powerful of these outward-bound images, *Standing Masthead* (2005, figure 4.6), is one of the masterpieces of the series. Like Naslund's Una, who goes to sea, Solien's Mrs. Ahab is now aboard a whaler—albeit in her ubiquitous hoop skirt rather than in the trousers that Una dons when she ships out on a whaler disguised as a cabin boy. Ishmael's masthead perch has been turned into a theater box and the sails into curtains, and Mrs. Ahab assumes Ishmael's lofty position, looking out over the ocean as if it is a theatrical spectacle being presented on her behalf. And what does she see? Her preferred version of Moby Dick, floating to the left of the

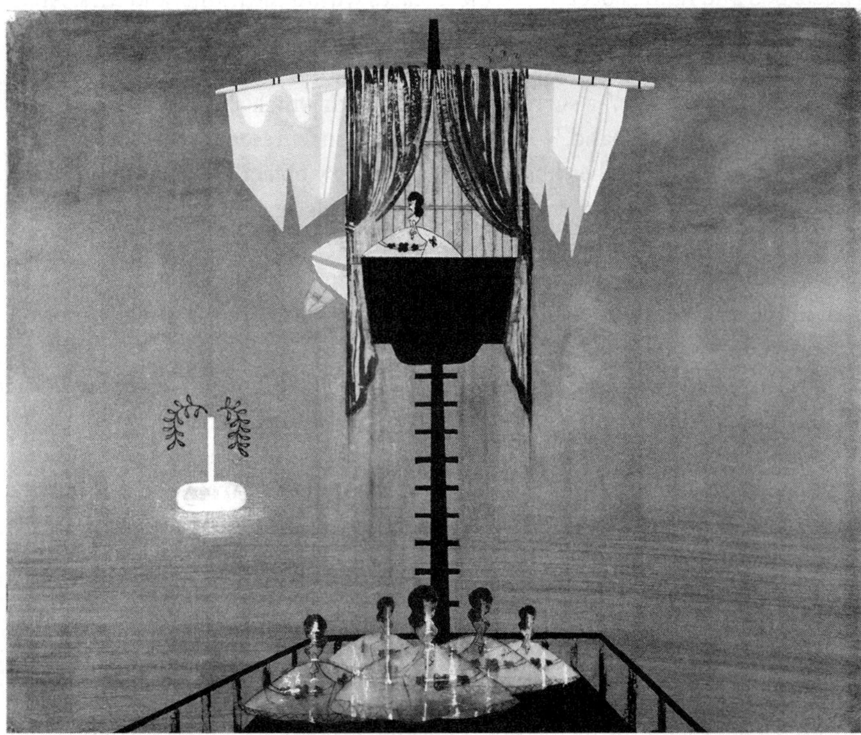

Figure 4.6. Women at sea, whale as vase.
T. L. Solien, *Standing Masthead*, 2005. Mixed media on paper, 31¾" × 38¼".

Source: Privately owned. Courtesy of José Carlino and Folliard Gallery.

frame, in which the White Whale is no longer a foe but a delicate white vase that spurts forth flowery tendrils. Meanwhile, below Mrs. Ahab, five versions of her own image, all hoop-skirted, glide over the deck. The hems of their dresses may be stained red by the bloody labor that occurs on whaling ships, but the women seem to float above the gore in female solidarity. Their huge dresses—formerly the symbol of cultural constriction and female immobility—are now akin to wind-filled sails as the boat's all-female voyage into the unknown and an open-ended future gets underway.

In contrast to Melville's all-male worlds, Solien also explores the possibilities of female-dominant domains in complementary images. *Long Branch 2006* nods to Winslow Homer's *Long Branch, New Jersey* (1869) with a nearly identical visual layout: Homer's female vacationers are recast as a covey of whalers' wives, nine women in contrast to the two foregrounded figures in Homer's painting.[26] These wives have just bid farewell to husbands or other male relatives aboard the small whaling vessel occupying the lower left of the image. The ship, about to pass over the horizon, is visible only as a silhouette, dark as the sea with which it is visually one. Occupying the foreground, the wives are clad in billowing hoop skirts, and some carry sun parasols (whose ribs were also commonly made of whalebone). Nor do they appear particularly mournful or immobile. Mimicking the movement of the clouds scudding across the baby-blue sky and the wind jostling their skirts, several have turned from the ocean view and are moving across the park in pure enjoyment. The revitalized energy that all these women apparently feel, freed of their husbands, resonates in the lively cut-out shapes and vibrating colors with which Solien imbues the landscape. As the nineteenth-century ballad "Nantucket Girl's Song" puts it,

> Then I haste to wed a sailor,
> and send him off to sea,
> For a life of independence
> is the pleasant life for me.
> . . . .
> But when he says "Goodbye my love,
> I'm off across the sea,"
> First I'll cry for his departure,
> then laugh because I'm free.[27]

Independence, freedom, laughter: All these emotions are latent in Solien's depiction of the wives in *Long Branch*. The idea of pleasure is literalized as play in *Croquette* (2006) as Mrs. Ahab and her hoop-skirted friends float across a croquette lawn (Mrs. Ahab, "haloed" by a giant croquette hoop, holds the mallet while in conversation with another woman). In contrast to the oil by Homer that inspired this scenario, Solien has eliminated the men. Another collage, *Island Park* (2009, figure 4.7), similarly features hoop-skirted women enjoying freedom of movement in an out-of-doors setting, a shady arbor crossed with walking paths. Three women float through the space in separate directions, each of their sight lines leading outside the frame into the viewer's world. In contrast, the sole male–female couple in the park has merged into a single black silhouette (like the ship and sea in *Long Branch*) as they follow a path that trails off into the background. Their shrouded darkness seems ominous, foreclosed, as opposed to the fully visible women flitting in multiple directions with complete freedom of movement.

Solien makes this energy vital to the images depicting Mrs. Ahab's life after she is widowed. A woman clearly on the move, Mrs. Ahab launches on a quest for self-expression and independence as she joins the mass migration to the plains and the American West launched in the name of Manifest Destiny. Sometimes the hoop skirt makes a guest appearance—at a resort hotel, in a prairie home, by the viewing stands at a horse-racing track, at the Wisconsin Dells, outside a

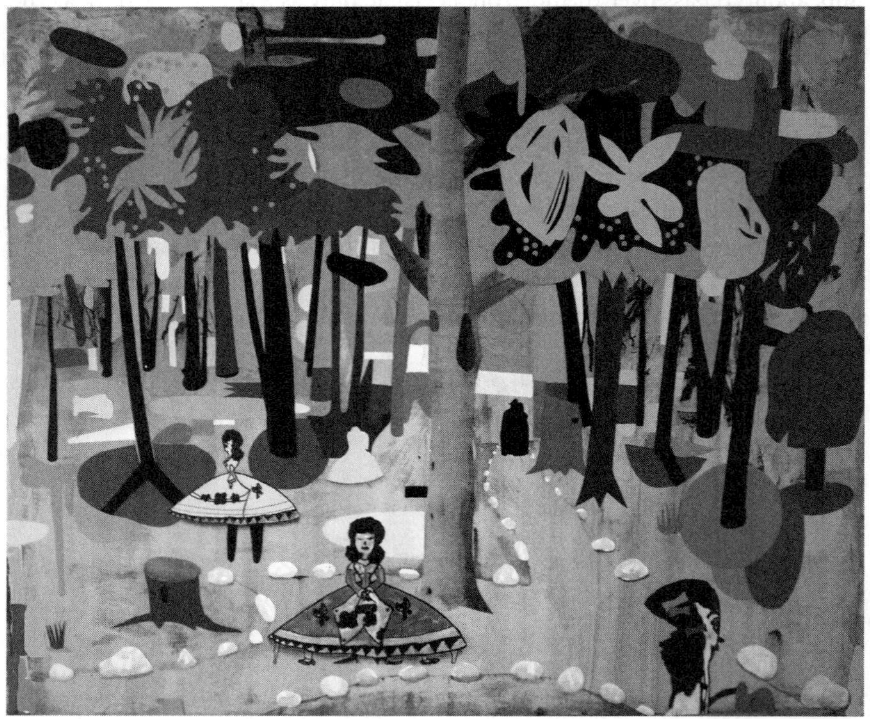

Figure 4.7. Female mobility and independence.
T. L. Solien, *Island Park*, 2009. Mixed media on paper, 30" × 36".

Source: Privately owned. Courtesy of Lauren Dybsand.

mining operation—but now she exercises the freedom to don *any* outfit she desires, from kimono to flapper dress, jodhpurs, cowboy clothing, even a Civil War reenactment uniform (she assumes the latter two costumes in male drag, wearing a deliberately fake-looking beard). As historical witness to the violence, hardships, and disasters of frontier life, Mrs. Ahab often emerges in this part of the series as a kind of hard-scrap pioneer hero. But Solien resists overly idealizing her self-actualization the farther she spatially removes herself from the East and the more she moves temporally into the twentieth century. This, perhaps, is the point of the poignant scenario in *Less* (2011), where, in a visual nod to Degas's *The Absinthe Drinker* (1875–1876), she sits at a café table, older, alone, sadder, but still with a knowing gleam—perhaps even a challenge—in her eyes as she squints directly at the viewer. Emancipated widow she may be, but we cannot absolve her of her complicity in the atrocities occasioned by settler-colonist expansion, any more than we can ignore Ahab's involvement in the capitalist industry of slaughtering whales to fuel yet more industry.

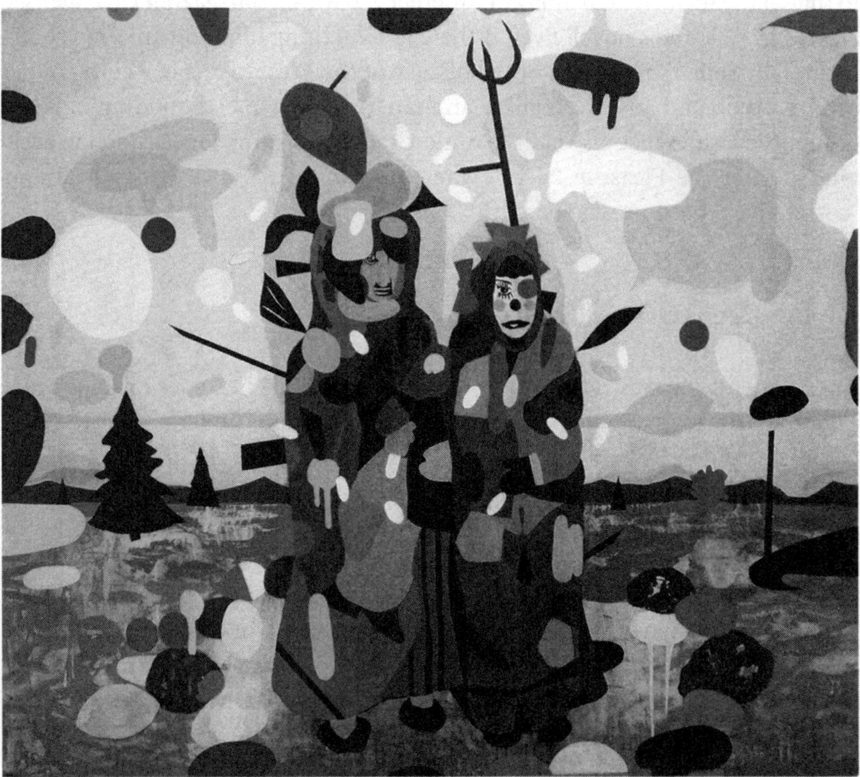

Figure 4.8. Wedding of cultures.
T. L. Solien, *Blanket Ceremony*, 2010. Oil and acrylic on canvas, 48¼" × 54¼".

Source: Courtesy of the artist.

Two images painted in 2010 and both titled *Blanket Ceremony* may indicate Solien's desire to forge a rapprochement between Mrs. Ahab's existence as a settler colonialist and the Native populations being decimated by such encroachments. In both images (the major difference being a change in seasons), a blanket-wrapped Mrs. Ahab stands beside a fur-and-blanket-encased Native American inside a circle of sacred stones, which seem to signify a bonding rite or marriage between the two (figure 4.8). On their backs are attached a multicultural array of weaponry from rifle to spear to harpoon, humorously including something resembling a whale tail rising behind the man's headdress. Dots of color decorate the surrounding landscape as if in celebration of the rite being performed within the stone circle. If, as I suspect, this mix of symbols and signifiers from multiple cultures reflects Solien's attempt to envision antagonistic worlds achieving coexistence, however counterfactually, his message hues close to that of the inclusive harmony of difference to which star-gazing Una Spenser aspires in Naslund's novel. Even if there is something too utopian, even sentimental, in Solien's rewriting of the history of the West to create a cozy couple of Mrs. Ahab and a Native American man, this cross-racial bonding of icons of supposed difference also calls to mind Urania's yearning for selfhood in Melville's "After the Pleasure Party," wherein splintered "halves" may heal and "co-relatives" become whole.

Diving Deep: Driscoll's Wife

As in Solien's collages, a gigantic, billowing hoop skirt becomes onstage presence and primary symbol for the myriad transformations undergone by the protagonist of Ellen Driscoll's theatrical performance piece *Ahab's Wife, or The Whale* (1998) as the title character dives into her psyche.[28] In this rendition of Ahab's partner, however, Driscoll is interested in the hoop skirt not only as a sartorial reminder of women's encasement in patriarchy; indeed, the enigmatic valences that this object accrues throughout the production are as multiple as the many moving parts that make this experimental work as diversely hybrid as Melville's famous novel. If mixed and multimediated art forms are especially conducive to contemporary artists inspired by Melville's amalgam of genres and modes, Driscoll's *Ahab's Wife* potently exemplifies multimedia's ability to travel alongside Melville in spirit while simultaneously contemporizing his vision. The piece was conceived as one facet of a series of exhibitions and events titled *Ahab's Wife: Harbor Soundings, Ocean Dreams* and held at the Snug Harbor Cultural Center on Staten Island in 1998. As part of this program, more than thirty of Driscoll's paintings, prints, and sculptures were displayed in Main Hall; a second room exhibited scrimshaw art; and Melville's personal collection of whaling prints were hung in a room that, uncannily, once served as the office of his brother Thomas from 1867 to 1884.[29]

Driscoll's presentation in the Music Hall provided the fulcrum for this assembly of overlapping parts. Even though Driscoll conceived the production, the staged performance was the product of intensely collaborative work that defies single authorship. Driscoll's husband, the poet Tom Sleigh, wrote its densely lyrical, sometimes comic, and often surreal script, but the script's words would signify little without the elaborate movement-choreography by Amy Spencer and Richard Colton that becomes the production's primary conduit of visual meaning. This dance element in turn depends on the highly elaborate lighting and set design (including the hoop skirt), along with music that abruptly shifts between classical and popular registers. The human actors—whose roles morph across bodies and centuries—share the stage with shadow puppets manipulated by human operators visible behind scrimlike half domes. The

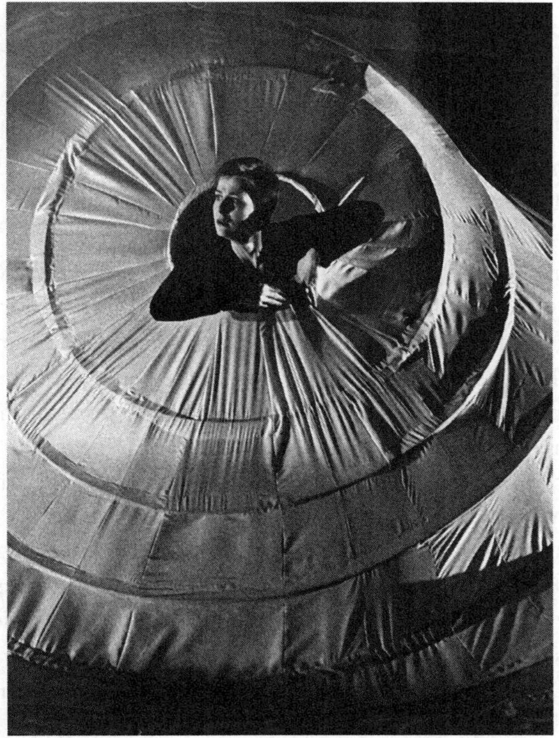

Figure 4.9. Hoop skirt as prop: cage, sails, whale's eye, diving bell.
Scene from Ellen Driscoll, *Ahab's Wife, or The Whale*, Snug Harbor Cultural Center, Staten Island, 1998.

Source: Courtesy of the artist.

overall effect is a sensorium equivalent to the dream state that inaugurates the protagonist's transition from her roles as spouse, waiting woman, and widow into a more active engagement with her past and present lives.

On Driscoll's stage, Melville's "hooded phantom, like a snow hill in the air" (*Moby-Dick*, 22), quite literally becomes the enormous hoop skirt, which initially encases a tripled avatar of Ahab's young wife in a cage of horizontal bars as she awaits her husband's return. Throughout the Snug Harbor performance, the function of the skirt constantly metamorphoses as it is manipulated by poles carried by dancers on stage. Even as it initially surrounds the wife, leaving only her arms free to move, wavelike, in the air, it also floats with a fluid buoyancy that hints at freedom, motion, the possibility of taking flight (figure 4.9). At times, it seems to waft like underwater creatures, jellyfish and anemone; at times, it becomes a globe, imprinted with a map of the world; at times, it mimics the waves of the ocean as well as the sails of ships. For a large portion of the performance, it hovers above the stage, reminiscent of a parachute, transforming into an omniscient cosmic eye gazing down on the actors and audience. It serves as the slipcover protecting the diving bell that takes the wife into the depths of the ocean for her epiphanic encounter with Moby Dick, and in this encounter the skirt becomes both whale's forehead and gigantic eye. As chameleon signifier, the hoop skirt is ever present, never denoting just one thing, as enigmatically multivalent in meaning as the White Whale.

As in Solien's collage paintings, Driscoll's choice to make the wife's psychological journey the focus of her meditation on Melville's novel brings the politics of sexuality and gender front and center as she dissects the marriage of Ahab and his wife. In the staged production, the whale delivers the prologue while meditating on his bifurcated vision; because of the positioning of a sperm whale's eyes on either side of his blank forehead, he can never see what is ahead of him, only the separate images that his eyes pick up to the left and right.[30] Intriguingly, an earlier draft subtitled "Or the Fan" opens not on the whale but on younger versions of husband and wife, isolated in separate pools of light, talking to but physically unaware of the other. However seemingly disparate, both prologue versions foreground the same theme—the split vision that develops in marriage, blinding husband and wife to the disastrous storms lying straight ahead, storms that rupture oceanic bliss. As the voice-over of a preacher (shades of Father Mapple) announces a sermon concerning "the hearts of two of our shipmates" since "we're all of us Jonahs in the belly of love" (1), Ahab's wife struggles to remember the nautical language her gone-to-sea husband has taught her. For each of her feminine expressions, he is adamant that she use the properly masculine equivalent: "A real sailor says, 'Yo ho,' not 'Yoohooo,'" he corrects her, then amends her "Ahoooey!" to "AHOY!" (2). Clearly, this Ahab privileges his masculine vernacular at the expense of the feminine. The scene ends with Ahab's nostalgic declaration, "Call me Ahab!"—a callback to the days of their courtship—to which she responds, "Call me Augusta! Or Gusty! Or Gus!" (3). The metamorphosis of "Augusta" to "Gus" evokes a playful fluidity in gender significations that countermands Ahab's desire that she speak only his language. The moment also primes us for the script's subsequent rapid tonal shifts from slapstick to sublimity, from poetry to whimsy—juxtapositions that echo the destabilizing shifts in mode and mood informing Melville's aesthetics.

One of Driscoll's innovations in placing a female character at the center of her project is to give the nineteenth-century context of *Moby-Dick* a simultaneously contemporary overlay, signaling the relevance of the dilemmas faced by this "Mrs. Ahab" to women of all times. Thus, the first act transports us to the late twentieth century, viewing a modern living room where Ahab's widow (now played by another actress), drinking heavily (perhaps self-medicating after the trauma of Ahab's disappearance), speaks of the "magnetic" force (opposite poles attracting) that at one time attached her heart to Ahab's. This force field allows her to tap into radio-like "frequencies" from across the world as she channels various "voices" and contemplates the fate of sailors like her husband, all sea "dogs" who begin their journeys "tail wagging," only to sink into "the doldrums" and "then—over and out. Sayonara. Charlie. Slam bam thank you ma'am. Hail and farewell" (4). Surreally, a "Mastman" appears, who speaks of the transcendental ecstasy of climbing the mast and letting "your soul slide right out of your body, like in a dream" (4). Ishmael's masthead reveries are clearly on Driscoll's mind, and as in the case of Melville's narrator-protagonist, this dreaming state proves dangerous should the watcher in the crow's nest slip and fall (as this Mastman immediately does). What may be deadly for others, however, in fact anticipates Mrs. Ahab's psychic readiness—perhaps primed by her inebriated state—to slip and fall into an imaginative reverie that initiates her own subconscious sea voyage, an interior journey to understand her marriage's failure, Ahab's fate, her own potentialities.

The wife's quest is first staged as a search for something she has "lost" ("It's true, I lost it" [7]) on a figurative sea voyage with her husband ("it was here, I know it. . . . I spread the net, but somehow it slips through undetected" [5]). Literally, the lost object is a lovely fan that Ahab gave her as a first-anniversary present, which has fallen overboard. (By the end of the performance it's clear that the marriage is this "voyage out," one that ends in shipwreck.) The motif of the lost object recalls Freud's theory of the origins of all narrative in the infant's game of *fort/da*, in which the child attempts to regain mastery (*da*—"there!") over that which they've lost (*fort*—"gone!"): symbiotic oneness with the mother and an oceanic state of preconscious bliss.[31] As Ahab's wife frantically hunts for her lost object, she simultaneously initiates the process of diving inward to confront her traumas, and this psychodramatic register is signaled in the surreal resonances that the setting and action assume—living-room couch transforms into a shark stealthily stalking her, a harpooner appears doing the same.

This surreality heightens the performance's sexual politics as the wife dons the costume of a sea-faring captain, replete with fake beard (recall Solien's depictions of Mrs. Ahab in male drag). Simultaneously another sea captain appears in the living room, dressed exactly like her and indignant at being confronted by this gender-troubling double. His response is to demonstrate his more masculine bona fides, "*flex*[*ing*] *like a bodybuilder*" and spouting hyperbolic language that ironically deconstructs his performance of superior masculinity: "Biiceps. Triiceps. Fooorceps" (6, original emphasis). Muscle groups give way to an instrument intrinsic to childbirth, as drawn-out, "erect" *i*'s give way to more open *o*'s. In this world of gender instabilities, "Gus" has again become "Augusta." Meanwhile, the stalking harpooner and shark transform into totemic guides that help the wife on her quest. The harpooner becomes a spinning compass, reminding her, "Magnetic north. That's where you left the fan he gave you," and the circling shark summons the wife to make the plunge: "Come on down here, *Sister*, where it's really deep" (7, emphasis added). The act ends with water filling the living room as she recalls her initial premonition, when Ahab presented her with the fan, that marital happiness is ephemeral: "This can't last, I wouldn't like it to last. The old in/out leading to God knows what complications" (8).

The hallucinatory quality of this scene's finale continues in act 2, which opens beneath the ocean as the whale laments in blank verse his condition of perpetually divided vision. All the while, the gigantic, unoccupied hoop skirt moves across the stage, turning to a perpendicular position to become a gigantic eye watching the wife, who intuitively understands the whale's visual experience of "perpetual post-mortem" (9), for this is also the condition in which whaling men's wives find themselves, their lives suspended in the anticipation of learning of the deaths of absent husbands. The whale and wife begin a rhythmic colloquy, a call-and-response, recounting their equivalent experiences of pain and loss. In this moment, Driscoll moves beyond simply filling in the missing narrative of Ahab's wife; in collapsing the worlds of human and animal, the text makes palpable the equally untold story of the hunted creature's trauma and pathos. Of his encounter with Ahab—projected on the scrim of the diving bell and enacted by shadow puppets (figure 4.10)—the whale reveals that he "felt no malice" when "my forehead / And the ship finally met" (10), and the wife confesses, "The further down I drifted, the more I was losing him. . . . I should have looked where I was going . . . when I heard what sounded like a ship breaking apart" (10)—that is, the figurative ship that has been their marriage. The exchanges swell to a shared epiphany in which the whale describes his pained descent, Ahab's harpoon digging into his side as the *Pequod* sinks. Then, at ocean's bottom, he not only sees Ahab's wife but also magically, impossibly, sees her whole, with *both* eyes: "I suddenly saw a face . . . *your* face in both my eyes" (10). In turn, the wife realizes the whale "see[s]" the way she "feel[s]," that they both know "*what it means to lose*" (11, original emphasis).

A dance of seduction between wife and whale (accompanied by the music of Irving Berlin's "Cheek to Cheek," which cheekily rewrites Ahab's fantasy of meeting forehead to forehead as romantic Hollywood musical) follows this moment of shared insight, as words and movements build to a climax. What first appears the mounting language of sexual congress discloses itself as a scene of childbirth—or, more accurately, the wife's eroticized rebirthing of herself: "And me the aftermath" (11). As whale and wife continue to identify with the other's loss and pain, their words not only enter into and speak from the consciousness of the other; they also channel the "frequencies" of Ahab's subjectivity, so that lines spoken by both whale and wife express *Ahab's* losses—of

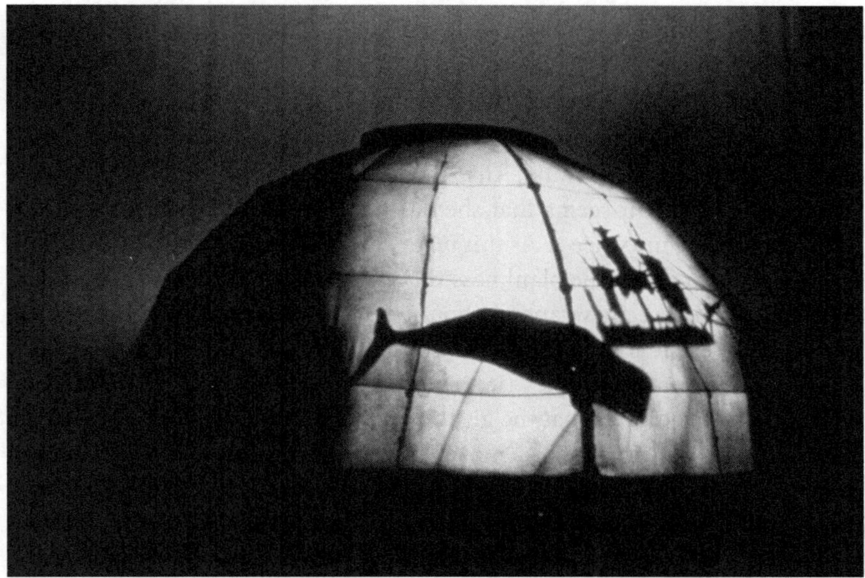

Figure 4.10. Hoop skirt as scrim.
Scene from Ellen Driscoll, *Ahab's Wife, or The Whale*, Snug Harbor Cultural Center, Staten Island, 1998.

Source: Courtesy of the artist.

vision, of spouse—and alienation as he weds himself to a maddened quest for revenge. As empathy for the whale now leads to empathy for Ahab, the scope of Driscoll's narration once again expands outward to include more than just the wife's story. The ethic inspiring Driscoll's imaginative reencounter with Melville reaches beyond the necessity of female representation to include attentiveness to all sentient things—a lesson also implicit in Ishmael and Queequeg's expansive humanity and foregrounded in contemporary environmentalist artists' questioning of the human–animal divide (see chapter 7).

Act 3 builds upon the wife's coming to understand the darker inner forces that have compelled Ahab on his doomed journey. Although Driscoll doesn't explicitly link Ahab's demons to his self-limiting masculine perspective, we implicitly sense that his emotional distance from his wife as he increasingly directs his energies into his vengeful quest is a defensive psychological response to an original loss of symbiosis that, as feminist psychoanalytic theory has shown, adheres in male individuation.[32] Thus, we learn that even before Ahab departs on his last voyage, he has begun an emotional leave-taking that *is* his death foretold. As the wife remembers, it is "as if he were lying in a coma, and inside his head someone were moving as in an empty house room to room . . . turning out light after light, stepping out the door, [until] everything inside

[was] still, dark" (14–15). The image resonates eerily with Solien's portrait of Mrs. Ahab looming over the emotionally vacated Ahab, and it foreshadows how Eckert's character Nathan will sink into a darkness that results from his self-imprisoning, monomaniacal, and overtly masculinized death-drive.

From the drama's beginning, Ahab's wife has been attuned to the lower "frequencies," and now it seems that she has telepathic access to her husband's thoughts. "Inside my voice . . . is this *other* voice," she says, one that allows her to compassionate with the blankness that has closed "its depths" around the drowned Ahab, "weeds wrapped about his head" (16, original emphasis) as he fades into existential nothingness. In response, the whale sounds a dirge-like song, "Bloooooowhooole" (16), as Ahab's wife climbs a mast. The final stage direction indicates that the gigantic hoop skirt "*ripples like waves of the sea*" (16, original emphasis), a movement recalling the words of the final chapter of *Moby-Dick*, when "the great shroud of the sea rolled on as it rolled five thousand years ago" (427). While Driscoll's conclusion maintains a Melvillean ambiguity, it appears that Ahab's wife has, like Ishmael, survived her deep dive and, raised aloft, now navigates her future direction from the masthead, even as the siren song of her whale/double hints at a "whooole"ness that follows wounds, rupture, and division.

The Diva's Star Turn: Eckert's *Whales*

"Whalebone corsets!"[33]

So sings a woman dressed in a full-length red dress as she channels the motley voices of the international world of street vendors crowding the streets of nineteenth-century New Bedford in Rinde Eckert's *And God Created Great Whales* (first produced in 2000), adding, "Shark tooth earrings! . . . Scented candles!" (97).[34] Minutes later she modulates into a Caribbean rhythm, the curvaceous movements of her hands outlining the built-in corset of her dress as she shimmies to the beat, her words underlining the economics linking nineteenth-century women's undergarments to the whaling industry: "You make some whalebone corsets and baleen combs . . . [take 'em] to the store, then sail back to de sea to get some more!" (98).

This striking woman is the imaginary Muse that Nathan, an ailing piano tuner who is desperately trying to complete an opera based on *Moby-Dick*, has summoned into being to keep him on task so that he can finish his magnum opus (figure 4.11). Although her lyrics remind us of the links among whalebone, women's costumes, and their gendered implications, Eckert channels the metaphoric associations of such garments rather than actual dress in his meditation on the roles of gender in Melville's imagination. In contrast to Solien and Driscoll, who highlight Ahab's hoop-skirted wife as a way of adding a

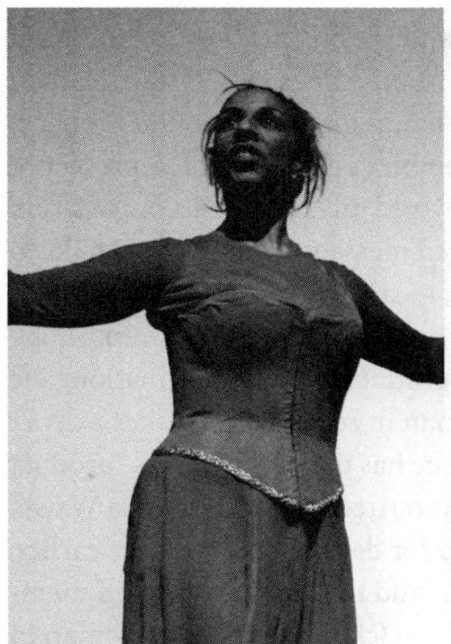
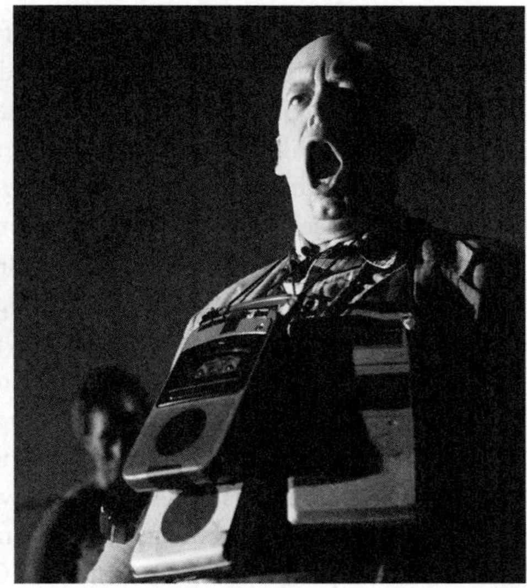

Figure 4.11 and 4.12. Corseted Muse versus "corseted" Nathan. Rinde Eckert, *And God Created Great Whales*, 2000, performance stills.

Source: Images reproduced with the permission of Rinde Eckert. Photographs by Caleb Wertenbaker.

female presence to their revisionist takes on Melville's male worlds, Eckert makes Nathan himself—as monomaniacally driven as Ahab—the locus in which female presence asserts its defiant refusal to be invisible or silenced or disembodied: first, as the Muse figure who exists as a figment of Nathan's imagination but whom the audience clearly sees; second, as the opera diva Olivia (played by the same actress), on whom Nathan has modeled his Muse; and, third, as the female element lacking in Nathan's opera—an element whose relevance neither Muse nor Olivia allow Nathan to forget. In the process, the dialectic of confinement/freedom that Solien and Driscoll locate at the intersection of whaling and women's dress takes on a broadly metaphoric resonance. At first, it appears that the female Muse is confined within Nathan's mind—if he dies, so does she. The further Eckert's narrative probes, however, the clearer it becomes that it is Nathan who is "corseted," as it were, in a limiting point of view that valorizes male heroics, violence, and existential doom. Not only are Muse and Olivia the only ones who can assure the completion of Nathan's opera, in effect becoming its authors, they are also the only ones who can lift Nathan from the dark abyss into which he, Ahab-like, is quickly sinking.

Nathan's monomaniacal sense of urgency, the audience immediately learns, is the effect of an irreversible brain disease from which he suffers. "You will remember less and less," a woman's voice-over announces. "One might say you will drown in your own ignorance" (86). The stage lights come up, and we see the Muse perched on a platform on stage left and Nathan helplessly clanging at his piano on stage right, until she commands him, "PUSH PLAY" (86). Nathan depresses a button on a cassette recorder that hangs on a rope around his neck. Duct-taped corsetlike across his body, it resembles a makeshift life preserver, an apt visual reference to the seafaring world of Nathan's composition (figure 4.12). Indeed, the recorder's prerecorded messages are designed to keep Nathan from "drown[ing] in ignorance" (86), to stay afloat as long as possible. "Today you will continue to work on your opera," the tape instructs him. "Look around the room. There is a woman. She is a product of your imagination. She will be helping you"—at which point the woman in red rises and takes a diva's bow—"She is infallible, so listen to anything she has to say" (87). This "product of [Nathan's] imagination" is based on the now retired opera star Olivia Walsh, whose career Nathan has obsessively followed for decades. A few years earlier, he had the fortune to become her piano tuner, and through a reenacted memory we become privy to the moment when Olivia (channeled by the woman in red) learns Nathan is composing an opera based on *Moby-Dick*. In her rich, lilting, ironic voice, she laughs, a bit ruefully. "Oh! Well, no part for me then!"

There may be "no part" for a female in the grandiose opera that Nathan has conceived, but there is an insistent place for women in Eckert's exploration of the monomania that drives men like Ahab—and Nathan—to self-destructive extremes. Visually, nothing is more immediately striking to spectators than the physical presence of its two actor-singers: Rinde Eckert, playing the part of Nathan, is quite literally one huge "white whale" of a white man, bleached out by the lighting and his ashen suit, wistful face childlike as he progressively loses memory and motor functions. Nora Cole, playing the corseted figment of his imagination as well as the real-life diva Olivia, is an arrestingly proud, self-possessed, statuesque African American woman—a female Queequeg who possesses something of Ishmael's arch tongue and plasticity of being. That she exists within Nathan's mind nods toward a psychic state of gender fluidity, an androgyny of being, as well as a complication of white privilege that exists within Nathan whether he cares to acknowledge it or not.

In giving women a central place in the world of Melville by means of this innovative scenario, Eckert channels *Moby-Dick*'s innovative textual energies on multiple levels, for if the woman in red is Nathan's animating muse, Melville remains Eckert's. On the level of word and action, the script manages quite remarkably to convey Melville's sense of the multicultural life of New Bedford and aboard the *Pequod*, especially when one considers that only two actors are giving voice to the entire "babble" of the novel's heteroglossic universe. On the level of genre, Eckert's creation—as impossible to pigeonhole as Driscoll's *Ahab's Wife* or, indeed, *Moby-Dick*—is at once opera, chamber piece, dramatic two-hander, mime, and dance piece in which spoken and taped voices as well as live and acoustic instrumentation intermingle. On the level of music, the score incorporates arias, ballads, street tunes, sea shanties, Caribbean rhythms, church-organ melodies, ukulele riffs, tambourine beats, synthesized sounds, recitative, and wordless vocalese. True to its postmodern sensibility, the stage set includes multiple modern modes of media and textuality: five color-coded cassette recorders, a television set (playing the Gregory Peck version of *Moby-Dick*), telephone message recordings, Post-It notes that festoon Nathan's piano, flashcards with words on one side and pictorial representations on the other designed to jolt Nathan's failing vocabulary. The sensorial world of *And God Created Great Whales* is as hybrid and multivocal and at times as demandingly dense and richly rewarding as Melville's text. Standing at the center of this multimedia event is the Muse/Olivia, whose presence, as Robert Wallace puts it, "lifts Eckert's opera into greatness," her equal time on stage with Nathan creating a degree of reciprocity on vocal, gendered, and racial levels that, as we will see, is extraordinary.[35]

In the unfolding psychodrama, however, Nathan resists such reciprocity. Instead, he frantically identifies with the masculine qualities he associates with Melville's world of the hunt. When the Muse suggests the opera could use "something feminine" as a "ballast for all that monomaniacal striving" (120), he emphatically shuts her down, offering a paean to "the slaughter, the men high on the kill, the water white with sharks tearing at the wounded, obliging flesh" of the "lanced and bleeding" whale (120). The telltale phrase "wounded, obliging flesh" hints at the traumatic underbelly of Nathan's identification with the hunt and with Ahab. Foremost, Nathan sees in Ahab's fixed desire to slay his foe a reflection of his own desperate desire to complete his opera, to conquer the blank page with which his loss of memory leaves him. Like Ahab, he justifies his obsession as an attempt to reach an ecstatic sublime, and he empathizes with Ahab as one whose attempts have been crippled by hateful circumstance. If Ahab's dismemberment spurs the captain's crazed quest for revenge, on an equivalent level Nathan's loss of memory is the wound that makes all the more pressing his mad desire to conquer his own white whale, this incomplete opera, and prove that he is in control once again.[36]

Part of the richness of Eckert's interpolation of a female presence into this Melvillean vortex resides in the way Nathan's Muse supersedes the role of the traditional female muse of male poets. Despite being a "product" of Nathan's imagination (87), this Muse exudes agency and self-determination. Feisty and self-aware, abrasive and challenging as needs be, spitfire and femme fatale in one package, Nora Cole's red-corseted woman emerges as a fully realized being. She actively resists Nathan's easy gender stereotyping; she valiantly attempts to redirect Nathan's monomania into more affirmative paths; and she poignantly expresses her desire to break away from his mind and become her own person, freed from his fantasies and, in particular, his fading memory.

Even though her existence is tethered to Nathan's, the Muse/Olivia figure played by Nora Cole emerges, arguably, as *the* dominant voice on both musical and performative levels in this two-person drama: *She* becomes the star, the diva who offers the hope that lifts Nathan's tragedy to new levels of understanding. In the process, she also becomes Eckert's means of affirming art's status "as proof against the ravaging entropy of it all" (106) that is mortal human existence. The importance that this female presence brings to Eckert's revisionist account is heightened by the verbal interactions, playing out on stage and in Nathan's mind, between this woman dressed in flaming red and the opera singer, Olivia, on whom her image is modeled. Over the course of the play, we witness the two women moving from wary distrust of each other to cooperation in attempting to lift Nathan from the abyss. A pivotal moment occurs in the second act as Olivia's voice on Nathan's tape recorder triggers his memories of their first meeting. The Muse, listening with Nathan, begins to channel the opera singer's voice and gestures, transforming herself *into* Olivia as she teases Nathan with the possibility of making an addition to his all-male cast: "Perhaps Ahab could have a vision. A dark woman appears to bring him a promise or a warning. Or maybe some heavenly creature at the end descending over Ishmael, floating on his coffin. She could look just like me, hanging there, on a celestial wire, singing of redemption or love" (95).

In the final act, the Muse realizes that embodying her alter ego may be the only way to bring Nathan, whose condition has vastly worsened, back to reality. Assuming Olivia's voice and mien, she asks,

> How is the opera going? . . . I was hoping you haven't forgotten my cameo. . . . I was hoping I inspired you! I still think it would be a good idea, this visitation. I mean, well you know—*all those men harpooning*, lancing, flaying. . . . Ahab in his cabin, pouring over his charts, *glowering, obsessed*. Then from nowhere I come in, sing some simple air . . . something exotic, a koto perhaps. Then I vanish, as mysteriously as I appeared, leaving . . . a promise or a warning. A penultimate lightness before the groaning sea collapses all, everything.
> (116, emphases added)

Magically, we sense that Muse and Olivia have merged as they strive to bring into being an alternative to Nathan's masculinist, destructive vision of obsession, violence, and the "collaps[e]" of "everything."

What follows are three melodies in what the Muse calls a "feminine air" (117), songs that are indeed digressions from—which is to say, *additions to*—Nathan's set text. Even though they may be only "marginal note[s]" (117), as the Muse quips, they work, like Ishmael's digressions, to expand the opera's metaphysical reach. The Muse's first inserted melody voices a message of peace and inclusiveness, leading to Nathan's violent outbreak, "[That's] not in the book. . . . It's a whaling ship for God's sake!" (117, 120). The opposition between "something feminine" (120) that the Muse advocates and Nathan's embrace of monomaniacal aggression leads to a shouting match that ends, ironically, with the Muse in full command, ordering Nathan to continue the opera with *her* addition intact: "It's the third Act and Ahab is hovering over his charts," she sets the scene. She then repeats Olivia's words *as if her own*: "And out of that provoking night a woman comes, an apparition . . .'I bring you a promise and a warning'" (121). As she speaks, the Muse rises in a vertical position behind the seated Nathan: she is now in ascendance.

Thus begins the second musical deviation from Nathan's score: an otherworldly duet in which Nathan joins the Muse in chiasmic lyrical exchanges that figuratively bind the two and lead on Nathan's part to the momentary recognition that his desire to be "innocent," to be a "child" again (123), is *both* the "promise" (of a lost wholeness) and the "threat" (of nothingness) that the future holds for him (123). As the melody drifts away, Nathan inadvertently pushes the on button of the cassette recorder on which he has saved Olivia's telephone messages, and Olivia's voice triggers his memory of a conversation where she explains she's left the world of opera behind in order "to simplify" (124), to experience "another kind of ecstasy" (125)—a decision that the Muse lauds as "heroic, full of epic feelings" (124). Ahab's mad quest, both women indicate, can follow an alternative "heroic" path, transform the story, rewrite Melville, if only Nathan would follow in his female idol's lead in learning to simplify, to find "ecstasy" in peace and calm.

At this crucial juncture, the Muse's recognition of the nobility and heroism of Olivia's gesture leads to her own tragic epiphany, expressed in the third off-the-book or "marginal" aria—namely, that she herself is "a woman with no history," just "every man's dream" (125), unless she finds a way out of the prison of Nathan's thoughts. The Muse's recognition, plaintively sung a cappella, compels her to take immediate action to move the opera to its completion: Nathan rises to the occasion to immerse himself in the role of Ahab as he gives up the spear, and the Muse swoons on the floor of the darkening stage, announcing "the yet yawning gulf" that consumes all as "the great shroud of the sea rolled on as it rolled five thousand years ago" (127).

The theater goes dark, and silence follows, but, as in Melville's text, an epilogue emerges from the darkness, lifting Nathan's drama, Eckert's opera, and the novel that has inspired this reenvisioning to new heights. First, through flickering light, we dimly perceive a robotic Nathan sitting before a television set on which John Huston's classic adaptation of *Moby Dick* plays. Seconds later, Nora Cole, now dressed all in white, enters as the flesh-and-blood Olivia Walsh, speaking with healing compassion to the mute composer as she retrieves the recorder containing the completed opera. Her celestial presence and radiant calm command the stage as she once again teases Nathan about the ending of his opera. In her description of his response, she proceeds to rewrite its conclusion: "Do you remember? I once asked you how you planned to handle the ending—all that grand violence, the monolithic whale, the sinking ship. 'How does one do that?' I asked you" (128). She then recounts the way Nathan has said the opera concludes—the scene that Nathan and the Muse have just enacted—and revises it with her own vision of the sublime. "'All subsides, the Leviathan, the cloth waves, the lonely coffin bobs in the center.' Then I descend on a wire like a baroque angel to pull Ishmael from the sea" (128).[37]

Adding her own ending to her quoted version of Nathan's rendering, Olivia brings her version to life as she now proceeds to "pull" Nathan "from the sea," from his own depths. For, as she begins to sing, her voice draws Nathan from the shadows at the rear of the stage, and he regains just enough cognition to join her in an extended wordless duet of vocalese in which her soaring voice elicits Nathan's sonorous response. Equal partners now, the two glide on a musical plane of pure transcendence, pure being—no words, just musical sound—that lasts three minutes as Olivia helps Nathan cross the threshold to the oblivion that faces everyone—"the ravaging entropy of it all" (106), as she has previously said. The haunting music is some of the most beautiful in the entire production, its lack of words making listeners all the more aware of the depths of meaning that linguistic signifiers—as Melville before Eckert knew so well—can never quite capture. The stage lights go dark as the two figures end by harmonizing on a high note.

While the whalebone constitutive of the hoop skirts on full display in Solien and Driscoll's work is mentioned only once in Eckert's script, in the Muse's reference to "whalebone corsets," on a metaphoric level the links among women, women's bodies, whales, and whaling couldn't be more profound: when Olivia finally appears in this final scene, she is clothed head to toe in shimmering white, lifting Nathan from blankness (one manifestation of whiteness as a lack of color) into a moment of sublimity (another version of whiteness). Bringing a woman's presence into intimate contact with Melville's metaphysics, Eckert posits love and redemption as an alternative "epic" (125), answers to the "hatred," the "vengeance," spurring Ahab's quest and segregating the world into gendered oppositions that, in the phrasing of Melville's poetic persona Urania, leave "selfhood . . . incomplete."

Pants Roles, Other Tactics, and Intersectional Musings

I want to conclude this chapter by commenting briefly on strategies other artists have used to usher women into the world of Melville. The earliest "solution" to Melville's "woman problem" was that of making Pip into what is alternatively called a "pants role" or "breeches part"—theater involving a woman playing a man's part as if she *is* a man. This is how the Young Actress in Orson Welles's *Moby-Dick—Rehearsed* (1955) gains her place on stage, taking on Pip's role because the director cannot find an African American boy to play the part. More recent forays use the opportunity to import another person of color in addition to a woman into Melville's shipboard world: giving the role of Pip to a Black female actor has become standard in subsequent adaptations of the novel as drama or opera.[38] Perhaps the most recent example is Jake Heggie's *Moby-Dick* (2010), proclaimed by Robert Wallace as a uniquely "twenty-first-century" opera.[39] Indeed, the addition of a woman's voice allows Heggie considerably more "vocal diversity" in the range of tonalities with which he can experiment, thereby expanding the emotional resonance of the score while diversifying the cast on racial and gender levels as well.[40]

A pants role is one thing; a female character who knowingly assumes male clothing (as Una Spenser does in the guise of Ulysses in *Ahab's Wife*) to enact a gender masquerade is another. The avant-garde German composer Olga Neuwirth's opera *The Outcast* (2012), billed as a "musicstallation in theatre with video," features a female version of Melville's narrator-protagonist, *Ishmaelle*, whose love of "sail[ing] the forbidden" has prompted her masculine masquerade as Ishmael.[41] So too the protagonist of the Chinese-born author Xiaolu Guo's recently published novel *Call Me Ishmaela* (2025) disguises herself as a cabin boy to go to sea on a whaler commanded by a freed Black man who has his own obsessions. Other artists, instead of turning to Ishmael, have made Queequeg the means of introducing a gendered critique layered with racial implications. Joseph Foster's black-and-white woodcut print *Queequeg* (2001) visualizes for the South Sea islander an androgynous body whose sinuous curves and taut muscles complement each other. The body's tattoos (white against black in the woodcut) refer to diverse religious systems (just as his pose evokes Hindu and Buddhist sculpture), suggesting the global worlds he encompasses. Abby Schlachter goes a step further in her cast sculpture *Queequeg in Her Coffin II* (1997). Using her own body to create the cast, the artist renders up a life-size female Queequeg, whose surface she emblazons with random bits of texts that hold personal meaning for her, just as Queequeg's tattooed skin inscribes a "treatise on the art of attaining truth" (*Moby-Dick*, 481).[42]

In another example of artistic self-identification, the textile artist Abby Langdon creates *The Warrior* (2016) from a photographic transfer, in which she assumes the pose of Queequeg—harpoon lifted over her head, face resolute (figure 4.13). The image is shot from above such that Langdon seems to lunge upward. Onto her flesh Langdon has stitched an intricate pattern of Māori tattoos. Thus, the traditionally female craft of sewing (even more visible on the rear of the image) combines with an Indigenous art form and an image of fierce female power, aligning Queequeg's racial otherness with women while granting an aura of invincibility to both. The White Whale, too, undergoes a gender reversal in some contemporary representations. Julia Oldham's video installation at the *Adrift in the Wonderworld* exhibition in Cincinnati (2016), *Speak,*

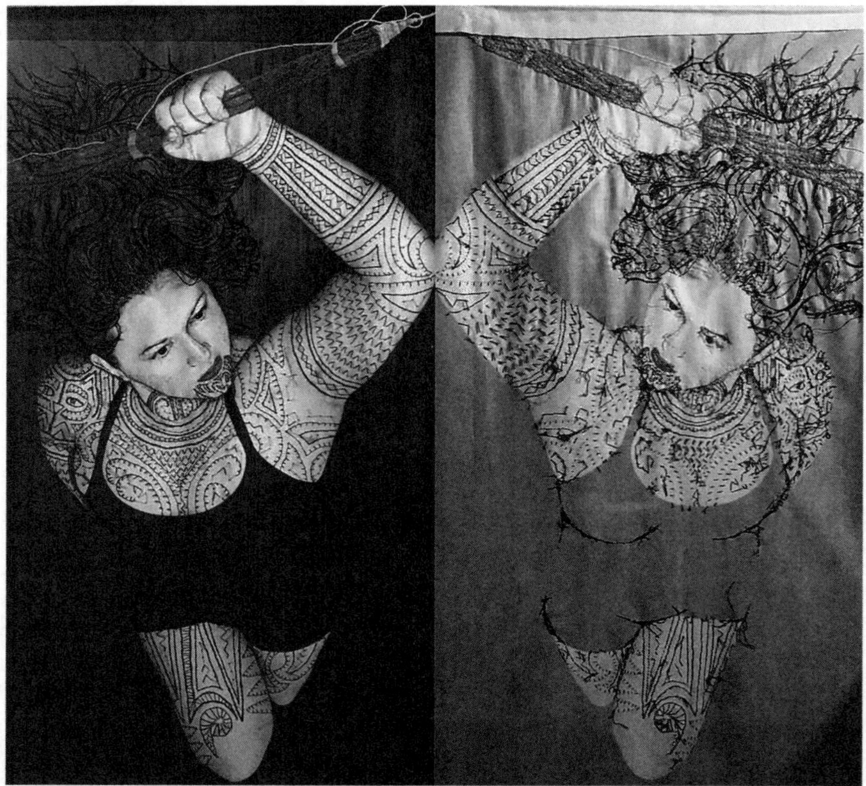

Figure 4.13. A female Queequeg in fabric art.
Abby Langdon, *The Warrior*, 2016. Fabric, photo transfer, embroidery. Front and reverse sides, 30" × 39".

Source: Courtesy of the artist.

Thou Vast and Venerable Head, makes the corpse hoisted aboard the *Pequod* in "The Sphynx" chapter a female whale who, when Ahab addresses her severed head, rebukes him in Oldham's own (female) voice. Aileen Callahan, taking her cue from Melville's paean to the maternal wonders of mother whales nursing their young in the enchanted calm of "The Armada" chapter, created the series *The Birth of Moby Dick* (2002), forty oils that depict the whale as fetus in the womb and birthing calf.[43]

The overlapping issues of gender, race, and life-forms beyond the human in several of these examples invite us to contemplate the varied, often intersectional desires, hopes, and musings that this revival of interest in Melville has activated. The Melville arousing today's outpouring of creative interest and engagement—in contrast to the Melville so attractive to literary scholars in the earlier twentieth century—is one who questions the constricting bounds of gendered categories and embraces the polymorphous fluidity of sexuality, one who exposes the patriarchal ideologies precipitating the war of the sexes, and one who damns racial oppression in no uncertain terms. He is also a writer whose critique of the mercantile economy and its unquenchable desire to extract energy resources—via the whaling industry—reveals the class disparities and environmental devastations left in capitalism's wake. Simultaneously, this "contemporary" Melville is a writer whose global vision surpasses national allegiance, a writer whose embrace of aesthetic hybridity, methods of pastiche, and self-interrogating reflexivity has more in common with tenets of twenty-first-century sampling than with the universalizing grand narratives of high modernism. It is fair to say that those artists now turning to Melville are finding in this forbearer's promiscuously rich imagination and eclectic formal iconoclasm a range of possible points of entry. These intersections across time and space inspire them to take creative risks while simultaneously anchoring their endeavors in the literary tradition of which Melville is now, ironically, a seemingly permanent fixture.

Moving the women so often absent in Melville to the forefront is one productive point of entry for such contemporary efforts, and it is an approach that Solien, Driscoll, and Eckert—in differing but complementary ways—exemplify at its best. Collapsing the distance between the materiality of the whaling industry and the materiality of women's existence, all three artists transmute their Melvillean encounters into creative collaborations with their source material that neither attempt to outdo Melville nor pay him unquestioning homage. Nor do these artists promote their additions to Melville as being in any way definitive. Something at once more magical and productive—something more indicative, perhaps, of the direction of twenty-first-century art as it enters an increasingly multimediated digital epoch and participatory culture—occurs as Solien, Driscoll, and Eckert pose open-ended questions about the place of women in Melville, ferreting out in his very omissions the traces, the trails of clues, the capacity for empathetic connection that result in the rhizomatic intersections between past and present that are not only true to the spirit of Melville but extend beyond his horizon of vision in directions relevant to this century.

CHAPTER 5

SIZE MATTERS

Of erections how few are domed like Saint Peter's! Of creatures, how few as vast as the whale!
—Herman Melville, *Moby-Dick*

Let us not take it for granted that life exists more fully in what is commonly thought big than in what is commonly thought small.
—Virginia Woolf, "Modern Fiction"

Matters of size, both literal and figurative, play an inevitable role in the responses of many contemporary artists channeling the spirit of Melville. Whether the effort involves Trisha Lowe's fifty-two-foot-long sculpture of inflatable woolen fabric, *Mocha Dick* (2009), which mirrors the average size of a sperm whale, or Sharon L. Butler's exhibition *Moby-Dick, Used* (2005), where bookshelves overflow with used copies of the novel in multiple editions, or Samuel Hunter's play *The Whale* (2012), in which a six-hundred-pound teacher assigns *Moby-Dick* to his online students, immensity and excess emerge as dominant foci for a number of artists contributing to today's Melville effect.[1]

Giganticism, of course, is a familiar topic in discussions of both Melville's titanic ambitions and *Moby-Dick*'s status as a candidate for *the* "Great American Novel." That whales are the world's largest living mammals encourages such speculations: Melville's subject is "big" in all senses of the word. So were his own ambitions, if we are to believe Ishmael's rhapsody about those bold writers whose "mighty theme[s]" make for "mighty book[s]": "One often hears of writers that rise and swell with their subject, though it may seem but an ordinary one. How, then, with me, writing of this Leviathan? . . . Give me a condor's quill! Give me Vesuvius' crater for an inkstand! . . . Such, and so magnifying, is the virtue of a large and liberal theme! We expand to its bulk. To produce a mighty book, you must choose a mighty theme" (*Moby-Dick*, 349). Granted, Ishmael's overblown rhetoric includes a healthy dose of self-parody, but his word choices—"condor's quill," "Vesuvius' crater," "magnifying" virtues, "expand[ing] . . . bulk," "ris[ing] and swell[ing]" themes—evoke the sheer *magnitude* of Melville's elastic imagination in creating "this Leviathan" of a book. The novel's aim, Ishmael continues, is no less than that of encompassing "*all* the generations of whales, and men, and mastodons, past, present, and to come, with *all* the revolving panoramas of empire on earth, and throughout the *whole* universe" (349, emphases added).

Such comprehensive inclusion is, indeed, a sizeable goal.

Matters of size or scale also attach to assumptions about *Moby-Dick*'s length. Contrary to perception, the text is no longer than the average midcentury triple-decker novel, but because of Melville's additive, digressive, kaleidoscopically shifting modes of narration, most readers experience its "bulk" not only as weighty but also as ever expanding: Its girth swells as one Ishmaelean riff leads to another, as scientific taxonomies splinter into subcategories, as ambiguities generate more ambiguities. "Excess" is, as critics have always realized, central to Melville's narrative aesthetics, in which nonlinearity, hybridity, and pastiche are the norm rather than the exception.

This chapter explores several contemporary artists who have internalized, responded to, or replicated such Melvillean levels of magnitude and excess. Whether creating a sculpture or a painting or a song or an essay to match every chapter or every page of *Moby-Dick* (and, in two cases, every word), or whether serially engaging Melville in works that repeat and refine their object of fascination to the point of exhaustion, these contemporary artists appear as monomaniacal as Ahab in the attempt to "magnify" their endeavors to monumental proportions.[2] "The encyclopedia quality of *Moby-Dick*," writes Jeffrey Insko, "seems to invite a similar procedure on the part of its admirers."[3]

To unravel why size matters so much to these artists—and whether it matters differently than in earlier twentieth-century iterations—it is helpful to recall the concepts of vastness that have always been integral to theories of the sublime. In the eighteenth-century philosopher Edmund Burke's estimation, the experience of the sublime—that frisson of terror and delight triggering one's highest aesthetic and emotional response—is most often attached to conceptions of vastness, immensity, infinitude: "Greatness of dimension is a powerful cause of the sublime."[4] Clearly, Melville's White Whale—in all its terrifying beauty—epitomizes a kind of Romantic sublime that attaches equally to the novel's audacious attempt to include "the whole universe" within its pages. Even though the novel's publication occasioned some harsh criticism, some early readers, such as the anonymous reviewer for the *London Mercury Advertiser* in 1851, acknowledged that the author "rises to the verge of the sublime."[5] Such sublimity, for such reviewers and readers, is intrinsically linked to Romantic aesthetic theories growing out of neoclassical precepts.

According to Burke and others, those "great" minds best equipped to express sublimity, to give birth to "great conceptions," possess imaginations that can encompass the overarching totality of sublime objects without being distracted by the particularities that might disrupt aesthetic perception. This relegation of detail to the realm of the decorative or inferior is central to Naomi Schor's analysis of the masculinist values often embedded in historical evocations of the sublime: "The sublime . . . can be seen as a masculinist aesthetic designed to check the rise of a detailism which threatens to hasten the slide of art into femininity" and to result in a "loss of [male] virility."[6] Artistic genius, it follows, is "big," singular, unique, virile—qualities traditionally associated with the male ego that defies convention and withstands the lesser tastes of the masses.

Whether these charges hold for the late twentieth- and early twenty-first-century reenvisionings of Melville examined in this chapter remains to be seen. (One might note right away that neither Ishmael nor Melville is afraid of distracting details, as the chapters on whaling lore abundantly evince.) But it is clear that perceptions about *Moby-Dick* have long been caught up in a discourse of size that, since D.H. Lawrence's pithy intimation that the White Whale is the great (white) American phallus, inevitably assumes sexualized dimensions: "Size matters" in a manner explicitly gendered as male.[7] Melville's winking jokes in the text encourage such assumptions. There are the explicit references to the sperm whale's penis—"black limber bone," "grandissimus," "unaccountable cone" (312, 325, 324)—and "The Cassock" chapter facetiously transforms its epidermis into a clerical garment that triggers Ishmael's innuendo about "archbisho*prick[s]*" and their "lad[s]" (325). There are the slyer references to the "size" of Johnson's Dic(k)tionary—Melville is quite aware of his wordplay—and to the "grand erections" of classificatory systems so immense they never reach completion (185).[8] The very *excess* of such puns is "sizeable" in its own right, swelling the novel's bulk. But as noted in chapter 4, emphasizing the phallic obscures the numerous ways in which the feminine, the androgynous, and the emotions figure prominently in Melville's textual erotics. Likewise, assuming these phallic references are unilaterally aggressive, destructive, or "phallogocentric" may blind us to the degree to which they often exist outside heteronormative terms. As is evident in the "Squeeze of the Hand" chapter, Melville's celebration of virility expresses something closer to polymorphous jouissance or, as Jennifer Doyle suggests, freedom from the genital imperative of normative heterosexuality and a valorization of collective identity over Cartesian singularity.[9]

In addition to these associations of both whale and novel with conceptions of immensity, notions of the sublime, and phallic power, considerations of size take a related form for another group of artists drawn to *Moby-Dick*—namely, that of *serial repetition*, in which the artists' multiple iterations over time and space manifest an obsessive tendency worthy of Ahab. Such a compulsive reaction is not unique to artists; it permeates twentieth-century scholarship on the novel as well. This is evident in the obsessive-compulsive aspects attending the midcentury scholar Hershel Parker's word-for-word transcription of *all* of Melville's marginalia into his personal copies of the same volumes that filled Melville's library as well as in the twenty-two years it took the editorial board of Northwestern University's Newberry Library to complete its edition of *Moby-Dick* because of an "obsessive compulsiveness to get everything right."[10] This scholarly compulsion also permeates Robert Wallace's otherwise exemplary work on Melville and Frank Stella (an artist this chapter examines later). If Stella's desire to create individual artworks for every chapter of the novel amounts to an obsession, Wallace's assiduous attempt to track down these pieces (dispersed around the globe) can be seen as a monomaniacal quest in itself (Wallace reports that he's viewed 129 of 138 titles and 177 of 266 unique artworks), and his recordkeeping of the abstract shapes forming the building blocks of Stella's pieces is obsessive in its sheer meticulousness (twenty-two "waves," thirteen Chinese "lattices," etc.).[11] Obsession, we might venture to say, is contagious. We witness immensity taking on a related dimension, that of duration across time, in the hands of John Bonham, lead drummer for Led Zeppelin. His improvisational riff for the group's song "Moby Dick" (1969) clocks in at forty-five minutes, making it the longest and most famous drum solo in rock music history.

To put it mildly: Melville's "big novel" encourages feats of almost superhuman endurance, repetition, and size.

I deliberately use the words *big novel* to call to mind ongoing debates about the Great American Novel." In *The Dream of the Great American Novel*, Lawrence Buell notes that *Moby-Dick* has been a "perennial G.A.N. candidate" since the 1950s.[12] Today's readers and scholars may question the assumption that "bigger is better" (an assumption also questioned by Virginia Woolf in this chapter's second epigraph).[13] But debates about whether this or that novel is *the*

GAN continue to engage serious reviewers and amateur commentators, feeding the eagerness with which the literate public awaits news of the latest "big" one—as if there can be only one or as if the criteria for "greatness" is universally accepted. Whence this fixation? As Buell notes, the desire to designate the GAN is closely tied to American myths of exceptionality (both of nation and of a robust national literature), and *Moby-Dick* tellingly achieved its status as a contender for GAN precisely as America emerged from World War II as the globe's dominant power. Just as the rediscovered Melville of the 1920 and 1930s became the repository for the projected values of that era's intellectual elite, the ascension of *Moby-Dick* to the status of national greatness in the 1950s expressed postwar America's hubristic confidence in its puissance on the world stage as well as in the value of its literary cultural capital.

A corollary of the myth of the great or "big" American novel is the myth that true artistic genius is one of a kind and overwhelming, a concept deriving from Romantic aesthetic theory that ego-minded modernists such as Gertrude Stein, James Joyce, and Ernest Hemingway did much to revivify. As noted in chapter 1, the idea that artistic "genius" rises sui generis fosters a set of aesthetic values—singular, self-actualizing, assertive, a force of nature that erupts rarely but whose molten overflow cannot be ignored—that dovetails with many early twentieth-century estimations of the rediscovered Melville but that many contemporaries educated in post-structuralism are likely to find suspiciously totalizing. In turn, humanist assumptions about "genius" and literary "greatness" are coded, as Kassia Boddy comments, as "relentless[ly] masculine," bolstering the assumption that candidates for the GAN must be literally as well as figuratively "big"—"work whose 'thickness' and 'length' will translate into 'muscularity' and 'febrility.'"[14]

Given these criteria, *Moby-Dick*'s "bigness" makes it an obvious contender for the "Great American Novel," however suspect that designation might be. What is relevant for my purposes is the degree to which these "size matters" have insinuated themselves into many contemporary artistic evocations of Melville and to what effect. Does the preoccupation with size reveal a hubristic degree of ambition that, in imitating, competing with, or even "outsizing" Melville, depends on retrograde aesthetic conceptions of monumentality and singular genius? Might a preoccupation with size point to a psychological compulsion caught in a state of repetition? Or does this fascination reveal something else altogether, a desublimation of normative conceptions of the sublime? Might an excess of detail, a rejoicing in particularity and exactitude for its own sake, become a marker of a post-postmodern aesthetic that embraces amateurism as much as if not more than mastery?

These are a few of the questions that inspire this chapter. To frame the extent to which scale becomes an important factor in the contemporary articulations of the Melville effect, the first section takes up two midcentury modernist artists, the stage and film impresario Orson Welles and the muralist and painter Gilbert Wilson, whose lifelong obsessions with adapting *Moby-Dick* to various media attest both to their own grandiose ambitions and to their angst at feeling that they were falling short of the mark. After a side glance at two contemporaries in the second section, Jake Heggie and Kent Stephens, who in large part succeed in fulfilling Wilson's and Welles's ambitions, I turn to a cluster of contemporary visual artists who have made *Moby-Dick* the basis for extensive engagements with their medium. I begin with Frank Stella, who from 1985 to 1997 created more than 1,500 prints, metal reliefs, and free-standing sculptures (266 of them originals, the largest weighing eight tons), each bearing a chapter title from *Moby-Dick*. Then I take up Robert Del Tredici, who in the late 1960s began producing absurdist, comic-book-style drawings that bear quotations from the novel. The artist returned to this project in the late 1990s in a series of colored silkscreen prints, then again in new formats in the 2010s, for an oeuvre of more than 200 works. Next I evaluate the 552 illustrations produced by Matt Kish and published in 2011 in one volume as *Moby-Dick in Pictures: One Drawing for Every Page*. Setting himself the goal of creating a picture a day for every page of his edition of *Moby-Dick*, Kish incorporates myriad found materials into his surreal, psychedelic images and pairs each composition with a quotation from the source page. The result, in Elizabeth Schultz's words, is a "monumental" volume (my softback copy weighs four pounds) that has become a collector's item for Melville aficionados. The fourth section of this chapter takes up a range of other projects that use *Moby-Dick*'s chapters as a source of inspiration and an organizing principle: a song cycle (2008–2012) by Patrick Shea, whose 138 compositions include everything from ballads and R&B to punk; George Cotkin's book *Dive Deeper* (2012), which makes each chapter the occasion for a virtuoso riff on Melville's impact on contemporary culture; and a collaborative mixed-media "installation," *Remaking Moby-Dick.1* (2013–2018), organized by Trish Harris and Lissa Holloway-Attaway, which invited artists in any media to contribute works inspired by the novel's chapters.

Not all these artists, admittedly, are "thinking" big—indeed several are absorbed by exacting minutiae in forming their responses. But even in the repetition of such detail, in the chapter-to-chapter or page-to-page or quotation-to-quotation reliance on Melville, they participate in projects that become if not monumental, at the very least immense in volume. Likewise, these artists evince a compulsive quality in their attachments to their projects that echoes the obsessive drives that Melville interrogates in characters such as Taji, Ahab, and Pierre. In diagnosing how obsession came to be classed in the nineteenth and twentieth centuries as a symptom of a disorder and nervous disease—not merely the "hobby horse," "Hypo," or "ruling passion" of previous eras—Lennard J. Davis notes the paradox by which "reason and passion exist on the same level" in the person driven by an idée fixe.[15] One finds this tenuous coexistence operating in many of the art projects analyzed in this chapter. These artists are consumed, as it were, by a passion for capturing an "essence" of Melville that is personally meaningful to them or that unlocks their own creativity, and yet they simultaneously subject the excess, the sheer volume of material, to which this zeal leads to curiously rigid rules: for Kish, a picture a day; for Stella, a finite slate of abstract shapes reconfigured in infinite ways; for Shea, the recording of a new song "every Saturday morning." Marina Van Zuylen has theorized that monomaniacal fixations are a means of "keep[ing] the arbitrary at bay," of resisting the "tyranny of the everyday."[16] True, the rules imposed by these artists bind their productions within exacting frameworks, but, pace Van Zuylen, these boundaries also become the means of giving play *to* the arbitrary, of seeing what *can* happen—what might serendipitously spring to mind or guide the paintbrush—within the imposed framework. The piling up of details, the repetition of a similar object approached from myriad angles, the relishing of particularity: All become a *gleeful* means of expression to many of these artists, for whom the monumentality of size is less consequential, perhaps, than the frisson of multiplicity, recurrence, and open-endedness.[17]

The erotics of such free play, born out of the fetishized bindings that contain them, share something in common with *Moby-Dick* besides "size." After all, Ahab isn't the novel's only obsessed monomaniac (though his fixation is of the decidedly destructive and authoritarian bent). When it comes to a love of detail, taxonomies, infinite sources of knowledge, riffs spun from a word or phrase, Ishmael is something of an obsessive as well. But it is Ishmael's ability to swerve from metaphysical flights to the materials of his everyday existence—or, as Jennifer Doyle puts it, his ability to be erotically turned on by his breathless recounting of what readers in search of action deem the tedious parts of the novel—that makes him the multiform subject whose capaciousness is lifesaving.[18] As the latter sections of this chapter suggest, Ishmael's postmodernist sense of fluidity crosses paths, intriguingly, with our digital age's post-postmodern embrace of amateurism as an aesthetic in which excess and size also matter, but matter differently.

Wilson and Welles Size Up Melville

The seemingly endless fixation on size, volume, and vastness among participants in today's Melville effect is foreshadowed in two midcentury modernists who, except for their midwestern roots, hypersexuality, and longstanding obsession with Melville, couldn't seem to be more different. One is the nearly forgotten painter Gilbert Wilson, who skirted the edges of national recognition with his populist murals in the late 1930s but quickly sank from public view. The other is Orson Welles, who in his teens achieved outsize renown as a "Boy Wonder," first in the theater as actor, director, and overall auteur and later in film and television: Everything Welles did or attempted to do was "big" in execution as well as notoriety. Wilson's homosexuality and reclusiveness seem worlds removed from Welles's reputation as a womanizer with a gargantuan sexual appetite and his unrelenting self-promotion. Despite these differences, both men shared a fanatical belief in their unique creative "genius" while suffering from crippling inferiority complexes, and both spent decades obsessed with the idea of adapting *Moby-Dick* to multiple formats—projects that, by and large, remained frustratingly unrealized. And, as the following pages suggest, in a curious if convoluted manner both men's psychosexual makeup—so different at first glance—colors not only their overweening creative urges but their lifelong infatuation with Melville.

Let's begin with Gilbert Wilson, an artist many readers may have never heard of, despite a career spanning nearly the whole of the twentieth century, in which he restlessly, relentlessly conceived one creative project after another in a wide variety of media: large-scale populist murals in the Diego Rivera tradition, paintings, drafts of novels and short stories, librettos, screenplays, a sexological treatise, blueprints for secular chapels, public-art projects. Born in 1907 in Terre Haute, Indiana—the birthplace of fellow Progressives Theodore Dreiser, Eugene V. Debs, and Ida Harper—Wilson, a socialist who liked to think of himself as a "gentle radical," died in 1990, leaving hundreds of paintings and drawings in a barn on his sister's farm in Kentucky. Most of this artwork is related to his decades-long ambition of transforming *Moby-Dick* into a modern multimedia production—a production that, Wilson enthused, "will be the biggest event in theatre history" and prove that "I am [the] . . . artist of my century."[19] The more Wilson fantasized about such acclaim, however, the farther he drifted into obscurity, despite his relocating to New York City, the epicenter of the art world. Edward K. Spann's biography of Wilson is suggestively titled *Unfinished and Unbroken*, and, ironically, the obscurity that dogged Wilson's life threatened to become the biographer's as well. Spann's manuscript, left unpublished at his death, appeared doomed to become a "lost book" until Robert K. Elder—inspired to learn more about the enigmatic artist after attending a local showing of Wilson's work—tracked it down and saw it through to publication in 2019. If not for Elder's efforts, the curse of neglect that Wilson shared with Melville would have become Spann's as well.[20]

From his sizeable artistic ambitions to the objects of his erotic obsession (namely, hugely overweight older men), Wilson manifested a manic energy and tendency to excess. Both are on full display in journal volumes that total nearly 2.5 million words and whose entries detail the intensity of his artistic aspirations and his bitterness at never achieving the renown that he felt his due.[21] While Wilson yearned for worldly acclaim, he was also stubbornly and willfully self-defeating, an iconoclast willing to flaunt convention and stay true to his vision, even when it meant losing projects and alienating potential sponsors. As such, he strongly identified with Melville as a creative genius "ignored by the public of his time."[22] Wilson came closest to the recognition he craved in the 1930s, when, after a brief sojourn at the Art Institute of Chicago (and even less time at Yale's School of Art), he executed a number of heroically dimensioned public murals. An article in *Scribner's* in May 1937 described the twenty-nine-year-old as a "young man with a formidable claim to recognition as one of the most potent mural painters in America," an artist whose work has "the audacity and self-assurance of a master."[23] Potency—audacity—master: Wilson was no doubt pleased to find himself tagged with the very attributes he revered in Melville.

For Wilson, the primary purpose of his murals was to foment social consciousness among the masses.[24] This belief in the political efficacy of art made him all the more attracted to what he saw as the radical politics of Melville's masterpiece. When Rockwell Kent, famed illustrator of the Random House edition of *Moby-Dick*, hired Wilson to work on a mural project in 1944, the younger man reread the novel with a fresh eye, perceiving for the first time its "great magnitude." Newly convinced it was the greatest book ever written, Wilson declared, "Melville is my first love, . . . and *Moby-Dick* is my Bible."[25] Reading and rereading this holy scripture, he increasingly interpreted Ahab's destructive pursuit of the White Whale as a grim prophecy of the nuclear destruction made possible by humans' irresponsible pursuit of nature's hidden powers.[26]

If Wilson felt he had found a kindred spirit in Melville's politics and refusal to bow to convention, this identification was strengthened by his perceptions of the homoerotic currents in Melville's work. For his time, Wilson was unusually forthright about his homosexuality, and he felt that, like Melville, he was channeling his libidinal energy into "potent" art. The psychosexual origin of Wilson's attraction to men is telling, especially given his obsession with the size and scope of *Moby-Dick*. Around age six, Wilson was sexually molested—though he insisted on calling it a "romp," a welcome initiation into same-sex desire—by an evangelist minister, a hugely corpulent man dressed in a white suit whom the boy idealized as "godlike."[27] This whale of manhood clad in white became the prototype for all Wilson's future love interests as well as the model for his representations of an oversize Ahab. Long before reading *Moby-Dick*, then, Wilson's nascent erotic imagination was already pursuing a "white whale" as the ultimate object of desire.[28] The ambivalence that the mature artist Wilson projects onto Ahab—as an object of attraction yet as a negative force of destruction—perhaps expresses, on a subliminal level, the darker underside of Wilson's insistence that his childhood seduction was consensual, innocent play. Note in figure 5.1 the way the captain's phallic power is canceled by his fatal pride. In the instance of baptizing his harpoon, its seemingly electrified point bisects his crotch, such that the harpooners' blood in the vessel on the floor below Ahab seems the production of Ahab's self-wounding. In another painting that depicts the naked, prone body of delirious Ahab after losing his leg, Wilson makes the former image's symbolic castration literal: Testicles remain intact, but the penis (like his leg) has completely disappeared, leaving a gaping wound.

Wilson's obsession with turning *Moby-Dick* into a contemporary masterpiece began in earnest in 1947 as thoughts of creating a ballet with multiracial dancers (Wilson was an ardent supporter of civil rights) morphed into the even grander conception of an epic-size musical drama, *The White Whale*, that would combine acting, singing, music, and Wilson's set designs. It would be, in Wilson's grandiose claim, "the *biggest* event in all theater history."[29] "Bigness," daring the limits of the possible, was part of the attraction. "Such a *tremendous* undertaking," he wrote to a correspondent, is "almost forbidding in *magnitude* and conception."[30] He immediately began a series of expressive paintings and drawings of characters, scenes, tableaux, and sets, eventually numbering in the hundreds, that show him working at the apex of his craft (see figure 5.2). Executed in various styles, tones, and media, some were fully finished paintings in the hyperrealistic mode of his earlier Rivera-influenced murals, some traditional pastels, some modernist renderings, some impressionistic sketches, some expressionistic portraits, others anticipating Keith Haring's antic figures. "What we witness" in Wilson's work, Elder writes, "is not just an evolution, but *an omnidirectional exploration* of the text as Wilson tested the bounds of his talent."[31]

This "omnidirectional"—let's call it rhizomatic—exploration of *Moby-Dick*, coupled with Wilson's facility in multiple genres, anticipates the contours of the contemporary Melville effect. Perhaps the most riveting of these more than three hundred artworks is the *Insanity Series*: portraits of Ahab as his face disintegrates, realism yielding to raw expressionism yielding to fractured cubism. In the third portrait, *I Am Madness Maddened* (c. 1950, figure 5.3), Ahab's features are still recognizably human, while the zigzagging scar on his countenance is pure abstraction. Something of Munch's *The Scream* (1893) reverberates in the hair standing on end and gaping mouth. The eye on the right is monomaniacally fixed on the doubloon in the upper-right corner, implying, as Elizabeth Schultz suggests, the man's intensified focus on the whale and hence his growing insanity.[32] By the fourth portrait, *He Who Has Never Felt Madness* (c. 1950, figure 5.4) the face has exploded, leaving us with two profiles confronting each other over the white gap that has replaced the lightning's scar. One eyeball floats surreally amid the

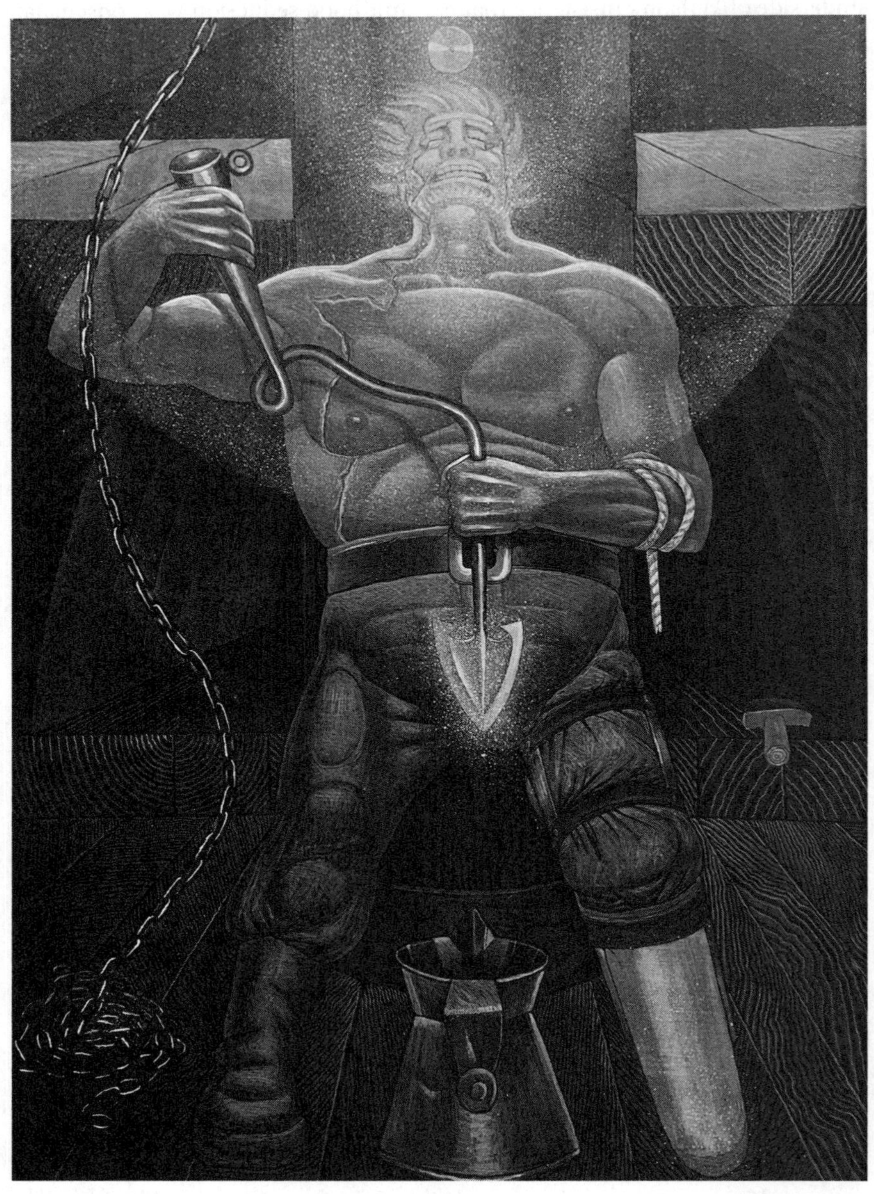

Figure 5.1. An electrifying self-castration.
Gilbert Wilson, *St. Elmo's Fire*, c. 1955. Acrylic and colored pencil on particle board, 34" × 36".

Source: Sheldon Swope Art Museum, Terre Haute, Indiana. Accession no. 1989.21. Courtesy of Swope Art Museum.

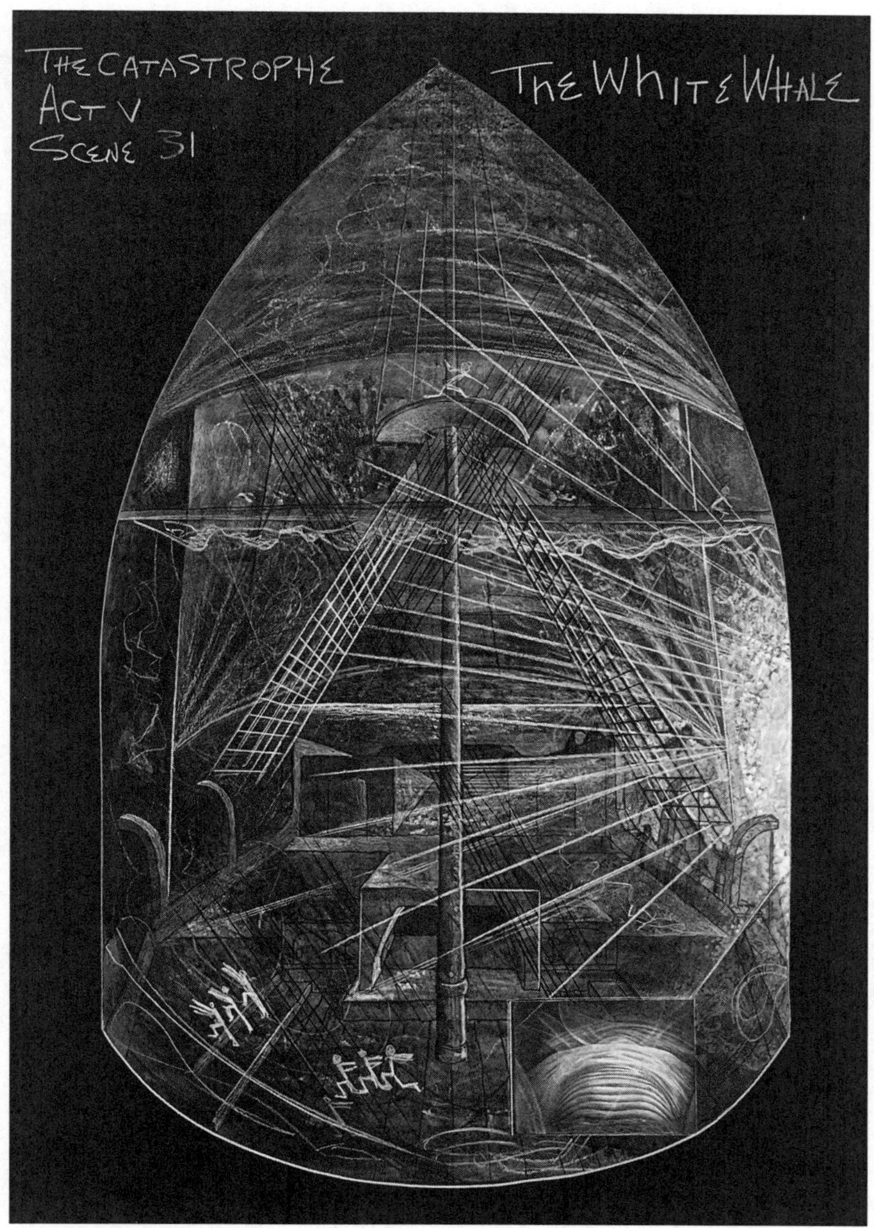

Figure 5.2. Set design for Gilbert Wilson, "The Catastrophe" in *The White Whale.*

Source: Sheldon Swope Art Museum, Terre Haute, Indiana. Accession no. 1989.58.16. Courtesy of Swope Art Museum.

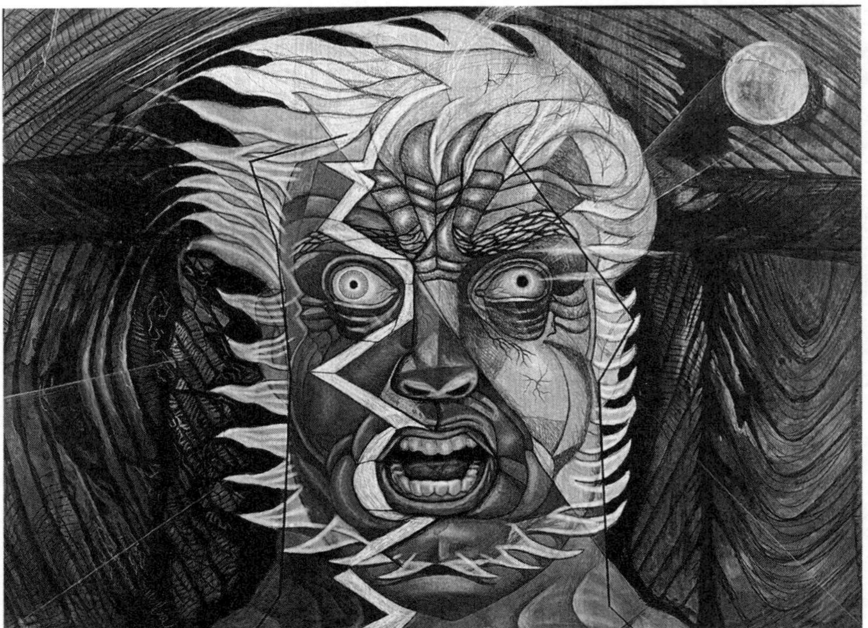

Figure 5.3. Eyeballing madness.
Gilbert Wilson, *Insanity Series #3: I Am Madness Maddened*, c. 1950. Gouache with colored pencil on paper, 21" × 29".

Source: Sheldon Swope Art Museum, Terre Haute, Indiana. Accession no. 1989.16.C. Image courtesy of Swope Art Museum.

fractured debris; faint lines, "like torn tree roots, or like bits of veinings and arteries," emanate from the eye on the viewer's left, forming the only organic matter remaining in this exploded world.[33] These character portraits were central to Wilson's psychodramatic set design; he intended them to be projected on a gigantic sail dominating the stage.

Wilson briefly fantasized getting Orson Welles to direct the multimedia production, and as he completed a libretto for what he was now calling an opera, he began casting about for a composer, considering Virgil Thompson, Aaron Copeland, George Menotti, Samuel Barber, Kurt Weill, and Dmitri Shostakovich. None signed on, but these plans were not merely empty pipe dreams: Despite his relative obscurity, Wilson was acquainted with Eleanor Roosevelt, Pearl Buck, Theodore Dreiser, Richard Rodgers, and Walter Huston during these years of intense creative foment. Increasingly obsessed with adapting the novel, Wilson toyed with alternative formats—radio play, television production, self-standing book pairing his illustrations with Melville's prose, independent film, spoken drama with background music, audiotaped play—but the idea of

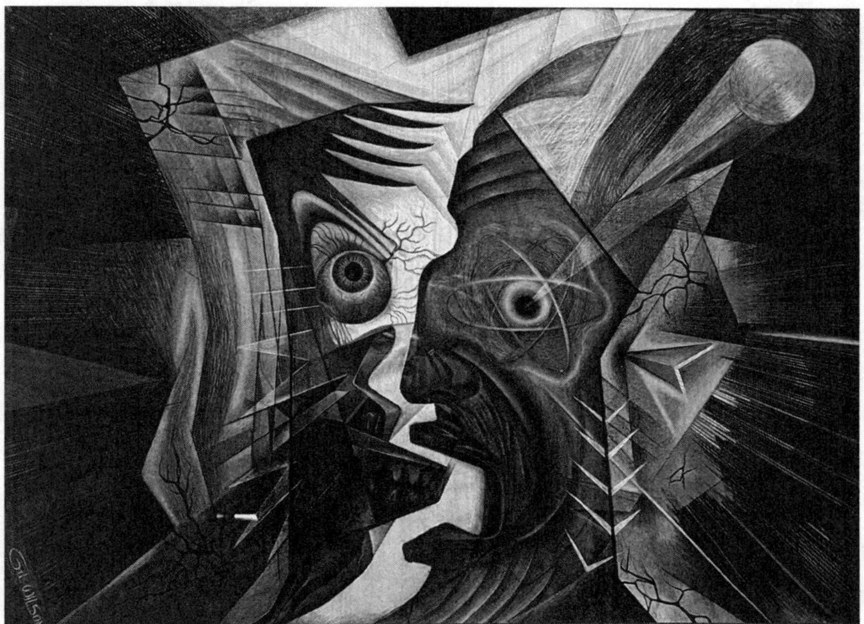

Figure 5.4. The self in fragments.
Gilbert Wilson, *Insanity Series #4: He Who Has Never Felt Madness*, c. 1950. Gouache with colored pencil on paper, 21" × 29".

Source: Sheldon Swope Art Museum, Terre Haute, Indiana. Accession no. 1989.16.D. Courtesy of Swope Art Museum.

a multimedia, operatic stage production remained the ultimate goal, the elusive White Whale to which he kept returning.

When Wilson dreamed, he dreamed big.

Perhaps the most heartbreaking of these invariably stymied projects involved his ideas for a film, which he shared with Walter Huston (one of his models for Ahab in his drawings). Learning that Walter's son, John Huston, was considering making a movie version of the novel, Wilson enthusiastically campaigned to be involved, preparing a 250-page shooting script and boasting in a letter to a friend that "this will be the greatest film ever made so far. . . . I expect to get an 'Oscar.'"[34] In a pattern that typified Wilson's manic bursts of creative enthusiasm, these grandiose fantasies collapsed to nothing as he found himself increasingly sidelined by Huston and Warner Bros. Presumably to get Wilson off its back, the studio paid for him to go on a six-month national tour promoting Huston's film in 1955. Humiliating as this outcome was, Wilson made the event his own, setting off (like Ishmael) from New Bedford in a white Chevrolet with a model whale on its roof, using the speaking engagements to

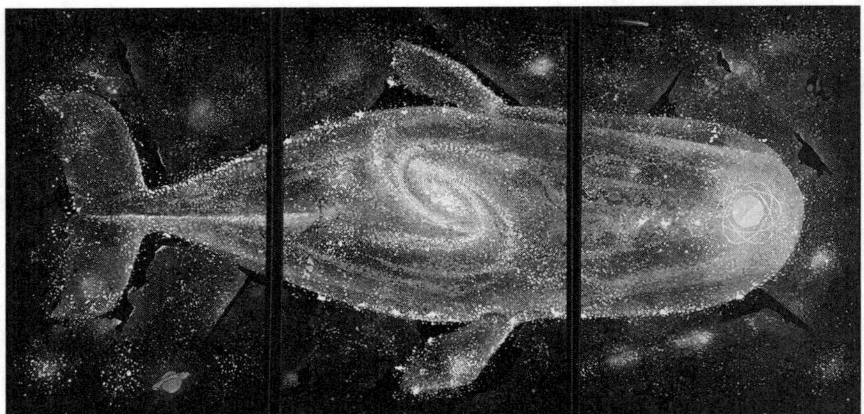

Figure 5.5. The White Whale and atomic catastrophe.
Gilbert Wilson, *The Cosmic White Whale*, c. 1970. Oil on particle board, 46¾" × 92".

Source: Sheldon Swope Art Museum, Terre Haute, Indiana. Accession no. 1989.35.A,B,C. Courtesy of Swope Art Museum.

display *his* artwork and expound upon *his* interpretation of Melville as prophet of the atomic age, barely referencing the film. "An artist with an obsession," reported the *Kansas City Star*; "a traveling evangelist of art," noted a Louisiana newspaper.[35]

Even as this evangelizer's oversized dream of collaborating with Huston was shrinking, he began work on a short film incorporating his paintings and drawings; in contrast to his ambitions, the result is fairly pedestrian and decidedly minimal—a narrator quotes just enough passages to give a sense of the novel's plot, and the only motion in the film is the camera zooming in and out of details of the artwork, a feeble attempt to add a sense of movement.[36] The completed thirty minute short (produced by Jerry Winters) briefly screened in 1955 but quickly closed—another disappointment for Wilson. Discouraged but defiantly indefatigable, he wrote in his journal, "I will never cease to see *Moby-Dick* as a catalyst." In 1958, back at work on the libretto for the dreamed-of opera, he muses in his journal, "What it is—*just what it is*—that holds me so relentlessly to this track. It will not let me go."[37] *Relentlessly*: This choice of adverb, equally descriptive of Ahab's maddened drive, sums up the degree to which Wilson's desire to mount his own monumental version of *Moby-Dick* had grown into an all-consuming monomania. Leaving New York to set up a studio on his sister's farm in Kentucky, he still dreamed of turning the novel that had now obsessed him for nearly four decades into some grand vehicle, preferably an opera or musical. Up to the end of his life, Wilson continued to paint dozens of scenes from the novel, increasingly larger in scale, including a haunting three-panel image (c. 1970, figure 5.5) of the whale sailing across the cosmos, a galaxy swirling at its center and a ringed planet in the bottom-left panel. True to Wilson's allegorical reading of the novel, the symbol for atomic power is etched in white on the whale's head, and the entire body is shaped to evoke the A-bomb. Seriality and repetition became so engrained in Wilson's consuming drive to create his Melvillean masterpiece that he fought on, defiantly optimistic in the face of multiple failures and if "unfinished" was also "unbroken" to the end of his life.

***

Even before Orson Welles's imagination seized on *Moby-Dick* as a vehicle for the exercise of his self-proclaimed genius, he was already being associated with whales, if only ironically. Behind his back, the crew working on *Citizen Kane* nicknamed him "Monstro" (the devouring whale in *Pinocchio*) because of his all-engulfing attempts to control every aspect of the production. Reviewing Welles's performance as Othello a few years later, the theater critic Kenneth Tynan rather cruelly likened Welles's corpulence to that of "a landed whale," a metaphor to which he returned in reviewing Welles's metatheatrical *Moby-Dick—Rehearsed* as a "piece of pure theatrical megalomania": "In aspect, [Welles] is a *Leviathan plus*. . . . The trouble is that everything he does is on *such a vast scale* that it quickly becomes monotonous. He is *too big* for the boots of any part."[38]

Orson Welles was, like Gilbert Wilson, a modernist to whom size very much mattered. Everything about Welles was BIG—ego, imagination, proclamations of genius, productions, sonorous voice, declamatory acting. Achieving international fame as a teen whose precociousness was matched only by his prodigiousness, Welles was both blessed and doomed by what a writer for the *Herald Tribune* later called his "gigantism of manner and mind."[39] Despite Welles's celebrated public image, his obsessive drive for near impossible achievements and belief in his genius barely papered over an ever-present sense of failure: of not being good enough, of not being revered by his peers, of never matching the early success that greeted his first years at the Mercury Theatre or his first movie, *Citizen Kane*—all achieved by his midtwenties. After these triumphs, the Boy Wonder of yesteryear had to contend with a growing reputation as "the world's youngest living has-been."[40]

Biographers have speculated about the psychological forces contributing to Welles's overweening confidence in his genius, the size of his ambitions, and his obsession with controlling every detail of projects that were already overly grandiose. One dominant factor was his compulsive need as child and youth for approval from powerful male authority figures who could affirm his already sizeable sense of self and talents. This resulted in a psychosexual etiology as fixated and sexually ambivalent as Wilson's. Blithely claiming, like Wilson, to have been "sexually interfered with" by an older man when he was ten years old, Welles happily promulgated a myth about his youthful desirability to adult men, gay or straight, throughout his life. "From my earliest years, I was the Lily Langtry of the older homosexual set. Everybody wanted me," he bragged.[41] As his biographer Simon Callow notes, it is impossible to establish truth from self-serving mythology in these matters. But it seems clear that throughout adolescence Welles set out to seduce—at least on a psychological level—male authority figures, often gay men, using his charm to secure their mentorship. For young Welles, to be viewed as a desirable object by male figures endowed with power translated into an affirmation of his precocious talents but hid the inadequacies that were to become the driving force behind his obsessive desire to succeed: to do everything better and bigger than anyone else had done it before.

While the quasi-homoerotic frisson of these male–male relationships were superseded by Welles's famously huge heterosexual appetites once he reached manhood, they nonetheless set the pattern for a narcissistic neediness and self-aggrandizement that veered, in time, into the outright megalomania that marked his colossal successes and equally colossal failures on stage and in film, radio, and television. If everything about Welles's ambition and personality was big, he likewise pitched his artistic projects to an increasingly gargantuan size and scale, from his failed attempt to condense seven Shakespeare plays into one vehicle to his success in negotiating the unprecedented Hollywood deal (total control over every aspect of production) that resulted in *Citizen Kane*. Not insignificantly, the heralded film focused on a protagonist who, in David Bordwell's analysis, falls "victim of the egotism of his own imagination": a description applicable to Welles himself.[42]

Such drive and immensity, ever teetering on the edge of failure or doom, inevitably drew Welles to Melville. Without question, Welles, like Wilson, personally identified with Melville as a genius whose great talents were ignored by his contemptible peers. The idea of adapting *Moby-Dick* to another medium began to obsess Welles in the 1940s, once he removed himself to Europe in hopes of reviving his flailing career on fresh terrain. His first conceit was to record a version on disc with Charles Laughton in the part of Ahab; then he readapted some of this material for a thirty-minute radio play broadcast on his *Mercury Summer Theatre of the Air* series in 1946, in which he voiced the part of Ahab. Next, he began to toy with the idea of an oratorio backed by a huge chorus and orchestra and accompanied by dancers—a multimedia extravaganza blending music, movement, lighting, and color, "a piece of total theatre."[43] Welles's vision of a mixed-genre vehicle of epic dimensions echoes Gilbert Wilson's desire to create "the biggest event in all theater history" with his mixed-media opera. An outline for Welles's imagined production, transcribed by a friend and collaborator, includes a description of Melville that reverberates with Welles's self-perception at this point in his career: "Recognition and acceptance of the work of a great creator seldom come in his own generation. . . . Melville, the untimeliest of American Titans, has only lately been properly appraised. A multiple personality, driven by neuroses to create works of libidinal intensity, he was inevitably rejected by the chill philistinism of his age[;] . . . he lived and died a magnificent failure."[44] Welles's ambitions were nothing if not "Titanic." His idea for an oratorio was commissioned by the San Francisco Theatre Association for production in 1947, in conjunction with the impresario Alexander Korda and a score by Bernard Herrmann (who had composed his own "Moby-Dick" cantata in 1940), then deferred to 1948.[45] But, in the end, like so many of Welles's projects, it dissolved before it ever got underway.

Welles's simmering Melvillean energies reemerged in a new form when in 1954 John Huston invited him to play the role of Father Mapple in Huston's film adaptation—the same film Gilbert Wilson so hopefully and then desperately attempted to become part of. Shortly after completing Mapple's sermon on Jonah and the whale (achieved in two takes), Welles began his own adaptation of Melville's classic: no longer as an over-the-top musical oratorio but—perhaps even more challengingly—as a piece of pure theater, with minimal props and costumes and no breaks in the action. The illusion of a heaving shipboard world and the terrifying chase scenes depended entirely on their staging, abetted by sophisticated lighting and intricate choreography. Premiering at London's Duke of York Theatre in 1955, *Moby-Dick—Rehearsed* was self-consciously metatheatrical: A troupe of turn-of-the-century players assembles on the bare stage to rehearse, so they think, *King Lear*—only to be ordered by the actor-manager, known as "the Governor," to read through a new script about *another* tragic figure driven mad by his demons: to wit, Melville's Ahab. At first hesitant, the actors gradually immerse themselves in their roles, bringing the action-charged world of Ahab's quest to life for thrilled London audiences. Welles, of course, played not only the nameless Governor but also the relentless Ahab. Critics raved, proclaiming "that [Welles] had found . . . a subject . . . *big enough* and rugged enough for his supercharged theatricality."[46] Typical of Welles's never-satisfied perfectionism, he continued to rewrite dialogue and rearrange scenes up to the final night of the relatively successful run.

Yet Welles wasn't done with *Moby-Dick*; the novel still obsessed his imagination. He immediately began shooting a televisual version of the staged production, intending to use innovative camera angles and rapid cuts to create the antithesis of a conventionally filmed stage play; the viewer's experience was designed to be "like reading Melville by lightning . . . the opposite of Huston's pulverisingly literal version." However, after a few days of shooting and some forty to seventy-five minutes of rough footage later (accounts vary), Welles abruptly abandoned the project, unsatisfied with the results. This sudden loss of interest was as typical of his artistic decision-making process as the obsessive micromanaging that accompanied those productions that made it onto stage or film. This unfinished footage, reputedly destroyed in a fire, has become the stuff of Hollywood legend, with rumors periodically resurfacing of a remaining copy stashed away in one place or the other, awaiting—like Melville himself—rediscovery and acclaim.[47]

Two decades of increasingly botched or abandoned projects followed this one moderate midcareer success, sealing Welles's public reputation as a has-been. Welles remained undeterred, however, in his fixation on bringing to fruition a series of gargantuan projects with larger-than-life protagonists: Lear, Falstaff, Don Quixote. Around 1980, his restless imagination returned to *Moby-Dick*, and he shot twenty-two minutes of sequences for a film in which he played *all* the parts, an endeavor that, like the others, came to nothing.[48] By this time in his life, the physical man was the opposite of "nothing," known as much for his obesity as for his talents: Welles had physically become the "white whale" that was Gilbert Wilson's eroticized manly ideal. In 1965, photographs taken on the set of *Chimes at Midnight* had captured this whale of a Welles as, in the role of Falstaff, he added padding to his already immense girth. But even as he became the butt of jokes on late-night television, derided for making Gallo wine commercials for quick cash, the film critic Parker Tyler noted that a younger generation was beginning to see in the man "a mirror of its own aspirations and adventurous near successes." Welles had become, in effect, the new avant-garde's modern-day Melville, "the quintessential type of the Big Experimental Cult hero—always achieving failure yet bringing it off brilliantly."[49]

Even failure, it appears, is a matter of size.

Heggie's Opera, Stephens's *Orson*

While their obsessions with Melville remained unfinished business for both Wilson and Welles—an elusive white whale they spent their lifetimes pursuing—today's Melville effect has produced two works that, to large degree, serve as fulfillments of these midcentury artists' thwarted ambitions: an opera staged by Jake Heggie in 2010 and a play put on by Kent Stephens in 2003. Just how these two productions begin to realize Welles's and Wilson's dreams anticipates the "size matters" preoccupying the contemporary artists examined in the following section.

We've seen that Wilson dreamed of creating a multimedia opera based on *Moby-Dick* that he claimed would be the "biggest event of theatre history." Many of his ambitions come to fruition in Heggie's widely acclaimed *Moby-Dick* in the first decade of the new millennium, whose staging wouldn't have been possible before this century's advances in digital technology. Robert Wallace praises the megaproduction as "a thoroughly twenty-first-century creation in

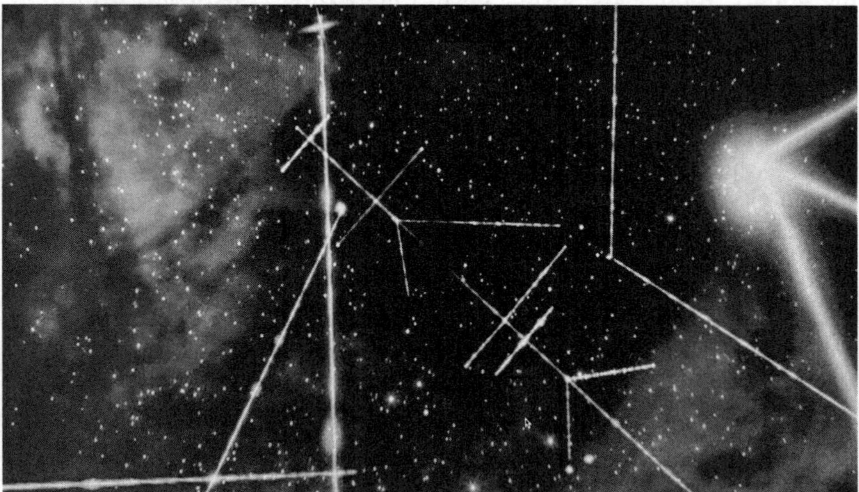

Figure 5.6. "Infinity! . . . We will harvest infinity."
Digital technology used at the beginning of Jake Heggie's opera *Moby-Dick*, 2010.

Source: Clip from the DVD of the October 2012 San Francisco Opera production (EuroArts Music Interntional 2013).

its technical requirements, multicultural scope, and global vision"—and he is right on target about the state-of-the-art technology.[50] The opera opens with a digitally projected expanse of rippling waves as they give way to a starry cosmos seen against the night sky. Uncannily, this visual effect echoes Gilbert Wilson's instructions in his libretto for how his imagined opera should begin, with "a widescreen cinematic rear projection" revealing "millions of stars—dark voids—galaxies—milky ways": "Slowly we move back to define the vast tail of leviathan seen in the sky from below. We scan the huge body up to the head where a spiral nebula resolves into its microcosm of an atom."[51]

Likewise, as the overture's pensive main theme slowly builds in Heggie's opera, white lines begin to streak across the galaxy, connecting one star to another. At first, the lines seem to be forming signs of the Zodiac, but then this heavenly skywriting begins to resemble navigational sea routes, and, finally, it transforms spectacularly into the three-dimensional outlines of a gigantic ship hurling through space straight toward the audience (figure 5.6). As the stage lights up, these outlines disappear into the actual stage set, where curved wooden beams simulate the hull of the ship, beneath which Queequeg and Ishmael huddle in their sleeping quarters. The awe that the audience experiences as this starry universe transforms into the *Pequod* charging through the cosmos is sublime, its scale planetary; one feels, indeed, as if "the flood-gates of the wonder-world" have "swung open" (*Moby-Dick*, 22), crossing the threshold to a realm that skirts the far edges of being and consciousness.[52] These numinous sensations are matched by Ahab's first words to his crew: "Infinity! . . . We will harvest infinity."[53]

This call to immensity, incommensurability, and awe aligns with what Heggie sees as music's unique ability: to travel beyond words, "to say what cannot be said."[54] Heggie thus approximates through musical idiom the effects that Melville achieves by wrestling with the ambiguity of linguistic signs. The librettist Gene Scheer underlines another equivalence between Melville's vision and Heggie's re-creation of that vision in music, comparing the omnidirectional nature of Melville's unfolding narrative to Heggie's "zig-zagging" method of scoring: "Things don't grow at once and they don't grow like a ladder; they grow *like a bush in all directions*. That's the way [Heggie's] themes and arias are conceived. . . . [His music] grows . . . organically, allowing the piece *to go in different directions*, and that is what Melville certainly did in the book."[55] Scheer's analysis is prescient, given the degree to which the contemporary Melville effect is rhizomatic; for many of its participants, "vastness" is neither monolithic nor monumental but rather the result of an openness to the proliferation of parts, to the sprawling outgrowths that spawn yet more offshoots.

Clearly, the production's "sublime" effects would not have been possible even a decade earlier, making it a uniquely *twenty-first*-century masterpiece. But there are features of this enterprise, despite Scheer's claim to rhizomatic complexity, that seem closer to early twentieth-century aesthetics than to postmodernist or twenty-first-century ones. Briefly accounting for these aspects may also tell us something about today's Melville effect. Heggie offers persuasive commentary about his incorporation of contrapuntalism, unstable harmonics, and wild tonal and rhythmic vacillations to evoke on the sonic level the messy hybridity of Melville's imaginative world of words. But many of the opera's musical motifs seem more firmly Romantic than contemporary in sound, which is why the music critic Mark Swed faults the score for playing it safe, "taking no chances."[56]

An equal taming of the polymorphous energies of Melville's prose infiltrates Scheer's libretto, whose arc—unlike the novel's—is linear and action driven. The radical queerness of Ishmael and Queequeg's bond has been stripped away, their relationship converted into the nonsexual one of teacher and pupil. Phrases such as Ishmael's earnest "Teach me" and Queequeg's solemn "Learn well" rely on a familiar plot formula: growth from youthful naivete (Ishmael goes by "Greenhorn" until the last words of the opera) to responsible maturity (Ishmael's acceptance of Queequeg's global worldview). Although this arc makes for a compelling story, its format is ploddingly traditional. In a curious fashion, the opera's contrary pulls between innovation (experimentally mixing media and state-of-the-art technology) and tradition (using tried-and-true musical and thematic rubrics) gloss a very real aspect of twenty-first-century aesthetics, in which innovation unashamedly embraces traditional values, as also seen in chapter 3's discussion of the "post-postmodern" turn in contemporary fiction.

Whatever one's reservations, Heggie's opera does fulfill the promise of immensity and grandeur that Wilson dreamed of achieving. Continuing to play at major houses around the world, it has achieved the acclaim and celebrity that always eluded Wilson ("What hell it is to be an obscurity," he lamented).[57] In contrast, Kent Stephens's inspired engagement with Welles's Melville obsession in his drama *Orson Welles Rehearses Moby Dick* (2003) has received a single production.[58] Nonetheless, this metatheatrical riff is one of the most compelling creative works spawned by today's Melville effect. In a "dizzyingly reflexive loop," Stephens imaginatively re-creates the event of Welles's rehearsal of *Moby-Dick—Rehearsed*, itself about a rehearsal of a play based on *Moby-Dick*; thus, in Stephens's drama, his actors enact the (fictionalized) lives of the (real-life) actors starring in Welles's London production.[59]

In this instance of art imitating life imitating art, the matters of size central to Welles's creativity and ego prove central to Stephens's enterprise. "And God created Great Welles" (25) a cast member quips, although we might well reverse the wordplay to "And Great Welles created God" since for most of the first act Welles maintains a godlike inscrutability as he barks out directions to the actors from a seat in the darkened rear of the theater; his omnipotence is all the more terrifying for remaining unseen but heard. When a cast member dares to ask, "What do *you* think the whale represents?" Welles gleefully roars, "An excuse for all of us to do some shamelessly *big acting*!" (21, emphasis added). The size of Welles's ambition, however, proves his Achilles' heel, so he is warned in a hallucinatory dream sequence, where Marlene Dietrich (Welles's costar in *Touch of Evil* [1958]) materializes to admonish him, "You're *too huge*. You have to think smaller" (99, emphasis added).

Hugeness, however, is to the "Great Welles" what the Great Whale is to Ahab. Both men, desperate to affirm their superiority and power, aim for the largest "catch" of all, even though it might sink them forever. Stephens's script captures this aspect of Welles's tormented psychology in a self-reflexive swirl of theatricality that deconstructs the monumentality upon which Welles stakes his claim to superior genius. "He's going to finish you off, Orson. The White Whale is best left alone" (62), warns Jack, a character who may or may not be real but functions as Welles's subconscious imp of the perverse. In essence, Stephens ingeniously takes Welles's formula in *Moby-Dick—Rehearsed* and does it one better by conveying the cost of consuming artistic obsession when tethered to egoistical claims of greatness.

Welles's play takes place in the late nineteenth century, and the cast has gathered, so they think, to rehearse *King Lear*; Stephens's play is set in 1955, and characters bearing the names of the real-life actors playing the roles in Welles's actual Duke of York Theatre production have gathered together to rehearse (so they believe) *The Tempest*. While both Shakespearean tragedies center on a maddened, vengeance-seeking former ruler, it is fitting that Stephens replaces Lear with Prospero, an artist figure who, like Welles, summons magical arts (which are also theatrical ones) against his perceived foes. The metatextuality of this Pirandello-like scenario—a play (based on Melville's novel) within a play (Welles's) within a play (Stephens's)—is underscored by Stephens's use of magic realism and an array of postmodernist elements. The latter include intertextual incursions of Welles's filmography into the diegetic flow, from characters to settings to musical scoring; the proliferation of surreal moments that may or may not be "real"; the breaking of the fourth wall by the actor playing Ishmael; the continual blurring of levels of fictionality and reality.

Stephens also blurs time levels by adding a twenty-first-century understanding of gender and race to events represented as occurring in 1955. He not only creates a backstory for the actress in Welles's production, Joan Plowright, that far exceeds Welles's representation of the unnamed "Actress" but also makes the Stage Manager a female character (Coral), and the two women unite in a solidarity that resists the male prerogatives rampant in the London theater world of the 1950s. Similarly, Stephens creates a new character, Percy, a Black South African hired to play the parts of the *Pequod*'s harpooners. In one of the play's most powerful dream-hallucinations, Percy delivers a stirring riposte to Melville's "Whiteness of the Whale" chapter as he recites "*Moby-Dick*, the Lost Chapter: On the Blackness of Blacks." Percy ultimately opts to "jump ship," quitting the production to "act" in the real world by fighting apartheid in his homeland.

This swirl of textual self-reflexivity allows Stephens to explore the monomaniacal obsessions that drive artists (Welles, Wilson, Melville) to challenge the limits of the possible. "Why MOBY DICK?," Welles roars when one of his actors asks why undertake "something so bloody hard": "Why did Hillary climb Everest? I doubt it's because he likes thin oxygen and brain edema. Nothing is worth doing if it's not worth doing badly! . . . I have no idea what the whale fucking represents. But I do know we're all of us chasing the Thing that bit us once that we have to track down again. And I'll chase it round Good Hope, and round the Horn . . . and round perdition's flames before I give it up" (24)

Welles's monologue, building to a crescendo that incorporates the same words that Melville puts in Ahab's mouth (*Moby-Dick*, 139), suggests that the "Thing" that once "bit" the speaker and that he is still chasing—akin to the whale that once "bit" Ahab and has now become his monomania—is Welles's "Rosebud": the originary moment he associates with the acclaim heaped on *Citizen Kane* that has eluded him ever since. But this "Thing" that "bites" "us" is also what the genre of the novel is to Melville *and* what stage magic is to actors seeking to re-create those moments of enchantment when everything comes together in live performance.[60] In a direct address to the audience, the actor playing Ishmael uses Melville's metaphor of the "higher truth" that exists in landlessness to explain the compulsion that drives all actors: "[We are] perpetually on voyage to another character: tracking it down, harpooning it, mastering it, riding out its flurry. . . . Because in [our] eternal journey is a truth that's almost intolerable; all deep, earnest work is just the effort of your unique soul to keep to the independence of her own sea" (41). If the "Great Hunt" is as inevitable as its prey is elusive for all actors, then for a megalomaniac as charged with supersized ambition as ego-obsessed Welles, the possibility of failure is near annihilating. "He's . . . going to take us all down with him," bemoans an actor in the flailing production. "Deliver us all from this self-obsessed disaster!" (36).

Welles's staged vision was neither flop nor shipwreck but a moderate success, garnering well-earned critical praise. But in the trajectory of his career, it provided at best a temporary lifeline. While Welles ingeniously used stagecraft illusion to bring Ahab's vengeful hunt "alive" for its audience, Stephens's version of this rehearsal achieves yet something more. Yes, like Welles, Stephens also captures life on the sea in the brief instances where we witness the rehearsal catch fire. But the metatheatrical levels of the production—a play within a play within a play—also give Stephens the opportunity to showcase Welles's contradiction-ridden psychology, illuminating the latter's attraction to Melville and megalomaniacal dreams of achieving ever greater triumphs. Welles's Governor has none of this self-reflexive density; he simply "is" the all-powerful Director, as caught up in his project as he is in his role as the monomaniacal Ahab.

Stephens's version of the writer-director-actor, in contrast, is both spectral and panoptic, showcasing a personality driven by demons that even more closely align Welles with Ahab in his pursuit of an impossible, self-defeating goal. Instead of the obsession with size that eats at Welles, Stephens lets the smaller moments—the cast gathering around a piano, meeting in a bar, awaiting reviews, managing off-stage personal crises—and flashes of magical realism to contribute additively to his diagnosis of debilitating conceptions of genius and success. In Stephens's reworking of Welles's rehearsal, matters of size fragment into partial truths in a manner that may be even more Melvillean than the modernist monumentality that Welles projected onto the author.

Chasing the Comic Sublime: Stella, Del Tredici, Kish

Visual artists have always been prone to producing closely related works that focus on a common theme, technique, image, or idea—many an exhibition consists of an individual artist's iterations of a prevailing concept. Nonetheless, the sheer intensity and volume of the repeated engagements of contemporary artists obsessed with *Moby-Dick* is eye-opening. This section examines three figures—Frank Stella, Robert Del Tredici, and Matt Kish—whose multiple encounters with the novel integrate its text into their visual art, including chapter titles, individual pages, and word clusters.[61] Renowned for his abstraction, Stella cemented his international reputation with his monumentally sized *Moby Dick* series, composed of hundreds of original works bearing the titles of every chapter of the novel. Robert Del Tredici and Matt Kish work on a comparatively miniature scale—eight-by-eleven-inch sheets of paper are their favored canvas. Yet they evince a similar obsession, using a comic-book-like aesthetics to insert bits of *Moby-Dick*'s text into serial creations whose immensity adheres in their sheer volume. If Stella's abstract style, experimentation, and playful combinations of form and color seem postmodernist expressions of the world of high art, Del Tredici's and Kish's unabashedly personal feelings about *Moby-Dick* and unselfconscious embrace of amateurism gesture toward a twenty-first-century post-postmodernist aesthetics worthy of investigation.

"Monumental," "utterly ambitious": Such descriptions seem apt for a project twelve years in the making and including a sculpture weighing in at eight tons and towering twenty-three feet.[62] Begun in 1985 and completed in 1997, the world-renowned Stella's Melville-inspired series includes artworks for each of *Moby-Dick*'s 138 sections, totaling 266 unique creations (with multiple works for some chapters). In addition, most of the prints and sculptures have been reproduced or recast dozens of times, meaning the series actually encompasses more than 1,500 objects.[63] This capaciousness is matched by Stella's use of multiple media and materials: silkscreens, lithography, bas-reliefs, freestanding sculptures, collage, paint, metal (cast aluminum, fabricated aluminum, etched magnesium), marbling, architectural forms. Stella's conception for the series was the happy conjunction of experiments molding wave-shaped forms in his studio and a visit to the Boston aquarium, where he was struck by the movement of Beluga whales: "[It] reminded me of 'Moby-Dick,' so I decided to go back and read the novel and the more I got into it, the more I thought it would be great to use the chapter headings . . . [as] titles of the pieces."[64]

Stella's fascination with Melville relates to the way the author explores conceptions of space through an interplay of form, content, and perspective, achieving, in Ishmael's words, the "rare virtue of interior spaciousness" (247). Indeed, the paradoxical play between spatially imagined totalities and the limits of human perception animates Stella's work as much as it does Melville's. As Robert Wallace perceptively notes in his book on the two artists, the critic trying to evaluate Stella's series as a whole is put in the position of all those artists and naturalists who (as Ishmael notes) inevitably fall short of their attempts to represent the living whale in its enormity.[65] The human eye simply cannot take in the scale of the whale, who, "in his full majesty and significance, is only to be seen at

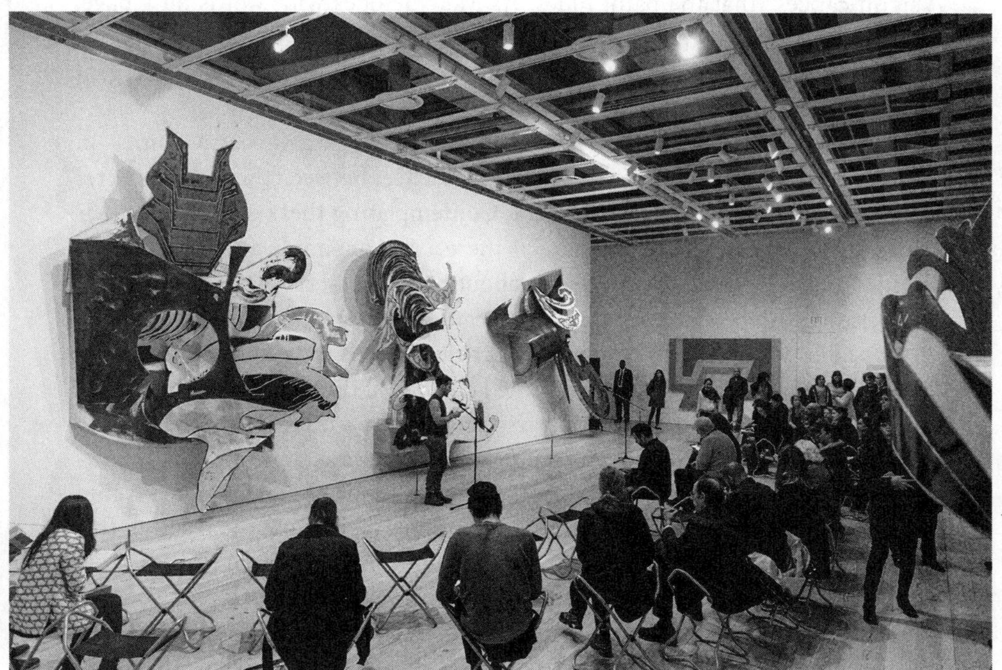

Figure 5.7. Multimedia Melville: reading *Moby-Dick* in front of Stella's sculptures. Public program, *Moby-Dick: A Marathon Reading*, Whitney Museum of American Art, New York, November 13–14, 2015, in connection with the exhibition *Frank Stella: A Retrospective*, October 30, 2015–February 7, 2016.

Source: Photograph by Filip Wolak, courtesy of the Whitney Museum of American Art.

sea in unfathomable waters; and afloat the vast bulk of him is out of sight" (216). This insight leads to Ishmael's famous declaration, "You must needs conclude that the great Leviathan is that one creature in the world which must remain unpainted to the last" (218). So, too, no one person will ever be able to access the totality of Stella's series, for its parts have been dispersed across the globe, towering in public spaces, displayed in distant museums, hanging in private collections, purchased by anonymous buyers (see figure 5.7).

Stella's huge cast-metal bas-reliefs—the predominant form in the series—play on this tension between the whole and the impossibility of apprehending wholeness. These wall pieces are entire objects unto themselves, but because of the three-dimensionality created by the overlapping shapes that compose them, the object that viewers see keeps changing as they shift angles of vision—hitherto eclipsed views open to sight, depths emerge, perspectives disappear or are fractured as other metallic pieces curve into view; vibrant colors clash from one angle and harmonize from another; overpainting suggests "significances" that the paint hides. As Melville does with words on a page, Stella presents dazzling visual surfaces that tease us with all that remains unseen, resisting fixed meaning and rendering all interpretation contingent on perspective.[66]

The question of "meaning" becomes especially resonant—and ironic—in assessing viewers' attempts to find correspondences between these abstract creations and the chapter titles they bear. Contemplating these objects and their titles, Cotkin, for one, is led to ask, "Is there a real or simply a capricious relation?"[67] Stella has always been frank about his process; from the inception of the series, he first created the abstract object, then assigned it a title from *Moby-Dick*'s table of contents.[68] Nonetheless, critics cannot resist the temptation to find "meaning" derived from the named chapter in the given object's abstract shapes, ignoring the potential arbitrariness or whimsy leading to Stella's choice of title once the object has been completed. Wallace has done more than anyone to elucidate the "spirit" of Melville in Stella's work, but he, too, reads into these artifacts narrative elements that sometimes seem more the result of free associations than Stella's intention. For example, meditating on the bas-relief *The Forge* (1988, figure 5.8), he links the "metallic wave" that horizontally crosses the relief with the content of Melville's chapter: "The industrial texture of the cast aluminum wave shape *reminds us of* the flaming heat with which the blacksmith forges his metallic creations in the novel." If this is true, should not *every* relief showing an aluminum wave shape remind us of the blacksmith? Next, observing the strips of paint highlighting the ribbed edges of the metallic shape, Wallace suggests they exist "as if to underscore the blacksmith's assertion"—now Wallace quotes Melville—that he can "smoothe" (*Moby-Dick*, 370) away all seams except that in Ahab's forehead. [69] But how can this "as if" be true if in creating these painted stripes, Stella has not yet even thought of *The Forge* as the title the work will bear?

Even critics warning against such literal correspondences are sometimes misled into a version of the same logical fallacy. Roberta Smith accurately describes the way Stella's shapes seem to "sweep and tumble"—creating the illusion of turbulent motion, which it's fair to say suggests bodies of water such as the ocean. But in her choice of verbs that follow "sweep and tumble," Smith veers into metaphoric equivalences that take their cue from the novel, averring these shapes not only "sweep and tumble" but also "*dive and breach*."[70] Whales "dive" and "breach," abstract shapes do not; Smith is now moving beyond a neutral description of Stella's goal into implicitly Melvillean terrain.

What Wallace correctly identifies—and here his study is invaluable in training our eyes to perceive Stella's visual repetitions—is the repertoire of images that migrate from one piece to another, creating a visual "narrative" of uncannily familiar shapes relating to other familiar shapes in ever-shifting tensions and contingent configurations.[71] The most recurrent image is the wave shape

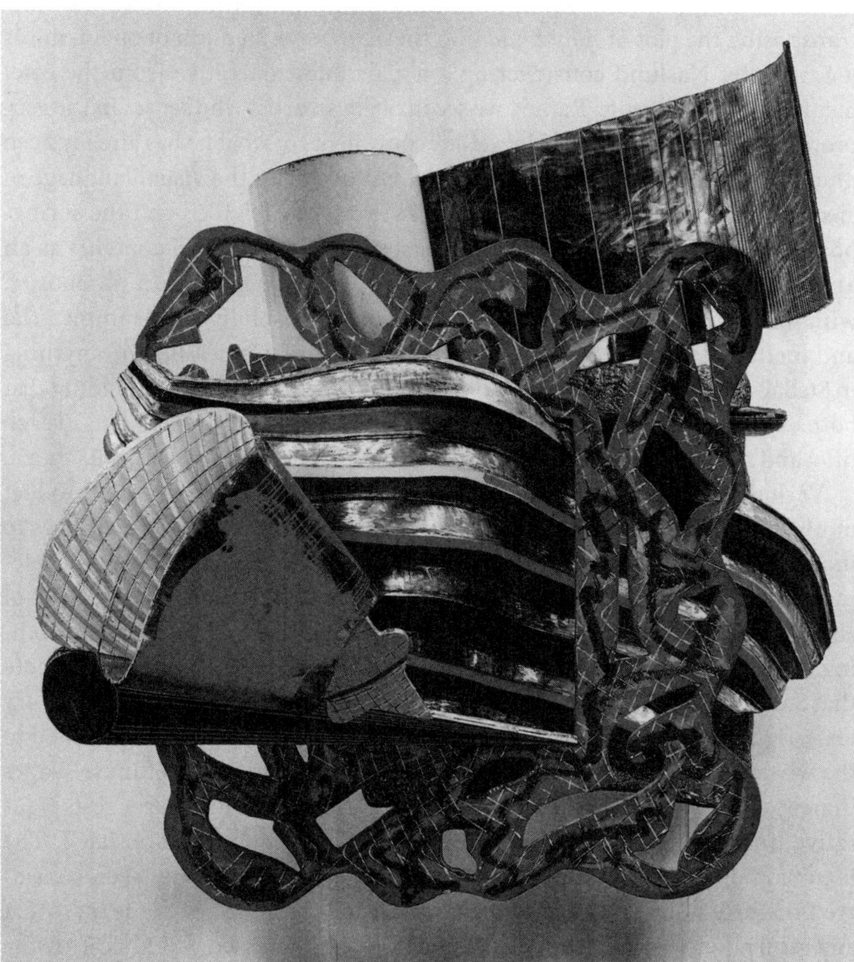

Figure 5.8. Abstraction and shifting perspectives in Stella's bas-reliefs.
Frank Stella, *The Forge (S-10, 3X-2d version)*, 1988. Mixed media on cast aluminum, 97¾" × 95⅝" × 64".

Source: Cat. No. 222.

that evokes ocean as well as whale; another pattern involves intricate, mandala-like Chinese lattices that impart a sense of underlying connectedness whose "stillness" or "calm" anchors the leaping play of curves and color animating the three-dimensional wall hangings.[72] As these shapes suggest, Stella finds in Melville a kindred artistic spirit equally interested in rendering a sense of cosmic vastness, of perpetual motion, in tactile materiality.

Stella's relation to Melville, then, is quite different from either conventional or innovative understandings of "adaptation"—this is not Benjamin Britten, say, transposing the plot of *Billy Budd* into the expressive medium of opera, nor is it Sana Jeter Naslund constructing a female quest narrative from the brief mentions of Ahab's wife. Rather, we see in Stella an artist who senses in the very proportions and rhythms of *Moby-Dick* equivalents of what he has already been practicing and what he wishes to push even further in the visual language of abstraction. Instead of making the actual words of Melville's text the springboard for creative reimagining, Stella uses Melville's table of contents as an armature for exploring his own obsession with movement, with immensity, with tongue-in-cheek humor and playfulness, with solidity made immaterial and ineffability made tactile. Rather than definitively "referring to" anything in Stella's so-named art objects, the chapter titles are part of the scaffolding that both establishes the rules of the project (you aren't done until you've used each title) and contains its infinite possibilities (more than 1,500 objects) in its frame.

Various commentators have noted Stella's growth as an artist as a product of his involvement in this series, marking his transition from flat surfaces to increasingly three-dimensional forms and his willingness to incorporate elements of figuration within the dictates of pure abstraction. A basic tenet of abstraction is that the artwork refers only to itself: Presence is everything; nothing about the object refers to a specific world exterior to itself. Yet the more that Stella's shapes recur (in a series, moreover, taking its name from a literary text), figurative associations—Is that a whale? Is that a tiny figure attached to the whale?—inevitably arise, and the continual intermingling of these shapes in new configurations creates a visual narrative that, if elusive, suggests figurative links to events and perceptions exceeding the abstraction itself. The incursion of "semifiguration" into abstraction has traditionally been considered the bête noire of the movement's advocates because "of the fear . . . that any return to the figuration that abstraction had repressed would destroy the authenticity of abstraction itself."[73] Here, under the influence of an emerging aesthetic to which the *Moby-Dick* series gives rise, Stella begins to break from orthodoxy. Because an artist inevitably "has a sense of living in the world," he tells Wallace, "associational things come through[;] . . . so even though you started with abstraction, figuration comes back in from the other side." His immersion in Melville, he continues, "made it possible for me to accept detail in a kind of way and then let it happen, let it be, let it build up. I think that these paintings . . . build up a sense of narrative detail. They come very close to telling a pictorial story . . . which I think is a new idea . . . because abstraction usually just wants to be itself. It's a different sense for me of making the parts relate, to tell the pictorial story."[74]

If Stella's investment in Melville thus rewrites the vectors of adaptation, then the figurative elements that intrude upon his abstractions—teasing viewer with the possibility of narrative meaning—share a trait in common with the more general aesthetic formulations arising among contemporary participants in the

Melville effect: a return of previously discredited "realist" possibilities of representation alongside postmodernist self-reflexivity and experimentation. Allowing for elements of "semifiguration" within abstraction is, of course, not the same as post-postmodernism's reembrace of fictional realism. But the latter's balancing of postmodernist tenets with a recommitment to something like realistic storytelling resembles Stella's movement toward a practice of abstraction that makes room for figuration and hence "story." In both, the messy mixture of categories and aesthetic priorities points toward new possibilities of creating avant-garde art that simultaneously attends to history and human concerns.

Stella's twelve-year obsession with working and reworking the visual tropes that animate his series—each work exploding with blasts of color, with the steely gloss of metal, with voluminous shapes, with literal as well as figurative weight—reveals an artistic determination that approaches something like monumentality in the sum of its parts. *Awe* is not too strong a word to describe the response generated by the immense wall reliefs and sculptures, in particular. How about *terror*, the other component of Burke's sublime? Instead, I posit that many viewers, after moving beyond feelings of initial incomprehension, experience something like joy or ebullience: Stella's is a *comic sublime*, if you will. This is a trait that the series shares with the next two artists I examine. For Stella, then, size matters not only in the sense of using shape, color, and form to create effects of turbulent motion, fluidity, and vastness in still objects but also as a way of demonstrating an aesthetic affinity with Melville, another master of the near impossible who, in a similar expenditure of delight, challenges the boundaries of representation itself.

In Robert Del Tredici's reenvisioning of *Moby-Dick*, there is no ambiguous gap between word and image, as in Stella's borrowing of chapter titles. Rather, Melville's prose becomes an integral component of each image, directly incorporated into the frames of Del Tredici's provocative compositions. While the size of Del Tredici's artworks (the pen-and-inks were executed on standard-size sheets of paper) pales in comparison to Stella's gigantic reliefs and sculptures, his output is nonetheless vast. It presently encompasses more than 200 works, including 85 drawings executed in the mid-1960s, 21 silkscreens created from 1990 to 2001, and around 100 more collages and paintings since 2016; with each phase, the artwork has grown more complex and multitextured. Like Stella, Del Tredici is fascinated with the effects of scale, in which the visual contrast of vast totalities, diminutive figures, and subjective points of view underlines the existential, tragicomic vision he shares with Melville.

Del Tredici's pathway to Melville is at once idiosyncratic and revealing. "Melville saved my life," he says of the crisis of religious faith that led him to drop out of seminary in the 1960s and enroll in graduate studies in philosophy and literature at Berkeley. As a teaching assistant, he encountered *Moby-Dick* for the first time, immediately identifying with Ishmael as a teller of "brutal truths in droll terms."[75] "It became my Bible; I couldn't have lived without it," he recounts, adding that it became "my guide on how to wander and how to see."[76] His words recall Gilbert Wilson's intense identification with *Moby-Dick* as his personal secular scripture; for both men, discovering the novel was akin to a numinous experience filled with revelation. Del Tredici immediately began creating pen-and-ink drawings that focused on the novel's philosophical ponderings and psychological puzzles, choosing resonant passages to illustrate in the comics aesthetic he had begun to practice as a seminary student. After completing a master's degree in comparative literature, Del Tredici began to "wande[r]" like his hero Ishmael, landing in San Francisco "in the dark finale of the hippie era." Those turbulent times fed his desire to use his sacred "guide" to penetrate to life's truths via his drawings ("I felt I could keep illustrating this book forever").[77] Del Tredici distributed photocopies of his early compositions free of charge; with the Melville pen-and-ink renderings, he used offset printing to make copies, which he sold for fifty cents each at Moe's Books.[78] These were not artworks designed for museum walls; they were messages meant to touch the masses.

If Del Tredici's was not the typical means of art distribution, neither was he the traditional figure of the "all for art's sake" artist. Indeed, he went on to become a teacher, then a scholar of the history of animation, and, finally, for most of his career a professional photographer. His most memorable photography is fueled by a grave concern with the abuses of atomic power akin to the worries obsessing Wilson.[79] In the 1990s, an invitation by Robert Wallace to lecture at his university inspired Del Tredici to return to his artistic renderings of Melville. Learning silk-screening techniques, he reworked eleven of his earlier pen-and-ink drawings (which now became four times their original size) and created nine new illustrations in this medium. These silk screens are infused with layers of vibrant color that push in more clearly abstract directions. During this period—again at Wallace's instigation—Del Tredici met Frank Stella (memorably at Arrowhead, Melville's home in the Berkshires), and he credits Stella with passing on to him the "torch of graphic mischief" that animates his work.[80]

From the early pen-and-inks to the more complex silk screens to his most recent work, Del Tredici's *Moby-Dick* series pioneers a distinctive aesthetic that complements his existential take on the novel. In the traditional practice of book illustration, the artwork appears above and separate from the captioned words being illustrated. Each of Del Tredici's visualizations does feature a quotation from the novel, but Melville's words intertwine with, wrap around, and interact with the image, deconstructing the typical format of illustration. The selected passages are predominantly ones that pose the big epistemological and ontological imponderables—How do we know? How do we see?—that obsess

Melville and Del Tredici alike. The stark images making up the pen-and-ink drawings are often animated by a comics-influenced style in which mysterious, whimsical figures are presented as two-dimensional outlines (Jill B. Gidmark likens them to cave art) whose surroundings pulsate with "jittery cross-hatching" that "evoke[s] mental states."[81] They frequently include fantastical and surrealist elements in which the "comic and cosmic" play off each other. The varied colors and diverse textures of the stock paper on which they are inked add a kaleidoscopic dimension that complements Melville's mix of genres and Ishmael's myriad viewpoints.[82]

A simple but effective example of the "comic sublime" occurs in *The Whiteness of the Whale* (1965, figure 5.9), in which the "subtlety appeal[ing] to subtlety" that leads the imagination on, seeking after "some chance clue . . . to the hidden cause we seek" (*Moby-Dick*, 162) is both graphically represented (the whiteness of the whale in the image is formed by the *absence* of ink, thus remaining subtly elusive) and sardonically parodied (there's nothing subtle, really, about the way the immensity of the whale dwarfs the tiny figure of the Ishmael figure swimming in its wake). *Inscrutable Tides of God* (2000, figure 5.10) depicts questions of scale and immensity on a more complex level. "There is no life in thee, now, except that rocking life imparted by a gently rolling ship," Melville writes in chapter 35 "imparted, by her, borrowed from the sea, by the sea, from the inscrutable tides of God" (136). In Del Tredici's rendering, a vast ocean envelops the earth, which "rocks" the ship atop it; this globe, meanwhile, is rocked or cradled by two streams ("tides," in one of which an entity resembling a whale swims). Other cosmic forces glint in the distance, emphasizing the isolation of the boat, its fate "rocked" by "the inscrutable tides of God." The jagged frame surrounding the white rectangular border gives the image the appearance of being an insert in a map, an enlargement, perhaps, of a mere dot in a larger, unseen and unending, oceanic universe.

The critic Jill Gidmark illustrates just how far Del Tredici's visual meditations veer from earlier twentieth-century illustrated versions of the novel by comparing Rockwell Kent's and Del Tredici's depictions of the same scene from chapter 48.[83] Kent's rendering of Queequeg's vigil by night in a whaleboat (1930, figure 5.11) is moodily realistic—yes, we feel the isolation of the men on this dark sea, but the candle's powerful rays (radiating outward like the sun's) suggest hope, even spiritual illumination, in the midst of this solitude (as does Queequeg's prayerlike posture). In contrast, Del Tredici's *Imbecile Candle* (1965, figure 5.12) is much more inward, psychological, and stark, far more in tune with the bleak existentialism of the excerpted prose describing the scene: "There, then, [Queequeg] sat, holding that imbecile candle in the heart of that almighty forlornness. There, then, he sat, the sign and symbol of a man without faith, hopelessly holding up hope in the midst of despair" (187).

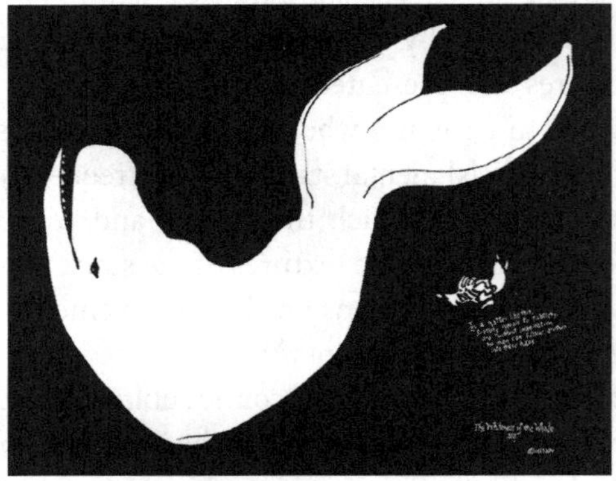

Figure 5.9. Questions of scale.
Robert Del Tredici, *The Whiteness of the Whale*, 1965. Pen-and-ink drawing on paper, 8½" × 11".

Source: Courtesy of the artist.

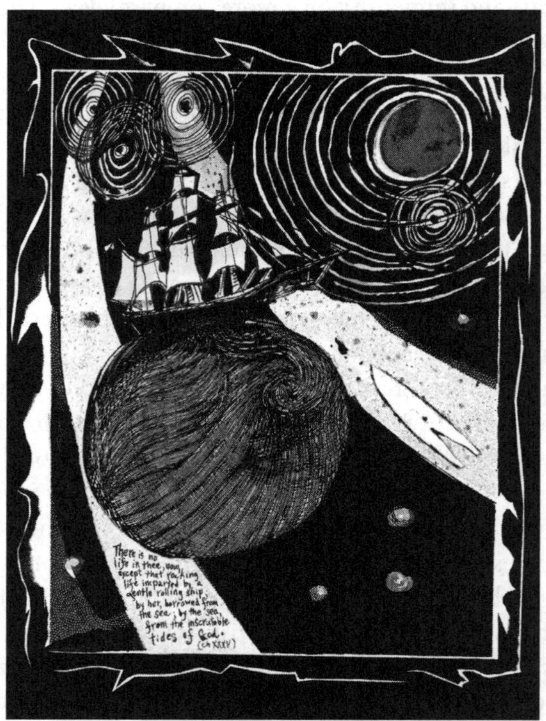

Figure 5.10. The precarity of cosmic voyaging.
Robert Del Tredici, *Inscrutable Tides of God*, 2000. Silkscreen print, 22½" × 30".

Source: Courtesy of the artist.

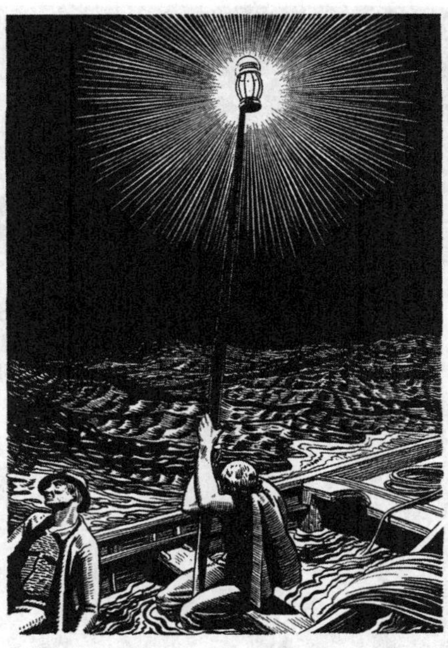

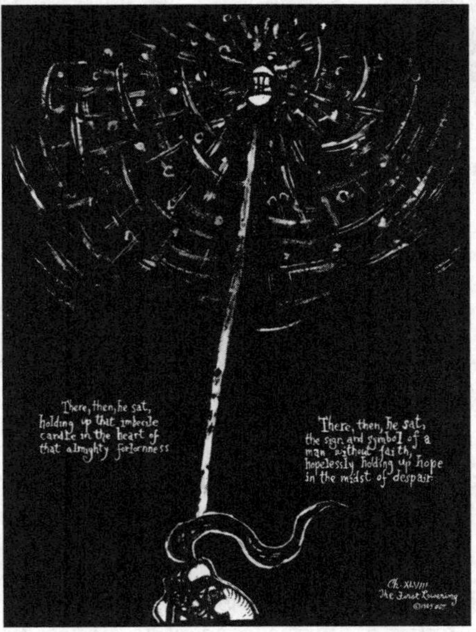

Figures 5.11 and 5.12. A ray of hope or hopelessness? Contrasting visions of chapter 48. *Top*: Rockwell Kent, *The First Lowering*, illustration for Herman Melville, *Moby-Dick* (Random House, 1930). *Bottom*: Robert Del Tredici, *Imbecile Candle*, 1965. Pen-and-ink drawing on paper, 8½" × 11".

Sources: 5.11: Courtesy of the Plattsburgh State Art Museum, Rockwell Kent Collection. 5.12: Courtesy of the artist.

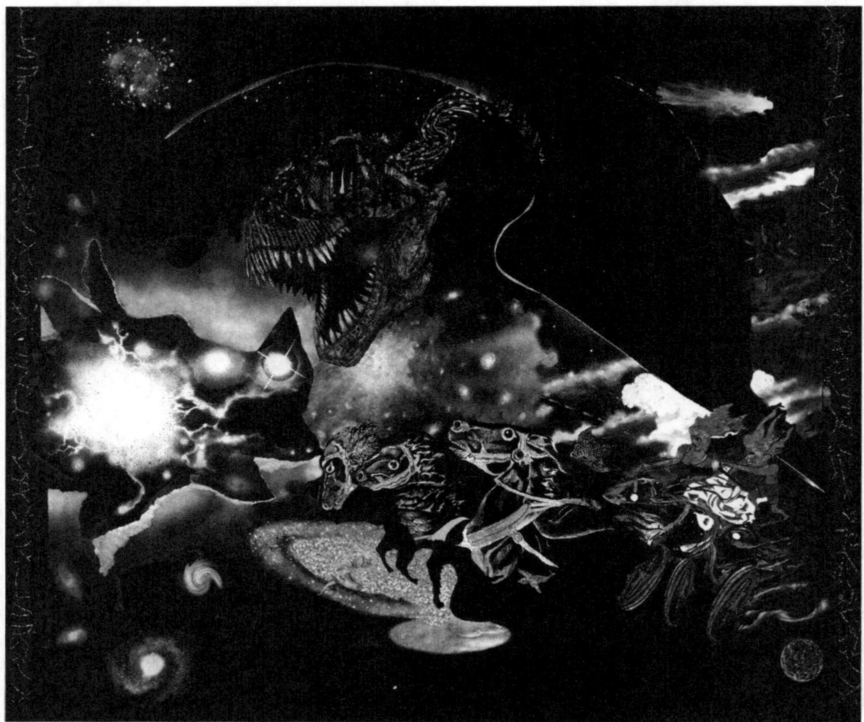

Figure 5.13. A darkening vision in the twenty-first century.
Robert Del Tredici, *Burning Immortal*, work in progress, c. 2025. Pen-and-ink, computer graphics, 8½" x 11".

Source: Courtesy of the artist.

Any hint of heavenly illumination is extinguished by Melville's reduction of the synonym for God, "Almighty," to the lowercase adjective *almighty*, heightening the degree of humanity's "forlornness . . . in the midst of despair." Del Tredici's "imbecile" candle is not only stupid (as Melville's word *imbecile* implies: How can a single candle illuminate such blackness?) but also diminutive, a mere flicker, a "sign" of all loss of "faith." While Del Tredici's image self-reflexively nods to Kent's by positioning the upright pole at the same angle, the light, instead of radiating outward, forms concentric circles dissolving into chaos, random sparks on the verge of extinction. And this flickering light reveals nothing of the surrounding natural world; sky and sea are part of the same black void. Meanwhile, Queequeg's presence is all but extinguished, reduced to his top-knot wafting in an invisible breeze. There is no boat, no companion, no kneeling in prayer, on this night watch—just the feeling of "imbecile" human consciousness fragmenting "in the heart" of an alienating universe.

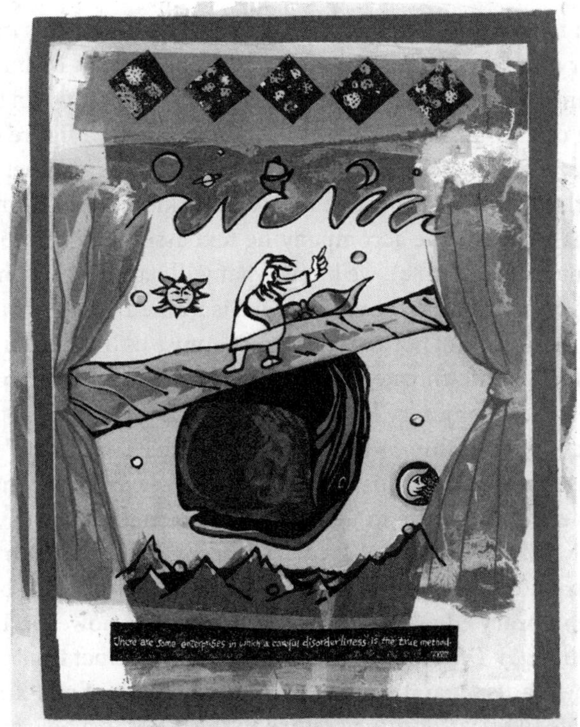

Figure 5.14. Life as a circus act: the comic sublime.
Robert Del Tredici, *Careful Disorderliness*, 2000. Silkscreen print, 22½" × 30".

Source: Courtesy of the artist.

This sense of existential despair is heightened in Del Tredici's latest outpouring of *Moby-Dick*–inspired art by his incorporation of allusions to disheartening twenty-first-century political events: the deadly U.S. involvement in Iraq, the rise of monomaniacal patriotism, atrocities at Abu Ghraib—events that resonate with Melville's critique of America's reckless tendency toward violence and destruction. In figure 5.13, the perils facing our age find expression in a work-in-progress illustrating chapter 48's commentary on a storm at sea: "The whole squall roared, forked, and crackled around us like a white fire upon the prairie, in which, unconsumed, we were burning immortal in these jaws of death!" (187). Here, Del Tredici combines the horrific and fantastical in a hybrid aesthetic evocative of Melville's mixture of genres: Note the *Games of Thrones* dragon bearing down on the seascape, the use of collage and computer-generated imagery, the surrealist depiction of what might be exploding galaxies, and the burst of Stella-like colors composing the horse-drawn chariot at the bottom right.

And yet in face of this darkness Del Tredici often infuses his images with a mordantly wry sense of humor: Tragedy and comedy, as in Melville's writing, go hand in hand. We've seen a glimpse of Del Tredici's ironic wit in the absurdist juxtaposition of gigantic whale and pitifully small man in figure 5.9. Another example, *Careful Disorderliness* (2000, figure 5.14), depicts Ishmael precariously treading a strip of burlap suspended high in the skies, beneath which looms a menacing whale.[84] If, as the accompanying text asserts, "a careful disorderliness is the true method" (284), we know what will happen if Ishmael loses his footing. Then we notice that the entire scene is framed by stage curtains—this is pure theatricality, meant both to terrify and amuse us like any circus act. And that's what Ishmael's life-threatening situation has been reduced to in this illustration: the occasion for jittery laughter.

Del Tredici's relationship to his Melvillean "Bible" or "guide" for living is overwhelmingly personal, intimate, and subjective—everything that New Critics warn readers of literature to guard against. Nonetheless—as we see elsewhere in the Melville effect—Del Tredici's reading of himself into Ishmael not only results in pictures that reverberate with Melvillean meaning but also gives them a contemporary edge. In one significant aspect, however, Del Tredici's obsession with *Moby-Dick* is unique. It has flared in distinct time periods, with a decades-long hiatus separating his initial proliferation of pen-and-ink drawings and his late twentieth-century return to the series in a new medium, then another fifteen years separating these silk screens and his latest images. At the same time as Del Tredici continues to extend the parameters of his oeuvre, he is extending the parameters of the novel: An as yet unpublished image, *Ahab's Last Stand* (2023, figure 5.15), illustrates a nonexistent chapter 136 in which the "horror" of Ahab's death (he has been swallowed by Moby Dick) is counterbalanced by the macabre humor of the punning title (this is indeed Ahab's "last stand," as his leg, severed from its whalebone prosthetic and leeching crimson blood, attests).

It is noteworthy that in transforming his earliest pen-and-inks into multihued silk screens, Del Tredici is, in effect, *adapting his own adaptations* of Melville. As Del Tredici puts it, "When I picked up the leviathan's shining trail again after thirty-odd years of other pursuits, the energy of *Moby-Dick* lay waiting for me, perfectly undimmed, as if freed from a time capsule. It straightaway returned me to my roots in art, taking me beyond black-and-white into a universe of color."[85] Going back ("to my roots") is also moving forward ("taking me beyond"), a double motion that lies at the heart of twenty-first-century reencounters with Melville and our rethinking of the work of literary history.

Like Del Tredici, Matt Kish's adoration of *Moby-Dick* is unabashed—there is little if any critical distance between himself and the object of his greatest enthusiasm. "I've been obsessed with *Moby-Dick* for most of my life," he

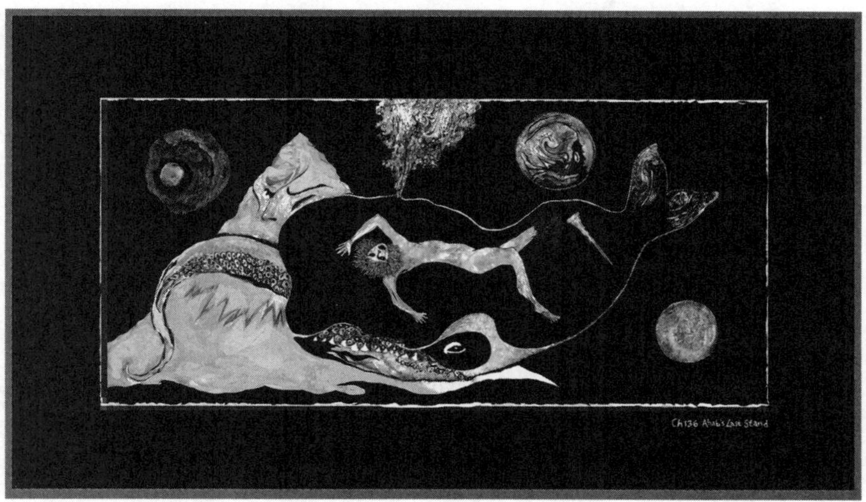

Figure 5.15. Painting beyond the end.
Robert Del Tredici, *Ahab's Last Stand*, 2023. Pen-and-ink, computer graphics, 8½" × 14".

Source: Courtesy of the artist.

guilelessly declares.[86] That obsession reaches back to Kish's youth. He was seven years old watching afternoon television at his grandparents' house when a screening of *Godzilla* was followed by Huston's *Moby Dick*. The shock of realizing that there are real-life monsters even more terrifying than sci-fi ones seared itself into the boy's consciousness. The specifically visual nature of this introduction to Melville was amplified soon after when Kish's father presented the boy with an abbreviated version of the novel, each page of text paired with a full-page illustration. Given this congruence of the written and visual, it's no wonder that Kish says his "lifelong obsession" with Melville has always been paralleled by an "equally obsessive, almost frantic appetite for images," one fixation feeding the other. When he read the unabridged novel in high school, he found himself "totally hooked" for life, and he has reread it religiously eight or nine times over the years, with a devotion (like Wilson's and Del Tredici's) bordering on the numinous.[87]

Kish found his immediate inspiration for his book Moby-Dick *in Pictures: One Drawing for Every Page* (2010) in the work of the punk artist Zak Smith, who undertook the challenge of illustrating every page of Thomas Pynchon's *Gravity's Rainbow* (1973), another Leviathan of a novel. Smith's "nakedly *ambitious*" goal, Kish admits, "appealed to me *enormously*." The rarefied label *artist*, however, is one that Kish abjures; in this respect, he is closer to Del Tredici than to Stella. "I do not consider myself an artist," he states, pointing to his lack of formal training, and in one videotaped interview he hints that the

Moby-Dick series may be his last artistic foray, the leaving behind of a "childhood innocent love."[88] Intriguingly, this forthright embrace of amateurism—viewing his art as child's play rather than professional mantle—proves generative for Kish's creativity. He finds the lack of training liberating rather than a limitation because he gets to make up all the rules.

And making up the rules is a task Kish assumes with a passion, revealing a tendency toward excess (both in coverage and ambition) matched only by the intensity of his obsession. The rules are simple. First, every day without fail he must create one illustration for each page of *Moby-Dick*, focusing on a sentence or group of sentences that inspires his creativity. That he is using a no-frills Signet copy—aimed at the everyday reader—rather than the authorized *Norton Critical Edition* complements his antielitist, self-proclaimed amateurism. Second, he must proceed through the novel in a linear fashion, not skipping a single page. Within these parameters, he allows himself to work in any medium: paint, crayon, ballpoint pen, collage, magic marker. The enthusiasm with which Kish throws himself into the project once he sets the rules of the game mirrors his desire for total immersion in the text, "to walk through every sun-drenched word . . . to smell, taste, hear, and see everything."[89] To attempt to savor "every" word, to grasp "everything," is obsessive-compulsive. It is also totalizing in its vacillation between the sensory experience of each particular and the wholeness that comprises "everything." And the more that Kish attempts, like the other artists in this chapter, to capture the "enormities" of vision that he associates with *Moby-Dick*, the more enormous his creative output becomes.

This interplay between the minute and the monumental is echoed in the workspace Kish devised for his *Moby-Dick* project. Converting a closet that barely accommodated his desk into a studio, Kish began his colossal task. Just as the limitations imposed by his "rules" create the conditions for serial excess, this cloistered space yields reams of art. Once launched, Kish recalls that the project became "all I could think about," and the closer the end loomed in sight, the more he found himself "obsessed . . . by the task of finally finishing the art and slaying the monster."[90] The visual language of Kish's 552 images is visceral and arresting, juxtaposing a variety of styles and artistic influences; each picture is conceived as a multilayered, expressionistic "extension and response to the text," rather than a realistic representation. These layerings—of media, of color palettes, of recurring symbols, of background paper, of superimpositions of text and image—are all part of Kish's visual effort to approximate Melville's verbal layering of surface and hidden depths, of creating more than one can see at a glance, an aesthetic that aligns him with Stella and Del Tredici, who are equally interested in the ambiguities of perception and ontological uncertainties that haunt Melville's pages.[91]

Although Kish shares with Del Tredici a fantastical aesthetic, his style is even more in sync with twenty-first-century digital media: technopsychedelic, popping with primary colors, and incorporating abstract designs, machinelike imagery, dashes of surrealism, what Elizabeth Schultz terms "shock and awe" tactics, and a hermeneutic visual lexicon that creates symbolic correspondences with elements of *Moby-Dick*.[92] Thus, Ishmael usually appears as a short robotlike object (rather like *Star Wars*' R2-D2) with a curlicue at the top of its head and waves at its base; Ahab resembles a kind of black tank riven by a crimson streak; the Queequeg icon is covered in overlapping, turquoise-colored, scallop shapes (Kish's equivalent for body tattoos).[93] The page's unpainted "negative space" often defines the White Whale, visible only because the surrounding wash of colors outlines its blank absence. Images from magazines are occasionally added, collagelike; a wide range of calligraphic styles are used for wordings incorporated into the image. The canvases for most of the pictures are "found" pages that Kish has collected, including pages from electrical grid instructions, Bible storybooks, biology texts, and more.[94]

Kish's pairing of image and page is often deliciously appropriate, adding a note of ironic self-reflexivity to the overall composition. Thus, the illustration that accompanies Ahab's declaration "I'd strike the sun" (140) is painted over the title page of the book *The Exploration of Space*, and Ishmael's conclusion that "the whale has no famous author" (100) is illustrated with a crayon-scrawled whale on a flyer advertising "First Books" (its list of book categories and titles as detailed as Ishmael's cetological classification system). The picture accompanying the passage in the chapter "Grand Armada," in which newborn whales are still attached by umbilical cords to their mothers, is painted over the page of a biology primer explaining the initial resemblance of all animal embryos.

The visual hyperactivity typical of Kish's images is on full display in the picture that accompanies a quotation from "The Counterpane" (figure 5.16), in which Queequeg presses his forehead to Ishmael's brow, clasps him around the waist, and declares them henceforth married. The viewer may first register simply a cacophony of angular lines, geometric shapes (triangle, rectangles, oblong, circle), horizontal bars, and one straight vertical line down the middle. Only on second glance does the viewer begin to discern the presence of two figures, a gray-toned "Ishmael" with zooming eyeball to the left and a scallop-whorled "Queequeg" with almond-shaped red eye to the right; their foreheads abut to form the vertical line bisecting the image. What might initially seem a confrontation (their massive foreheads bringing to mind Moby Dick's battering ram) turns out to be a sign of the indivisible bond uniting the two, a bond reenforced by what we now recognize as their arms in an embrace in the lower half of the image. Looking carefully, however, it becomes apparent that three of the limbs belong to Queequeg and only one to Ishmael. The

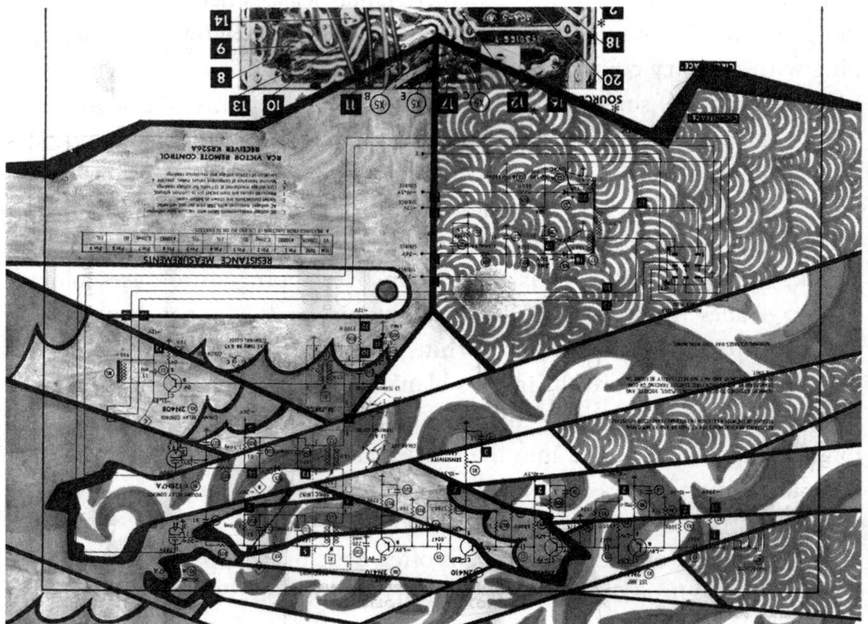

Figure 5.16. A meeting of bodies.
Matt Kish, *He pressed his forehead against mine*, September 25, 2009. Ink and marker on found paper. 11" × 7¾".

Source: Courtesy of the artist.

bond (indicated by their meeting foreheads) may be that of equals, but Queequeg is clearly taking the lead in initiating this "marriage." The found paper that forms the canvas for this amorous interlude adds a characteristically humorous note—it is a diagram of the resistance units involved in wiring an RCA receiver. Indeed, the ultimate sign of the two men's union is their ability to communicate, which is of course what receivers facilitate, but such heartfelt communication doesn't occur without a bit of initial resistance.

A different mode of visual hyperactivity is apparent in the picture (figure 5.17) accompanying the quotation "As yet, however, the sperm whale, scientific or poetic, lives not complete in any literature. For above all other hunted whales, his is an unwritten life" (116). Here, words alone populate the image. The shapes of the tails of the two white whales escaping the right and left margins of the page are created by the *absence* of words—as such the whales remain literally "unwritten." The swelling and diminishing wave shapes consist of run-on phrases about whaling (two are particularly relevant: "pretend to put the living Sperm whale before you" and "an easy outline one for the present thereafter to be filled in" [116]). The "easy outline" yet to be "filled in" becomes,

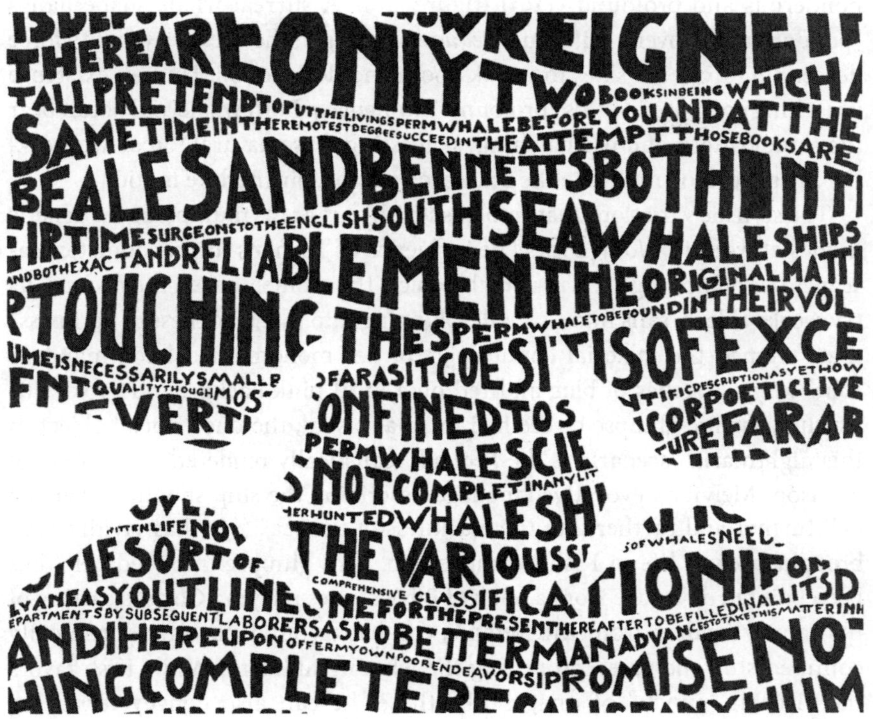

Figure 5.17. Escaping an ocean of words: "unwritten" whales.
Matt Kish, *As yet, however, the Sperm Whale, scientific or poetic, lives not complete in any literature*, January 15, 2010. Ink on bristol board, 8½" × 7".

Source: Courtesy of the artist.

cleverly, the negative white space in the image that depicts the "living Sperm whale"—and only its tail, at that. If the psychedelic script making up this image is reminiscent of rock concert posters of the 1960s, the use of lettering in figure 5.18 calls to mind a war-propaganda poster. Below the bloody letters that spell out "Death to Moby" (the exhortation by which Ahab rallies the crew to his cause), there appear three horizontal rows of silhouetted, armored figures that look more robotic than human as they hoist spears and spades, wielded as one by Ahab's demagoguery. At the very heart of this mob, second row center, Ishmael, too, casts his allegiance to the captain's mission of vengeance. He is the one individualized figure in the group (his eyes open), yet he has also become part of the mass. "I, Ishmael, was one of that crew, my shouts had gone up with the rest. . . . Ahab's quenchless feud seemed mine" (152). Del Tredici's tragicomic play with the incommensurability of scale in *The Whiteness of the Whale* is echoed in Kish's three-toned rendition of the phrase "He is both ponderous and profound" (293) (figure 5.19). A surreal whale shape hangs "ponderous[ly]" over a miniscule *Pequod* bobbing in the ocean, a weighty force descending from the skies to wreak doom and destruction. Human existence is nothing compared to this "profound" immensity. Both whale and ocean bear the same pattern of cross-hatching, suggesting these natural forces are working in concert to annihilate the unaware boat in a pincherlike motion.

The stylistic variations that embellish Kish's art are as multiple as the generic modes at work in *Moby-Dick*. The influence of Turner's impressionistic seascapes lies behind figure 5.20, which depicts the moment when the *Pequod*, its try-works ablaze, sails into a squall, "plunging into that blackness of darkness" that "seemed the material counterpart of her monomaniacal commander's soul" (327). Blotches of blue and red on a lurid pink background evoke this psychodramatic glimpse of the hell in Ahab's soul; the one "black" object in this nightmarish scenario is the *Pequod*, realistically rendered on a splash of crimson. Melville's evocative language describing the ship shooting "her red hell further and further into the blackness of the sea" (327) has vividly been brought back to life in Kish's composition. This glimpse into "red hell" has been painted on a page from a book of Bible stories relaying Christ's casting of the money lenders from the Temple; the background page thus ironically comments on the greed propelling the whaling industry. While Kish favors the visceral "punch" of images like these, he can also convey terrifying insights with just a few strokes. Figure 5.21 accompanies the passage in chapter 126 describing the half-asleep sailor who falls from the mast to his death. As in Japanese ink drawing, three curved brush strokes suggest the mast, and the black streak of ink midpage represents the "falling phantom in the air" (393). The simplicity of the image amplifies the horror of the moment, freezing it in time. No less chilling is the found page on which the image is painted: The dedication page of this unknown book is addressed to one W.N.H., "who would rather stay on the ground." All these elements combine to render an arresting visual equivalent of Melville's existential allegory.

The monumentality of Kish's endeavor is undeniable; the pressure of producing an image a day as well as the sheer length of time (552 consecutive days) it took to achieve this diverse, richly multivisual experience are daunting. The size of Kish's obsession with Melville's book thus results in a picture book that is as sizeable as Melville's novel. But whereas Melville (like Orson Welles and Gilbert Wilson) broods on the public's neglect of his artistic genius, Kish seems to thrive outside artistic institutional structures or approval, embracing his "nonartist" status as a badge of honor. In what is perhaps a prototypically early twenty-first-century twist, Kish seems to value more than renown the sheer opportunity to pursue his passion in a gargantuan project that to others may appear indulgent or excessive.[95] Rather than courting recognition, success came to Kish unexpectedly, the result of the daily posting of his creations on the

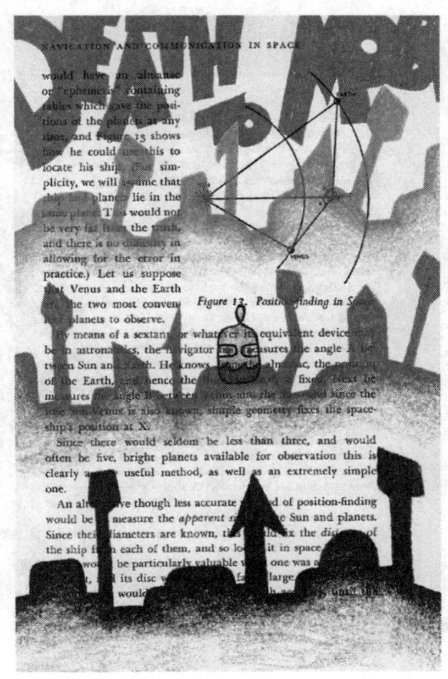

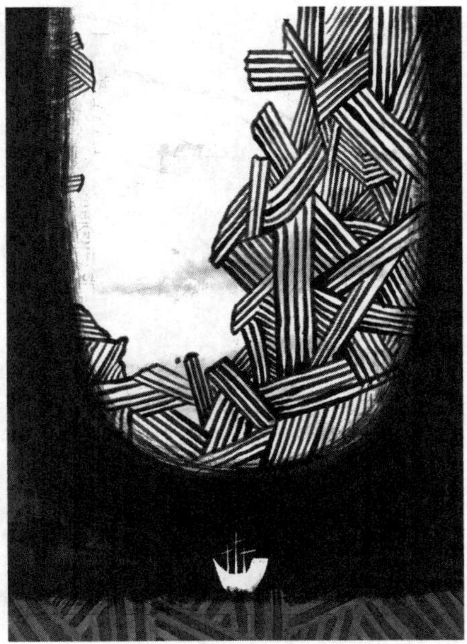

Figures 5.18 and 5.19. Propaganda's appeal: pondering a weighty profundity.
Top: Matt Kish, *I, Ishmael was one of that crew*, February 21, 2010. Colored pencil and ink on found paper, 5" × 8". *Bottom*: Matt Kish, *He is both ponderous and profound*, August 31, 2010. Acrylic paint on found paper, 7¾" × 10¾".

Source: Courtesy of the artist.

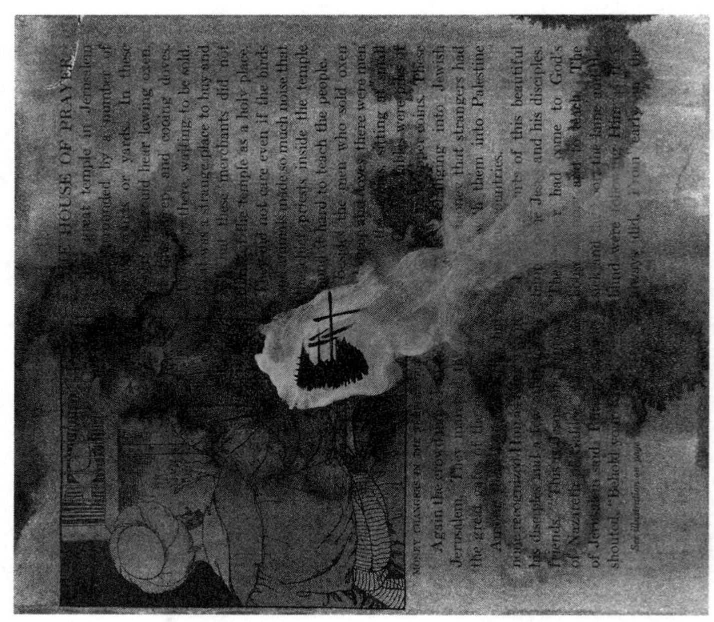

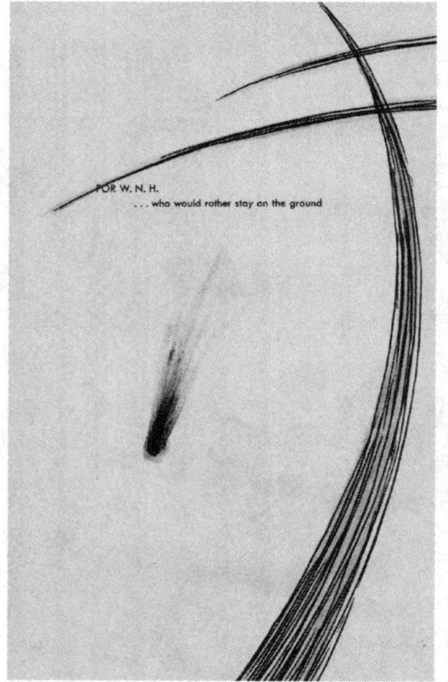

Figures 5.20 and 5.21. Red hell and a phantom fall.
Top: Matt Kish, *As the wind howled on, and the sea leaped, and the ship . . . shot her red hell further and further into the blackness*, October 17, 2010. Acrylic paint and ink on found paper, 9" × 7½". *Bottom*: Matt Kish, *At sun-rise this man went from his hammock to his mast-head at the fore and . . . they saw a phantom falling through the air*, December 21, 2010. Acrylic paint and ink on found paper, 7¼" × 12".

Source: Courtesy of the artist.

internet. These postings began to generate a virtual fan base whose growing numbers brought critical attention to Kish's outpouring and ultimately resulted in its publication in one volume. The "cosmic comedy" that Kish finds in *Moby-Dick* clearly resonates with an audience who knows how to look for art in untraditional venues, an audience for whom conventional aesthetic labels and categories have little purchase.

Multiplying Mobys: Music, Prose, Multimedia

The challenge of creating artifacts to match *Moby-Dick* chapter by chapter has inspired more than visual artists, as the following examples of a songwriter, an essayist, and a collaborative team illustrate. In each instance, an extended engagement with the novel based on its sequence of chapters results in projects whose proportions vie with the intensive labor that has gone into their creation.

From 2008 to 2011, the songwriter Patrick Shea committed himself to writing a song per week based on a chapter of *Moby-Dick* and posting it to his blog every Saturday. Within this framework, he could take up any chapter, which added an element of free play within his general rule of one composition per week. He also allowed himself the freedom to range widely among popular musical genres: ballads, R&B, gospel, working-class postpunk, country, bouncy show tunes, heavy metal, dance music. "*Moby-Dick* lends itself particularly well to multi-genre work," Shea writes in the book where he collected these songs' lyrics, "because the story itself is something of a multi-genre piece."[96]

Although Shea majored in English literature, he freely proclaims his amateur status vis-à-vis the novel: "I don't consider myself an expert. . . . I haven't spent any extraordinary amount of time studying the book."[97] This casual disclaimer of literary expertise is of a piece with Kish's foreswearing of the label *artist*—being a novice, existing outside the art establishment and its categories of value, becomes a badge of honor (see chapter 1 on "deviance prestige") for several contemporary creators inspired by Melville's work. Like Kish and Del Tredici, Shea prioritizes a relation to the novel that is overwhelmingly personal and subjective. The process of funneling to the core idea of a given chapter, he writes, is also narrowing to a "core idea of myself." Perhaps, then, it is no surprise that Shea—like Del Tredici, Kish, and Wilson—elevates the novel to the status of scripture; he reads *Moby-Dick* like he reads the Bible, "out of order, one chapter at a time."[98] This unabashed embrace of the text as the site for self-reflection and self-revelation goes hand in hand with Shea's praise of pop music as a "less traditional but no less powerful" mode of artistic expression. Valorizing popular culture over high art and subjective reading over critical exegesis, he participates in a particularly twenty-first-century democratization of artistic goals and aesthetic values.[99]

Shea comments that in preparing for his weekly song posting, he felt like a pastor or priest selecting the biblical text for the upcoming Sunday sermon. While much has been made of conceptions of the godlike authority of the omniscient novelist and of the pastor as God's ordained mouthpiece, little of these values accrue to Shea's use of such terms; if anything, his stance is that of the anonymous missionary selflessly disseminating the gleanings derived from his "out of order" reading of his secular scripture, *Moby-Dick*, to those willing to lend an ear. While the task that Shea set for himself as a composer was considerable, extending over nearly three years, the motivating desire of the song cycle seems anything but grandiose. True, a degree of obsessive-compulsiveness (setting rules to "discipline" his focus) motors this desire, but Shea revels in the ephemeral, the trivial, and the everyday intrinsic to contemporary pop music's aesthetic—that is, of producing sounds that please and words that convey feeling with no high-cultural pretensions. He isn't obsessed, like Wilson or Welles, with creating "big" art as a monument to his unique genius.

One might argue, of course, that composing within such rules creates *too much* material and that the inevitable repetitiveness results in a degree of mediocrity (unless the musician truly *is* a "genius") or, for the listener, boredom (so much repetition!). But one person's boredom may be another's turn-on, and Shea, I suspect, isn't too worried about what others may think about the excessive amount of material spawned by his tribute to *Moby-Dick*. Rather, his personal pleasure in fulfilling his goal far outweighs its public reception. Size may matter to Shea, but it matters more as a reminder of the diffuse pleasures that art offers when freed from expectations of greatness. "There is a subtle line," he writes in the lyrics to "The Fossil Whale," "Between the scale of the subject / And the thoughts brought to the mind." So, too, composing the lyrics for Ishmael's meditations on immensity in the chapter "Measurement of the Whale's Skeleton," Shea reminds us, "Don't call the sum of all a whale / The sum will surely fail."[100] For this composer, learning *not* to look for the "sum" (or the summa of summas) is intrinsic to his participation in the Melville effect.

Melville's chapters also come into play as a structuring device for the historian George Cotkin's work *Dive Deeper: Journeys with* Moby-Dick (2012). The conceit underlying this essay collection is that of linking each of its 138 essays to one of Melville's chapters. Cotkin's subtitle indicates something of the size and extent of his ambitions. The noun *journeys* suggests that the volume records (like Melville's novel) a quest and that this voyaging forth occurs "with" *Moby-Dick*—Cotkin's musings and Melville's narrative occupy an equal plane as companion voyagers. The main title is even more suggestive. "I love all men who dive deep," Melville famously wrote to Evert Duyckinck in 1849, and

Cotkin's substitution of the comparative *deeper* for Melville's *deep* suggests that his look at "perhaps America's greatest novel" through the lens of the material it has inspired—material at once "brilliant and bemused, enduring and ephemeral, insightful and muddled"—may increase its "greatness."[101]

Cotkin begins by repeating Melville's claim that "to produce a mighty book" the writer "must chose a mighty theme." Dipping, as it were, his own pen into "Vesuvius' crater for an inkstand," Cotkin states his equally ambitious goal of creating a new version of the "intellectual chowder" that Duyckinck used as a metaphor to describe *Moby-Dick*, a goal he will realize by tracing "Melville's signal contribution to modernist and postmodernist creativity"—namely, *all* those twentieth- and twenty-first-century scholars, writers, thinkers, and makers and breakers of culture who have been inspired by his example. Cotkin creates this chowderlike mix of tasty morsels by writing short essays that reveal their links to *Moby-Dick*'s chapters "by dint of phrase, symbol, context, or rhythm." Reading *Dive Deeper*, then, involves two simultaneously unfolding journeys: an exegesis of Melville's chapters, paired with Cotkin's musings on the array of modern artistic expressions and cultural references that have now become "part of the biography of the book and its readers."[102]

What surprised me, in diving deeper with Cotkin, is how absolutely engaging he makes each plunge. The comprehensiveness of his knowledge is outstanding. There isn't a Melvillean influence in high or popular culture that Cotkin hasn't come across, and his suppleness in moving between his meditations and Melville's chapters yields constant surprises and fresh insights. Noting that *Moby-Dick* was written in an age, like ours, in which "imperial hubris and a cocky sureness reigns," Cotkin credits Melville with honoring his "readers by shaking their foundations" and expresses his hope of doing the same by breaking the scholarly mold that has been his usual métier. Aware that there's little new he could do with a novel that's "already attracted a universe of commentary," Cotkin decides "to try for something more creative."[103] *Dive Deeper* is the felicitous result, an amalgam of creative interpretative energies written in lively prose in which every entry enlarges the reader's perception of Melville's imprint on culture past and present.

The congruences Cotkin establishes between his essays and Melville's chapters are at once bold and subtle. Sometimes historical context provides the link; sometimes it is Cotkin's free association, running with a word in Melville's text until the riff bleeds into the more recent event or inspiration; sometimes Cotkin's reading of Melville creates an independent metaphor that opens onto the contemporary example. And sometimes the wording of Melville's chapter title is all Cotkin needs. Thus, chapter 88, "Schools and Schoolmasters," seamlessly leads to Cotkin's analysis of Melville's incorporation into the curriculum; the chilling commentary accompanying "The Dart" traces the evolution of harpoons into explosive killing devices fired by canons at their prey; chapter 67, "Cutting In," motivates Cotkin to examine "cut-up" (e.g., heavily edited) versions of *Moby-Dick*.

The insights that spring from the connections that Cotkin forges among *Moby-Dick*, history, and popular culture are everywhere on display. Taking up the novel's second chapter, "The Carpet-Bag," Cotkin recounts Ishmael's accidental entry into a Black church in New Bedford, whose parishioners are listening to a sermon on the blackness of Blackness, noting that Melville himself was in New Bedford on a similarly cold evening in 1840 looking for a post on a whaler. Next, Cotkin notes that in the same decade the former slave and abolitionist Frederick Douglass lived in New Bedford, where he found employment unloading supplies from ships like the one on which Melville was seeking a posting; by 1841, the record shows Douglass was honing his oratorial skills as an "exhorter" in one of the town's Black churches. This leads to Cotkin's whimsical but thought-provoking question: "Is it entirely fanciful to imagine that the black minister quickly glimpsed presiding . . . in the New Bedford church, mentioned in this chapter, was Frederick Douglass?" We'll never know, of course, but the coincidence of these "two giants of nineteenth-century American culture" being in the same place at the same time is fascinating to savor, "intellectual chowder" at its tastiest.[104]

Events occurring contemporaneous with the novel's publication also enliven Cotkin's comments on chapter 22, "Merry Christmas" (the day the *Pequod* launches into the wintry Atlantic). On December 24, 1851—the year of *Moby-Dick*'s publication—one Sidney Willard Jr. signed his name to a first edition housed in Northwestern University's Rare Books Room. Given the date, Cotkin reasonably infers that the book was a Christmas present to Willard. Did this youth ever read the novel? We'll never know: its pages are tantalizingly clean, lacking marginalia or underlining. What we *do* know, Cotkin adds, is that Sidney Willard Jr. "was slaughtered, along with over 1,200 of his comrades, at the Battle of Fredericksburg in the War Between the States, almost exactly eleven years after he inscribed this volume." Within this telling, the novel becomes a thread in the web of worldly events and lost lives that so deeply traumatized Melville in the 1860s.[105]

Other meditations bring popular culture or contemporary events into conversation with the novel. Chapter 64, "Stubb's Supper," features the shipboard cook Fleece's sermon to the sharks, and "Fleece," it turns out, was the code name assumed by Gudrun Esslin, a member of the Baader-Meinhof Gang, a confederacy that terrorized cities in West Germany throughout the 1960 and 1970s. Esslin assigned aliases to her fellow revolutionaries that were also derived from *Moby-Dick* (Andreas Baader, the comrade most fixated on crushing "the White Whale of the imperialist powers," was nominated "Ahab"). Ironically, as

Cotkin notes, in choosing her own code name, Esslin *misread* Melville; she assumed Fleece was a dedicated ship officer rather than a buffoonish character whose preaching of Christian love to the avaricious sharks is laced with irony.[106] And while the self-immolating sharks (they begin feeding on each other) might well reflect Melville's caustic attitude to capitalism consuming itself, he would have been equally repelled by the violent anarchism advocated by Baader and Esslin, who saw the totalitarianism practiced by Ahab as a version of their own fanaticism, but that is the antithesis of the democratic brotherhood embraced by Ishmael.

In addition to historical and cultural intersections, Cotkin finds a place for commentary on almost all the scholars and intellectuals who promoted the first Melville revival as well as twentieth-century literary figures and artists who pay homage to the author. Amid these notables, Cotkin includes proliferating manifestations of Melville in popular culture, from M. C. Lars's "post-punk laptop" rap video *Ahab* to Sam Ita's inventive "pop-up" book. *Dive Deeper* swells in volume in recounting these Melvillean encounters and journeys. But the overall effect is less that of promoting its own achievement than of expanding the breadth and depth of readers' perception of the novel's history of readership, reception, and afterlives. Like the figure of the rhizome, this conversation between text and its history spreads in diffusive, crisscrossing shoots that put past, present, and future in nonhierarchical interplay.

Trish Harris and Lissa Holloway-Attaway's *Remaking* Moby-Dick*: A Multivocal Project* (conceived in 2012 and ongoing through 2018) sounds like the perfect example of the multimedia ambitions I have been attributing to the contemporary Melville effect. Both in its scope (inviting the participation of as many creators as possible in all forms of media) and its structure (art inspired by *Moby-Dick*'s chapters), the project merits pride of place in this chapter's meditation on "size matters." The gap, however, between the project's ambitions and its execution raises interesting questions about the liabilities of dreaming "big" and about contemporary aesthetic practices that privilege inclusion, access, and nonsingularity.

Harris makes the project's ambitions explicit in the opening sentence of her prefatory comments. "The curator's statement for a project as ambitious as this one," she begins, "should open as a sort of hymn to Melville." However tongue-in-cheek, the comment's use of religious language reveals a worshipful enthusiasm in excess of typical critical objectivity, and the "hymn" that follows elevates Melville to godlike status: "We thank you, oh Mighty, for the inspiration, for the gift of a wondrous start point." Harris's original conception was to create a "post-text project" of "videos, images, and sounds" corresponding to Melville's chapters, but, as she "confesses" (note the continuing religious imagery), most of the incoming contributions turned out to be textual artifacts—poems, stories, essays.[107] With more outreach, videos followed, albeit in a much smaller number. Harris's ambitions are echoed in a second preface by the collaborator and project director Lissa Holloway-Attaway, who sees in "this massive Moby-sized text" the occasion for a yet "larger exploration of digital art, public space, and mixed realities": What is already "massive" is designed to become even "larger" by adding "more voices and echoes" to the novel, "increas[ing] exponentially" what Melville facetiously refers to as its "joint stock-companies" (*Moby-Dick*, 103).[108] Adding more, "increas[ing] exponentially": again, wittingly or not, the emphasis is on size.

The results were published in a print version in 2013, comprising what Harris terms "a sort of group exhibition of 90 writers, artists, and computer programs," with QR codes added to direct readers to online videos. For all its ambitions, the multimedia project doesn't quite measure up to the size of its claims. Of its 161 entries, less than half are original "remakes." Fully 59 of the chapters are covered by photographs by one Ida Avebro, and although I don't mean to demean her talents, most have little to do with the *Moby-Dick* chapters with which they are paired—seeming to serve as filler to make up for the lack of contributions on those chapters. Another 24 entries are machine-generated texts or word clouds, providing a digitalized form of padding. The remaining individually authored entries (less than half the 161 total) skew disproportionately to poetry (41) and prose (16), vitiating the collection's goal of being innovatively multivocal and inclusive of all media in its reach. The online version contains a number of videos that are rudimentary—music over still images—at best.[109]

I don't mean to be overly critical. In both print and online versions, there are gems worthy of attention. Several poetry entries are quite evocative. In "ishmael, new bedford, 2013," Jim Mezzanotte's bleak portrait of the run-down condition of today's port city is haunting:

> ishmael tweets and smokes a cigarette
> trying to catch a break
> because the city is dead
> and the fish are gone.[110]

Also effective (and effectively placed) is the poem accompanying the epilogue, A. J. Huffman's "I Am Classic," in which Ahab, whale, and Ishmael give sobering testimonies to their "classic" status; we move from Ahab's "I am cold / distance," to Moby's "I am repeated / injury, phallic manifestation of primal male / aggression," to Ishmael's

> I am professor and prophet . . .
> welcomed or not. I am history's accountant.

> My only purpose is to transcribe those events that
> I alone survived.[111]

Among the video submissions, Charlotte McGowan Griffin's looped installation (first displayed as a one-hour film in Berlin in 2009, paired online with the "Whiteness of the Whale" chapter) offers a mesmerizing play of light and shadow over white shapes. Accompanied by Peter Liljeqvist's haunting soundscape, these forms gradually reveal themselves to be cut-outs and hangings of white paper. Although not originally created to illustrate Melville's meditation on whiteness, its components come together to breathtaking effect, evoking the terror and awe that Ishmael attributes to the albino whale. By its end, one feels as if one has sunk to the bottom of a milky sea inhabited by the skeletal remains of an extinguished world.[112]

Some of the most successful videos are those that don't take themselves too seriously and in "messing" with the "master" text prove themselves masters-in-miniature of the comedic. *Moby Mix: A Hollyweird Production* by Jonas and Joshua has disappeared from the online postings, probably for copyright reasons, but setting Disney's Donald Duck version of the novel to the music of *2001: A Space Odyssey*, followed by "In the Navy" by the Village People and "La mer" as crooned by Maurice Chevalier is as irreverent as it is inspired. So, too, is the eight-minute video *Moby and Ahab Visit Toronto* by Heather Wilson and Michael Dubrule. Beginning by noting the discovery of the vertebra of a killer whale in freshwater Lake Ontario in 1987, the infectious video imagines a stovepipe-hatted Ahab and a cuddly Moby (played by Wilson in shark costume!) taking in the sights of Toronto.[113] The playful use of title cards, a bouncy soundtrack, sprightly choreography, and clever camera work make the video a delight to watch, all the while posing a conundrum that Melville would have relished: How *did* a killer whale end up in one of the globe's largest freshwater bodies of water?

Moby Richard: A Comical Remake also makes the most of a gleefully amateur cast and no-frills budget. Filmed as if a promotion reel for a major motion picture, this self-referential romp features an all-female cast of exuberant teenagers (wearing wigs as deliberately fake looking as the beards worn by Solien's cowboy-disguised Mrs. Ahab and Driscoll's sea-captain-impersonating Ahab's wife) who are clearly enjoying themselves as they spoof the novel's main characters. Having begun with a giggly chorus of voices declaring over a title card, "PREVIOUSLY ON WHALE WATCHERS!" the video reaches its climax in a swimming pool, and the dedication in the credits to "Ms. Rogers and Mr. Reed for being the best teachers ever" leads one to suspect the actors and director are high-school students whose reading of *Moby-Dick* for English class inspired this creation: If so, they do their teachers proud.[114]

Amateurism and Excess in a Digital Age

The latter examples as well as those of Del Tredici and Kish in the preceding section lead me to ponder two recurring motifs in my analyses. The first concerns the status of the "amateur," a term I've found myself using increasingly: Who gets to designate what an amateur is? When does amateurism become a positive identity for some creators? To what ends and for whom? The second is the growing presence of what I've referred to as a "comic sublime" at play, which, I suspect, may more accurately be a *desublimation* of an aesthetics of the sublime, one that is rooted in contemporary digital culture.

In the case of Harris and Holloway-Attaway's *Remaking* Moby-Dick project, the question of amateurism breaks two ways. Including everyone's submissions is central to the editors' ethos of encouraging a more genuinely participatory culture in the arts. The more voices included and the more diverse the media employed, so the argument goes, the more we are empowered to appreciate the inherent multivocality of all texts and the elasticity inherent in the history of the creative arts. Toppling the primacy of the authorial signature by making room for the amateur (an effect underlined by Harris and Holloway-Attaway's choice of alphabetizing the contributors' biographies by their given names rather than surnames) not only democratizes access to the project but blurs the line among reading/viewing/creating. The proliferation of bloggers and self-published books certainly feeds into this changing horizon of what counts as an "amateur" or "professional," an "artist" or "author." But, as both the *Remaking* volume and its online version demonstrate, the editorial decision to accept all submissions means that some work is bound to be half-baked, naive, or simply not very good. Harris and Holloway-Attaway might legitimately argue that even those submissions that I deem to be "not very good" are valuable in increasing our understanding of how a "classic" such as *Moby-Dick* is always-already contemporary, how it continues to command high cultural capital, how "remaking" is part of all reading and all acts of interpretation. But this nonhierarchal inclusiveness also risks alienating or boring potential readers and viewers to the degree that the sheer excess of contributions creates a kind of white noise that ironically can drown out perceptions of the diverse paths of inspiration that are such a project's goal. Then, again, I might be underselling younger audiences, who, attuned to the internet's supersaturated layers of information and adept at disappearing down online rabbit holes, may take such excess as a given and are satisfied with finding (if they are lucky) the particular entries that speak to them while skipping the rest. Weirdly, size *doesn't* always matter for a generation that has grown up in a world of digital information and telecommunication that is infinitely large, multilayered, and rhizomatic.

As I hope my praise of some of most spirited and savvy if "amateur" videos included in *Remaking* indicates, I want to distinguish between works that are unthinkingly simplistic and a praxis or aesthetics of the amateur that is self-aware, knowing, and tongue-in-cheek. The latter endeavors remind me of that repeated moment in old Hollywood films in which a group of enthusiastic youngsters or teens decides to put on a play, and the ultimate production, however unseasoned the performers or makeshift the sets, thrills with vitality and creative spunk. This amateur creative energy, too, is part of the Melville effect inspiring so many enterprising artists today. Flaunting one's nonprofessional status or lack of sophisticated resources and making the most of it, sampling this and sampling that, speaking in multiple rather than singular authorial voices: all these contemporary trends creating a place for the unrecognized or noncanonical creative endeavor may sound familiar because they align so closely with Melville's practice and aesthetics.

This brings me to the second motif connecting many of the artists included in this chapter. From Stella to Del Tredici, from Kish to Shea, from *Moby and Ahab Visit Toronto* to *Moby Richard: A Comic Remake*, one senses a degree of wit and wry irony that approaches comic existentialism. Although *Moby-Dick*'s humor has never been in question, modernist Melvilleans tended to emphasize the novel's more tragic elements, its weighty portents of doom, its immensities of despair, its riddling ambiguities. Such a focus coexists with a long history of privileging the sublime as the greatest aesthetic goal of all. However, the strain of "cosmic comedy" that runs throughout many of these postmodern and post-postmodernist works begins to tilt the balance in favor of recognizing the comic absurdity of overcontemplating the vastness, scope, and unknowability of reality; there is plenty to mull over and ponder and laugh at in attending to the messy details, the jumbled particulars, the insignificant minutiae that are our daily bread. In the process, Romantic and modernist aesthetics of the sublime find themselves undergoing a process of *de*sublimation, resulting in an altogether different aesthetic understanding of scale and vastness that gives rise to comic perception as temporary catharsis. And the amateur can laugh, as knowingly and loudly as anyone else. Size matters now because its scale allows us to perceive cosmic comedy in the disparity between our minute existences and the vast metaphysical and epistemological imponderables that, like Melville's White Whale, threaten to engulf us.

Along with these shifts in the meanings of artistic amateurism or professionalism in singular or group authorship, in increasingly populist modes of distribution and recognition, one also senses a change shared by several of this chapter's subjects in their attitudes toward fame or renown. To be sure, dreams of celebrity status and fandom have only been amplified in our digital epoch, but artists such as Kish and Shea do not seem to be compelled by the desire to be recognized as *THE* great painter or composer of the decade, someone whose genius is (or should be) lauded by all. Ambition still motivates these creators, of course, as does an obsessive-compulsive devotion to their focus on Melville, which indeed may be excessive in its execution. But the size of the ambition resides in the scope of their projects, not in the anticipation of public applause or universal recognition. Once again, we see that size matters, but matters differently for contemporary artists fascinated with the immensity of *Moby-Dick* and charged with the desire to evoke reality in all its infinite particulars and vast infinities.

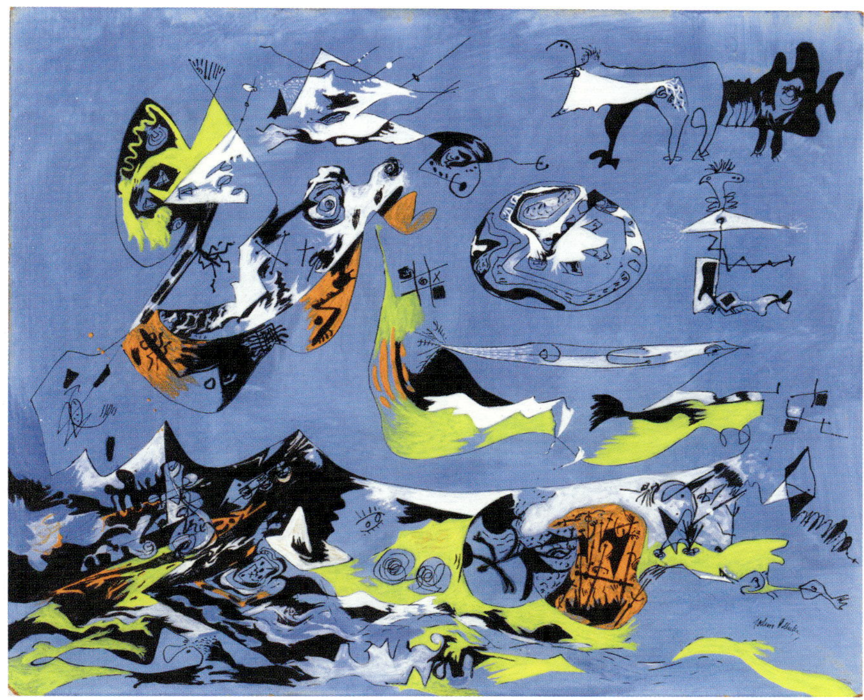

Figure 1.1. Modernist moody blues.
Jackson Pollock, *Blue (Moby Dick)*, c. 1943. Gouache and ink on composition board, 18¾" × 23⅞".

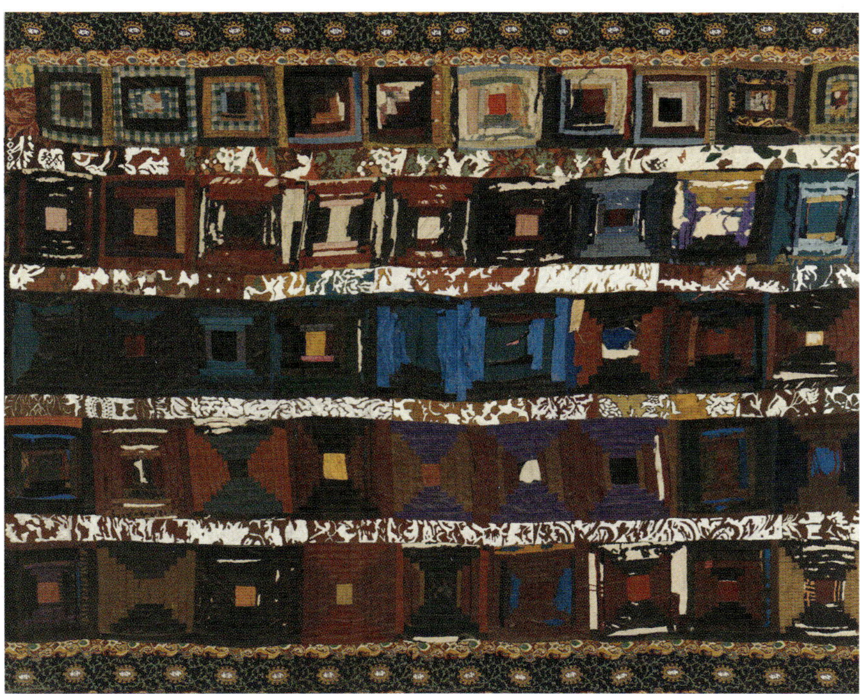

Figure 1.4. From page to painting: patchwork aesthetics and Melville.
Ann Wilson, *Moby-Dick*, 1955. Acrylic on found quilt mounted on canvas, 66¼" × 84".

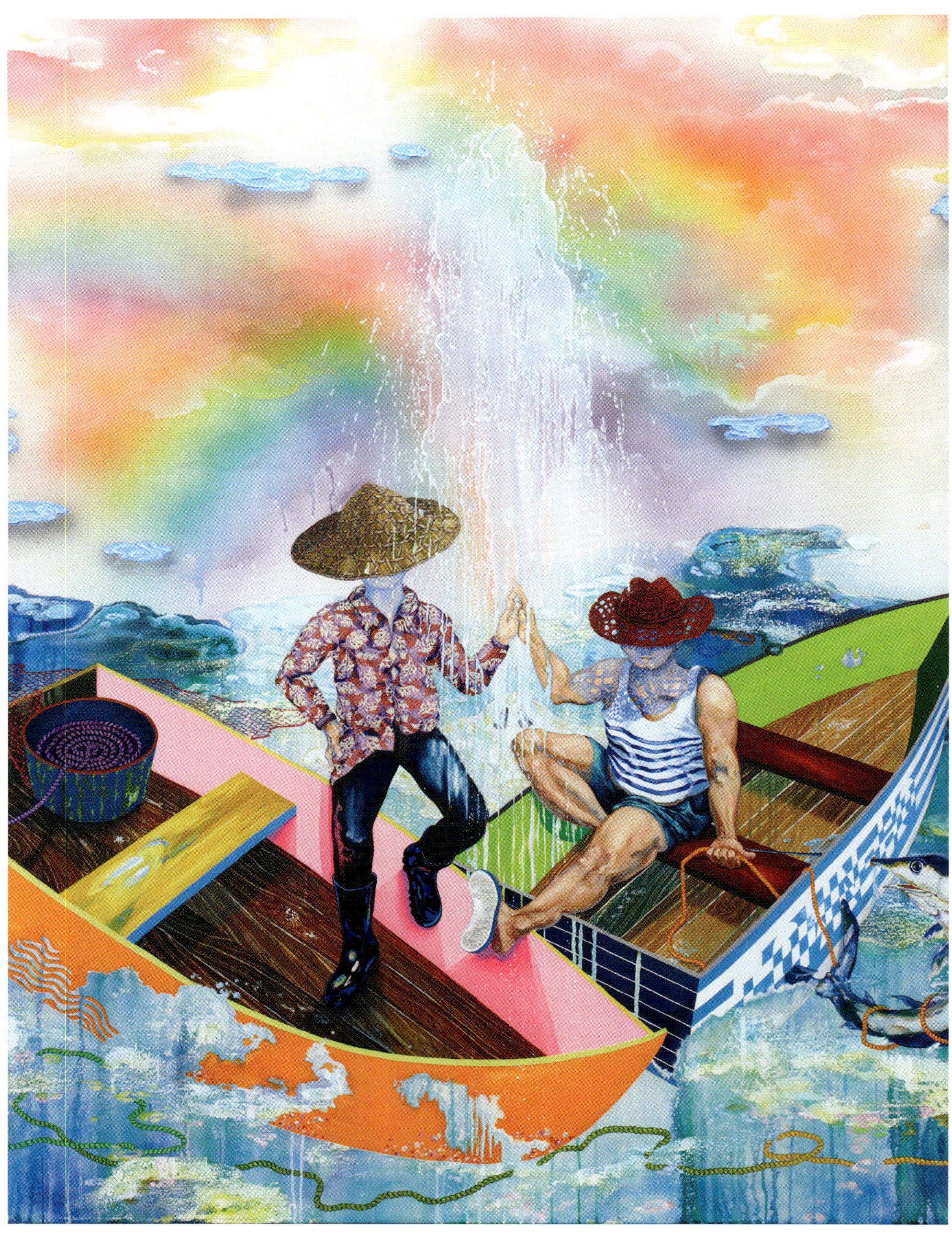

Figure 2.19. Sea gams as gay fantasia.
Eleen Lin, *Meet. Greet. Fleet*, 2018. Oil and acrylic on canvas, 72" × 96".

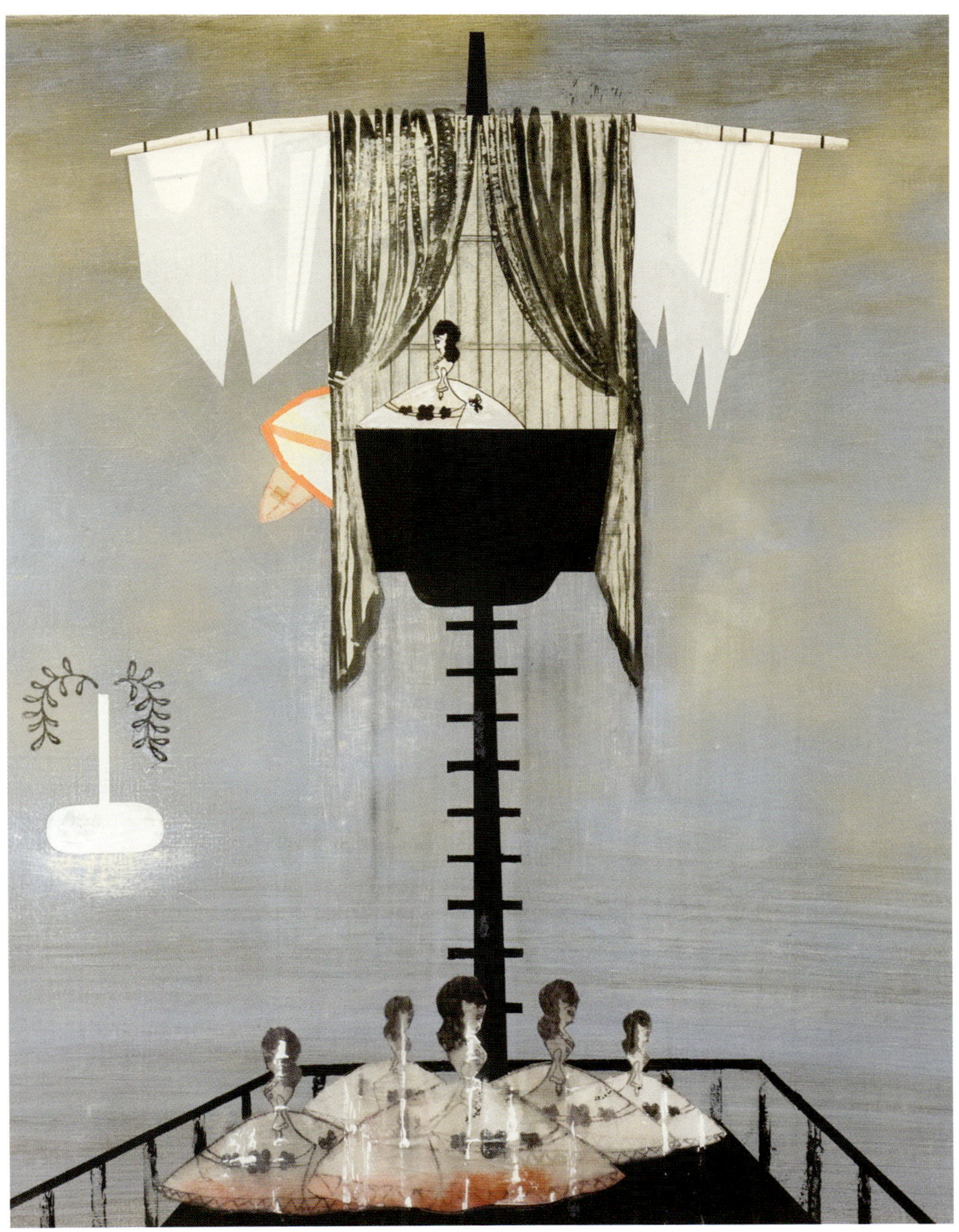

Figure 4.6. Women at sea, whale as vase.
T. L. Solien, *Standing Masthead*, 2005. Mixed media on paper, 31¾" × 38¼".

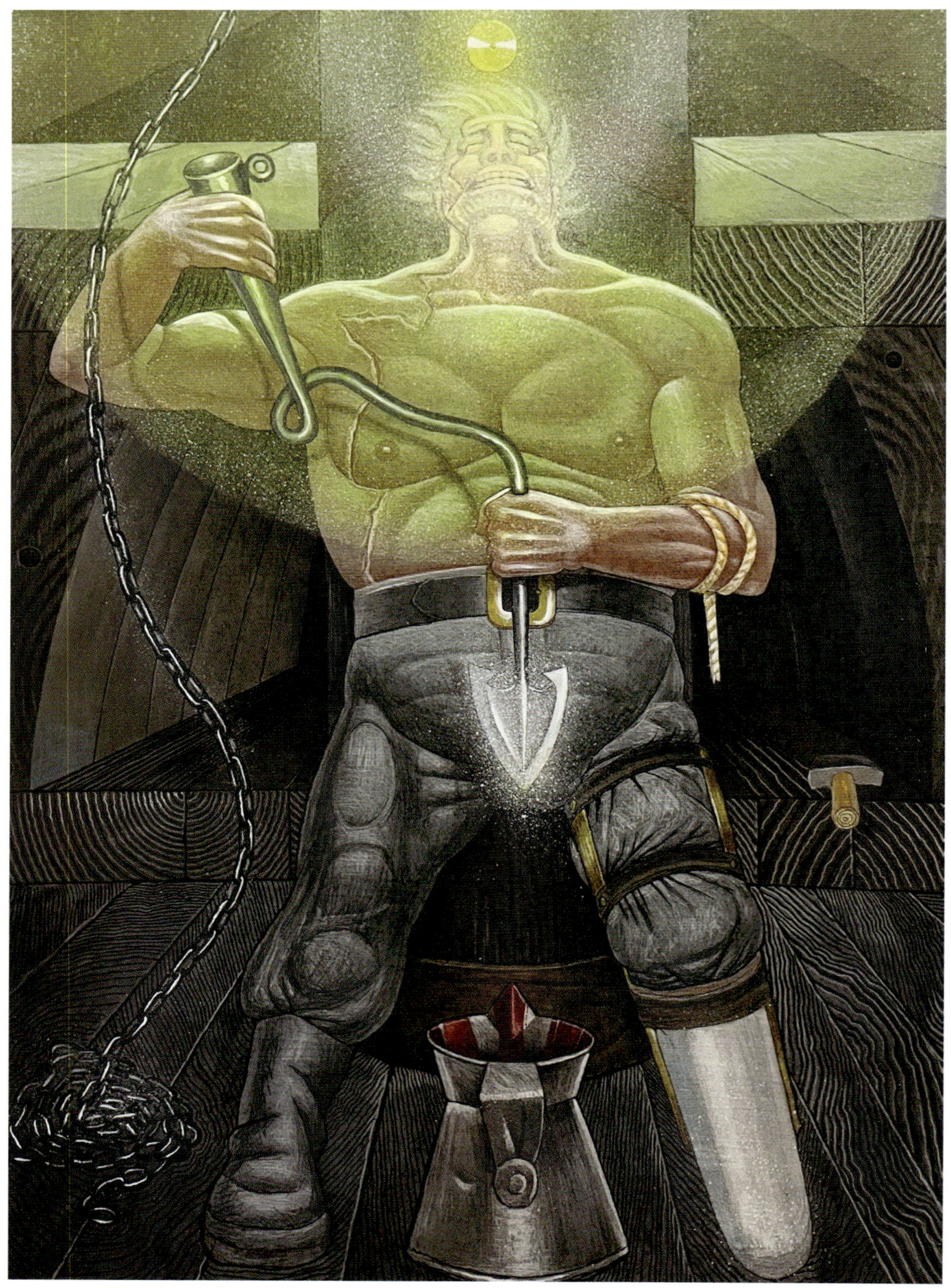

Figure 5.1. An electrifying self-castration.
Gilbert Wilson, *St. Elmo's Fire*, c. 1955. Acrylic and colored pencil on particle board, 34" × 36".

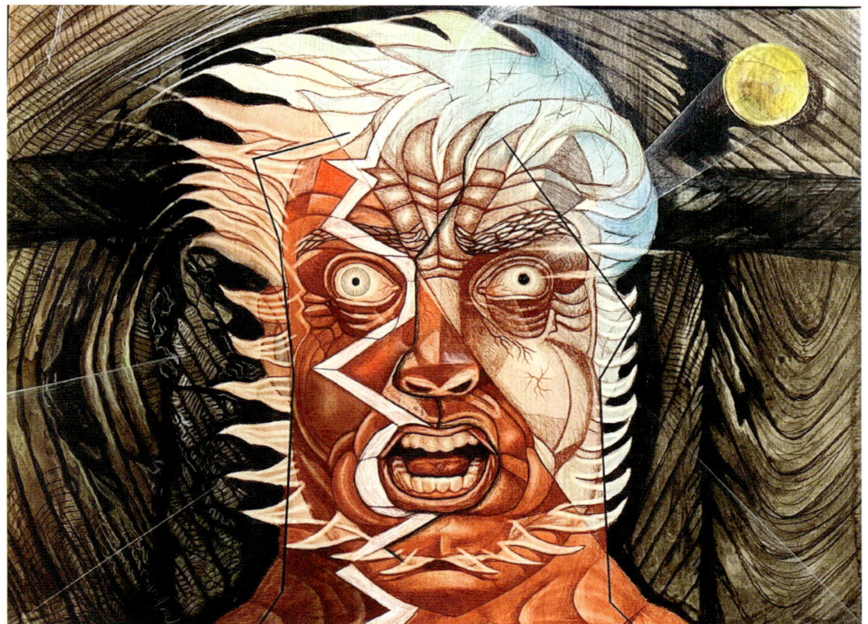

Figure 5.3. Eyeballing madness.
Gilbert Wilson, *Insanity Series #3: I Am Madness Maddened*, c. 1950. Gouache with colored pencil on paper, 21" × 29".

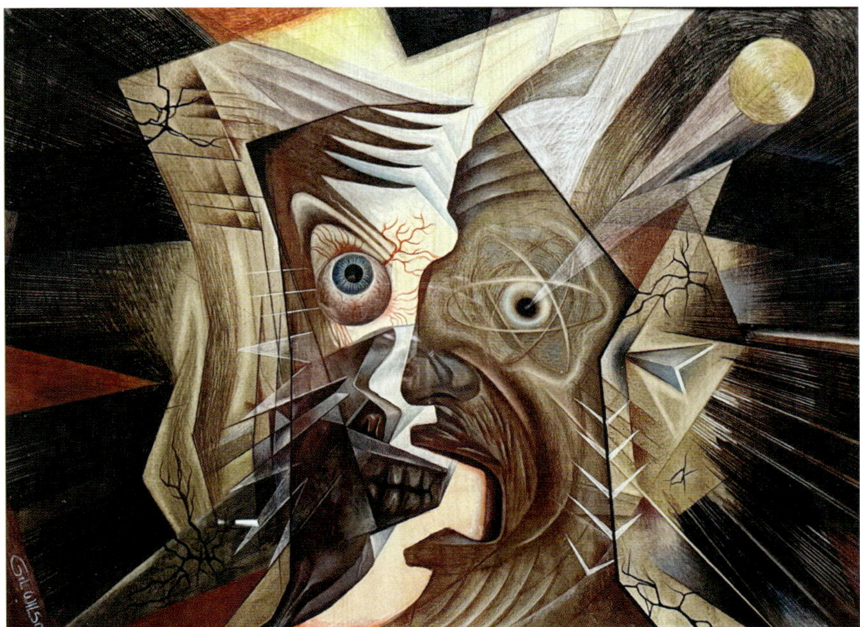

Figure 5.4. The self in fragments.
Gilbert Wilson, *Insanity Series #4: He Who Has Never Felt Madness*, c. 1950. Gouache with colored pencil on paper, 21" × 29".

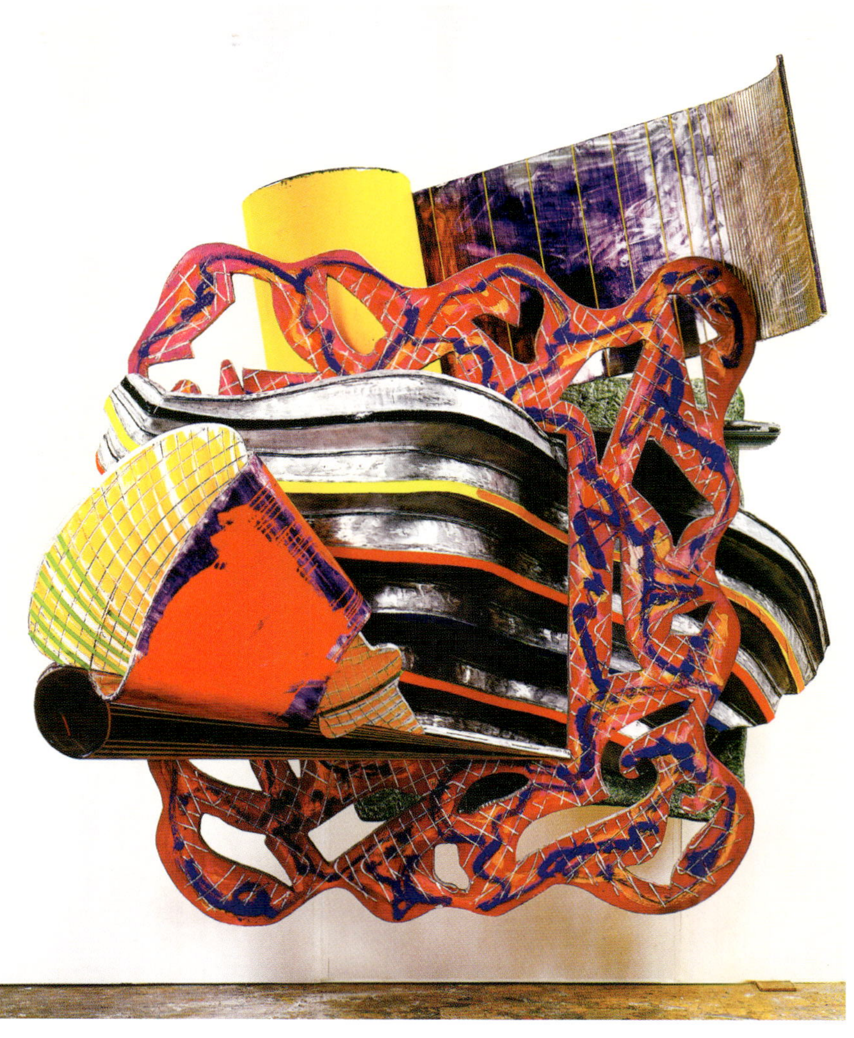

Figure 5.8. Abstraction and shifting perspectives in Stella's bas-reliefs.
Frank Stella, *The Forge (S-10, 3X-2d version)*, 1988. Mixed media on cast aluminum, 97¾" × 95⅝" × 64".

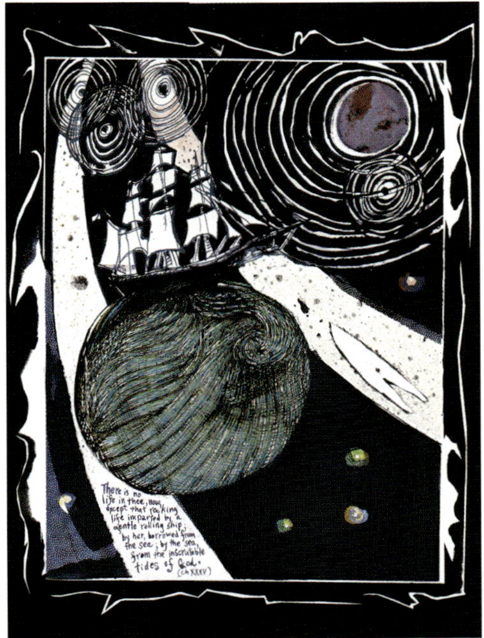

Figure 5.10. The precarity of cosmic voyaging.
Robert Del Tredici, *Inscrutable Tides of God*, 2000. Silkscreen print, 22½" × 30".

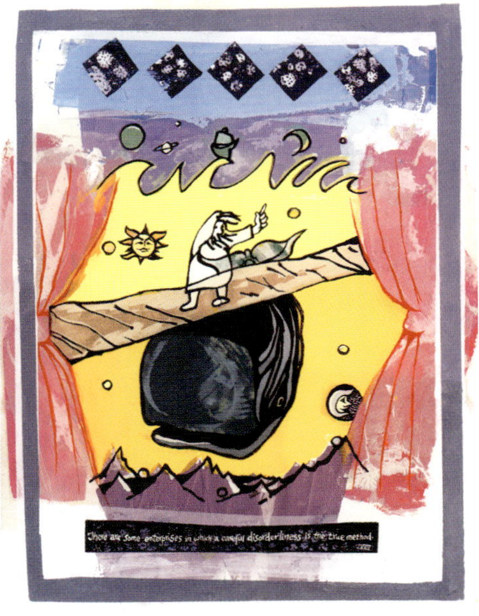

Figure 5.14. Life as a circus act: the comic sublime.
Robert Del Tredici, *Careful Disorderliness*, 2000. Silkscreen print, 22½" × 30".

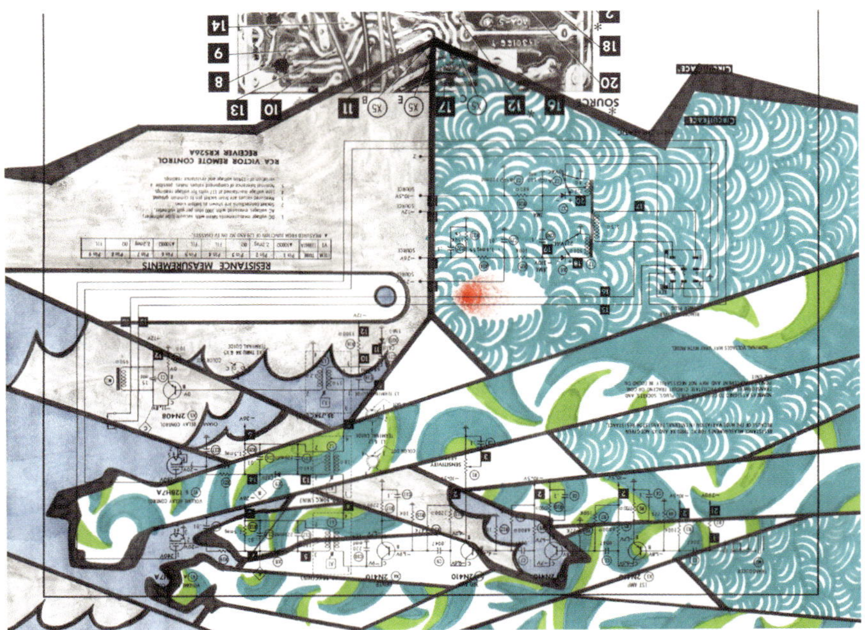

Figure 5.16. A meeting of bodies.
Matt Kish, *He pressed his forehead against mine*, September 25, 2009. Ink and marker on found paper. 11" × 7¾".

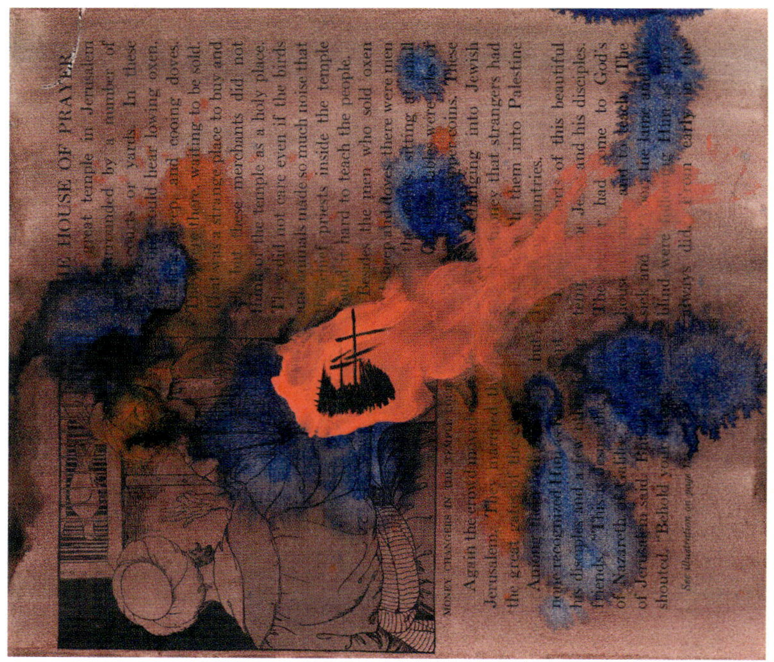

Figure 5.20. Red hell in black night.
Top: Matt Kish, *As the wind howled on, and the sea leaped, and the ship . . . shot her red hell further and further into the blackness*, October 17, 2010. Acrylic paint and ink on found paper, 9" × 7½".

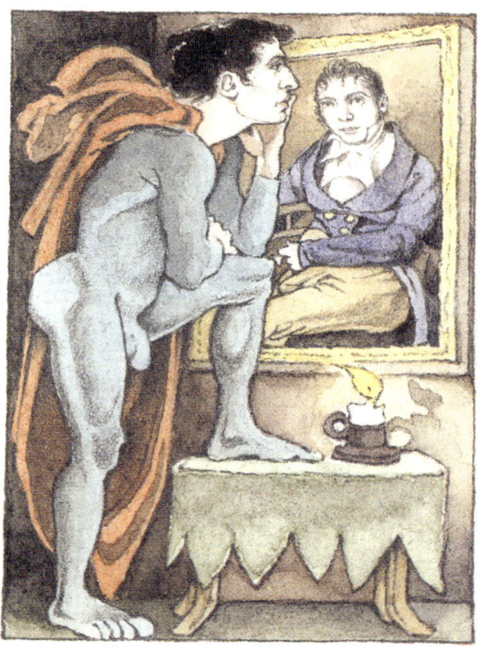

Figure 6.11. Erotic reveries beholding the closet portrait.
Maurice Sendak, *Youth is hot, and temptation strong*, in Melville, *Pierre, or the Ambiguities*, ed. Parker, illus. Sendak, illustration facing p. 119.

CHAPTER 6

PERVERSE MELVILLE AND THE SUB-SUB'S QUEER INVESTMENTS

So if I seem queer to you, be sure, I am not alone in my queerness.
—Melville to Evert Duyckinck, February 12, 1851

Such a provoking perversion of talent.
—*Graham's Magazine*, review of *Pierre*

Nearly all the fictional worlds created by Melville give powerful expression to elements that hover ambiguously between the *perverse* and the *queer.* Scholars today are well aware that attempting to define either term is a notoriously slippery enterprise, whether one considers the words in their historical contexts or their use in theories of psychology and sexuality. But this ability to elude fixed definitions is precisely the quality that Melville's fictional worlds embrace in their excursions into the darker, unruly, indeterminate underbelly of desire, sexuality, subjectivity, and consciousness. And these subterranean channels of the queerly perverse running throughout Melville's canon—in particular those animating *Pierre* (1852) and *Billy Budd* (1924)—have inspired a number of contemporary artists.

If Melvillean perversity has proved a stimulus for recent artists, intimations of its presence did not go unnoticed by many of the author's original readers. Throughout Melville's career, reviewers registered profound unease with what they perceived as a disturbing tendency toward the perverse or "unnatural," sensing the threat to the established order of things portended by these textual undercurrents. Even the early South Sea fictions, where the perverse is displaced to foreign climes, aroused such uneasiness. *Typee* and *Omoo* may have marked a sensational literary debut, but their depictions of islander eroticism nonetheless raised concerns that the author's "prurient" depictions might "imbrut[e]" readers by stimulating "unchaste desires."[1] By the time of *Mardi* and *Moby-Dick*, reviewers were more convinced than ever that Melville's creative imagination, however often it approached the sublime and poetic, not only "perverted" truth but was deeply aberrant in form as well as subject matter.[2] *Pierre* confirmed their worst fears, its undisguised demonstration of strange and estranging writing deemed as "crazy," "loathsome," "monstrously unnatural," "objectionable," and "repulsive" as the author who had imagined its deranged protagonist and themes into being.[3] As a reviewer wrote in *Graham's Magazine*, the novel's exploration of the "phenomena of morbid emotions" signals a "provoking perversion of talent and waste of power" precisely because, as another contemporary commented, it "deviated from the legitimate line of the novelist."[4]

Implicit in such comments is a diagnosis of Melville's self-destructive impulses: Here is a writer of immense talents who can't help but violate moral taboos and aesthetic conventions. Why? Just because they are there to be defied, to be "deviated" from and thus rendered deviant. In a word, Melville falls victim to his imp of the perverse.[5] Moreover, this irresistible urge to do the "wrong" thing precisely because one should not shares affinities, as we will see, with psychoanalysis's theory of the perversions—those instinctual drives that reason barely and not always successfully holds in check. Melville's stubborn, often self-destructive resistance to normative expectations is well known; he himself writes of that "tyranny of an usurper mood" that mysteriously causes one to do what's worst for oneself.[6] Likewise, his fiction gives expression to taboo desires that seem to arise unfiltered from his unconscious, emerging via oblique modes of expression and obfuscating ambiguities. But it is equally true that much of the time Melville is perfectly in control of his "imp of the perverse"; he often seems to relish taunting his readers with these perversities, daring us to acknowledge that the ambiguities at which his prose insistently hints *are* reality.

The general reader might expect *Moby-Dick* to be the Melville work most greatly inspiring artists who channel his embrace of the nonnormative, given its excess of homoeroticism. Interestingly enough, though, until Wu Tsang's *Of Whales* multimedia project in 2023 (taken up in chapter 7), no contemporary artist of note (not including those submitting sketches to sites like DeviantArt .com) has fully "queered" the Ishmael–Queequeg relationship, nor have I found anyone capitalizing on David Leverenz's intriguing assertion, made decades ago, that Ahab is a "flaming queen."[7] The most penetrating and daring reenvisionings of Melvillean perversity, rather, have been reserved for contemporary retellings of *Pierre* and *Billy Budd*, as we will see in this chapter. This, however, doesn't mean that *Moby-Dick* is lacking its share of queer perversities. Two minor yet exemplary instances involve the teasingly coy descriptions of the purported creators of the novel's opening two sections, "Etymology" and "Extracts." A closer look at how the queerly perverse insinuates itself into the portraits of the late grammar school Usher and the Sub-Sub Librarian anticipates the varied uses to which "perverse Melville" is deployed by artists today: as trigger of narrative desire, as point of view, as authorial self-positioning, as formal aesthetics.

The first page of *Moby-Dick* confronts the reader with neither the story of Ahab nor the story of the White Whale but with a page titled "Etymology." A parenthetical line identifies the "Late Consumptive Usher to a Grammar School" as its "supplier" (7). Deceased this "late" Usher may be, but he is immediately, paradoxically resurrected from the dead by an unidentified biographer whose description in the following headnote ("I see him now") freezes the Usher's otherwise forgettable existence into an eternal present. Occupying this liminal space between life and death, between section title and following etymologies, the Usher is relegated to the very margins of being as well as of text in this short notice. So dismissed and diminished (as peripheral, as textual deviation, as "late" in all senses), the "pale" and "threadbare" ghost of a man is rendered even more inconsequential by his employment as a minor school official whose job it is to open doors, announce visitors, tidy up, and dither away the hours "ever dusting" his beloved "lexicons and grammars" (7).[8]

Here is where perversity enters the portrait of this marginal figure. Dotingly attending to moldering books that "mildly" remind him of his own mortality (and whose "dust" likely worsens his consumption), the solitary figure manifests an obsessive-compulsive fixation that is both fetishistic (overinvesting in these seemingly unused and undervalued books) *and* masochistic (devoting himself to unrewarding and, perhaps in his case, deadly labor). To wit, he strikes us as a very queer soul, inhabiting a marginal narrative space that deviates from fictional norms and forestalls the story proper. Melville winks at the Usher's "queerness" in a campy description of the "queer handkerchief," "mockingly" decorated with "all the gay flags" of the world, with which the man lovingly dusts his "lexicons and grammars" (7). Lexicons are dictionaries, and, as Jennifer Doyle remarks, a nineteenth-century slang expression for people in love with pompous dictionary language was "swallowing the dick."[9] Melville's own love of words and wordplay, of "swallowing the dick," is legendary. As such, the fetishized objects of the Usher's care (lexicons or "dicks") anticipate the story of Moby *Dick* himself, a dick-tionary of infinite significations that not only consumes Ahab but "swallows" all signifieds in its destructive wake. The perverse decision to begin *Moby-Dick* with this odd portrait thus foreshadows the deviations and deviancies that proliferate as Ishmael's first-person tale gets underway.

Once is not enough, however, not for Melville's imp of the perverse. The "Etymology" section's disruption of narrative expectations is followed with an even queerer deferral of narrative: an encomium to the "Sub-Sub-Librarian" (8) who provides the section's eighty "extracts." Like the description of the Usher, that of the Sub-Sub verges on camp: extravagantly over-the-top, winking at us without our being sure that we are in on the joke.[10] This "poor devil," delegated to the twice-diminished status of a "mere" "sub" of a *sub*ject, belongs to that "hopeless, sallow tribe" of librarians and book lovers who submit to the ignominy that a "thankless" world heaps on them. Like the Usher, the Sub-Sub is both a fetishist whose objects of desire are books and a masochist who converts his submission to the world that devalues his work into a source of pleasurable pain, a "not unpleasant sadness." "*Give it up*, Sub-Subs!" the Librarian and his suffering brethren are perversely exhorted: "For by how much more *pains* ye take to *please* the world, by so much the more shall ye for ever go thankless!" (8, emphases added). The Sub-Sub, like the Usher, is pale to the point of fading away into nothingness in a mean world where "splintered hearts" hopelessly "strike" at one another; and, as is also the case with the consumptive grammarian, death is figured as this subordinate's only release.

If the Sub-Sub's submission to ignominy ("Give it up . . .!") isn't perverse enough, even queerer is the manner and method by which the man goes about gathering his extracts on whaling. In combing the world's store of books for "whatever random allusions" he may find of whatever "has been promiscuously said, thought, fancied, and sung of Leviathan," he practices a methodology that, as suggested in chapter 1, is quintessentially rhizomatic, for he is figured as a "burrower and grub-worm" haphazardly tunneling his way through "the Vaticans and street-stalls of the earth" (8). In the process, the statements that he assembles "higgledy-piggledy" (8) anticipate the messy mix—of styles, of genres, of modes—that composes Melville's authorial signature, in which the perversion of norms becomes a pleasurable aesthetic in itself. "At least we can promise ourselves that pleasure which is wickedly said to be in sinning, for a literary sin the divergence will be," Melville winkingly says of one such "sinful" digression in *Billy Budd*.[11]

Like the networks of interconnected roots formed by the rhizome, the underground and mazelike tunnels created by "burrower and grub-worm" are potentially endless, creating intersecting and diverging pathways without clear beginning or end. What I would like to emphasize now is the degree to which the concept of the rhizome is evocative of Freud's description of the perversions that teem in the unconscious and drive human desire. In *The Three Essays on the Theory of Sexuality* (1905), Freud famously begins his investigation into the nature of the libido by examining the myriad "deviations" from "what is assumed to be normal" in the psychosexual life. First demonstrating that the libido is initially independent of any particular goal, Freud proceeds to examine "the deviations described as 'perversions'"—sexual activities that involve parts of the anatomy other than those strictly required for copulation, that linger over intermediate zones, or that fixate on substitute objects (as in fetishism). Next, he demolishes the line separating "normal" and "deviant" sexuality by showing that these perversions are almost always *also* present in activities that society deems normative. In other words, one does not *become* a pervert—one *remains* a pervert from birth onward. Having deconstructed conventional assumptions about sexual aims and objects, Freud declares his revolutionary hypothesis—namely, that the sexual instinct is "put together from components which have come apart again in the perversions" because the perversions in their myriad manifestations are "of a composite nature." Later in his analysis, Freud draws on the image of rivers to describe the component instincts; whenever the main channel is blocked, the excess water overflows its banks into any number of tributary channels that have hitherto lain dormant. Analogously, blockages in the subconscious may reactivate perverse dispositions always present but hitherto kept contained by the main river's embankments.[12]

This universal "disposition to perversion" is precisely the truth of human nature that Melville's fictions, through oblique pathways and tributary channels, ambiguous hints, and teasing innuendo, demonstrate time and again. When Melville jestingly writes to his friend Evert Duyckinck, cited as this chapter's first epigraph, "So if I seem queer to you, be sure, I am not alone in my queerness," he is articulating the same insight to which Freud gives expression half a century later in his theory of the instinct or libido: "The disposition to perversion is itself of no great rarity but must form part of what passes as the normal constitution."[13] And the list of the so-called perversions surfacing in Melville's fiction is legion: most notably, "inverted" or same-sex desire (in *Moby-Dick* and *Billy Budd* but also in *Redburn*, *Typee*, and *Clarel*); mother–son, brother–sister, and father–son incest (*Pierre*); narcissism (*Moby-Dick*, *Pierre*); fetishism (from the brown skin of South Sea islanders to the tattooed corpus of Queequeg, from whalebone legs to phallic chimneys, from the Usher and Sub-Sub's overbeloved books to Ishmael's fixation on cetological detail); scopophilia and voyeurism (think of Taji's desire to glimpse behind the veil in *Mardi*); masturbation (the closet "reveries" of *Pierre*; the rapturous sperm-squeezing hands of *Moby-Dick*); transvestism (Goneril's suspect masculinity in *The Confidence-Man*; suppositions about Steelkit's whispered secret in "The *Town-Ho*'s Story" in *Moby-Dick*); pedophilia (the Missouri Bachelor's desire to purchase boys in *The Confidence-Man*); symbolic castration (Ahab's missing limb, Billy's stutter, Pierre's myth of Enceladus); polygamy (South Sea sexuality, the *ménage à quatre* in *Pierre*); sadomasochism (Claggart's rage in *Billy Budd*, the asides on lashing in *White Jacket*); cannibalism (*Typee*, Fleece's shark sermon in *Moby-Dick*).[14]

"Perverse Melville," this chapter's title, thus comes to signify a number of overlapping understandings of perversion. It nods to the psychological imp of the perverse that causes Melville to react against anything normative, even to his detriment; it indicates his intuitive grasp of what Freud theorizes as the component instincts that "have come apart again in the perversions" and the deleterious effects of repression; it encompasses the "sinful" deviations from novelistic convention that subjected Melville to charges of having perverted his talents and, in so doing, of having perverted fictional norms (and potential readers); it suggests transgressive desires that remain taboo not only in culture but within consciousness itself. Finally, "perverse" aptly describes the Melville who takes perverse pleasure in everything that is odd, errant, shoved to the margins, made strange or estranging: the Melville who delights in everything that is, in a word, *queer*—a word that his texts repeat incessantly and with obvious relish.

Melville, of course, wasn't privy to the early twentieth-century rise of the word *queer* to signify homosexuality or to the late twentieth-century revival of the term to indicate a range of nonnormative gendered and sexual dispositions. But the recurrence of *queer* throughout his writings, viewed in tandem with his penchant for libidinally charged language connotating the perverse and the deviant, retrospectively gives Melville's use of the word an uncannily contemporary feel. Note the Carpenter's soliloquy in chapter 108 of *Moby-Dick* as he shapes a new whalebone leg for mad Ahab: "Stubb knows him best of all, and Stubb says he's queer; says nothing but that one sufficient little word, queer; he's queer, says Stubb, he's queer—queer, queer; and keeps dinning it into Mr. Starbuck all the time—queer—sir—queer, queer, very queer. And here's his leg! Yes, now that I think of it, here's his bedfellow! has a stick of whale's jawbone for a wife!" (360–61).

Repeating the word *queer* eleven times, the Carpenter attempts to reassure himself that Stubb's characterization is correct: that this "one sufficient little word" can pinpoint, once and for all, the strangeness that is Ahab. But this attempt at fixity (like Ahab's own attempt to assign definitive meaning to the White Whale) immediately undoes itself as the sheer repetition gives rise to a plethora of possible signifieds, and the linguistic sign dissolves before our eyes.

So too with the Carpenter's repetition of Stubb's repetition: Queerness can't be pinned down—indeed, unfixability is what makes queerness so queer. It's no coincidence that as the Carpenter's ruminations spin out in a veritable stream of consciousness, he moves from this elevenfold repetition to a contemplation of the jawbone leg he's carving—a substitute, in symbolic terms, for Ahab's castrated phallus, the consequence of Moby Dick's having bitten off his leg (an action that intriguingly combines associations of "swallowing the dick" and *vagina dentata*). The Carpenter first figures the stump as Ahab's "bedfellow," then as Ahab's "stick" of a "wife." Through this process of association, the initial iterations of *queer* now attach themselves to the realm of sexual inferences:

oedipal fears of castration by the devouring mother; the homoeroticism latent in bedding with a "bedfellow" (wording that evokes the "heart's honeymoon" shared by Ishmael and Queequeg at the Spouter Inn); and, finally, heterosexual coitus, whose castrating threat is implicit in the identification of "wife" with a bone taken from the sea monster's devouring "jaw." One perversion after another attaches itself, through this process of association, to these assertions of Ahab's "queer" strangeness.

The spectrum running between perversion and queerness forms the space within which several contemporary artist-writers adapt or reenvision Melville. First, I take up James Creech's *Closet Writing/Gay Reading: The Case of Melville's* Pierre (1993). Though a work of literary criticism, Creech's wish-fulfilling recasting of *Pierre* as a gay coming-out novel amounts to an act of creative fiat on par with other artists participating in the Melville effect. In turn, Creech's "rewriting" of the novel depends on multiple media in that his ingenuous interpretation hinges not only on artwork referenced in the text but on other extratextual visual sources—namely, portraits of Melville's father. In the process, Creech's reading of *Pierre* dissolves the boundaries separating fiction and biography, fantasy and desire, past and present. The "perversity of my angle of vision," Creech writes, is "warranted by the far more perverse manner in which Melville smuggled his homoerotic desire into the novel."[15]

Remaking *Pierre* to fit one's desires also lies at the heart of the Melville scholar Hershel Parker's Kraken edition of the novel in 1995, rather deceptively marketed on one website as "Melville's never previously published, original manuscript."[16] In his role as editor turned author, Parker eliminates entire sections that he feels aren't part of the book that Melville originally meant to write; as such, he becomes, like Creech, author of a "new" novel.[17] What interests me most about this Kraken edition, however, is not Parker's amended text—since eliminations rather than creative additions are its principle—but rather the illustrations executed by Maurice Sendak, most well known for his quirky children's books (including one featuring a boy named Pierre). The resulting volume is an inspired example of mixed media in which the illustrations not only create a dialogue with Melville's words but are also in conversation with multiple nineteenth-century visual artists; this palimpsest layering of citations enables Sendak to bring into the realm of the visible a tortured gay subtext far exceeding Melville's printed words.

The elements of mixed media contributing to Creech's and Sendak's "perverse" readings of this novel also pervade the avant-garde French filmmaker Leos Carax's controversial film *Pola X* (1999). The title forms an acronym of the French translation of Melville's title, *Pierre, ou les ambiguities*. And the X? Officially, the Roman numeral indicates the number of drafts Carax wrote before filming; unofficially, it suggests the X rating the film received for its graphic depiction of unsimulated sex. Carax relocates Melville's plot to late twentieth-century France, framed within the politics of East European immigration, the Bosnian War, urban decay, paramilitary cults, and a dying aristocracy. As much a crazy mix of styles and genres as Melville's writings, Carax's heterogenous blend of forms (the pastoral, urban dystopia, surrealism) also includes a veritable concert documentary: industrial-rock cyberpunk musician-terrorists banging out music by the avant-gardist composer Scott Walker. As in the case of Creech, a very personal identification with *Pierre* bleeds into Carax's film adaptation; reading the novel at nineteen (Pierre's age), he immediately made it his "personal testament."[18] This overidentification goes even deeper, as Carax's career arc—early praise followed by midcareer damnation—echoes that of Melville (and, by proxy, that of the fictional Pierre): In defying convention, all three artists find themselves crushed by the homogenizing demands of the marketplace. The blurring of lines between Carax and Melville, film and book, enfant terrible auteur and enfant terrible protagonist render *Pola X* a porous artwork whose overflow evokes Freud's description of the repressed instincts filling subsidiary channels of perverse desire.

Another French director, Claire Denis, provides this chapter's fourth iteration of perverse Melville. Her film *Beau travail* (1999, loosely translated "Good Work") transports the lineaments of the plot of *Billy Budd* to East Africa, where an isolated band of French legionnaires in Djibouti fight out their differences on desert wastes as vast and empty as oceanic expanses with no land in sight. Elliptical in structure, visually poetic, foregoing words for silence, sensuous and unworldly—*Beau travail* has aptly been called a metacommentary on "the labor of adaptation."[19] In addition to its debt to *Billy Budd*, it also self-reflexively extends the "life" of Jean-Luc Godard's earlier film *Le petit soldat* (the actor who played the earlier film's protagonist is cast as Denis's Captain Vere equivalent and bears the name of Godard's character), and it incorporates the score of Benjamin Britten's operatic adaptation of *Billy Budd* (1951/1964) into mesmerizingly choregraphed scenes of the legionnaires' ritualistic exercises, stripped to the waist and glistening with sweat under the relentless sun.[20] This nod to Britten adds a homoerotic intensity that, as in *Billy Budd*, erupts in eroticized violence between Galoup and Gilles, Denis's versions of Claggart and Billy. The result is an unleashing of the polymorphous perverse in Galoup, which is manifested in increasing acts of sadism, frustrated voyeurism, obsessive fixation, delusional projections, and the collapse of life- and death-drives into a final act of mind-blowing cinematic jouissance.

"Give it up!" the Sub-Sub Librarians of the world are admonished, and to differing degrees all the subjects examined in this chapter submit to the erratic flow of the polymorphous energies they find in Melville, and by doing so, they transgress or reformulate the boundaries of genre, be they of scholarly writing, book illustration, or film. Intriguingly, Creech, Sendak, and Carax's strong overidentifications with *Pierre* dissolve the usual lines of demarcation between author and work. This intense degree of identification renders their creations particularly porous, open not only to the overflow of the "perversions" but also to incorporations of the extratextual. Like these men, Denis also identifies

Melville as a spiritual *frère*, but, unlike them, she remains coolly distant from the drama she sets loose before her camera.[21] The powerfully idiosyncratic compulsions and overidentifications apparent in Creech, Sendak, and Carax's authorship are transferred in *Beau travail* to the fluid operations of the film medium itself and to the porous psychic domain of Galoup, whose point of view "authors" the unstable text that the audience views; it is only through Galoup's deeply subjective, unreliable, warped recall that we perceive the hallucinatory events surrounding his confrontation with Gilles, the Billy character. Our senses thus lodged within Galoup's perverse subjectivity, *we* have no choice but to "give it up," give ourselves over to the deluge of intensities, the dissolution of boundaries, the proliferation of ambiguities that mark Denis's achievement and distinguish all four of these explorations of the perverse in Melville.

Pierre's Closet, Creech's Pierre

Pierre, or The Ambiguities is one hot mess, and Melville pulls no punches in piling perversity upon perversity as he conveys the title character's feverish descent into the depths of his psyche in rhetoric and imagery as fervid and frenzied as Pierre's state of mind. Passage after passage makes it clear that Melville is attempting to articulate what Freud would later classify as the unconscious, home to the instinctual drives and desires subliminally motoring conscious action. From the beginning, Pierre senses the presence of transgressive "invisible agencies . . . ye things I have no name for" (37), lying in wait to wreck his world. Soon enough, inchoate "emotions" that have hitherto lain "subterranean in him" begin to stir, taking "hold of the deepest roots and subtlest fibres of his being" (48). The cause? His perversely incestuous attraction to Isabel Banford—the mysterious woman who surfaces out of nowhere, like a forbidden thought, pressing her claim that she is his illegitimate half-sister. Immediately, Pierre loses his bearings, "wandering" (40) in "infernal eternal catacombs of thought" (51), while the "solid land" that previously was his "veritable reality" is invaded by "bannered armies of hooded phantoms, disembarking in his soul, as from flotillas of specter-boats" (49).

This return of the repressed, spectrally arriving by boat, is figured in imagery uncannily evocative of Freud's envisioning of the component instincts as flows of water. Melville writes of the "streams" of unthinkable desire that roll through Pierre's "thought-channels," evanescent "streams of . . . reveries" that leave no "conscious sediment," no conscious recognition of the "alluvial stream" that has come and gone (85). This "thoughtful river," the narrator asserts, is as "unending, ever-flowing," as it is inscrutable to human reason: "These [unconscious biddings] never unravel their own intricacies, and have no proper ending" (141). And the narrator warns that only way to fathom Pierre's subconscious motivations is to follow "the endless, winding way—the river in the cave of man" (107). These libidinal streams also become the nightmarish geography through which Pierre travels in the last act of the novel. Arriving in Manhattan in the middle of a dark night of the soul, he finds himself plunged in a hellish nightscape, wherein the city's main thoroughfare is likened to the mysterious Orinoco (South America's great river, flowing sixteen hundred miles from the Andes to the Atlantic), while its "long, narrow, dismal" side streets (or "side-glooms," as Isabel evocatively calls them) are likened to "thin tributaries" flowing "from the far-hidden places"—places haunted by society's *dejecta*, "sneaking burglars, wantons, and debauchees" (231–32). These collateral channels, now lapping at Pierre's feet, teem with all matter of perversions.

All of this is to say that Melville was profoundly aware of the psychological terrain he was attempting to put into words. What happens when these irrational instincts break through the walls of repression is, in essence, *Pierre*'s story. Even the barest summation of that story reveals the workings of the perverse and the unconscious at every juncture. Ironically, Melville had promised his publisher that he was now writing a "regular romance" calculated for popular appeal, and he described *Pierre* to Sophia Hawthorne as befitting a female readership as a "rural bowl of milk."[22] To the contrary: Although the novel opens in a pastoral setting—Pierre's ancestral estate in the countryside—the perverse is already on the prowl, contaminating every relationship in sight. Not only does Melville's own imp of the perverse impel him to parody the language of sentimental fiction in over-the-top prose hardly designed to win over "female" readers, but the dyad formed by Pierre and his widowed mother also reeks of transgressive eroticism. The narcissistic, domineering Mrs. Mary Glendinning breathes sexual energy; she is a coquette who, despite her years, is confident that her beauty is still capable of attracting "a train of infatuated suitors little less young than her own son" (5). But the "reverential and devoted" (and at this point utterly submissive) Pierre is "lover enough for this widow Bloom" (5), and the two not only overtly flirt with each other in the "lover-like" language of suitors (16) but also "call each other brother and sister" with "that strange license" that intimacy has "long bred between them" (5). The sexual suggestiveness embedded in Melville's word choices—"strange," "license," "bred"—charges this relationship with taboo incestuous energy, and the "brother–sister" banter prepares the reader for the next perverse turn of plot, when Isabel, Pierre's presumed half-sister, mysteriously appears and makes her own overly ardent claim on his affections. Thenceforth, a "strange, mysterious, *unexampled* love" (189, emphasis added) quickly grows between the two: Again, Melville's word choices suggest that more meaning attaches to this "unexampled" ardor than simple sibling devotion.

As Golden Age pastoral gives way to Gothic psychodrama, the plan of action that Pierre proposes to the woman he immediately and without question accepts as kin is downright *queer* in its perverse logic: not only that the two siblings run away and live together but also that they do so as nominal "husband and wife" to protect their bond from the world's calumny. Assuming this disguise in the name of preserving Isabel's purity only opens more floodgates to the illicit, for it gives the siblings' transgressive desires a proper name that allows them to evade their own mental censors. What's really going on, however, reverberates in the charged sensuality with which Melville depicts the pivotal scene in which Pierre unfolds his plan. Evoking Milton's Lucifer pouring temptation into Eve's ear, Pierre's lips sensuously "wet" Isabel's lobe as he "tremblingly" whispers his "strange" proposal with seductive assurance: "I holding thee, thou canst not fall" (193). When, in response, Isabel presses herself into Pierre with the "*inexpressible* strangeness of an intense love, new and *inexplicable*," Pierre's countenance lights with "a terrible self-revelation." The "burning kisses" and fervid embraces that ensue culminate in the serpent imagery Melville has borrowed from *Paradise Lost*: "They coiled together, and entangledly stood *mute*" (193, emphases added). Not only is the degree of explicitness with which the scene depicts this sexual "fall" striking, but so too is the way that the words *inexpressible*, *inexplicable*, and *mute* illustrate the mind's (Pierre's, Isabel's, the contemporary reader's) ability to censor or evade by not naming the "mute" desires nonetheless being communicated.

Intriguingly, by the time Pierre and Isabel leave the country for the city as man and wife, the dyad has morphed into a ménage à trois as they've decided to take a seduced dairymaid, Delly, with them; this threesome becomes a *ménage à quatre* when Pierre's fiancée, the angelic Lucy Tartan, defies social convention by joining the group in the city. Her desire that Pierre introduce her to the world as his "cousin" only extends the ripple effects of the incestuous currents first set into motion by mother and son parading as "brother and sister," then by brother and sister parading as "husband and wife," and now former lovers parading as blood relatives. The more Melville explores the inscrutabilities of instinctual desire, the more queerly perverse his novel becomes. This sliding scale of incestuously figured relations occurs in tandem with a swarm of adjacent perversions: narcissism, autoeroticism, fetishism, sadomasochism, psychic self-mutilation, and homoeroticism (the boy Pierre's "much more than cousinly attachment" to his cousin Glen). As Pierre becomes prey to increasing delusions of grandeur and solipsistic enclosure in his tormented thoughts, his psychological state deteriorates, and his final acts of homicide and suicide bring the novel to an abrupt, grisly end. Pastoral romance deviates into haunting Gothic that becomes a Dantean descent into the lurid "night-world" of Manhattan, detouring into urban documentary and satire of the literary marketplace until, in this final twist, morphing into Jacobean revenge tragedy and a melodramatic bloodbath. This frantic narrative careening between genres and formats is as formally perverse and perversely executed as the ultimately unhinged plot. Melville may begin in control of his imp of the perverse, working perversity to his own ends, but one cannot help but wonder whether by the time he completes *Pierre* the imp is in control of the writer. The reviewer for the *Washington National Era* was not wrong when he wrote, "Mr. M. has evidently taken hold of a subject which has *mastered him*, and led him into all manner of vagaries."[23]

Give it up, Mr. M!, one might imagine the Sub-Sub-Librarian roasting his creator.

Out of this textual surplus of polymorphous perversities run amok, the literary scholar James Creech discerns a substratum or counterplot in which Melville's camp rhetorical stratagems both conceal and winkingly inscribe a clandestine gay story. What is remarkable about Creech's *Closet Writing/Gay Reading*—hailed as "remarkable," "brilliant," "scintillating," and "exhilarating"—is the degree to which it is not solely literary criticism.[24] Its writing style and method presage what is now called "autotheory," in which the interweaving of personal narrative and criticism becomes a method for formulating theory at large. In addition to its functions as literary analysis, memoir, and critical theory, *Closet Writing* is also an act of creative fiat, writing into existence the "gay" novel that Creech argues Melville could only suggest in coded language. The result of Creech's rewriting gives us a new novel, a new *Pierre*, altogether.

Underlying his entire enterprise, Creech confides, was an intuition that he couldn't shake: "my unbidden but overwhelming sense that *Pierre* was, not to put too fine a point on it, a gay novel."[25] This gut reaction persists, despite a training in deconstruction and Foucault that warns him against making identarian, anachronistic claims. And it persists despite the fact that *Pierre* is the least obvious of Melville's novels in which to look for homoeroticism, given its pretense of being a sentimental domestic fiction in which women, romance, and marriage figure prominently. In face of these obstacles, Creech's intention remains that of "*restor*[*ing*] the repressed to its *rightful* place within the work" (26, emphases added) and figuring out how to do so without being accused of theoretical naivete or reductiveness.

His solution, ultimately, is to "*augment*" Melville's text "by *retrieving content* [Melville] had only the option of either encoding *or omitting*" (45, emphases added). "Augmenting," I want to stress, is not simply an act of interpreting or attempting to make sense of a complicated work of literature. By providing what isn't there—"omit[ted]" content—as well as restoring and "retrieving" what is hidden to its "rightful" place, Creech's reading fundamentally re-creates *Pierre*. This ambition is spelled out in a rousing manifesto: "We must make [the homoerotic] speak where it is silenced, and we must answer back where it manages, despite everything, to speak" (45). Creech "speaks" and "answers back" with the passion of a defiantly gay reader-writer, filling in the gaps created by textual "omission" and "silence" with a narrative in which Pierre emerges as a gay man.

Creech's creative effort succeeds, by and large, giving us a *Pierre* that we never before glimpsed. Creech achieves his goal by defending the productive roles that personal identification and projective fantasy may play in teasing out the homoeroticism closeted in nineteenth-century fiction.[26] By acknowledging his erotic response to a text like *Pierre*—"owning up to my practice of identificatory reading for minoritizing, or full, homosexual meaning" (47)—Creech suggests that the act of projecting contemporary "homosexual" desires onto past literatures, however anachronistic in terminology or as identity construction, may in fact bring into clearer focus the hermeneutic codes that authors such as Melville found to be their only means of expressing prohibited sexual feelings.[27] This method of encoding, Creech argues, approximates modern understandings of camp sensibility, which, following Susan Sontag, "*identifies with* what it is enjoying," winking at those who share similar feelings. Like camp, Melville's hermeneutic code, states Creech, "is designed to produce . . . a discriminatory effect of recognition and collusion among readers open to the wink" (111). By undertaking to "perform a camp reading" of *Pierre*, Creech accepts his position as "the novel's right narratee," the empathetic reader to whom Melville, consciously and unconsciously, has directed his wink.

Closet Writing not only opens the way for retrieving a "gay *Pierre*" but also provides a personal narrative of Creech's evolution as a critic who is also a gay-identified man. In an epilogue evocatively titled "Essaying in a Different Voice," Creech explains his growing desire to "to read and write as the gay man I am": whence this attempt to try or "essay" a "different voice" in scholarly writing "that would bear some resemblance to the life behind the work" (186). "This is Creech's 'coming-out' book," Caleb Crain declares, pointing to this autobiographical element.[28] Or, as Neill Matheson notes in a thoughtful review essay, one of the book's most dazzling aspects is the degree to which Creech has made his academic coming-out story *converge with* the personal coming-out narrative that he attributes to Pierre/*Pierre*: "His unambiguous claim for Pierre's gay identity is simultaneously an avowal of a whole [critical] approach no longer in conflict with his own sexual identity."[29] Looking back on his intellectual history, Creech frankly addresses his growing unease as a gay man with the poststructuralist methods of analysis in which he had been trained. Such methods, based on meaning's ultimate unknowability, undecidability, and difference, made it impossible for Creech to avow his identification with a *specific* difference—same-sex desire—in texts that resonated deeply with him. Coming to grips with this "not-very-happy [intellectual] history beyond which I felt it was time to move" (186), Creech began to explore the possibilities of erotic identification and projection as a productive rather than reductive means of "gay reading," and this theoretical turn underpins the "gay novel" that Creech restores and augments in his reading of *Pierre*.

Foremost, the counterplot of this "gay *Pierre*" hinges on Creech's bold declaration that "the novel's incest theme may be a Trojan horse for homosexual meaning" (88). That is, the overt intimations of mother–son and brother–sister incest smuggle a disguised homoeroticism right into "the very heart of the bourgeois family"—whose structure is organized around the Oedipus complex and its heterosexual incest taboo. In essence, one transgressive perversion (incest) masks and gives oblique voice to another (same-sex desire). The logical chain that emerges as Creech methodically decodes Melville's "winks" forms a remarkably convincing narrative whole. This queer narrative begins with Pierre's odd mourning of the "one hiatus" (7) or omission marking his otherwise halcyon upbringing, his desire for a sister—which is odd because, as Creech points out, the youth's *actual* loss and source of mourning involves his father, who died (as did Melville's father) when he was twelve. The "loneliness" of being "companioned by no surnamed *male* Glendinning but the duplicate reflected to him in the mirror," Pierre now admits, is "still stranger" than "the strange yearning" for a sister (7, emphasis added). As Creech rightly notes, the "shift to desiring a sister is, then, an unmotivated gender leap in the object of Pierre's homoerotic yearning" (117). And underlying this yearning, Creech adduces, is an intensely incestuous homosexual desire, manifested first in the son's erotic fixation on his absent father and culminating in the "transvested incarnation of the father" (155) in Isabel, who claims to be his father's illegitimate offspring. Having made the decision to abjure all ties and cast his lot with this half-sister, Pierre speaks a truth when, even within a nineteenth-century understanding of the term *queer*, he declares, "I look rather queerish, sweet Isabel, do I not?" (188).

Pierre's literal closet, fascinatingly, becomes the privileged site where the homoerotic valences of this "queerish" desire become legible. In this locked little room off his bedchamber, Pierre hides a banished portrait depicting his father while still "a brisk, unentangled young bachelor, gayly ranging up and down the world, light-hearted, and a very little bladish, perhaps, charged to the lips," sitting in his chair "lightly, and as it were airily . . . or rather flittingly" (72–73). "Flitting" and "bladish," "airy" and "unentangled": A dandy's sensuality and knowingness suffuse the rakish portrait and Melville's rakish prose alike. Just as Melville's sexual encoding in general works simultaneously to reveal and to hide its forbidden content, so too does this mesmerizing portrait. For, as Pierre stands gazing in a reverie (Melville's neologism is "trancedly") at the image, sometimes for hours and sometimes "all day long," his father's "ardent" face and "unchastened" gaze tease the youth with ambiguities: If sometimes Pierre feels "as if there were nothing concealed" in his father's look, sometimes it seems, "*yet again, a little ambiguously and mockingly, as if winking*" (80, emphases added). Why has this portrait been banned from public view? First, Pierre's father, upon viewing the portrait, fears it might too candidly "publish" (79) to the world his innermost secrets (including his premarital, clandestine love affair with Isabel's foreign mother); second, Pierre's mother abhors the portrait because it so openly hints at sexual desires preexisting their marriage and thus excluding her.

Pierre, in contrast, is not only transfixed by the portrait's hints of transgressive sexuality but *attracted to* his father's "bodily form of rare manly beauty" (131). This attraction is manifested in the youth's trances before the portrait, which, as Creech decodes, have all the markings of masturbatory reverie, in which Pierre is egged on by the come-hither saliences he *projects onto* his father's gaze. "Look again," he imagines the portrait speaking to him. "Consider this *strange, ambiguous* smile . . . this *too ardent* and, as it were, *unchastened* light in these eyes. . . . Youth is *hot* and *temptation* strong" (131, emphases added). In effect, the father's imagined voice is offering his image up, in a blazon of erotic language, to Pierre's delectation: "Probe a little, Pierre. Never fear, never fear. . . . Probe, probe a little, see, there seems one little crack there, Pierre, a wedge, a wedge" (84). As Pierre alternately (actively) "probes" and (passively) "throw[s] himself open" to these "ineffable hints," he starts up from "these reveries and trances" with a masturbator's guilt, "upbraiding himself for his self-indulgent infatuation" and promising himself he'll "never again fall into" midnight reveries (84–85) before the seductive chair portrait. A "fall into" incestuous homoerotic desire—flooding this locked closet space—is the secret concealed in full sight, barely masked by the novel's overt plot of incestuous heterosexual desire.

The next, ingenious turn in Creech's gay re-creation of the novel's perverse currents involves the way this eroticized portrait gives birth to a transgendered and transcoded realization of Pierre's homoerotic desires—the sister, Isabel—that in turn spurs Pierre to forgo his solitary onanistic reveries, leave his closet behind, and at last "embrac[e] the homosexual object in the flesh," as Creech puts it (167). This development in Creech's "counterplot" pivots, quite brilliantly, on his incorporation of an extratextual source that erodes the divide not only between art and life but also between modes of media, blending visual art with Melville's fictional writing. In the novel, two portraits of the Glendinning father are described: the clandestine chair portrait of Pierre's closet and an official portrait of the man in his patriarchal, married prime, proudly displayed in the drawing room at Saddle Meadows. As Creech's research reveals, *both* fictionalized portraits have real-life correspondences in two existing portraits of *Melville's* father; real and fictional portraits match to the last detail. Simultaneously, another boundary, that separating *critic* and fictional protagonist, dissolves, for in a "meta-Melvillean twist," as Caleb Crain notes, *Creech's* meditation on the *actual* chair portrait of Melville's father repeats Pierre's own meditation on *his* father's portrait: Creech has become Pierre attempting to decipher the portrait's secret.[30]

In this act of imaginative merger, Creech finds the "key" that cinches his homoerotic counternarrative by placing the novel's passages describing the chair portrait against his own observations of John Rubens Smith's portrait of Allan Melville, now housed in the Metropolitan Museum of Art (figure 6.1).[31] The results of this side-by-side scrutiny are revelatory. Take the ambiguous wording that describes Pierre "standing guard, as it were, before the mystical tent of the picture; and ever watching the strangely concealed light of the meanings that so mysteriously moved to and fro within" (85). Figuring the picture as a "mystical tent" seems inexplicable unless we consider it in light of the larger military metaphor at work, implicit in the description of Pierre "*sentineling* his own little closet" and "*standing guard*" before this "tent." Army tents are made of canvas, oils are painted on canvas, hence the metaphoric link. Consider one further passage as Pierre discerns the hidden resemblances between the portrait and Isabel's features: "Painted before the daughter was conceived or born, like a dumb seer, the portrait still seemed leveling its prophetic finger at that empty air, from which Isabel did finally emerge" (197). Taken on the level of prose, the referent of "that empty air" would seem to be the future in which Isabel will magically appear as a player in Pierre's life.

So far, so good. But when Creech links these prose details to the visual elements of the actual portrait, a whole new level of meaning inundates the text. In Smith's portrait of Allan Melville, a "prophetic finger" is indeed pointing, discretely leveled in the direction of the sitter's crotch (figure 6.2). The detail that rivets Creech's eye is described as "a bulging fold in the breeches which produces a clear, ithyphallic form. As an extraordinarily exaggerated fold in the breeches of a seated man, created by the downward pressure of the forearm posed laterally just above the site, this blousing bulge would ordinarily be perceived as an empty fold which the artist must have intended as innocent sartorial realism" (140). Recall the novel's figuration of the picture's "mystical tent," under whose canvas cover "mysterious" meanings move "to and fro," and recall Melville's description of the "prophetic finger" leveled at "that empty air, from which Isabel did emerge." The implications are uncannily queer: The invisibly tented or concealed phallus upon which Pierre longingly gazes becomes the fount of his newborn object of desire, the living Isabel. Yet this embodied object of desire is a cipher, a mystery, her own ambiguities concealed behind her surface, as the erotically cascading dark veil of hair so often obscuring her appearance connotes.

This equation of Isabel and phallus makes us reconsider Melville's wording when Pierre, clandestinely meeting Isabel to hear her story, accepts her as sister: "Pierre, have no reserves, this being is thy sister; *thou gazest on thy father's flesh*" (112, emphases added). Overtly, *flesh* appears to be a synonym for *offspring*. But in light of the winkingly phallic connections Creech has traced among Pierre's autoerotic reveries, the portrait's suggestion of the father's phallus, and the emergence of a new incestuous desire from that "exaggerated fold" in the breeches, the word *flesh* might also be taken literally. As Creech puts it, the father's "much desired 'flesh'" has been "displaced onto and incarnated in the person of Isabel" (155) as symbolic bearer of the desired phallus. Like Proust's Albertine, Creech concludes, Isabel is a literary instance of "a direct transgender encoding" (118), and, as "transvested incarnation of the father," her being

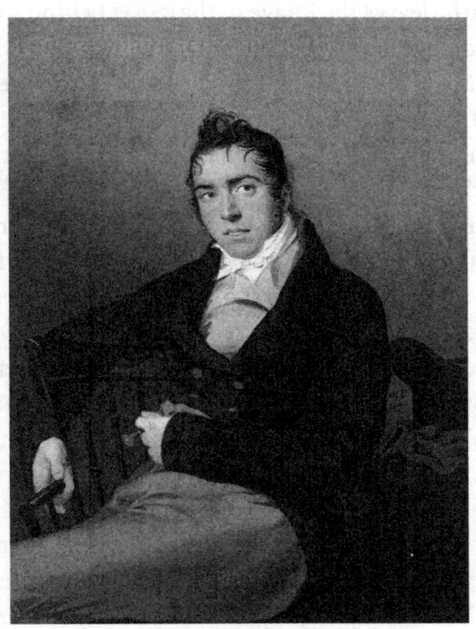

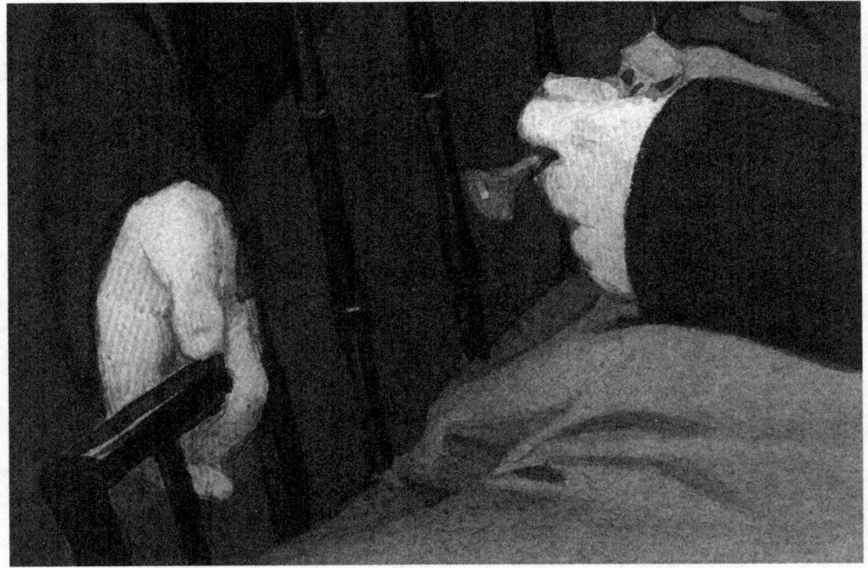

Figures 6.1 and 6.2. The chair portrait and detail.
Top: John Rubens Smith, *Allan Melville*, 1810. 8⅞" × 6¾". *Bottom*: Detail of the "blousing bulge."

Source: Metropolitan Museum of Art, Bequest of Charlotte E. Hoadley, 1946. Obj. no. 46.192.40. Met Open Access.

allows Pierre, once he leaves the image in the closet behind for the "real" thing, "to embrace the homosexual object in the flesh" (167).

Let's return to Melville's winking reference to the "strangely concealed light of . . . meanings" stirring within the "mystical tent" and "empty air" that Creech associates with the father's phallus. One might rephrase this to say that—following the logic of the closet—what is hidden or "concealed" is simultaneously revealing itself, coming to "light" to display its "meanings" in its very concealment. Earlier in the novel, the narrator raises the unsettling thought that one's innermost secrets may not be as secret as one fondly believes, for the "casket" protecting these treasures may "be picked and desecrated at the merest stranger's touch, when we think that we alone hold the only and chosen key" (69). Ironically, the actual portrait of Allan Melville, as Creech points out, contains a *literal* key. While one arm of the sitter is "loungingly thrown over the back of the chair" (*Closet Writing*, 72) in which he sits—this is the left arm from which the "prophetic finger" points toward his crotch—the right arm conspicuously toys with a watch seal and key dangling above the sitter's lap. The observer who catches Herman's wink thus becomes the "stranger" who holds the interpretive "key" to these secrets and whose "touch"—"prob[ing] a little," just as Pierre imagines his father commanding him to do—picks the "chosen lock" in the passage by linking it to the visible lock in Smith's portrait. Once again, through these perverse relays, the typically discrete boundary between fictional text and extratextual artifact gives way, one object's partial meanings flowing into and informing the other object in a "to and fro" movement that blurs the line between printed word and painting, between fiction and biography, between reader and text. What has been unlocked, in Creech's gay reading, is a surplus of queer meaning that cannot be contained, that spills over the dams of prescribed norms.

Thus, the decisive moment in Creech's "gay *Pierre*" occurs when the protagonist leaves his closet behind and burns the portrait that he has hitherto worshipped in "guilty thralldom," as Creech puts it, "stuck in an impossible mourning and desire" (146). The portrait, Pierre now realizes, is just surface, a two-dimensional illusion created by paint, whereas Isabel offers him the father's "flesh" in its three-dimensional materiality. This destruction of the portrait, Creech adds, removes the very "keystone of the novel's closet structure" and enacts a "decisive rejection of every virtue enshrined in the patriarchal order of the bourgeois family" (165, 167). In siding with his illegitimate sister's claims against those of his mother and his fiancée, Lucy, and, indeed, against his entire upbringing, argues Creech, Pierre liberates himself from "the whole compromise structure of family life"—the Oedipus complex and incest taboo—"that the closet enabled" (168) by leaving it behind.

Defiant rebel that Pierre now believes himself to be, freed from social convention or taboo to act on his (homo)erotic desire through his illicit relationship with the transcoded and transgendered Isabel, he declares his intention, upon arriving in New York, to become a serious writer who will "gospelize the world anew. . . . I will write it, I will write it!" (273). The subject of this promised tome, Creech believes, is "the illicit, erotic passion which he has made the new center of his life" (172).[32] But, paradoxically, the freedom he thinks he's found in leaving one closet only ushers another into being. This, in essence, is the paradoxical logic of the closet; coming out only attests to the ubiquity of the closet, its power to proscribe and prohibit. Most overtly, of course, Pierre's illicit incestuous relationship with Isabel is disguised as marriage of husband and wife. But, more pervasively, as the rest of the plot demonstrates, patriarchal and homosocial culture will not allow Pierre's desires to exist openly: With cousin Glen's appearance in New York as Pierre's double and rival, Creech points out, "the homosocial norm thus returns to destroy something unacceptable" (173). Having rejected one closet, Pierre attempts to escape into another private space—his writing chamber, tellingly figured as a "lonely little closet" and a "fatal closet" (339, 346). Trapped in the solipsistic confines of his unorthodox, antisocial thoughts and his increasing rage against the world's hypocrisies and lies, the would-be writer churns out page after page of a "gospel" that is unreadable—his publisher decries it as trash—and that will remain unread—the publisher refuses to print it—because the world refuses to grant transgressive sexuality any social legibility. Pierre's gospel must remain "closet writing." In a metatextual wink, Melville acknowledges the same about his own gospel (Creech's "gay *Pierre*") when he says of Pierre's authorial efforts, "*Two books are being writ, of which the world shall only see one*, and that the bungled one. The larger, and the infinitely better, is for Pierre's own private shelf" (304, emphasis added). In Melville's saying as much, Creech avows, "Melville publishes that he is publishing secrets" (174), with the "gay" version of his novel remaining on the private shelf. Such textual winks and encoding are as explicit as the author can be when writing of desires granted no legitimacy or legibility in his world.

Neill Matheson offers his own superb reading of Creech's reading in a lengthy review essay in *Diacritics*. While he salutes with admiration Creech's "bravado" and "willingness to dispense with caution" in following through on his surmises, he also points out some ways in which Creech's hypotheses may overlook "interpretative problems." To the extent that we read *Closet Writing* as *literary* analysis, I tend to agree with Matheson, but what such criticism underlines for me is the degree to which Creech's most outstanding achievement is, indeed, a *creative* act of imagination, a mesmerizing rewriting of the novel he imagines Melville as being unable fully to write. Some of Matheson's points, however, are worth mentioning. One has to do with the way Creech, in attaching the Allan Melville portrait to the text, "locat[es] *a* very specific and loaded visual referent" for all of *Pierre*'s ambiguities and Pierre's forbidden desires in one concrete object: "the father's penis." While the evidence of the pointing finger convinces me that Melville is consciously encoding a phallic innuendo into his prose, coded language to which only he (as possessor of the actual portrait) has access, I, too, am struck by Creech's exorbitant enthusiasm at this point in his reading. Yes, I can see what might be a fold in the father's breeches, but whether it is the "blousing bulge" or the "extraordinarily exaggerated" shape that Creech claims it to be is rather questionable: Creech may be the one who is exaggerating here, at least as far as size goes.

Matheson makes a related point about Creech's phallic emphasis. Pierre speaks repeatedly of a "peculiar trait" (teasingly left unidentified) in the portrait that father and Isabel share: "Isabel had inherited one peculiar trait nowhither traceable but to [the portrait]" (196). Creech claims that Melville has "indicated [this singular trait] in . . . [t]he portrait['s]" representation of and the text's reference to the pointing finger leveled at the father's crotch, concluding that "the inherited trait is the phallus itself" (145). Creech hedges a bit here. On the one hand, he suggests that "Isabel is a masturbatory fantasy come true" for Pierre precisely because "she share[s] the phallic trait with the portrait . . . making her the incarnation of the homoerotic object" (146) that hitherto has been the focus of Pierre's gaze; on the other, he never goes so far as to say that the "transvested" Isabel is, in fact, a male in disguise. Matheson correctly notes that Creech ignores the narrator's comment that this singular feature is "visible in the countenance of Isabel," meaning that it must be a facial resemblance. But Matheson, too, overreaches in claiming that, "for Creech, this shared trait is literal, identifiable, specifically phallic: Isabel has a *penis*. . . . Her possession of the peculiar trait identifies her as *biologically actually male*."[33] Creech never states that Isabel is actually a man disguised as a woman; for all his suggestiveness, Isabel is for Creech a transvested projection of desire who, whatever her embodied form, remains in Lacanian terms the "bearer of the phallus," ever present and ever absent.

Two additional points made by Matheson are relevant here. In building the case that Pierre's burning of the portrait and choice of the father's "flesh" made manifest in Isabel are signs of his "coming out," Creech overlooks the potential homosexual panic that may simultaneously mark Pierre's act of choosing Isabel over the father. On first meeting Isabel, Pierre is simply struck with the way that the enticingly subtle expression in his father's image "intermarryingly blend[s]" with some "foreign feminineness" in Isabel (112). But now, the "certain lurking lineament" (197) that he has discerned in both appears in the father's portrait to be "loathsome," "detestable," and "repugnan[t]," whereas the same feature in Isabel seems "sweeter" and "nobler" (196). Pierre's turn to Isabel and his sudden disgust at the portrait seem ambivalent at best, homophobic at worst. Might he be turning to a heterosexual object of desire out of homosexual panic and self-loathing? Matheson's second point concerns Melville's larger questioning of fixed identity. The protagonist of Creech's reimagined "novel" is at heart a gay man who, despite his lack of a vocabulary for his same-sex desires, comes to identify himself, in today's parlance, as homosexual. I agree with Matheson, however, that rather than *securing* an identity, Pierre's embrace of the perverse assures that his identity, like everyone else's, *unravels*—the ambiguity of identity, indeed, lies at the heart of Melville's novel, as its subtitle implies. And one result of this struggle to "know," to unravel imponderable mysteries, is an unleashing of destructive inner forces that can't be attributed solely to the repressive forces of institutionalized heterosexual conformity.[34]

In a word, what I've been calling the perverse lies as much at the heart of the erotic ambivalences that wreak havoc in this novel as does the homoerotic, for the homoerotic is just one among its many manifestations. Creech's construction of a "gay *Pierre*," however enlightening, comes at the expense of acknowledging the sheer range and play of instincts and urges that flood this novel specifically and, as Melville was intuitively aware, human nature more generally. Perhaps the novel's most radical move, Matheson writes, lies in its "blurring of the distinction between sexual and nonsexual relationships, and a corresponding expansion of the erotic."[35] Such blurring and expansion are also functions of the polymorphous perverse in all its unfixity and range. In the process of attempting to evoke this realm, indeterminacy itself becomes erotically charged, as Melville's "strange" language, oblique approaches, and errant plotting in *Pierre* demonstrate.

If Creech overlooks some of *Pierre*'s perversities to make space for his gay reading, the payoff is nonetheless immense. At the most basic level, his take on Melville's deployment of the incest motif simply feels right: "Converting homosexual desire into incestuous desire allow[s Melville] at a minimum, to preserve homoerotic feeling, feeling which still remains palpable behind the disguise" (122). At its most ambitious, Creech's "gay *Pierre*" is an astonishing demonstration of creative fiat—in essence, Creech has imagined into being a new version of the novel, one equal to other artworks spawned by today's Melville effect. Any reader who revisits *Pierre* after having read Creech's reenvisioning, I wager, will discover a text they never before knew existed.

Sendak and Pierre's "Pierre"

Bringing the homoerotic subtexts of *Pierre* to the surface is also Maurice Sendak's mission in illustrating the 1995 Kraken edition of Melville's novel. This edition is notorious for Hershel Parker's drastic textual excisions, resulting in what he avers is "a reconstruction" of "the original" manuscript that Melville presented to his publishers in January 1852. In Parker's surmise, the demeaning terms of the publishers' contract led the author to add the scathing passages about the publishing industry in the last third of the novel, where the reader belatedly learns that Pierre is an author whose attempts to write the "truth" are savaged by an industry geared to profit and public tastes. In deleting all these sections (some 13 percent of the text), Parker claims his edition restores the novel to its original unity. But Parker's conjectures raise as many problems as they attempt to solve. First, without documentary evidence, there is no way to establish Melville's "intentions." Second, any attempt to pinpoint origins or originals is doomed to fail (indeed, *Pierre*'s narrator states that there are no proper beginnings or endings, either to life or to fiction, for the "profounder emanations of the human mind . . . never unravel their own intricacies" [141]). Third, as John Bryant asserts, "all editions interpret," but Parker's desire to impose a more streamlined coherence on the novel runs counter to Melville's own unconventional aesthetics: "Melville often broke with conventional novelistic practices, made late additions to his texts, and digressed in his fictions to discuss fiction . . . and of course these 'botches' are what make Melville so compelling."[36]

If Parker's emended *Pierre* thus betrays a fondness for textual unity, based on the assumption that everything seamlessly "fits" within a well-written text's form, Maurice Sendak's artwork champions the novel's deconstructive spirit by prying those seams apart. Foremost, Sendak makes *Pierre* a point of departure for a highly personal meditation on the trauma, among other horrors, of growing up gay in the late twentieth century. Reenvisioning the novel for his contemporary present, Sendak, like Creech, taps into the novel's latent homoeroticism. But where Creech inserts a reconstructed "gay Pierre" back *into* Melville's fiction, Sendak creates a Pierre who *also* stands *outside* the text: a visual allegory charting the plight of gay men at the height of the AIDS crisis.[37] Nor do Sendak's thirty-two renderings function like book illustrations in any traditional sense.[38] Rather, Sendak's intra- and intertextual visual encounter with Melville records a dialogue of similarly attuned minds: "A great artist illustrating a great writer is an event in and of itself, but in this case," Bryant explains, "the event is not just the visualization of a text; it is an artist [Sendak] finding revealing explaining himself in response to a writer [Melville] who was finding . . . explaining himself" equally revealing. Emerging from this "doubly interpretive venture," Sendak's illustrations "achieve their own Melvillean aesthetic"—the inspiration is Melville's, but the result is Sendak's own.[39] This relation between Melville and Sendak, as Dana Seitler demonstrates, is also a radical form of erotic attachment, one in which the artist reactivates the past—here, his response to *Pierre*—as "a queer form of relation in the present," one whose "associative, non-empirical, joining together" creates "a potential history" whose queer energies exist in its "potential unfolding."[40] Reactivating the past in the present, Sendak's illustrations enact, as Seitler suggests, a new way of doing queer historiography; such reactivations are intrinsic to today's Melville effect, whether its remediations are explicitly queer or not.

Melville's influence on Sendak began when Sendak avidly started collecting first editions and other Melville memorabilia in his twenties. In an interview published four years before the Kraken edition's appearance, Sendak identifies Melville as a "guide" and "grappling spirit" reaching "all the way through my growing life," inspiring him "to try to come to grips with the thing in your work that has eluded you before." As a painter, Sendak loves "surfaces that are skins that conceal something else," a commonality attracting him to Melville, where the elusive always lurks beneath the surface.[41] Beginning with the publication of *Where the Wild Things Are* (1965), the consistent subtext of Sendak's children's books has been the trauma faced by youngsters forced to cope with a threatening world on their own. This nightmare of childhood is alleviated only by the child's inner resources of irony, fantasy, and imagination. In the *Pierre* illustrations, Sendak goes a step further, visualizing the trauma of growing up—or, perhaps more accurately in Pierre's case, the *failure* to grow up, adapt to the rules of the adult world, accommodate its hypocrisies.

Despite Melville's role as "a great model," Sendak, when asked in 1991 whether he intended to create any art with Melville in mind, responded that he'd "accepted long ago that you can't illustrate Melville," for all he "sees" in Melville is "subtext" ("You see one thing and sense another"), which by definition defies direct representation.[42] Yet within the next two years, Sendak found himself increasingly preoccupied with *Pierre*, a response in part to a more public acknowledgment of his identification as gay and in part to his dismay over the oppression and demonization faced especially by homosexual men in the wake of the AIDS crisis. In a comic strip featured in *The New Yorker* in 1993, Sendak drew a caricature of himself declaring that he's now "illustrating [Melville's] most *meshuggah* [insane] book, 'Pierre,'" and his comic-strip companion exclaims in disbelief, "You're doing a book for *grownups*?" This revelation comes after his cartoon self has explained that the darkness of his just-released book *We Are All in the Dumps with Jack and Guy* stems from two simultaneous recent events: mourning "young friends dying of AIDS" and "studying Melville."[43] On the thematic level, the illustrations that resulted from this overlap evince Sendak and Melville's shared commitment in exploring "the dark places of the psyche."[44] On the aesthetic level, Sendak finds a companion spirit in *Pierre*'s perverse narrative form, for, as Jed Perl points out, Sendak's "stylized histrionics" and formal eclecticism capture in visual form *Pierre*'s over-the-top style, its "oddest possible amalgam of pastoral, gothic, romantic, realist, and tragic conventions."[45]

The hyperbolized eroticism that suffuses Melville's language and imagery seeps into virtually every frame of Sendak's illustrations, reinforcing his portrait of Pierre as a youth beleaguered by sexual confusion, queer desires, and a punitive world of stifling convention. These erotic meanings are bolstered by Sendak's dense layering within his thirty-two illustrations of visual references to nineteenth-century artists who defied contemporary aesthetic conventions in their quests to represent psychosexual states of being. William Blake figures conspicuously among these influences, as can be seen in the first of the only two Kraken illustrations lacking captions linking them to any specific moment in the text.[46] This lack bestows them with a generality that makes them especially significant; taken in tandem, the two illustrations may well be said to form Sendak's equivalents of *Songs of Innocence* and *Songs of Experience*.

The first of these two illustrations faces the opening of book 1 and depicts Pierre as an ebullient man-boy bursting with virility in a pastoral setting (figure 6.3). The composition self-consciously echoes that of Blake's Piper in *Songs of Innocence* (figure 6.4). Both men are framed by the twisting trunks of

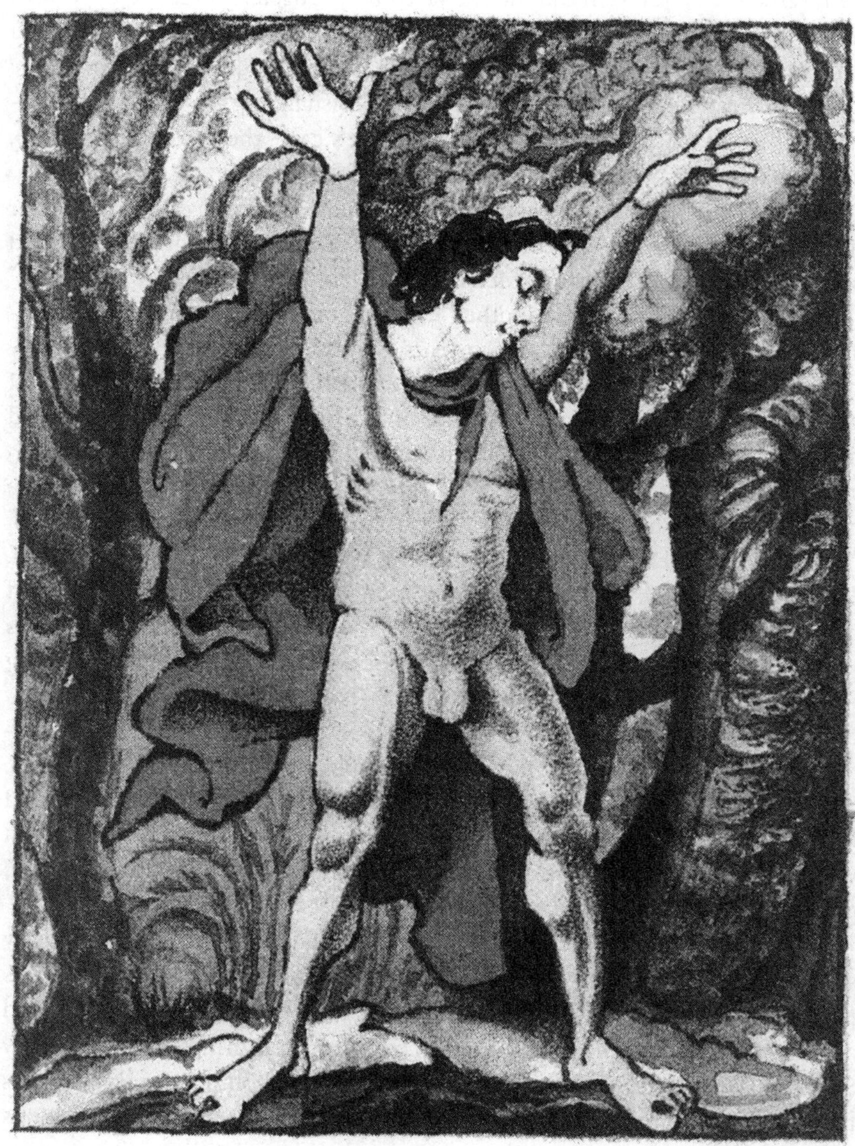

Figures 6.3 and 6.4. Sendak's songs of innocence and experience. *Left*: Maurice Sendak, uncaptioned illustration in Herman Melville, *Pierre, or the Ambiguities*, ed. Hershel Parker, illus. Maurice Sendak (HarperCollins, 1995), illustration facing book 1, p. 4. *Right*: William Blake, *Frontispiece* to *Songs of Innocence*, copy Y, plate 2. Relief etching in orange-brown ink and hand-colored with watercolor and shell gold. 6 3/16" × 5 9/16."

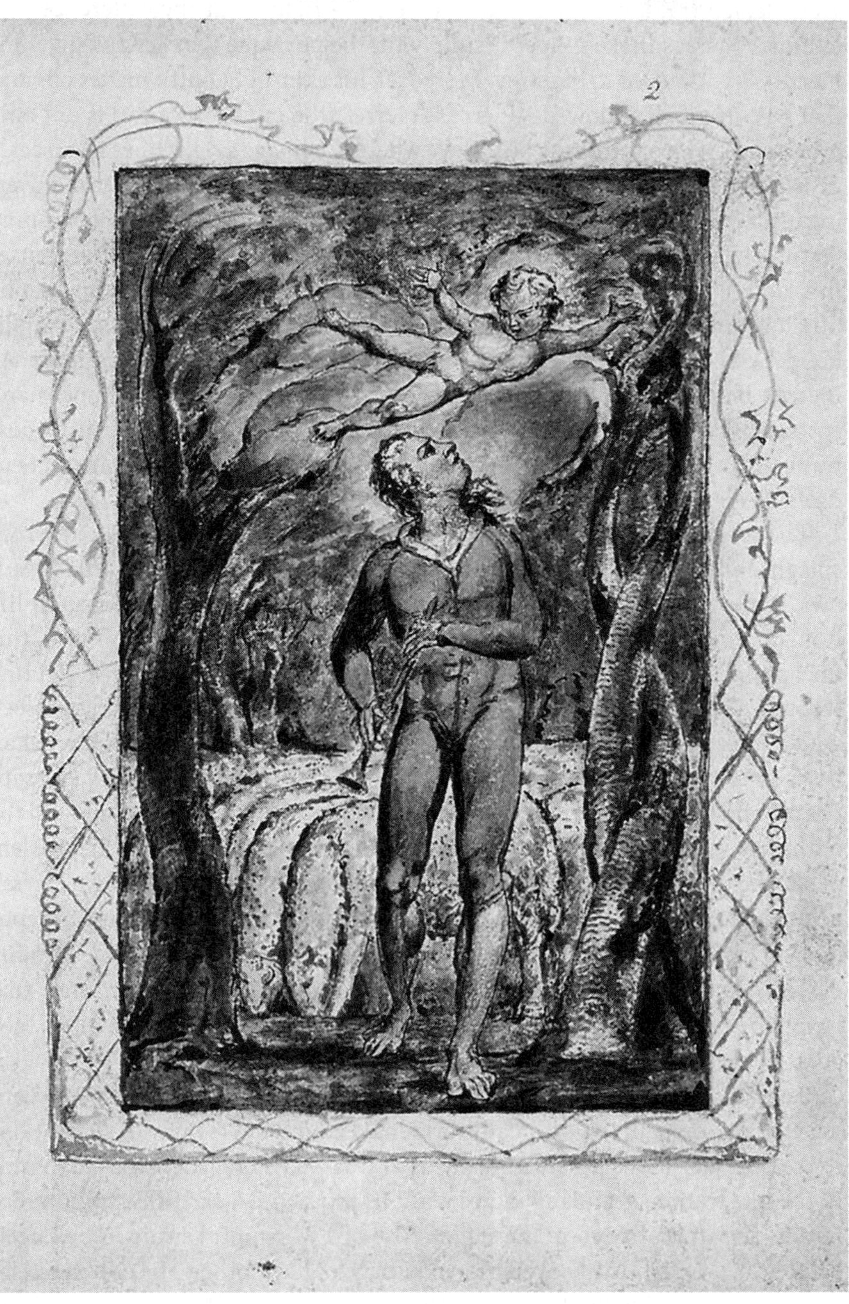
2

green-leafed trees, both are clad in blue body tights. But the differences are telling. Whereas Blake's Piper is simply fit, the physique that Sendak gives his Pierre is gym-buffed to bursting. Moreover, his skin-tight outfit makes obvious that he's very well endowed—Pierre's "pierre" (the pun is Bryant's) is not only prominent, it also forms the bull's-eye where the image's sight lines intersect.[47] This is Pierre in all his untested phallic glory. Instead of Blake's cherub hovering just above the Piper's head, Pierre's arms are flung to the sky in a preening gesture, head tilted and eyes shut as if he hasn't a care in the world—one senses this lad is a bit too confident, too filled with his own glory, to imagine that he might soon have need of celestial guidance in making the transition to adulthood. A final difference adds a contemporary gloss to Sendak's hero: As Pierre's blue tights and red cape suggest, he's basically wearing Superman's costume. At this stage, he may think he's Superman, but in fact it's just a costume. Elizabeth Schultz puts it beautifully: "A young Apollo in a wet-suit Sendak's Pierre might be, but Superman he is not."[48]

The second of these uncaptioned images faces book 14's account of Pierre's entrance into New York City upon his self-enforced exile from Saddle Meadows. Although he might still envision himself as a defiant, larger-than-life Romantic hero flaunting convention in the name of some higher Truth, this uncaptioned illustration depicts an absurdly gigantic, solitary figure striding through a surreal, emptied-out, miniature cityscape.[49] His weary face is crossed with a look of perplexity accentuated by hands raised to his brow rather than flung to the open sky, as in the first image. The red Superman cape has disappeared and with it his virility; the blue bodysuit sags on an aging body, and the outline of his genitals is no longer visible. In place of the red cape, an emblem of blazing desire, Plotinus Plinlimmon's treatise, ominously floats above Pierre's head (its pages on moral relativity have encouraged Pierre's rash zeal in repudiating family for Isabel). Empty philosophical conceits have replaced bodily desires. Dazed and confused: This illustration augurs the emotional state that weighs down overly zealous and equally naive champions of lost causes as they cross the threshold into the Blakean realm of "experience."

Sendak's renditions of Pierre's mental state as he moves from the overweening egotism of youth to psychically tormented adulthood teem with suggestions of the polymorphous perverse. Oedipal drama—as literal spectacle—abounds in the illustrations featuring Pierre with his mother. An early illustration represents the youth frozen in the stagey pose of a worshipful swain as he kneels before the proportionally overenlarged image of his mother. His crotch bulges conspicuously in his tights, while Grecian-coifed Mary Glendinning, wearing a see-through negligee, coyly commands her son, "Come, help me finish my toilet." A yellow ribbon forms a Möbius strip looping the two together. In another illustration, spent autoeroticism limns Pierre's bodily posture (modeled after a Fuseli male nude sketch) as he sits, legs spread, on his fiancée Lucy's bed; as thunderclouds glower through the window frame behind him, the white light spilling between his splayed legs and down the coverlet hints that an act of masturbation may have just occurred. Both Lucy and Isabel appear on separate occasions as reclining odalisques, breasts thrust forward in aggressively sexual poses, highlighting our hero's incapacity or unwillingness to respond to their siren call. An image featuring a submissive Isabel bowing on the floor is dominated by the sweeping Medusaean hair that subsumes her features. The only other object in the room is her mother's guitar, whose dark orifice reveals what the whorl of dark hair hides (if the guitar functions as fetish object for Isabel, her hair serves as fetish object for Pierre). Other images evoke the sadomasochistic underbelly of Pierre's attachments (a harpy eating out his liver), fears of castration, neutering, self-mutilation, and the death-drive.

Particularly fascinating are the queer resonances that seep into those illustrations that nod to the younger Pierre's *heterosexual* attractions and inveiglements, notably those featuring him and Lucy in the same frame. Especially odd—one might say perverse—is the image Sendak creates (figure 6.5) to illustrate Pierre's vexed ponderings as he realizes that in order to fulfill his resolve of providing Isabel with "lasting fraternal succor" (177) through the fiction of a nominal marriage, he must not only abruptly sever his engagement to Lucy but do so without any explanation. On the one hand, in deciding to "sacrifice" his "earthly felicity" (179) for this lofty cause, he freely "submit[s]" (179) himself, with a masochist's eagerness, to the social opprobrium that he knows his elopement with Isabel will entail. On the other, he knows that breaking ties with Lucy will break her heart. As Melville's narrator sardonically notes, too often there "is an inevitable keen cruelty in the loftier heroism" (178): Pierre the self-sacrificing martyr, that is, must also play the role of sadist. Intriguingly, Sendak illustrates Pierre's dilemma by not focusing on the episode or Pierre's emotional state but rather on a metaphor that likens Pierre to the "restless sailor who breaks from every enfolding arm" to seek the open seas, only to come to regret the ties he's forfeited; these ties return to haunt him in the form of an "avenging dream" and transform him into a "self-abrading sailor, the dreamer of the avenging dream" (181). In Sendak's depiction, a completely naked, neoclassically sculpted Pierre rides something between a surfboard and the mast of a (perhaps sinking?) ship over churning seas, lightning piercing the stormy skies, red pennant blazing, with only the words "this self-abrading sailor, the dreamer" forming its enigmatic caption.

Curiously, though, this nude sailor seems the opposite of "self-abrading": His face is suffused with heroic determination, his arms upraised as if to combat all the hypocrisies of the world. One arm holds the fluttering pennant as if leading a battalion of knights to battle. The other arm holds aloft a woman who seems to float across the stormy sky as if a guiding spirit or angelic force urging him onward and forward to victory. Yet, against expectations, the woman

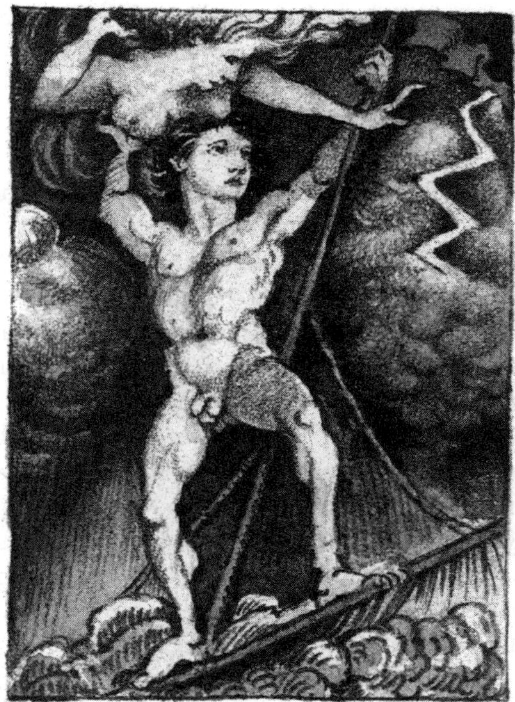

Figure 6.5. Pierre wages heroic war on convention, with Lucy as his missive. Maurice Sendak, *This self-upbraiding sailor; this dreamer*, in Melville, *Pierre, or the Ambiguities*, ed. Parker, illus. Sendak, illustration facing p. 257.

he appears to be championing isn't raven-haired Isabel but blond-haired and bare-breasted Lucy. For all of Melville's (deliberately clichéd) descriptions of Lucy's angelic insubstantiality, Sendak's "flying" Lucy is as well rounded as a Titian nude—indeed, a fulsome breast provides Pierre's handhold as he lifts her on high. One begins to suspect that Pierre isn't holding Lucy aloft to champion her—he's getting ready to throw her, like a spear, at his foes. And this is precisely what the textual Pierre is readying to do: By sacrificing Lucy's happiness to wage war on the world of convention that would deny Isabel's existence, he has made Lucy into a weapon. As Melville writes, in place of "the real Lucy," Pierre in his scheme to rescue Isabel has "substituted but a sign—some empty *x*" (181). Sendak's Lucy, however, reminds us that this *x* is not just a function to be fitted to Pierre's cause but a living, breathing body. By turning Lucy into an abstraction, an "empty *x*," Pierre's ratiocinations betray the baser instincts—Isabel's erotic pull—motivating his purportedly noble, self-sacrificing intentions.

A homoerotic undercurrent subtly undercuts the resonances of Pierre and Lucy's courtship in the volume's second illustration, which depicts Pierre wooing Lucy beneath her window (figure 6.6). Much like the hyperbolic language Melville uses to parody domestic romantic fiction in the novel's opening passages, Sendak deploys the visual tropes of sentimental love only to undercut their ostensible meanings. The tableau formed by the two lovers blatantly evokes the balcony scene of Shakespeare's *Romeo and Juliet* as Lucy gazes down at her supplicant.[50] The Shakespearean echoes are reinforced by the way in which the vines climbing up the walls on either side of Lucy's window suggest stage curtains, a reminder that this chivalric lovemaking is a performance, a surface that hides different realities. This sense of surfaces being not quite what they seem accrues to the pastel colors in the image, which belie the dark fates awaiting Shakespeare's lovers; likewise, the springtime verdancy surrounding the lovers forestalls any foreshadowing of the suicides and deaths littering Melville's tragic conclusion. But the illustration is most subversive in the way it directs the viewer's gaze to Pierre's muscular backside, visible through his Superman tights, and particularly to his hefty buttocks. In effect, we find ourselves cruising Pierre's ass.

This coy "wink" at a potentially appreciative gay audience becomes even clearer when we compare this image to one in book 5 featuring Pierre's bare buttocks (figure 6.7). The caption, "Guide me, gird me, guard me, this day" (*Pierre*, 106), repeats Pierre's resolve as he dreamily wanders in a "primeval woods," awaiting "the *fall* of day" (109, emphasis added), the twilight hour when he has agreed to meet Isabel and hear her story. Innocently embracing a Romanticist's faith in nature, he prays to the "god-like population of the trees" to "drop heavenliness" (106) on him as he abjures the "lies . . . of the diving and ducking moralities of this earth" (107). Sendak's illustration of Pierre plunging into this forest of contemplation and resolve is decidedly more somber and more ironic, evoking the ominous setting of the opening lines of Dante's *Inferno* ("I found myself in a forest dark"). There is also something Luciferian in Pierre's declaration that he will "make war on Night and Day" if the "invisible" (107) powers of Nature desert him on his quest. Sendak's woods are dark, the moon less than half full, and the stars in the sky eerily resemble spying eyeballs as Pierre lunges away from the viewer into the gloomy forest. He is entirely nude—no Superman outfit to bolster his courage now—and Sendak shades the contours of his body so that his rounded buttocks (full moon, as it were) outshine anything else in the entire picture. As Pierre steps into the unknown, the greatest danger that seems to face him, metaphorically speaking, is penetration by the viewer's gaze (the phallic dagger he wears at his side emphasizes this vulnerability to penetration). Sendak's statuesque, heroically proportioned Pierre

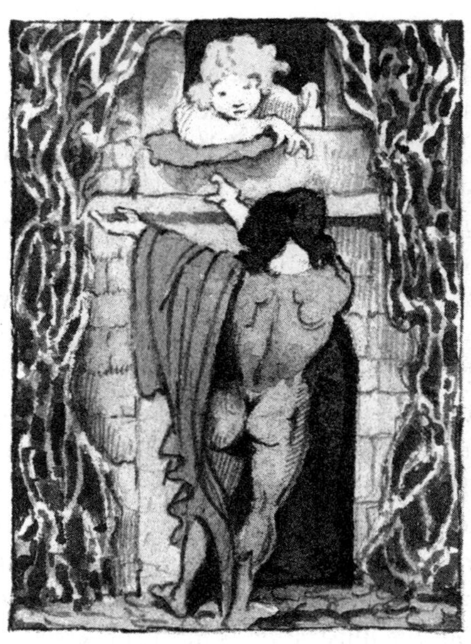

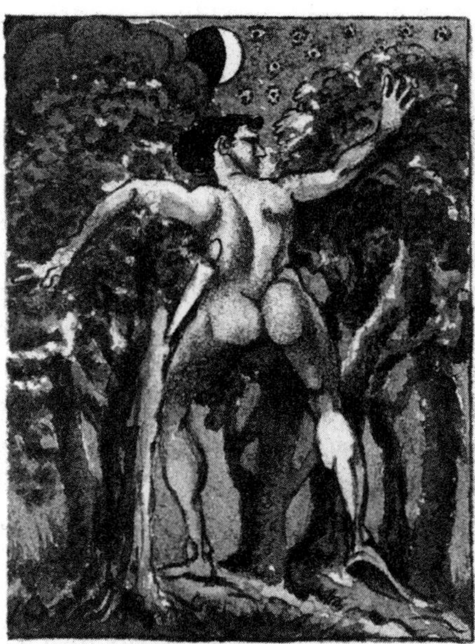

Figures 6.6 and 6.7. Sendak's rear assessments of Pierre.
Top: Maurice Sendak, *Bravissimo! Oh, my only recruit*, in Melville, *Pierre, or the Ambiguities*, ed. Parker, illus. Sendak, illustration facing p. 11. *Bottom*: Maurice Sendak, *Guide me, gird me, guard me, this day*, in Melville, *Pierre, or the Ambiguities*, ed. Parker, illus. Sendak, illustration facing p. 155.

thus becomes a homoerotic icon unwittingly on his way to martyrdom—not unlike the pierced and penetrated Saint Sebastian of Renaissance painting.

If these hints were not visual evidence enough of Pierre's psychic tug of war between heterosexual convention and taboo homoerotic desire, others playfully nod to the polymorphous fluidity that has always been part of Pierre's makeup. When Pierre announces his engagement to Lucy's brothers, the moon-struck lover embraces them all with joy. Sendak's illustration, however, makes clear that the "joy" depicted in "a hug all round again" (29) is a bit more suspect than Melville's wording reveals: His Pierre surreptitiously uses the occasion to sneak a hand behind Lucy's back and grasp at the palm of the brother who sports a body as sexy as Pierre's.

These homoerotic subtexts are most explicit in Sendak's rendering of the novel's passage in which Pierre's "much more than cousinly attachment" to his cousin Glen is likened to "the empyrean of a love which only comes short, by one degree, of the sweetest sentiment entertained between the sexes" (216) (figure 6.8). Sendak eliminates that discrete "one degree" by posing Pierre as a nude Cupid aiming an arrow at the heart of the equally naked Glen under a beneficent full moon. The red cape now drapes the sleeping Glen, indicating a successful transfer of desire from subject to object. All is not as halcyon, however, as this image makes such passion seem. Sendak's composition alludes to Henry Fuseli's *Der Kronenräuber* (1771), a depiction of *Hamlet*'s Claudio *poisoning* his brother, the king of Denmark (figure 6.9); this betrayal of brother by brother foreshadows the deadly homosocial rivalry between cousins Pierre and Glen that will displace their adolescent love. Ironically, the arrangement of the figures in Fuseli's drawing is modeled on a vase by the Dinos painter at the British Museum (figure 6.10), in which the standing ephebe places a leg on his lover's chair as if readying to mount the latter's erection. As Elizabeth Schultz succinctly notes of this complex relay of visual citations, "Sendak, reinterpreting Fuseli's Shakespearean scene, restores it to its Greek origins, redeeming the satyr as Cupid, a love-smitten, passionate Pierre."[51]

This rich citationality also characterizes another of Sendak's most homoerotically charged renderings—the closet scene in which Pierre autoerotically fixates on the enigmatic portrait of his father as a "gayly . . . bladish" (73) bachelor (figure 6.11). We've seen how Creech makes the portrait of Melville's father, Allan, central to his extra- and intertextual reading of *Pierre*'s gay codes. A year before the publication of Creech's book, Sendak made the same link (compare his representation to the portrait of Allan Melville, figure 6.1). Never has Pierre's "pierre" looked as plumped, and the squat candle (its flame pointing at Pierre's pierre), in addition to Pierre's left knee pointing to and nearly touching his father's crotch, only amplifies this incestuous homoeroticism. The unsettling quality of father–son desire is heightened when we view Sendak's composition in light of John-Auguste-Dominique Ingres's painting

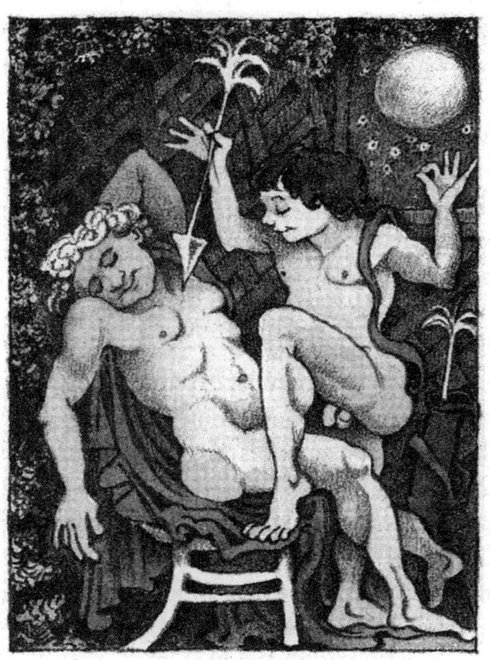

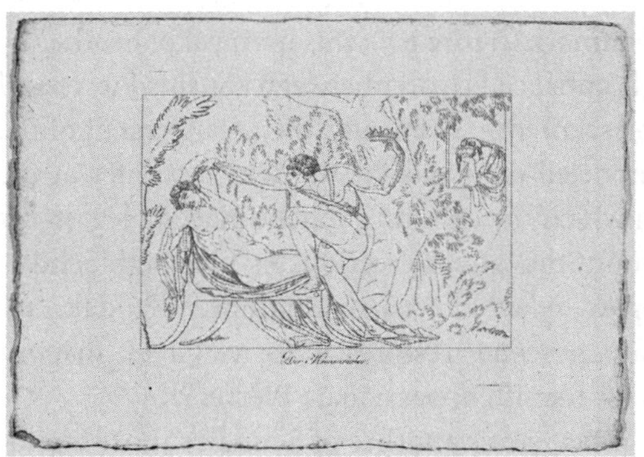

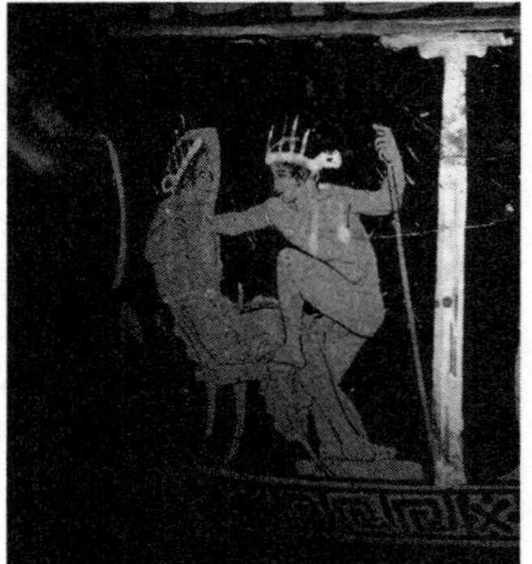

Figures 6.8, 6.9, and 6.10. Palimpsest readings of Pierre's "more than cousinly attachment."

Top: Maurice Sendak, *The friendship of fine-hearted, generous boys*, in Melville, *Pierre, or the Ambiguities*, ed. Parker, illus. Sendak, illustration facing p. 309. *Bottom left*: Johann Heinrich Lips, engraving (1807) after Henry Fuseli, *Der Kronenräuber*, 1771. *Bottom right*: Vased painted by the Dinos painter. Depiction of homosexual youths on reverse side of Bell Krater, Attic, Attica, Capua.

Sources: 6.8: Introduction and reconstructed text copyright © 1995 by Hershel Parker. Pictures copyright © 1995 by Maurice Sendak. Used by permission of HarperCollins Publishers. 6.9: Gift of Jenny Philippsohn. Obj. No. 55.526.6. Met Open Access. 6.10: © The Trustees of the British Museum. Asset No. 74684001.

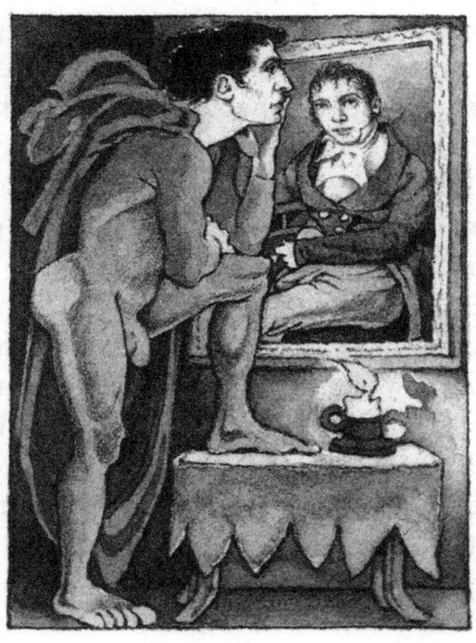

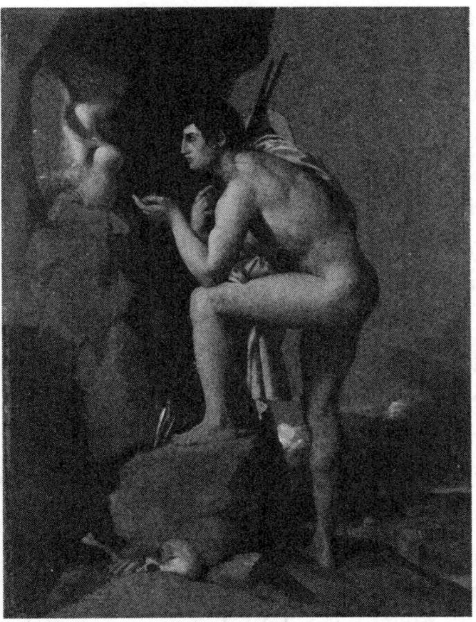

Figures 6.11 and 6.12. Erotic reveries beholding the closet portrait, with a wink at Oedipus. *Top*: Maurice Sendak, *Youth is hot, and temptation strong*, in Melville, *Pierre, or the Ambiguities*, ed. Parker, illus. Sendak, illustration facing p. 119. *Bottom*: Jean-Auguste-Dominique Ingres, *Oedipus and the Sphinx*, c. 1808/1827.

of Oedipus questioning the Sphinx (begun in 1808, completed in 1827, figure 6.12). Sendak has obviously copied the pose of Ingres's Oedipus, who even sports a cape worn over one shoulder, as does Pierre. But Oedipus is looking for answers from a female monster, unlocking the taboo of mother-son incest that, in Freud's terms, paves the way to normative heterosexuality. In contrast, when Pierre takes the position of Oedipus as he gazes at his father's sphinxlike mystery, the taboo revealed is that of phallic Pierre's closeted yearning for a male companion.

One precept of Eve Kosofsky Sedgwick's epistemology of the closet is the degree to which homosexuality exists as an open secret. The closet and its open secret are made literal in two images by Sendak that serve as companion pieces: One is the Kraken edition's front-cover illustration depicting Pierre and Isabel in an illicit embrace, and the second is an almost identical illustration placed midway through the volume bearing the caption "He whispered it" (figures 6.13 and 6.14). Both pictures depict the pivotal scene in which Pierre, Lucifer-like, whispers his temptation (to live together as nominal husband and wife) into Isabel's ear, upon which the two "coil" together, struck "mute" (192) in recognition of the unspeakable nature of their love. Reading the visual details of Sendak's two images against each other suggests the psychological transfers by which Isabel as an object of incestuous *heterosexual* desire surfaces from Pierre's incestuously *homoerotic* contemplation of his father. And what emerges "hiding in full sight" is as much a key to Sendak's interpretation of *Pierre* as the "pointing finger" of Allan Melville is the key unlocking Creech's reading of the closet portrait of Pierre's father.

Cover illustrations are chosen to tease readers with a glimpse of what a book is all about, and Sendak's roseate-hued portrait of a nude man and woman locked in a carnal embrace promises, not unlike the covers of mass-market romance novels, a torrid tale of passion. But it does so with a difference, as John Taggart perceptively notes. Paperback romances generally feature an impossibly attractive couple in a steamy clutch, with plenty of cleavage on display, teasing us with the promise of "more" if we purchase the novel.[52] But Sendak's cover is almost too hardcore for drugstore-shelf comfort. Modeled on the eighteenth-century sculptor Johan Tobias Sergel's drawing (circa 1770–1780) of a nude man and woman swirling in an embrace (figure 6.15) but departing from Sergel's kinetic romanticism, Sendak's lovers are rooted to the ground, completely naked, and rather bulky (and hence not immediately "attractive" in the conventional sense). Moreover, the angle of Pierre's pelvis meeting the thrust of Isabel's hips (abetted by the pressure of his right hand) suggests that actual penetration may be occurring. And if genital copulation has not quite yet occurred, penetration of another kind is subtly suggested. As the shocked yet titillated reviewer of the Kraken edition in *Lingua Franca* noted in 1995, one of Pierre's fingers seems to have disappeared between his female partner's

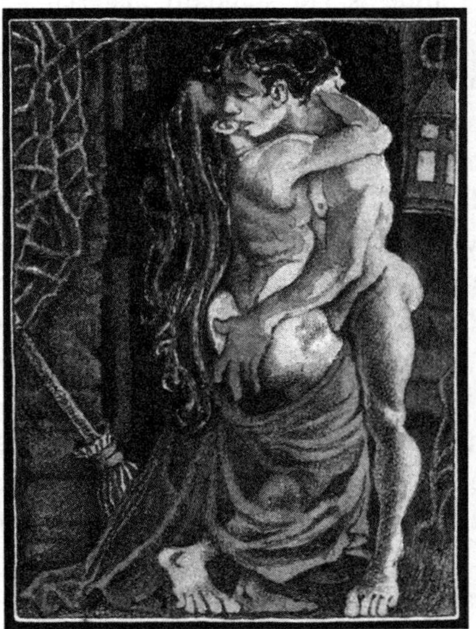

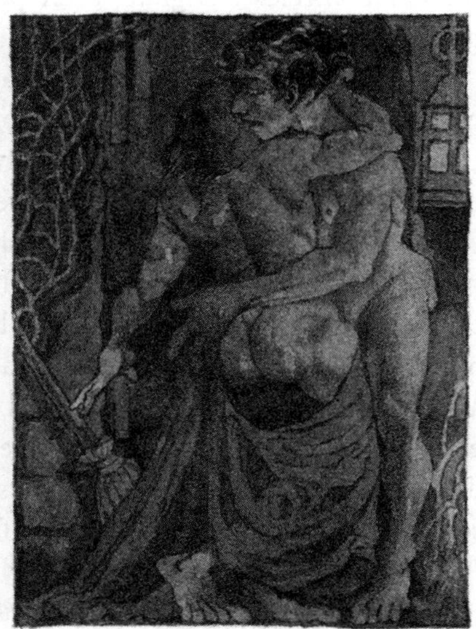

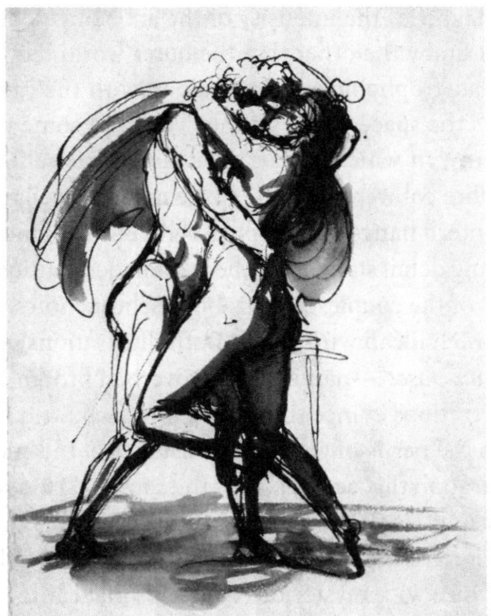

Figures 6.13, 6.14, and 6.15. Repetitions with a difference.
Top left: Maurice Sendak, *He whispered it*, in Melville, *Pierre, or the Ambiguities*, ed. Parker, illus. Sendak, cover. *Top right*: Maurice Sendak, *He whispered it*, in Melville, *Pierre, or the Ambiguities*, ed. Parker, illus. Sendak, illustration facing p. 275. *Bottom*: Johan Tobias Sergel, *Passionate Couple*, c. 1770–1780.

Sources: 6.13–6.14: Introduction and reconstructed text copyright © 1995 by Hershel Parker. Pictures copyright © 1995 by Maurice Sendak. Used by permission of HarperCollins Publishers. 6.15: Nationalmuseum Stockholm. NHM A 45/1970. History and Art Collection / Alamy Stock Photo.

muscular cheeks.[53] Digital rectal penetration is not standard material for paperback romance covers.

In the companion interior illustration, the dusky shades of the dust jacket have become darker, more foreboding, as Pierre whispers his audacious plan that the two deceive the world by living as man and wife in name. But the darker hue is not the only difference. Either Isabel's hair has been chopped off, or it's been swept over her left shoulder. Regardless, its absence and her now visible, backward-stretching left arm reveals a massively muscular torso that, along with the fully revealed buttocks, could well lead a viewer who hasn't read the novel to think they are seeing a man's body, hence that they are witnessing a male couple locked in a carnal embrace.[54] Beneath the heterosexual surface (or "cover") of the dust-jacket image, Sendak thus makes dimly visible a transgendered, transvested Isabel—an Isabel who, in more senses than one, has become her "father's flesh," the embodied fantasy of Pierre's "closet" yearnings.

And where is this taboo act of incest taking place? The way the couple's bodies press against the image's frame creates a sense of claustrophobia, of being wedged in, that magnifies the intensity of the act being depicted—this couple is so utterly swept up by the other that the outer world has ceased to exist for them. And this claustrophobic intimacy, along with the random details with which Sendak fills the space, suggests they've found some private dark nook, some hidden cranny, in which to carry out their lovemaking. A rough stone column and macabre cobwebs hint the space may be a cellar or perhaps a garden shed, and a lantern hangs in the upper-right corner. One seemingly inconsequential but telling detail stands out: the broomstick leaning against the stone column to the left of the couple. As Elizabeth Schultz notes, the broom is "the give-away" or the Melvillean wink here: "Both illustrations place Pierre and his beloved *literally in a closet*"—namely, the proverbial broom closet.[55]

Two more illustrations evince the degree to which Sendak's paintings allegorically allude to the perils of gay men's existence at the end of the twentieth century. The illustration that accompanies the caption "Hooded phantoms, disembarking in his soul" is particularly evocative (figure 6.16). The occasion is the aftermath of Pierre's first sighting of the as-yet-unknown Isabel's anguished face, which "stirs" him with mysterious emotions that cause him to "lose" himself in "wonderings" that "baffle" reason (48–49). Given the degree to which Melville makes this moment a pivotal narrative threshold in Pierre's self-revelations, it is striking that Sendak represents the subconscious phantoms "disembarking in his soul" (49) as grim reapers of death who hold the youth's pale, naked, collapsed corpse. Pierre's drooping body recalls various representations of the pietá and Christ's deposition from the cross: He is a sacrificial martyr. Thus allegorized as a beautiful young man dead before his time, Pierre also suggests the senseless death of all the gay young men in the arts community

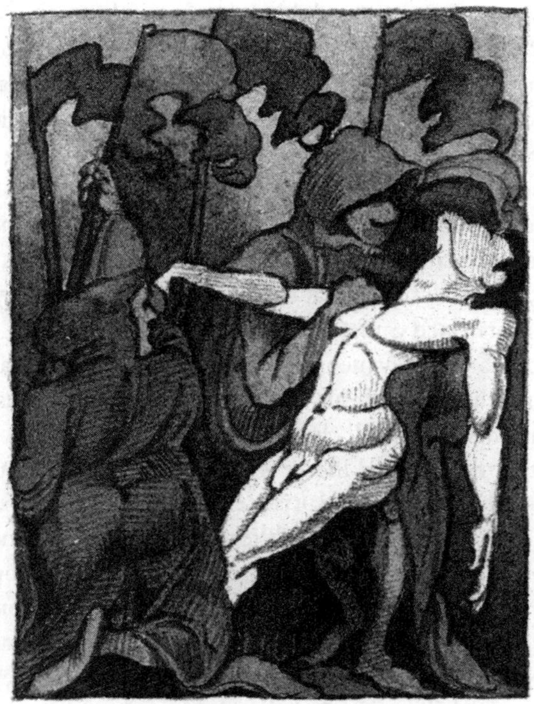

Figure 6.16. The specter of AIDS.
Maurice Sendak, *Hooded phantoms, disembarking in his soul,* in Melville, *Pierre, or the Ambiguities*, ed. Parker, illus. Sendak, illustration facing p. 73.

sickened by AIDS and cast out by an unfeeling homophobic world, "the hooded phantoms" of this reading.[56]

The "self-imprisoning and self-wounding" that ensue as a result of internalizing society's homophobia is implied in the final illustration in the Kraken edition.[57] Its caption, "Untimely, timely end," refers to the solitary confinement Pierre undergoes after murdering Glen. Chained in a "low dungeon of the city prison," whose "cumbersome stone ceiling almost rested on his brow," this physically depleted and psychologically defeated Pierre feels as if the pressure of the entire edifice is "piled on him" (361). Sendak's illustration captures this intense effect of claustrophobia and captivity, but it does so without portraying a literal dungeon cell. Rather, Sendak imagines Pierre in a cavelike space whose rocky surfaces close in on him from all sides. The rendering adeptly evokes the psychodramatic quality of the scene, while simultaneously referring to an earlier passage where Pierre lies beneath a rock overhang in the forest near his home, the Memnon Stone. Sendak's depiction of this earlier event depicts a healthy, virile Pierre in his body tights prone beneath the perilous slab, his protuberant phallus almost seeming to hold the overhang at bay. This is the prefallen Pierre, filled with masculine bravado before experience castrates him. In *Untimely, Timely End*, however, Pierre's nude, crouching figure has collapsed in on itself, his phallus is out of sight, and his eyes register horror and fright. As Wendy Stallard Flory and Schultz point out, the rendering evokes both Blake's Urizen facing self-destruction and John Flaxman's illustration of Ugolino in hell.[58] Sendak's Pierre, at the end of his failed journey to manhood, finds himself imprisoned and tortured not only in body but also in mind, again evoking the fates of gay men stigmatized or completely erased from public recognition for their HIV status throughout the 1990s. Just as the closet is a symbolic prison, this prison cell closets Pierre all over again.

Moments later, the shackled Pierre is visited by Isabel and Lucy, who identify themselves to the guards as the prisoner's "wife" and "cousin." To these two former objects of desire, he declares, "Pierre is neuter now," and the distance created by referring to himself in the third person seems to confirm his psychic castration or desexing—first, by the mad course of action to which his perverse desire for Isabel has led him and, second, by a social order whose perversion of sexuality has deemed nonnormative desires unacceptable. Pierre's death seconds later is followed by Isabel's dying statement, "Ye know him not." Pierre's suicide thus forms the tragic end to his defiant but failed attempt to shake off the shackles of sexual repression and societal oppression and liberate a self that yet, as Isabel intimates, remains unknown. Instead of freedom, he imprisons himself in self-hatred and punishes himself with self-inflicted wounds that leave him "neutered." Likewise, Sendak implies, for many late twentieth-century gay men demonized at the height of the AIDS pandemic, the epistemology of the closet—rendering invisible the knowledge that Sendak's illustrations insistently bring into the viewer's line of vision—remains gruesome reality.

Pola X's Pornographic Perversities

Leos Carax's film *Pola X* (1999) opens with a voice-over intoning Hamlet's line "The time is out of joint" as grainy black-and-white footage from World War II shows bombs raining down on European cities and gravestones exploding. By the end of Carax's film, time isn't the only thing out of joint in this unsettling, uneven, and explosive homage to Melville's novel, whose actions have been relocated to France in the 1990s. *Pola X*'s unnerving look into its artist-rebel's self-destructive unraveling, his descent into rage, madness, and despair as he irrationally pursues the siren call of his imp of the perverse, has widely divided viewers. If Melville's novel makes ambivalence a central theme, Carax's adaptation arouses ambivalence in viewers on almost every level, from its dangling plot threads to its jarring shifts in tone, from its kinetic camera work to the sonic noise that fills its soundscape, from nods to German expressionism to dense cinematic citationality that "feels like the history of modern cinema . . . tossed into a blender."[59] If Melville is sometimes productively "messy," then Carax is even more so.

At its Cannes premiere, the audience jeered and booed the film, declaring it a bomb; over the years, though, thoughtful critics have seen flashes of brilliance in its controversial subject matter and avant-garde approach to cinema. Despite the mental "shell-shock" incurred by Carax's bombardment of their senses, the film is a "carefully synchronized hangover" serving as this "millennium's mortifying epigraph," writes Chuck Stephens. The same commentator also quips that *Pola X* attains "a level of ignominy to which only *perverted* greatness or *pornographic* self-indulgence could inspire."[60] In the following pages, I use Stephens's throwaway references to the perverse and pornographic as signposts pointing to Carax's intentions. To these two alliterative *p* words, we might also add *politics*, for Carax's perverse tendencies as filmmaker and cinephile give him access to Melville's "perverse" in a way that places the "pornographic" *and* the "political" of this X-rated film at the symbolic center of its bleak meditation on the intersecting vectors of artistic genius, mania, psychosis, libidinal desire, and the anarchic reign of the instincts.

The personal significance that *Pierre* holds for Carax is as deep-rooted as Creech's and Sendak's attachment to the novel. Upon reading *Pierre* at the age of nineteen, Carax embraced as his personal credo its allegory of the defiant artist beset by conventionality.[61] (Carax's enthusiasm echoes that of Gilbert Wilson, Robert Del Tredici, and Matt Kish, who also unabashedly treat *Moby-Dick* as spiritual guide or "Bible.") Carax's investment in *Pierre* is not simply the usual case of empathy for a fictional character: "I am not above Pierre. I am with Pierre," he insists.[62] For Carax, that is, there is no ironic distance separating protagonist and auteur: Pierre is his fellow traveler in art's battle to rip away the masks that hide existential truth. This highly subjective mirroring is also echoed in the parallels that film critics have noted between Carax's "trainwreck of a career" and Melville's descent into ignominy after publishing *Moby-Dick* and *Pierre*. Widely regarded as the enfant terrible of 1980s–1990s French cinema, Carax's trajectory has been as rocky as Melville's. His early films, if not commercially successful, were lauded by critics as adding a bold new language to cinema, helping to usher in the French New Extremity movement. But by 1999 Carax's career had sunk to an all-time low, and *Pola X* was frequently derided, much like *Pierre*, as the product of a "mad," "deranged" mind whose embrace of creative defiance at all costs was judged not only "an act of hubris" but also downright "commercial perversity."[63]

The uncanny echo of Melville's downward-spiraling career in Carax's tumble from grace carries over into the way *Pierre*'s jarring shifts in tone are echoed in the film's uneven careening among modes. In both creations, flashes of brilliance coexist with embarrassingly banal or simply boring stretches of narration, and both seem to be reaching for mythical heights that neither Melville's pen nor Carax's camera ever manages to bring into sustained focus—perhaps because both are attempting to tap into something so anarchic, so preconscious, that it cannot be adequately represented in any medium. The lack of ironic distance in Carax's identification with Melville means that *Pola X* is, as William L. Brown puts it, "no ordinary transfer of a nineteenth-century literary work into the current of the twentieth's signature medium, film. Rather, it seems that the director sought to cast himself in Melville's mold by creating a sky-assaulting work." That is, Carax finds himself *in* Melville, just as Melville already exists *in* Carax, waiting to be found and molded to express Carax's similar existential and aesthetic vision. "*Pola X* is not so much Melville's *Pierre*," Brown concludes, "as it is the beating of [one] heart's genius to another's cracked monochord."[64] This intense, identificatory relationship—one heart rhyming to another's "cracked" beat—supersedes traditional models of literary or film adaptation; casting oneself "in [the] mold" of another artist's aspirations unleashes an unboundaried interchange of energies characteristic of the rhizomatic formations generating and generated by the Melville effect.

Carax's version of *Pierre* articulates, even more explicitly than Melville's original, the imp of the perverse driving its antihero to give up everything he's known once Isabelle's revelations offer him the opportunity. "*All my life* I have been waiting," the film Pierre tells his half-sister, "for something that would *push me beyond*".[65] (Carax's script uses the French equivalents "Isabelle" and "Lucie" for "Isabel" and "Lucy." "Mary" has been rendered "Marie," and, ironically, the surname "Glendinning" has been changed to "Valombreuse," or "Brave.") As unrealistic as it might seem for him unquestioningly to accept Isabelle's story as truth, the reaction he expresses is as psychologically apt as his wording is revealing: On the subconscious level, he's simply been itching "all [his] life" to blow up the entire edifice—from the oedipal family to the patriarchal system built on it—that has kept him suspended in a state of unquestioning, pampered safety, submissive to everyone's whims. And in blowing up that world—here the imp of the perverse comes into play—he's also priming himself to self-destruct if that's what it takes to "push beyond" the boundaries that have cocooned him in prisons of propriety. Outside those boundaries, Pierre will discover, exists a realm of anarchic desire and spontaneous action that defies reason. More so than in Creech or Sendak's renderings, Carax's film narrative associates this instinctual realm with the enigmatic figure of Isabelle (played by Katerina Golubeva). As Pierre's dark other, his shadow self, his doppelgänger, she personifies the return of the repressed that, now surfacing to consciousness in Pierre's tamped-down life, wreaks havoc on fictions of coherent subjectivity and a just social order: Both are fabrications veiling the inner and outer chaos that is the ultimate truth of human existence.

If Sendak's "priapic Pierre" strikes "the proper anarchic note," Brown writes, so too Carax's antihero "tap[s] into the erotic and creative energies" of Melville's novel.[66] A plethora of tracking shots of Guillaume Depardieu, who plays Pierre, straddling his father's phallic motorcycle and charging at breakneck speed through the Normandy countryside, evokes a similarly "priapic" élan—and, indeed, in the film's notorious lovemaking scenes, we see the actor's erection in action. But, strangely, Carax's version of Melville's "man-boy" appears stuck in more of an anarchic than a phallic state of being for most of the film. He is a sex symbol, yes, walking around shirtless or half-naked in numerous scenes, yet in these moments he's the passive object of the camera's gaze. From the film's beginning, the viewer is made privy to the unsettling incestuous currents binding him in a preoedipal dyad with his voluptuous mother, played by Catherine Deneuve. Calling each other "brother" and "sister," as in Melville's text, they exist in a fluid world without boundaries: Marie is as apt to walk into Pierre's bedroom as he sleeps naked in bed (figure 6.17) as Pierre is to walk into her bathroom as she lounges in the tub, breasts bobbing above the water line. "I don't get a last cigarette?" she flirtatiously asks her son as the two recline, as if postcoitally, on her bed (figure 6.18), she in robe and Pierre again shirtless as she quizzes him about the state of his sex life with Lucie.

Pierre's engagement to and sexual relationship with the girl-child Lucie, who lives in a neighboring chateau, poses no threat to this mother–son dyad; in fact, Lucie's passivity supports it, as Marie makes clear in taking charge of Lucie and Pierre's wedding arrangements. In one memorable image, the compliant Lucie is seen standing veiled on a stool in the garden, still as a statue as she is being fitted with her white wedding veil (figure 6.19); Marie supervises, confident in the knowledge that she is extending her control of Pierre by wedding him to this pale mirror image of herself. The doubling effect of mother–fiancée is driven home at the film's beginning as Carax cuts from Lucie and Pierre's morning tryst to a blond-haired woman viewed from the rear as she lounges on the lawn. For all the viewer knows, this might be Lucie—until the woman turns her head, and we see it is Marie, nonchalantly awaiting Pierre's return: She is happy to encourage the love affair since she knows Lucie's passivity won't interrupt her domination of Pierre. Of course, unlike Melville's angelic Lucy, this modern day, sexually experienced Lucie is no virgin. But she remains ethereal, disembodied. In a visually arresting image that occurs after the two have had morning sex, Carax's camera catches the reflection of the lovers talking to each other in a foggy bathroom mirror that shows their nude bodies but obscures

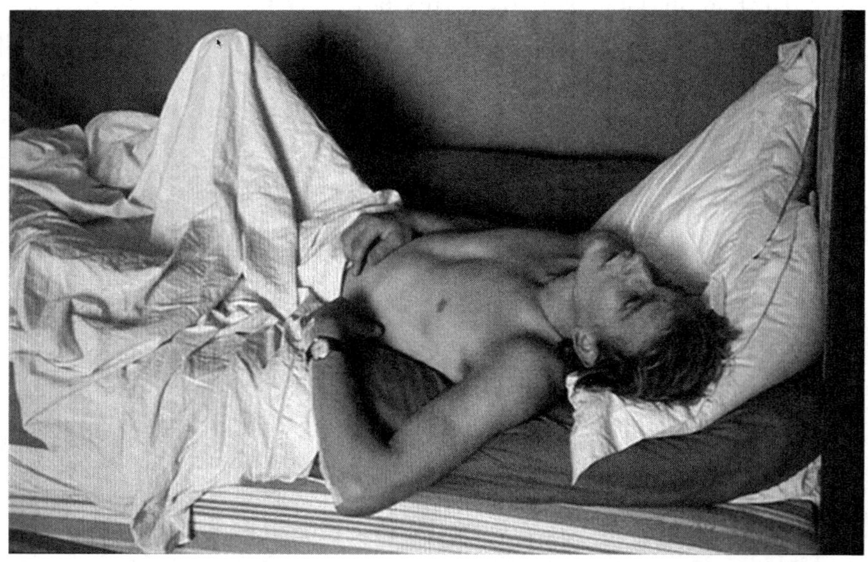

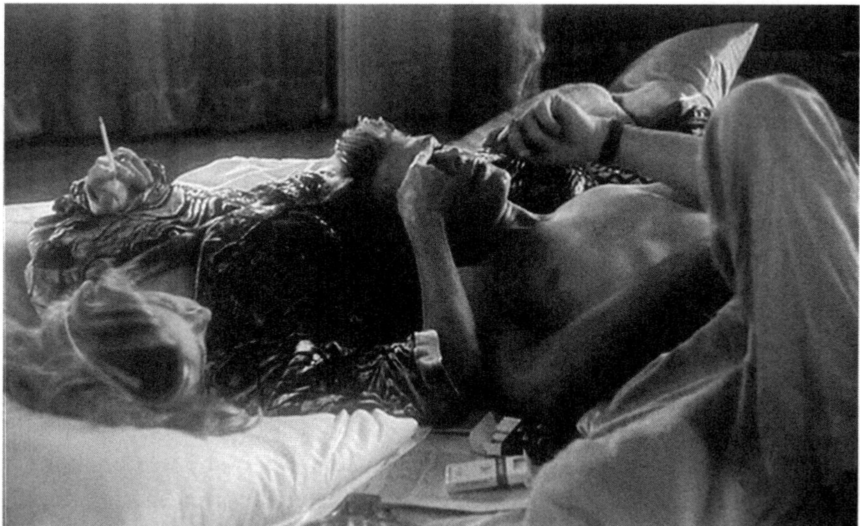

Figures 6.17 and 6.18. Carax's Pierre as recumbent object; "postcoital" cigarettes. Stills from *Pola X* (Leos Carax, 1999).

Source: United Artists GmbH / Alamy Stock Photo.

their faces (figure 6.20); seconds later the mist on the mirror has cleared, but as Lucie pulls a thin sweater over her head, masking her features, Pierre begins kissing her through the fabric (figure 6.21). This is "blind" or faceless love, indeed.

When Carax's Pierre tells Isabelle that "all his life" he's waited for "something" to happen that might "push me beyond all this," one senses his subconscious rebellion not only against upper-class conformity but specifically against the web of preoedipal desires in which he's been emmeshed. Yet, ironically, breaking out of this incestuous bond does not free Pierre to work through the Oedipus complex in a way that assures maturation and manhood. Rather, in unleashing the anarchic desires so long repressed by circumstance and upbringing, he trades one metaphoric womb for another, entering into an equally dyadic, suffocating intimacy with his half-sister. In Romantic poetry, incest—especially fraternally figured incest—is traditionally employed as a trope for the dangers of narcissism, for the drowning of self in the mirror of likeness. Living with Isabelle *is* Pierre's plunge into this mirror of self-sameness—a self-sameness that ironically dissolves all sense of self: "I'm another Pierre, now, thanks to you," he tells Isabelle. Likewise, Isabelle's only wish is to be with Pierre. Nothing but a world of two, and two alone, suffices to satisfy her yearning: "I want only you," she says. Her "want" is more than desire; it is pure need, without which she will cease to be. Not only is Pierre the "only" (sole) object of her "want," but "only" she will have him—singly, by herself, in a solipsistic world where twoness dissolves into oneness, as he ("you") supplies the lack ("want") without which she ceases to exist.

Carax gets a good bit of visual play out of doors and doorways as markers of the movement to "push beyond" or dissolve the incest taboo standing in the way of the half-siblings' fulfillment of their desires. In the hostel where they first stay in Paris, Pierre repeatedly pauses outside Isabelle's closed door, stopping himself just short of entering. In the derelict warehouse where they next take up residence, Pierre and Isabelle laboriously hang a huge, squeaking metal door onto the empty door frame separating their bedrooms. Whereas Pierre and his mother in their vast chateau seem to exist in a fluid interior realm where they move with ease in and out of each other's private spaces, Pierre and Isabel go through the charade of erecting this physical barrier to their incestuous desire. Such attempts, of course, prove useless in the psychodramatic world beyond boundaries that they have by now entered. Significantly, when Isabelle invites Pierre to cross the threshold to her chamber in the pivotal scene where they make love, she first cradles him on her lap like an infant eager to crawl back into the womb (figure 6.22), an effect furthered by the mane of dark hair obliterating her face as she bends forward to kiss him. She has become as anonymous as the featureless Lucie he kissed in the earlier scene when her face was shrouded by her stretched sweater.

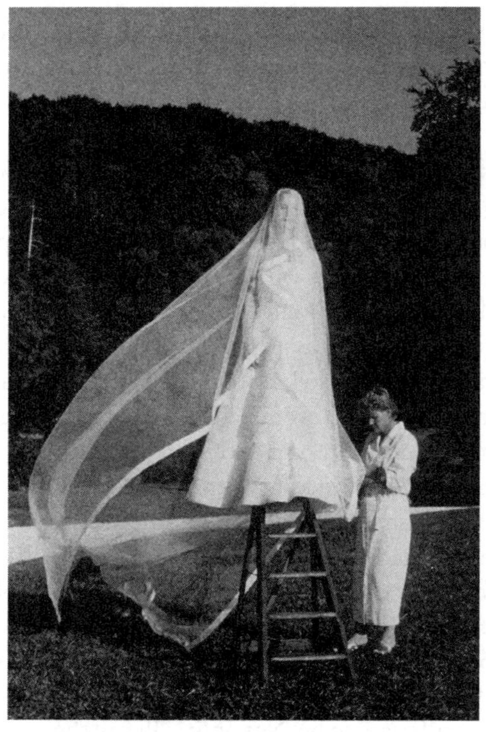

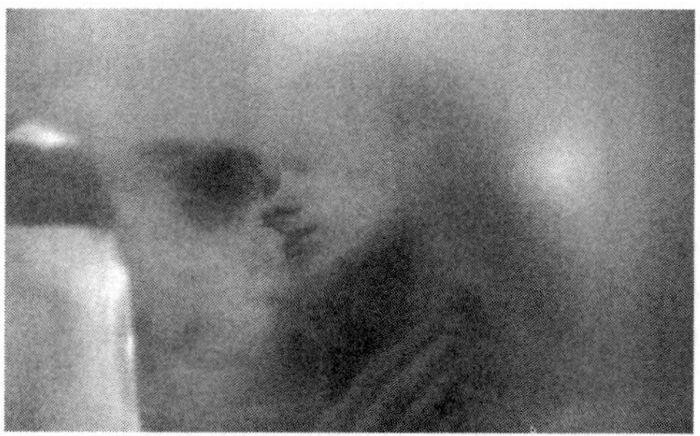

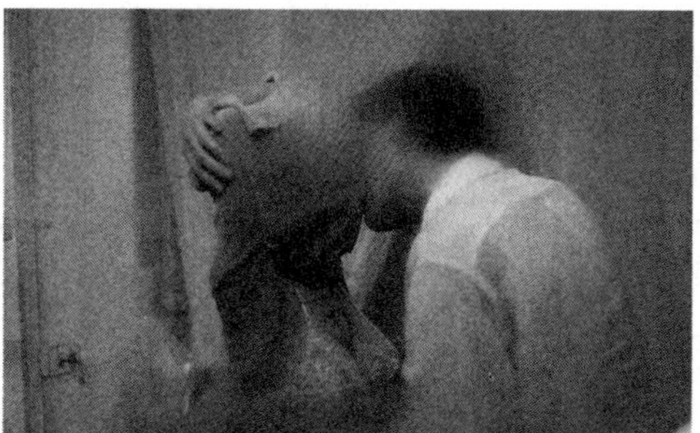

Figures 6.19, 6.20, and 6.21. Veiled bride, obscured faces, veiled kiss. Stills from *Pola X*.

Source: United Artists GmbH / Alamy Stock Photo.

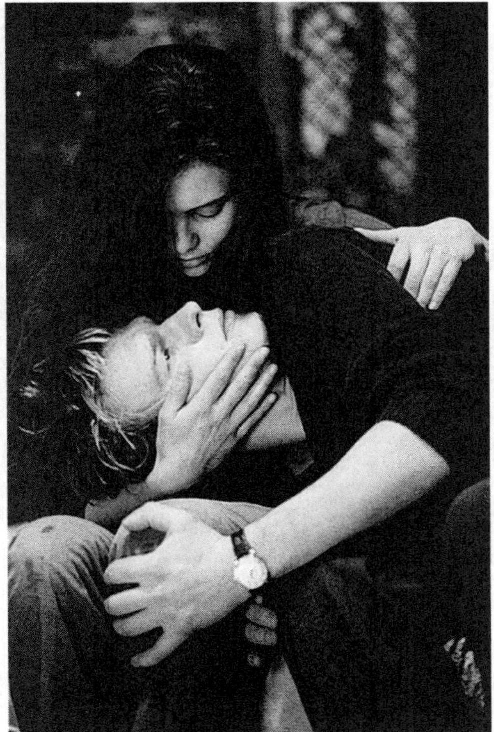

Figure 6.22. Isabelle's invitation to incest.
Still from *Pola X*.

Source: United Archives GmbH / Alamy Stock Photo.

That Isabelle embodies the realm of the repressed and the unconscious is signified throughout the film. Haunting the woods near Pierre's family chateau by night before being caught by Pierre, she appears feral, half-human, dressed in tattered clothing. Recalling her temporary sojourn in the chateau as a child, she explains she was expelled for supposedly attacking the infant Pierre "like a dog."[67] Like an abandoned animal, she resides in a rail tunnel (in the company of an equally ragged immigrant young woman Petruska and nameless girl who tag along with Isabelle throughout the film), and the three scatter like feral beasts at Pierre's approach—that is, until the night that Pierre finally catches Isabelle as he chases her through the forest.[68] The night is so black that their bodies are barely visible during the extended sequence; tree limbs whip by as if out of a Gothic nightmare (figure 6.23). Like Dante's pilgrim, Pierre has indeed entered a dark wood and thus opened the doors to both Heaven and Hell in the instant of Isabelle's revelation that she is his disavowed half-sister.

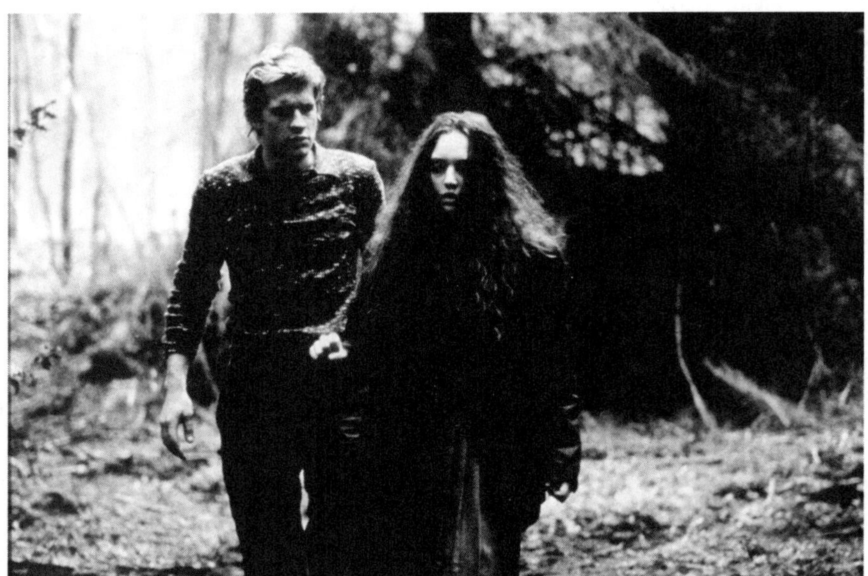

Figure 6.23. Gothic return of the repressed in the forest of the mind. Still from *Pola X*.

Source: United Archives GmbH / Alamy Stock Photo.

The degree to which Isabelle represents something prehuman is also registered in the grating, zombielike, broken French that she speaks in a little-girl voice in the eight-minute-long monologue that ensues once Pierre stops her, and she explains their putative kinship. In Gothic fiction, interpolated narratives are common, but Carax's film equivalent of the inset tale defamiliarizes the trope, subjecting us to an almost unbearable standstill in narrative time. Spoken in near blackness, Isabelle's monologue exemplifies, for some film critics, the height of Carax's folly because of its sheer tedium; for others, it is a stroke of genius, forcing us into a kind of mind-numbing limbo while this embodied return of the repressed unleashes in Pierre all that he desires (his heaven) and all that he hates (his hell), for the ultimate outcome of Isabelle's revelation of her castaway status is to fill Pierre with destructive and ultimately self-destructive rage at the world's hypocrisies and lies.

In Freudian parlance, the recovery of what has been repressed (in Pierre's case, his father's dirty secret and Marie's complicity) ought to abet a cessation of neurosis and portend the recovery of a coherent self. To the degree that Carax's Pierre emerges from the encounter with Isabelle as a self-proclaimed Romantic rebel ready to defy familial expectations and worldly conventions, he becomes an active agent for the first time in his life. But his headlong, impulsive plunge into exilic freedom, followed by his mounting wrath at the existing social order, only leads to an increase in unchecked neurotic behavior, violent outbursts, mounting paranoia, and obsessive mania. This careening out of control has been anticipated in the many tracking shots of Pierre barreling away on his motorcycle in the countryside, and it is repeated in the frenetic pace with which he maniacally strides the sidewalks of Paris's suburban wasteland in the film's third act. Once Isabelle—as doorway to the unconscious, the realm of instinctual drives—comes into Pierre's life, the anarchic nature of those drives subsumes his being, pushing him to the depths of solipsistic introspection and the dissolution of a coherent sense of being: "Nothing's left to save!" Pierre rages to Isabelle and Lucie as he storms out of their quarters in the film's penultimate scene. "You're rid of me!" More accurately, he might have said, "*I'm rid of me.*"

A recurrent motif in Melville's writing is the quester's futile attempt to penetrate to the "core" of meaning, often expressed in the symbolic imagery of empty centers, caskets, tombs, and other enclosed spaces. I suggest that Carax's film has not one but two such symbolic centers—the "private/pornographic" and the "social/political"—around which the film's meanings coalesce and disperse. If Melville's fictions repeatedly demonstrate the *emptiness* that lies at the heart of things, Carax's symbolic centers brim over with *plentitude*—but it is the plentitude of the polymorphous perverse in which chaos and anarchy proliferate without check. In the first instance, this anarchy is unleashed in the phantasmic or "pornographic" realm of private sexual desire; in the second, it occurs in the "political" realm of revolutionaries engaged in acts of anarchy. In the first, pure silence assails the ear; in the later, pure noise. Each modality forces the viewer into a sadomasochistic entanglement with cinematic temporality and spatiality that is perhaps Carax's greatest approximation of Melvillean perversity.

The erotic heart of *Pola X*—the sexually explicit representation of Pierre and Isabelle's lovemaking—occurs two-thirds of the way into the film. Reverse shots show the two standing on either side of the heavy door separating their rooms at the derelict factory, each staring at the metal barrier as if they are willing themselves to see through it to the other. Pierre opens the door, and they now look directly into each other's eyes. "What are you thinking?" Isabelle asks. "Everything," Pierre answers, to which Isabelle responds, simply, "Come," upon which invitation Pierre crosses the threshold into her room. I've already described how, sitting on her mattress, Pierre lowers his head to her lap, looking like a distraught child as he laments his failure to give her "everything" he intended. "We're together. That's everything," she comforts him. "But where?" he asks. "*Outside it all,*" she answers (emphasis added). Indeed, both have now "pushed beyond" to occupy a zone "outside" social norms or intelligibility. At this pivotal point, Isabelle lowers her head to kiss Pierre, inaugurating the sexual coupling that follows in the next cut. Four minutes pass without words, broken only by animal-like moans and sighs as the two, suddenly naked, grope each other in darkness, bodies visible in the darkest of blue hues. Literally, we are now watching a "blue movie," as old-style pornography was once called. Despite Roger Ebert's quip that the movie contains "a sex scene that would be shockingly graphic if we could quite see it," even in this dimly blue light we actually *do* "see" everything, including Depardieu's erection, Golubeva's vulva, oral sex, and coitus.[69]

This extended sequence defamiliarizes viewers on any number of levels. The artifice of fictionality is broken by the unsettling visual evidence that the sex isn't being faked—this is the "real" thing. As we witness these groping bodies, we may also uneasily feel that we have exited the story time of the film and entered a realm of taboo in which actors are no longer acting but *doing*, in which the boundaries of art and life have hopelessly blurred. (The fact that the two actors were off-screen lovers at the time adds to this effect.) The convulsive urgency of the lovemaking, moreover, is cinematically defamiliarized by virtue of being too stark, too guttural, and therefore perhaps too real to incite fantasy or pleasure; this "blue movie" lacks Hollywood's conventions for scenes of sexual coupling (rhythmic cutting from one partner to the other, titillating glimpses of perfect body parts, warm lighting, orgasmic moans). In effect, Carax forces us into an uneasy voyeurism to which we must submit.

The disconcerting feeling that, as viewers, we are witnessing urges more instinctual, more primal, than "just sex" is abetted by Carax's blocking of the sequence. One moment we are watching Isabelle cradle Pierre's head in her lap as if he is a child in a fairly well-lit room; the next, the camera is moving over naked, blue-lit bodies in the dark. The first "sexual" action we see is Pierre's face moving in to suckle Isabelle's breast. The next is his hand trailing down her torso, across her pubic hair, as his fingers push into her vagina. While these actions occur in conventional lovemaking, here they take on a heightened oedipal emphasis: the man-child suckling at the mother's breast, fingers probing the entrance to the womb from which he has emerged. Freud's hypotheses about the origins of adult heterosexual desire in unconscious infantile instincts couldn't be more explicit: Incestuously libidinal desire, no longer repressed, is perversely driving Pierre back to his origins, to the womb that is metaphorically the tomb. Hence, from this point forward, in increasingly surreal, unfolding narrative action, Thanatos is as ever present as Eros. This drive toward annihilation—*le petit mort* writ large—emerges as the existential "meaning" that resides at the pornographic core of Carax's embrace of the Melvillean perverse. Committed to using art to strip away the world's lies, Carax no less than Melville reveals the "chaotic darkness," as reviewer Stephen Holden puts it, that is the "unbearable truth that must be pursued, even if it proves to be beyond the grasp of art."[70]

If chaos and anarchy compose the psychological "truth" ushered into realization by the return of the *repressed*, so too the film's "political" core reveals anarchy as the one viable response of the *oppressed* to the structures of power that render them outcasts, aliens, colonized others, relegated to the fringes of society. Paralleling her function as emblem of unconscious desire in Pierre's psyche, Isabelle also becomes the vehicle by which Carax injects this level of political critique into the film: Her presence literalizes war-torn eastern Europe as the West's own repressed. The details remain ambiguous, but Isabelle seems to be a refugee from the Balkan conflict of the 1990s, traumatized to the point of psychosis by the genocide and devastation she has witnessed. Before Isabelle's appearance, we learn that Pierre's father, a resistance fighter in World War II, later became a famous diplomat in eastern Europe, where he presumably met and had an affair with Isabelle's mother. When the young woman dies in childbirth, the infant is foisted on two sadistic caretakers who raise her in total silence. Once Pierre takes up Isabelle's cause as his own, abandoning his idyllic existence in the countryside for their shared, squalid life in an increasingly nightmarish Paris, he awakens to the daily prejudices encountered by the homeless, outsiders, and refugees like Isabelle and her two female companions, and in the process of choosing them over a life of privilege, he finds himself othered in the society where he used to circulate freely. Hotels refuse to admit him because of his bedraggled companions; a taxi driver tells him his friends "aren't clean"; the little girl dies of a concussion because her companion, as an undocumented "alien," is terrified of contacting a doctor or calling the police. As these incidents mount, Pierre's rage reaches a boiling point, leading him into increasingly violent outbreaks. Thus, he is primed for the anarchist lessons that come his way when in the last act of the film he and Isabelle move into the derelict factory building located in an industrial wasteland on the periphery of the city: one of Paris's infamous, ethnically populated banlieues.

With the group's entrance into the abandoned factory, they literally step into a new world—a vast alternative reality or whirring "brain" invisibly operating within the city—and the tone of the film becomes increasingly surreal and dreamlike.[71] Like Melville's hodge-podge mix of literary genres in *Pierre*, Carax veers into yet another cinematic mode: one that is part futuristic (with echoes of the factory set in *Metropolis* [1927]), part revolutionary propaganda, part ear-splitting concert documentary, part Escher-like spatial nightmare (the factory space is crossed with catwalks leading everywhere or nowhere) (figure 6.24).[72] The interior of this warehouse complex forms the film's beating heart or political core, a black hole into which meanings disappear and from which all subsequent action emanates: It is, Holden asserts, the "film's *coup de cinema* . . . a giant, festering pandora's box that harbors all the emotional, spiritual and political ills of the world."[73]

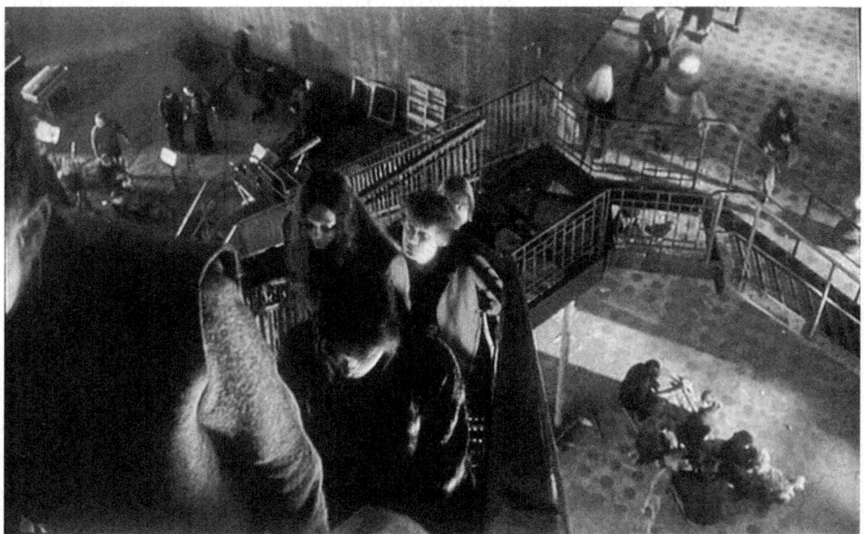

Figure 6.24. Escher-like stairs to nowhere in the heart of the anarchists' factory. Still from *Pola X*.

Source: United Archives GmbH / Alamy Stock Photo.

The complex is occupied by an unidentified, black-clad terrorist group of cybercultists whose object is anarchy: exploding the superstructure beneath whose surface they have constructed their alternate universe. The group's makeup is ambiguous, an amalgam of illegal immigrants like Isabelle's younger female companion, Petruska (her knowledge provides entrée to this world), fascistic thugs (with menacing black guard dogs), zombielike techies manning banks of computers, militant sharpshooters who use store-display dummies for target practice, survivalists (farm animals roam the structure), and an Aryan-blond cult leader with ice-blue eyes who conducts a group of musicians playing Scott Walker's grating industrial rock music from the pit of the building's atrium.[74] Pierre's doppelgänger in appearance, this cult leader proceeds, in intense conversations whose words we never hear, to seduce Pierre with his doctrines. Declaring that this man has pierced "the great lie hidden behind everything," the increasingly delusional Pierre makes him the model for the hero of the "serious" novel he is now maniacally writing on reams of white paper, a novel whose message he swears will reveal "truth" but which his publisher deems the ravings of a madman.

Some of the film's reviewers—rightly, I think—find the film's political subtexts forced, but Carax does manage to convey that the anarchist politics to which these outsiders gravitate is the inevitable outcome of their being made into alien others by society at large. The "dark other" of Pierre's psyche, the product of sexual repression that makes its return in the form of Isabelle, is thus mirrored in these oppressed societal others, who return—like the repressed—to wreak havoc on the political structures that deny their existence. On both the level of the individual psyche and that of group mentality, the result is anarchy: in the former internally expressed and in the latter externally directed. But in each case the result is the same: a violent and destructive explosion of polymorphous perversity. Within Carax's vision, these political and psychic levels are never far apart. If the trauma of genocide has led to Isabelle's psychosis, Pierre's newly awakened political consciousness leads to an increasingly narcissistic, solipsistic vision of himself as victim of a hypocritical world; his subsequent rage, coupled with the artistic impotence he feels at not being able to broadcast his message to the world in the form of the book he's been writing, unleashes the death-drive that culminates in his murder of his cousin (named Thibault in the film) and arrest.[75] The final image of Pierre sitting mute and dumbstruck in the back of a police van (symbol of the state's soul-crushing power) fades into images of the nightmarish forest where Pierre first encountered Isabelle. Thus, the film ends where his awakening to the darker truths began, in the murky realm of the unconscious, the place where, in the spectral form of Isabelle, Pierre embraces instinct, banishes reason, and sets into motion his own imp of the perverse.

Some critics of French New Extremity cinema, with which Carax has been associated, have likened the movement to "torture porn." The phrase is intriguing to consider in light of aesthetics of *Pola X*. "Torture," of course, carried a specific resonance in the 1990s, given the atrocities enacted by Serbian forces on their ethnic others. The anarchist cult in the factory, we sense, has no ethical problem with plotting terrorist acts on its perceived colonial tormenters. But perhaps the most "torturous" aspect of *Pola X*, at least in terms of its effect on the spectator, is its sexually "pornographic" element. Witnessing the scene of unsimulated sex between the actors playing Pierre and Isabelle is, I suspect, excruciating for many. And this is true not only because of Carax's command of our field of vision, which borders on the sadistic, but also because its depiction, like some of the other temporally dilated moments in this long film, threatens, ironically enough, to bore us. As Jennifer Doyle has noted in discussing *Moby-Dick*'s "boring" bits, pornography's focus on the fetishized detail, its repetition of the same again and again, is nothing if not tedious; yet what one person finds agonizingly boring is someone else's erotic turn-on.[76] Carax on some level seems to have imbibed this truth, getting off on making his audience squirm uneasily in their seats, and the effect is uncannily akin to Melville's perverse play with his readers in *Pierre*: We don't always want to look at this "train-wreck" of what the *New York Times* calls a "sometime intoxicating, often infuriating film," yet we can't turn away.[77]

Making "Good Work" of Depraved Desire: *Beau travail*

"Handsomely done!"

So John Claggart of Melville's novella caustically observes when Billy Budd—known familiarly to his fellow tars as the "Handsome Sailor"—accidentally spills his soup across Claggart's path as the sergeant-in-arms is passing by.

"Beau travail!" is the translation of Claggart's quip in the Gallimard edition *Billy Budd, marin* (1980), and the phrase—literally meaning "good work"—becomes, intriguingly, the title of Claire Denis's film released in 1999.[78] By reimagining the shipboard world of *Billy Budd* as a group of French legionnaires stationed in contemporary northern East Africa, Denis indeed puts Melville's text to "good work," creating a visually poetic rumination on the consequences of desire and envy, infatuation and irrationality, and guilt and remorse when unleashed within an insular, homosocial world of men. It would be a mistake, however, to consider *Beau travail* either a literal "translation" or straightforward "adaptation" into film of Melville's fable of innocence confounded by depravity. Rather, the themes and rhythms of *Billy Budd* function as "personal talismans, aesthetic aphrodisiacs, inspirational reference points, incantations," in Denis's meditation on the perversities created by repression and desire-become-hatred.[79]

The incident of the spilled soup in *Billy Budd* highlights the complex crossing of queer desires and perverse motives that Denis turns into cinematic reverie or dream. Many readers have noted the sexual charge of Melville's description of Billy's accidental "spill[ing] of the entire contents of his soup-pan" onto the deck, its "greasy liquid stream[ing] just across [Claggart's] path," like a spontaneous sexual discharge. Likewise, Claggart is about to "ejaculate" a retort when he stops himself, pausing a beat before he instead says, "Handsomely done, my lad! And handsome is as handsome did it."[80] On the surface, his play on the soubriquet that the other sailors affectionately use for Billy, the "Handsome Sailor," renders Claggart's words a witty rejoinder everyone can laugh at; on a deeper level, his repetition of "handsome" highlights the degree to which he is morbidly obsessed with Billy's beauty. And it is not just Billy's outward appearance but also his inner beauty that consumes Claggart—the very quality that Claggart knows that he himself lacks and will never possess.

When Denis takes the phrase "handsomely done" one step further by making its French translation, *beau travail*, her title, its meanings ripple in multiple directions. Not only does Galoup (her Claggart figure) attempt in his revenge plot to make "good work" (*beau travail* at its most ironic) of this "good work" (Melville tells us that *beau* Billy is "such a fine specimen of the genus homo" that "in the nude [he] might have passed for a statue of young Adam before the Fall" [94]); Denis also raises the provocative question of whether one as sickened in spirit as Galoup can ever be redeemed by "good work(s)"—that is, by feeling remorse or making amends for the tragedy he has precipitated.[81] On a metatextual level, to the degree that the film is a subjective record of Galoup's memories of his obsession and jealousy, the story that he is telling himself by writing it down in his journal and that we are watching unfold on the screen comprises a "working" through of perverse desire that may or may not augur a "good" end: *beau travail* indeed.

In addition to the transformation of Melville's all-male domain of a British man-of-war at sea during the perilous era of the French Revolution into that of French legionnaires stationed on a remote outpost in Djibouti in postcolonial East Africa, other aspects of Melville's fable undergo telling alterations in Denis's reenvisioning. When in the presence of Captain Vere Melville's Claggart falsely accuses Billy of inciting insurrection, the new recruit finds himself unable to respond verbally (he stutters in moments of crisis) and spontaneously lashes out with his fist, inadvertently striking Claggart dead. Although Captain Vere sees Claggart's death as God's punishment and intuits Billy's innocence, he feels compelled by duty to apply martial law, according to which Billy must hang. In Denis's retelling, Sentain (the Billy equivalent) strikes Galoup (the Claggart equivalent) *after* the latter has slapped him, the sergeant having just accused the youth of insubordination for what's in fact a humanitarian act (more "good work"). Galoup does not drop dead, nor is Billy sentenced to death on the spot. Instead, Galoup bides his time to take his revenge, effectually condemning Sentain to death by stranding him in the desert with nothing but a broken compass to find his way back to camp. Denis also reverses the sentencing of innocent Billy to death: The commandant, Bruno Forestier, court-martials Galoup instead, expelling him from the sole "family" he has ever known.

Despite these shifts, the focus on the ambivalent, troubling nature of Galoup's feelings toward Sentain forms the crux of *Beau travail*. As in Melville, we witness the tragic perversion of desire as it warps and shatters lives, transforming what might otherwise have been love into hatred.[82] And, as in the case of Claggart and Billy, the staff sergeant's perverse fascination with the fresh recruit exudes a homoerotic current. Yet Galoup's possibly closeted sexuality is just one component of the torments that eat away at his soul and cause him to project his feelings of inner emptiness, alienation, and self-loathing outward onto others. As Jonathan Rosenbaum perceptively notes, "In fact, [while] 'homoerotic' might superficially describe a few strains of the polytonality Denis is working with . . . it isn't an adequate label for [this] material."[83] That is, what drives Galoup literally and figuratively mad with depraved longing and bitter despair isn't *simply* the result of a frustrated erotic attraction to the handsome Sentain. Rather, he is most obsessed—and angered—by the younger man's possession of those qualities of inner grace that Galoup lacks: the comradeship, calmness, and openness that immediately make Sentain the favorite of the entire troop of men. The homoerotic dimensions of Galoup's desire just happen to be the trigger that sets off the explosion of the polymorphous perverse, shattering the rigid self-discipline that has hitherto allowed him to skate over the chaos that roils his inner world.

If another's "beauty" is a negative trigger for Galoup, the adjective *beautiful* perfectly describes Claire Denis's film. Reviewers and critics were unanimous in singing their praise of its sheer visual beauty. Arresting images and panoramic vistas are woven together in a lyrical flow whose sensuous, kinesthetic effects approach that of a dream. "A hypnotic, homoerotic effort fraught with a rare sense of the sublime—and, rarer still, without pretentiousness." So notes Lawrence Ferber in his review, adding a list of salient adjectives repeated by other commentators: "beautiful, majestic, forbidden, dangerous—and most of all, mesmerizing."[84] Denis creates these effects by keeping her camera at a tantalizing distance so that it seems as if the movie is merely "eavesdropping on or directly absorbing life," not distinguishing between major or minor events as they flow past the camera's field of vision. Rather than impose interpretations, Denis places her faith "in the ability of observation to reveal." For viewers, the sensation is simultaneously that of watching a documentary and that of experiencing a trance that unfolds at a "deliberate, hypnotic pace," lulling us into its largely wordless rhythms.[85] The opening sequence is representative. The camera slowly pans a vividly colored, crumbling mural that depicts legionnaires, then moves into a disco, where the native women are blowing air kisses while soldiers dance with them; then it cuts to the shirtless soldiers, sculpted torsos glistening as they do mesmerizing group exercises in the sun. The silent long shots of these ritualistic movements dilate narrative space and time: We have entered the world of choreographed dance, in which these sensuous bodies, primed with discipline and desire, are all we have of traditional "plot" (figure 6.25).[86] The succeeding images of the soldiers going about everyday tasks on their outpost, from "feminine" domestic ones such as hanging clothes to dry to more "masculine" ones such as breaking unyielding stones with pickaxes, are strung together associatively, so that we must read them as we would a poem, obliquely and elliptically. In entering this self-enclosed, all-male world, we have stepped into (in more ways than one, as I will show) a hallucination where subconscious desire trembles across the surface of the screen. The effect approximates the impressionism of Melville's indirect, lyrical prose in *Billy Budd*.

Abetting this "fluid impressionism" is the film's self-referentiality, blurring the boundaries between itself and other creative works.[87] French-film cinephiles are not likely to miss the fact that the commandant's name, Bruno Forestier, belongs to the protagonist of Jean-Luc Godard's film about the Algerian Revolution, *Le petit soldier* (1960). Moreover, Michael Subor, the actor who played the young, counterterrorist agent Forestier in Godard's film, now plays the role

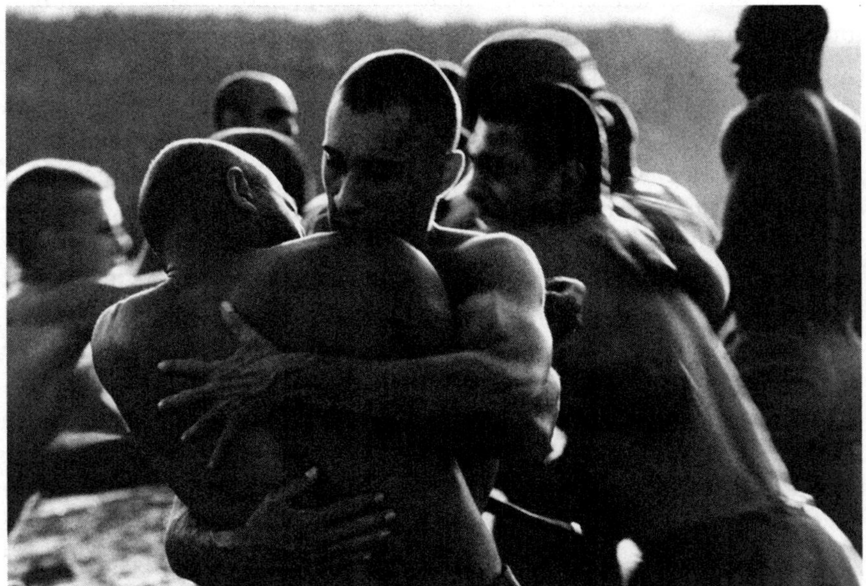

Figure 6.25. Discipline and desire in the desert.
Still from *Beau travail* (Claire Denis, 1999).

Source: TCD/Prod.DB / Alamy Stock Photo.

of Commandant Forestier, forty-some-years older, in *Beau travail*: Godard's young and idealistic agent has become in Denis's resurrection of the character a world-weary, disillusioned military professional reluctant to interfere in the actions of his men until Galoup's crime finally forces his hand.[88] By casting Subor to play a character bearing the name of a character he played four decades earlier, Denis creates a multitiered conversation between the anti-Algerian French colonial politics represented by Godard and the postcolonial world of Djibouti (throwing the purpose of the French Foreign Legion into question), between idealism abandoned and idealism perhaps partially regained, between anti-Algerian racism and the happily polyglot racial world of this contemporary legion. In a sense, then, Denis's film asks to be read not as a singular work of art but as part of an ongoing dialogue among artists. Another intriguing aspect of the film's intertextuality, given this chapter's reading of *Pola X*, is the casting of Denis Lavant as Galoup, an actor who made his mark playing the feral-like protagonist Alex in Leos Carax's first three films (Carax's actual first name is "Alex"), and those performances bleed into that of Galoup; to wit, the Romantic rebel of Carax's films has become a self-hating, internally raging man who looks as if life has given him a beating and left him, in J. Hoberman's simile, with "a face like a Tom Waits song."[89]

These metatextual references include another famous adaptation of *Billy Budd*: Benjamin Britten's opera, whose score is used first to highlight the scenes in which the men wordlessly perform their ritualistic exercises, moving in choreographed unison. E. M. Forster, who wrote the libretto to Britten's opera with Eric Crozier, explicitly aimed to highlight the "redeeming power of homoerotic love" (which Claggart rejects), although in the final opera Britten shifts the emphasis to Vere because that role was sung by Britten's lover, the tenor Peter Piers.[90] It is no coincidence, then, that Britten's score soars in precisely the most homoerotic moments of Denis's retelling—as the men's half-naked bodies gleam under the relentless sun and as they bounce onto and off each other in an ambiguous interplay of rigid discipline and sensuous beauty. The homoerotic frisson attributed to the film exists in these images of beautiful men communally and affectionately engaging in acts of intimacy that reach from violence to tenderness, from the most masculine to the most domestic of daily chores. But what is perhaps most intriguingly *queer* about the homoeroticism that viewers sense in *Beau travail* is that this homoerotic relay between image and spectator is the result of the collaboration of two women—female director and female cinematographer (Agnes Godard)—asking us to enjoy these sensuous male bodies seen at a distance *as if* parlayed through a homoerotic gaze. Thus, Sentain's collapse onto the body of the downed helicopter pilot that he has rescued from the sea visually reads as two beautiful men in a postcoital embrace; the tableau formed by the soldiers as they tenderly pluck stinging spines from Sentain's bloody foot after a sea-diving exercise combines the erotic (these tanned bodies could have stepped right out of an Abercrombie and Fitch ad) and the spiritual (the image also evokes paintings of Christ's deposition from the cross); a shot of the men shaving together, bodies touching, gives the quintessentially "masculine" act (shaving facial hair) a shared domestic and sensual familiarity (figures 6.26–6.28).

Especially in the seductive images of the exercises where the men move together in unison, the balancing act between disciplining the flesh and a bodily sensuousness verging on the ecstatic highlights the paradoxical extremes embraced by those recruits who choose to submit to the circumscribed world and rules of the French Foreign Legion. The makeup of its corps is unique among France's military: Men of all nationalities are encouraged to join, and three years after enlistment they can earn French citizenship, but their foremost loyalty is to the legion itself ("Serve the good cause and die," the legion's slogan, is tattooed on Galoup's chest).[91] The Foreign Legion has historically attracted recruits from among the dispossessed—those with no ties or future, those who wish to escape their pasts, those who wish to re-create their identity (legionnaires were encouraged to assume a new name). Before the 1970s, the legion's primary mission was that of protecting France's colonial interests,

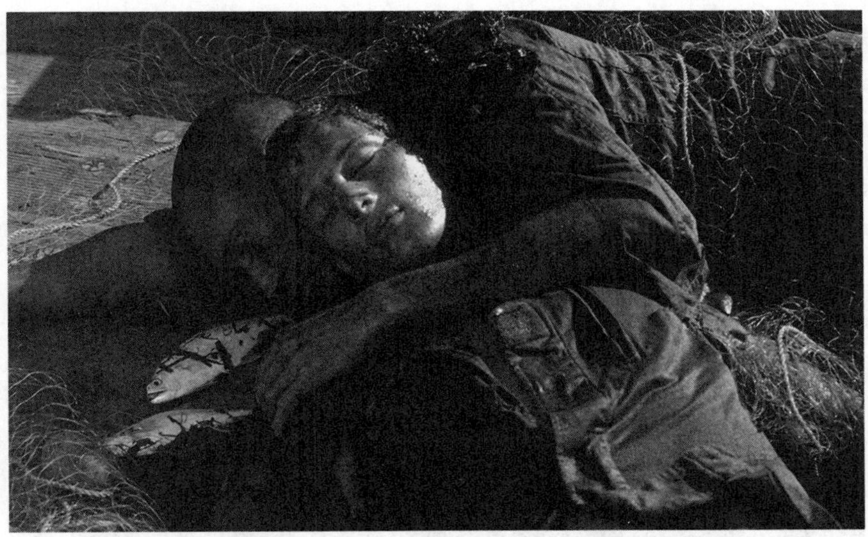

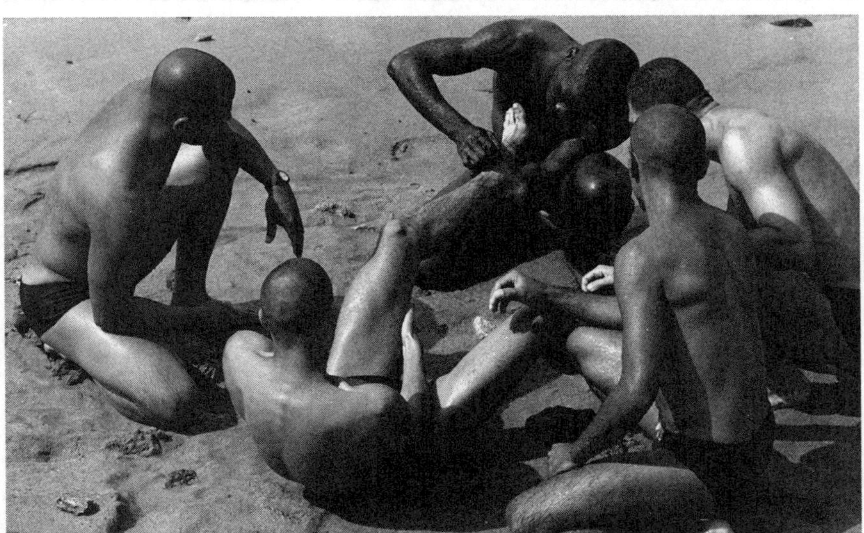

Figure 6.26 and 6.27. Visual lyricism and the (homo)erotic gaze.
Stills from *Beau travail*.

Source: TCD/Prod.DB / Alamy Stock Photo.

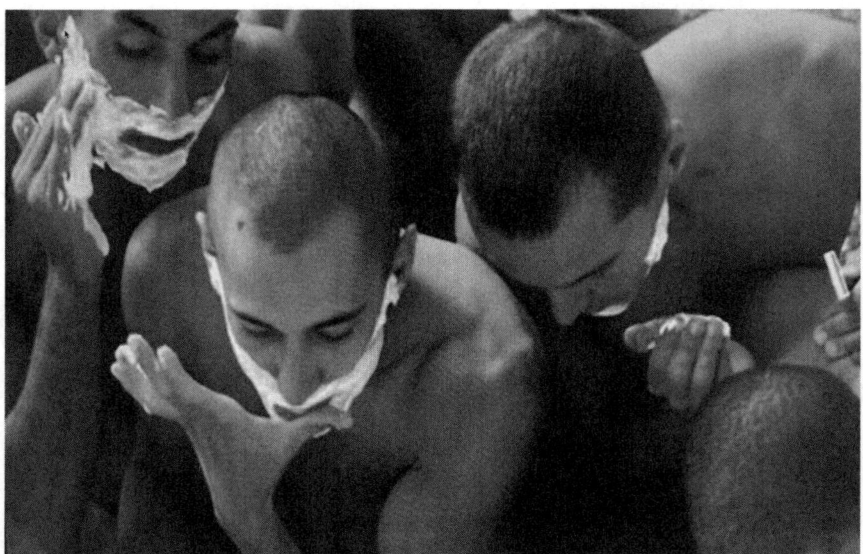

Figure 6.28. Intimate masculinities.
Still from *Beau travail.*

Source: TCD/Prod.DB / Alamy Stock Photo.

particularly in North Africa. However, in the postcolonial order following Algeria's successful independence movement, its soldiers have been reduced to peacetime activities, manning far-flung outposts like the one depicted in the film. Charles Taylor thus describes Denis's legionnaires as "military penitents" seeking to find "discipline in a void," and her panoramic shots of Djibouti's seemingly desolate desert and coastline emphasizes this sense of an existential void, a wasteland within which the soldiers create an enclosed, cut-off world buttressed by self-imposed rules and discipline.[92] While the camera's long, silent pans of this inhospitable landscape support a sense of existence being lived on the edge and possibly without meaning (ironically, the soldiers expend their greatest physical labor—"good work," indeed—chiseling out of rock a road that leads nowhere), this viewpoint is carefully framed to pertain only to the legionnaires; Denis strategically includes glimpses of ongoing, productive indigenous Djibouti life, whose inhabitants pause every now and then to gaze at the alien legionnaires, as if witnessing a curious spectacle being staged for their amusement (figure 6.29).[93]

From the beginning, *Beau travail* marks Galoup as one of those loners who has sought out the Foreign Legion because he feels he fits nowhere else in society; submitting to its harsh discipline allows him to control his feelings of

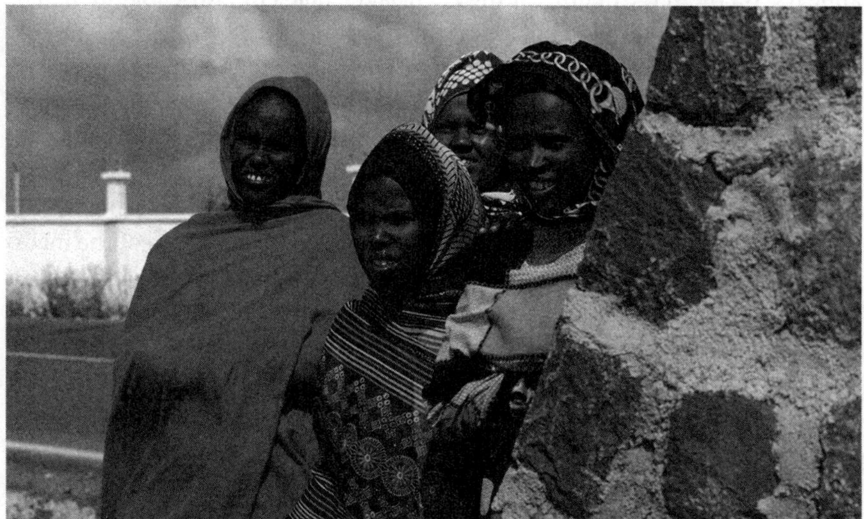

Figure 6.29. Djibouti women as bemused spectators and silent chorus. Still from *Beau travail.*

Source: TCD/Prod.D8 / Alamy Stock Photo.

inner chaos. What he gains by being "the perfect legionnaire," as he describes himself, is a sense of belonging and a reason for living. Just how bereft Galoup is without the structure of the military is evinced in the present time of the film, after he has been expelled from the legion. Six minutes into the film, his voice-over delivers the script's first significant words: "Marseilles, late February. I have plenty of time to kill. I screwed up. . . . [This is] the story of . . . a soldier . . . unfit for life. Unfit for civil life." Faced with this crushing sense of not belonging and "time to kill," Galoup moves through his day trying to re-create the discipline that, without a band of brothers sharing the same tasks, has lost significance. Making coffee, ironing clothes to create the "perfect crease," methodically stubbing out a cigarette, Galoup's every action is executed with excruciating care, almost in slow motion, each an attempt to fill the empty hours. A loner and a lost soul drifting without purpose or meaning in the civilian world, Galoup may nostalgically remember his days as a legionnaire as a time of belonging, but the truth of the matter is that even then he remained an outsider to the legion's self-created family, always watching, always commanding, rarely being one with his men. As a result, Galoup, not unlike Carax's increasingly isolated and maddened Pierre, is a volcano of seething repressions waiting to erupt. Lavant masterfully embodies these tensions in his fierce performance as Galoup. For Taylor, Lavant always appears "on the verge of unleashing . . . what he holds in"; Rosenbaum memorably likens him to "a switchblade ready to spring open."[94]

And spring open Galoup does, his emotions keen and murderous as a razor, when the parentless Sentain joins this chosen family of "brothers." Several minutes into the film, after long panning shots of the exercising legionnaires' sensuous bodies, a close-up of shimmering ocean water dissolves into the image of a fountain pen writing in a journal—Galoup in Marseilles recording his memories of Djibouti. Next, the camera cuts a series of close-ups of the meditative faces of several young soldiers gazing off-screen as they bob in a boat. The last face is Sentain's, and the next cut reveals that he is the object of Galoup's glowering scrutiny; in contrast to the youthful countenances of his charges, the sergeant's face is gaunt, caved in, marked by inner turmoil. Galoup's voice-over informs us he has taken note of this new recruit "who stuck out. . . . He had no reason to be with us in the legion. *That's what I thought.* I felt something *vague and menacing* take hold of me" (emphases added).

Thus begins Galoup's queerly perverse fascination with Sentain, whom he accuses of "seduc[ing]" all the others: "He attracted stares: all notice him, drawn to his calmness, his openness." The result is Galoup's increasing anger: "Deep down I felt a sort of rancor, a rage brimming. I was jealous." From "deep down" within, something indeed is "brimming" to the surface, something "vague and menacing" precisely because it is a projection of desires he prefers not to name or acknowledge. In describing Sentain as "attract[ing]" and "seduc[ing]" others, Galoup is projecting his own feelings outward; *he* is the one who is seduced and attracted, the one most intensely "star[ing]" at Sentain, and his jealousy is a by-product of the impossible distance that separates him from this object of fascination. These taboo desires symbolically unman Galoup. This fear of being "less than a man" for what he desires may explain the seemingly incongruous image that accompanies the voice-over at this point, as he angrily lops branches off a tree in present-day Marseilles: He is at once futilely attempting to control "nature" *and* enacting the self-mutilation incurred by repression (images of castration, as Melvilleans know, are rife in his fiction). After days and nights spent stealthily watching Sentain in hopes of finding the "chink in his armor," Galoup will spew out in his journal in second-person direct address, "We don't need guys *like you* here" (emphasis added); the potentially homophobic insinuation in Galoup's phrasing again reveals him in the act of projecting onto Sentain his personal sense of difference and self-disgust.

Tellingly, the "something vague and menacing" that Sentain's appearance rouses in Galoup is qualified by the sergeant's tacit admission, in the same voice-over, that this feeling is entirely subjective: "*That's what I thought*" (emphasis added). This degree of partiality is Denis's first hint that nearly all the camera's seemingly objective images of life in Djibouti are being filtered through Galoup's subjective point of view as he retrospectively canvases his memories. The camera's focus on what initially seems random images thus turns out to be significant markers of what Galoup is selectively remembering. In this light, the aside he makes in his initial voice-over about having too much time on his hands as a civilian takes on added significance: "I screwed up *from a certain point of view, and viewpoints count. Angles of attack*" (emphases added). Then he continues, disingenuously, "My story is simple." Simple it is not.

Retrospective narratives generally attempt to make sense of the past by discerning the meaningful patterns that link up to anticipate one's end; retrospection imposes order over events that otherwise appear random, chaotic, without meaning.[95] But first-person retrospective narrative, especially when it purports to be confessional ("I screwed up") is especially subject to distortions of memory as well as to conscious manipulation. Thus, when Galoup says that "viewpoints count," he inadvertently reveals his hand: He wants to tell a story that exonerates himself, a story that the audience sitting in judgment will "count" as true. His story is anything but "simple" since, as he also admits, all viewpoints, including his own, are "angles of attack." An "attack" may simply be an approach to a subject, but it can also be a violent assault on truth. Galoup is still thinking like a soldier ("attacking"), despite having been drummed out of the legion. Indeed, his discharge makes all the more imperative his attempt to control the story by shaping the viewer's reception of the perverse cruelty that culminates in his present exile.

Freud suggests that telling one's traumatic past may allow one to move on, to put away shame or guilt, perhaps even to experience catharsis. Whether this is true of Galoup's "confession" or not is left as open-ended as any Melville story. Early on Galoup notes that "maybe freedom begins with remorse," intimating he may wish to free himself from the burden of complicity that he carries for the virtual death sentence he's imposed on Sentain. However, he immediately adds the qualification, "I heard that somewhere," leaving ambiguous whether he's embracing or dismissing the sentiment. Midway through the film, he also confesses his regret that "I was that man, that narrow-minded legionnaire"; his single-minded focus on Sentain kept him from noticing the daily rhythms of life in Djibouti that he now finds himself missing. While this comment sheds light on the film's inclusion of multiple seemingly inconsequential shots of Djibouti life, allowing us to understand them as Galoup's attempt to recuperate what he previously failed to see, the admission of his having once been "narrow-minded" hints that his narrative viewpoint might still be partial, selective, incomplete: in a word, unreliable.

But even if Galoup is an unreliable narrator desperately attempting to control his story, the very act of remembering opens the floodgates to unconscious instincts and passions that refuse control—the same inchoate desires that have fueled his tormented obsession with Sentain. As suggested by the first image of Galoup's pen writing in his journal, emerging from underneath the previous image of rippling water, the sergeant's "story" both emerges from and is overdetermined by those floods of unconscious desire that have been triggered by memories of his obsession and, with such memories, the irrational libidinal impulses underlying his increasingly violent actions. This influx of the polymorphous perverse, in turn, accounts for the surreal, dreamlike aura imbuing the Djibouti scenes: In watching *Beau travail*, one has the sensation of witnessing a hallucination, a mirage rising in the desert, as much as any objective "reality." Justin Vicari notes a schizophrenic quality in Galoup's journal musings.[96] At the very least, I suggest, the juxtaposition of his emotionless voice and the charged imagery on-screen suggests the disjunction of a mind teetering on the brink of madness. Galoup's perverse infatuation with Sentain—both its occurrence in the past and its recurrence in the present retelling—thus warps Galoup's *and* the film's frame of reality, ushering the viewer into the realm of fantasy or dream.

Likewise, Denis interjects into her film moments whose spatial and temporal coordinates are impossible within the narrative logic of realism.[97] Tellingly, these narrative impossibilities almost always involve Galoup's emotionally heightened memories of Sentain. The first noteworthy example—ominously introduced by Galoup as "a harbinger of things to come"—occurs during Ramadan as the soldiers go out on the town. As they stroll the streets, we see Galoup lurking behind them, unseen, watching and longing from afar. The narrative "impossibility" here involves Galoup's clothing. At first, he (like his troop) is seen in uniform; as his stalking continues, however, *with no apparent time lapse* he appears in black slacks and black shirt (his "disco" clothes, we later learn; he is shown carefully ironing the same shirt in the present time of the film). The outfit, as Vicari notes, is suggestive of the "urban homosexual" in the 1990s.[98] Earlier, Commandant Forestier identified himself as a shepherd watching over his flock; Galoup—whose name contains the French word for "wolf"—is the *loup* preying on these innocent sheep.

What Galoup's voyeuristic gaze witnesses during this evening stroll also undergoes a strange transformation. First, the happy soldiers elevate a Black legionnaire, resplendent with red scarf accenting his bared torso, to their shoulders; next we see the same Black soldier lifting Sentain to his shoulders, at which Galoup's voice-over laconically comments: "In triumph they carried one of their own." The sequence uncannily evokes the opening of *Billy Budd*, where, as a prelude to Billy's intradiegetic introduction as the "Handsome Sailor," the narrator vividly recollects seeing an exemplar of the prototype paraded down the streets of Liverpool fifty years ago: a Black sailor "ebony of chest" with "gay silk handkerchief" (43) around his neck, escorted by an admiring bodyguard of worshipful comrades. As Denis replaces the Black soldier with Sentain, one cannot help but wonder whether this is a hallucination or fantasy produced by Galoup's desires, rendering the beloved as elevated, as idealized, and as maddeningly untouchable as a troubadour's lady on her pedestal.

For Galoup, the immediate results are feelings of both rage and exclusion. These roiling emotions are exacerbated in the next sequence, when Sentain rescues a pilot from a crashed helicopter, an act of heroism that Galoup perversely personalizes as "the end of me." Galoup converts his bilious anger into sadistic action, pushing the physical limits of the troop as Britten's choral music swells. Ironically, however, the more Galoup seeks to "punish" the men with drills and hard labor, the more they take a sensuous pleasure in their bodies' ability to perform the tasks; even more ironically, Galoup's sadistic discipline only increases his masochistic suffering, for he is forced to watch all this muscular beauty on display without being able to be a meaningful part of it. As the perverse takes its revenge on Galoup's attempts to repress his desires, he finds himself in a position not unlike that of Melville's Sub-Sub: "For by how much more *pains* ye take to *please* the world, by so much the more shall ye for ever go thankless!" (*Moby-Dick*, 8, emphasis added).

The next surreal moment occurs once Galoup orders the troop to move to a makeshift outpost far from their base camp for more punishing labor: building a road out of rock in the midst of seemingly nowhere. Between the relentless, Sisyphean task, the exercises continue until, without warning, we find ourselves watching Galoup and Sentain circling each other, shirtless, warily glaring at each other as Britten's music intensifies (figure 6.30). The scene lacks narrative motivation—we don't know whether this is another military exercise or we are witnessing an intensely menacing personal encounter between the two, for they appear to be entirely alone (only toward the end of the sequence does the camera draw back and reveal that the other legionnaires, watching, have formed a circle around this spectacle). A sense of impending violence mounts as the orbits traced by Galoup and Sentain grow smaller and smaller until the two men come to a standstill inches apart, locked in a "who will blink first" stalemate. Charged emotion and personal challenge light their eyes. But because of what? Are we witnessing homoerotic desire or unmitigated disgust? Brianna Beehler hypothesizes that the scene is another of Galoup's mental fabrications in which he summons into being a *mutual rivalry* with Sentain in order "to justify his insane feelings of jealousy."[99] Although everything in the film suggests these feelings are one-sided and that Sentain feels neither rivalry nor desire nor threat (like Melville's Billy, he shrugs off his comrades' concern that Galoup has it "in" for him), Galoup *needs* to believe that he and Sentain are engaged in something more intensely personal, something that emotionally involves both men. In Beehler's suggestive reading, this imagined fantasy

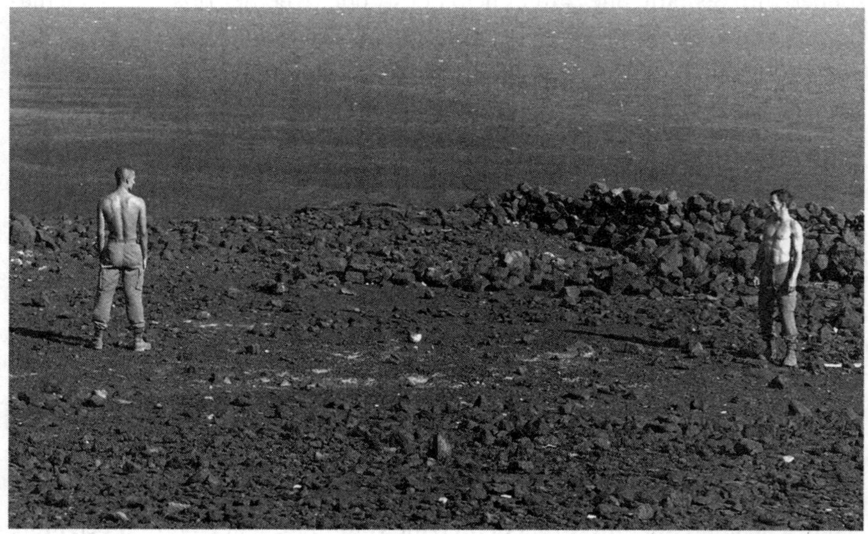

Figure 6.30. The face-off: love or hate. Still from *Beau travail.*

Source: TCD/Prod.DB / Alamy Stock Photo.

gives him the closeness he needs to justify his feelings as they increasingly tilt toward irrational, sadomasochistic violence.

The same question regarding what is real and what is fantasy clouds Sentain's fate, which unfolds after Galoup has slapped Sentain for giving a drink of water to a Muslim comrade being forced to dig a hole (the latter is being punished for having walked off guard duty to attend mosque during Ramadan). When Sentain strikes his superior back (echoing the crisis in *Billy Budd*), Galoup is more than ever obsessed with bringing Sentain down ("I'll kill you. . . . You are in my power," he narrates in his journal). His revenge is to strand Galoup in the desert with a malfunctioning compass to find his way back to the camp. The camera shows Sentain collapsing on the salt flats on the edge of the Red Sea as Galoup's voice-over drily informs us, "He never came back," adding that he *may* have died or he *may* have deserted, escaping over the mountains to Ethiopia. Once Galoup's treachery is discovered, and Forestier court-marshals him, however, the film silently presents yet another, open-ended possibility. The camera returns to the shores of the Red Sea, where a camel-mounted caravan discovers Sentain's salt-encrusted body; then, after more cuts to Galoup in Marseilles, it depicts Sentain unconscious but alive, aboard a public bus and tended to by a woman who feeds him drops of water. "For all we know," Rosenbaum writes, this rescue "could be happening in Galoup's imagination." Likewise,

Beehler notes that the film offers "no explanation for this disclosure of . . . events" nor any evidence "for how Galoup could know what happened to [Sentain]."[100] Because the African scenes have been presented as filtered through Galoup's memory, Beehler suggests that the bus scene is also Galoup's fantasy, a fabrication or (to use his earlier militaristic phrase) an "angle of attack" that partially allows him to "absolv[e] himself of this crime"—if Sentain survives, maybe his deed isn't so bad, after all. However, as Beehler also suggests, "Confessing [his] crimes to the viewer does not preclude the possibility of any further dishonesty. . . . Galoup may actually be as unreliable of a narrator as he was a sergeant."[101] The extremity of Galoup's need to exculpate himself points to the sheer power of the unconscious and polymorphous instincts now commandeering his narration. Both conscious and unconscious motives, I suggest, intersect in this fantasy of Sentain's survival. Likewise, the break that its insertion creates in the film's diegetic flow underlines the degree to which the perverse overflows created by Galoup's repression of desire (manifested in his acts of voyeurism, violence, sadomasochism, fetishistic obsession, and irrational behavior) have utterly splintered his psyche, such that reality and fantasy are no longer separable.

These hallucinatory "out-of-time" sequences culminate in the movie's final scene, one that again confutes narrative linearity and hovers in the ambiguous space between fantasy and actuality. Over the course of three minutes, Galoup literally and figuratively breaks loose—or loses it—on the dance floor of an empty disco. This final scene "comes out of the blue," as Taylor notes, "summing up the movie and blasting it to pieces at the same time." Up to this point, we have watched the tightly wound Galoup do everything in his power to maintain the rigid self-discipline of the "perfect legionnaire." But in this final sequence, he "proceeds to shred it to pieces before our eyes." Taylor expresses a sentiment—"It left me stunned, not believing what I'd just seen"—likely felt in the gut of most viewers of *Beau travail* as the final credits roll.[102]

The actions in Marseilles that immediately precede this climactic explosion on the dance floor make its appearance all the more arresting. Having completed the ritualistic ironing of his black party shirt, Galoup proceeds to make his bed with exacting military precision. He lies down, face up and shirtless, pistol in hand and resting just above his crotch; the camera pans to the "serve and die" tattoo on his right pectoral. All signals point to an impending act of suicide.[103] But as the camera continues to move from the tattoo to a vein pulsing in Galoup's bicep, this "life beat" of blood pumping through his body is matched by the faint sounds of the Europop hit "The Rhythm of the Night" by Corona. Without warning the camera cuts to an empty disco with a mirrored back wall as the soundtrack swells and Galoup, dressed in his black "disco" outfit, begins to dance, tentative steps at first, then his body jerking in kinetic "fits and stops" and finally whirling at break-neck speed like a possessed dervish.[104] Not only is Galoup's body breaking free of the rigid discipline he has hitherto scrupulously imposed on it, his *unsyncopated* movements are breaking free of the rhythm of this song *about* rhythm. For once, his body registers unrestrained, wild rapture as he hurls himself around the space, rolling across the floor, springing into manic spins and whirls, bouncing off his splintered reflection in the mirrored wall. Dispossessed of all constraints, he expresses pure libidinal release. "Give it up, Sub-Subs!": Galoup has become the living embodiment of the injunction addressed to the archivists of the world in the "Extracts" section of *Moby-Dick*.

This surreal conclusion encloses the spectator, like Galoup, in what Vicari terms a "site of fantasy," a space both in and out of time: This *could* be a nightclub in Marseilles; it *could* be the nightclub in Djibouti where the film's action begins; or it *could* be a space that exists only in Galoup's mind.[105] Here, for at least this one moment, Galoup discovers, in Elena Del Rio's words, "a life-beat that stands outside control and ratiocination." The result is an experience of jouissance, moreover, that includes the spectator as intimate participant; the erotic union that has never materialized between Galoup and Sentain becomes, Del Rio suggests, an intimate, tactile, libidinal relationship between Galoup and viewer, between his bodily spectacle and our visceral sensations. And if Galoup's solo dance is "dislocated from any intelligible lines of causes and effects, intentions and results," as Del Rio describes it, its "life beat" also takes Galoup—and the spectator—to a queer place that exists outside the binaries of life and death, of Eros and Thanatos, as traditionally theorized.[106] Rather than suggest that Galoup has suddenly chosen life over death (by forgoing suicide), Denis offers an alternative that, as Taylor suggests, "blurs the line between freedom and bondage, between release and torment."[107] In the process, the negative perversion of desire created by repression and envy gives way to pure jouissance, an explosion of polymorphous perversity that is euphoric rather than destructive. Galoup's escape from the constraints of ego allows him, at least for this dilated moment, to create *and* fully inhabit his own, singular, kinetic "rhythm of the night." Galoup may not find redemption or absolution, but his remorse does seem to allow him (unlike Melville's Claggart or Billy) to experience a temporary freedom that may—or may not—be a breakthrough from the straitjacket of self-torment and regret.

In this final scene, Galoup's frenetic body, Del Rio writes, "seems capable of breaking free of its own frame."[108] It also seems on the verge of breaking free of the cinematic frame itself. As with Galoup, so with the film: In *Beau travail*, Claire Denis's queerly perverse achievement is that of finding, in Taylor's beautifully chosen words, the cinematic means to "perch the rigid fetishism of order"—implicit in the technical and formal control that has gone into making this mesmerizing film *seem* unplanned—"right on the edge of chaos and, in the final moments, to dance suspended over the abyss."[109] Stripping *Billy Budd* of its trappings of Christian allegory, Denis has distilled Melville's fable down to its existential essence, revealing the imp of the perverse that keeps beating on in the face of meaninglessness.

CHAPTER 7

PLASTIC SEAS, PASTEBOARD MASKS, PLANETARY FUTURES

The great flood-gates of the wonder-world swung open, and . . . there floated into my inmost soul, endless processions of the whale.
—*Moby-Dick*

The only whale left to see may soon be the constellation Cetus—the distant, starry outline of a beast we loved and hated enough to place in the sky while removing it from everywhere else.
—Kathleen Rooney, "No Firm Fortress, No Retreat"

We are still tempting Ahab's unknowable gods and flouting signs and portents of extinction.
—Christopher Volpe, "Artist's Statement"

Now horror everlasting
Has come to visit.
Yet I am still a wild wonder-world
Ungraspable by mortal men.
. . . .
Call me not Ishmael but
The Sea.
—J. Martin Daughtry, "Loomings," in *Call Me Not Ishmael but the Sea*

In her richly suggestive column "Sea Trash, Dark Pools, and the Tragedy of the Commons" (2010), the *PMLA* editor Patricia Yaeger opens with a provocation: "How liquid are we?" Combining the oceanic turn in literary studies with what she dubs ecocriticism$, Yaeger challenges us to reimagine our planet and its global flows from the perspective of its interconnecting bodies of water rather than of its lesser, state- and nation-boundaried land masses. Such a shift not only irremediably alters our perception of land-based geopolitics, Yaeger writes, but also demands a reconceptualization of the relation of the human and the more-than-human—issues preoccupying contemporary artists tapping into the spirit of Melville in order to create environmentally inspired works of art. Taking these relations seriously can transform our understanding of the multiple agencies—human, animal, mineral, microbic, technological—at work in a world hurling toward climate catastrophe.[1]

In describing the ocean as a "commons"—a collectively owned space open to all—Yaeger leans on Garrett Hardin's terminology to describe the tragic fate of the once thriving English pasturelands known as "the commons": In a world of limited resources, the freedom of individuals to draw on natural resources held in common has led to their overuse and depletion.[2] In terms of the earth's oceans, romanticized ideas about their supposed "boundlessness" as well as figurations of their sublimity have abetted the process of environmental degradation by obscuring the degree to which, ever since the rise of civilization, human interaction with the world's waterways has rendered the ocean's ecosystems "always already technological" rather than "natural" or "infinite." Indeed, Yaeger continues, the earth's waters are perhaps "more techno than ocean" in this late-capitalist epoch.[3] The vast mass of plastic waste material, now twice the size of Texas, currently trapped in the Pacific gyres and in turn entrapping multiple species, is grim evidence of this technological imprint on ocean ecology.

As a "floating factory" engaged in the extraction of an energy source from the ocean commons and rendering it into a worldwide domestic and industrial commodity, the *Pequod* of *Moby-Dick* epitomizes this interface of the technological and the oceanic, the human and the nonhuman, the animate and inanimate. Likewise, the fact that the course charted by the *Pequod*'s voyage is at once transnational, transglobal, and ultimately planetary makes this novel richly suggestive for contemporary studies of world ecology, environmentalism, and energy resources. Brady Krein suggests that the novel's elliptical narrative form is particularly "well suited to attempting to understand and interpret the environmental crisis that is the Anthropocene"; its tacking back and forth between modes, subjects, and points of view forces the reader to undergo constant "mental course corrections" that reveal the enmeshment and interdependence of energy systems operating at the border of the human and the nonhuman.[4] Harnessing wind, a natural energy resource, and taking advantage of ocean currents, another natural source of energy, allowed whalers to hone their skills in successfully hunting down their prey and extracting the reserves of potential energy existing in the whales' organic makeup. In turn, converting blubber to oil yielded the commodity that lubricated factory machines producing steam and other sources of energy. Even the dried-out epidermis of the slaughtered whales participated in this economy, serving as fuel firing the try-pots where the whale fat was rendered.[5] The round-the-clock efficiency with which the workers on these floating factories expended (human) energy to extract oil made whaling, along with chattel slavery, into antebellum America's most lucrative shipping enterprise; producing whale oil became the "first American industry to make a global economic impact."[6]

If the discovery of petroleum in 1859—an extractable mineral resource—led to the collapse of the American-based whaling industry, so too the engine-driven ships replacing whalers' former sailing vessels, along with newly mechanized weaponry such as gun-harpoons, only advanced the near extinction of whale populations in the following decades. The exploitation of the ocean's resources epitomized in the mid-nineteenth-century whaling industry thus qualifies, following Yaeger, as a "tragedy of the commons," one in which the profit drive in the unregulated sphere of the ocean's "wilderness" tragically led to the depletion of a resource imagined as infinite but in fact is limited in quantity. Ironically, with the shift from whale oil to petroleum extraction, it is now the plastic waste produced by the conversion of petroleum into disposable objects that most greatly threatens the eco- and biosystems of the ocean, accelerating the pace of climate change. Consider, again, the size of the plastic-waste dump in the Pacific gyres: twice the size of Texas.

Moby-Dick, given its anticipations of these intermeshed energy systems, forms "an ideal novel of the Anthropocene," writes Krein. Whereas this scholar sees Ishmael's methods of reading and writing at "a variety of scales" as a usable model for making sense of global systems today, Kathleen Rooney describes her recent rereading of the novel in more apocalyptic if elegiac terms. She proposes that revisiting the novel at this point in human history creates an occasion for "thinking about and grieving the Anthropocene." In the present moment of planetary crisis, she muses, this text may help us come to grips with all that we have lost: "We probably can't atone for causing the horror, but we can consider Melville's novel as a conduit for processing our complicity, as well as for seeing the wonder in the ecology we were part of and destroyed."[7] Her use of the past tense says it all. In sum, the whaling industry both critiqued and celebrated in *Moby-Dick*, as Jeffrey Insko notes, inaugurated the epoch of "fossil modernity" in which the extraction of hydrocarbons, first from an organic source (whales), then from a mineral one (the earth), has abetted the environmental and planetary crisis signaled by climate change in the epoch of the Anthropocene.[8]

The artists examined in this chapter make Melville an eloquent "conduit for processing our complicity" in the life-threatening changes to the global ecosystem that have rendered environmental, energy, and oceanic studies such urgent fields of study; simultaneously, they make Melville the occasion for reseeing the "wonder" of the "ecology we were part of and destroyed." We have encountered anticipations of these environmental concerns in several of the reenvisionings discussed in earlier chapters. The scientific-driven compulsion to "crack" nature open in order to unleash new forms of energy underlies Gilbert Wilson's association of Ahab's monomaniacal hunt with America's self-destructive pursuit of atomic energy (chapter 5). It also lies at the heart of Marianne Wiggins's Melville-infused epic vision of twentieth-century America, *Evidence of Things Unseen* (chapter 3), whose scope moves from Kitty Hawk (the harnessing of air for flight) and the establishment of the Tennessee River Authority (the damning of rivers to produce electrical energy) to the uranium-enrichment experiments at Oak Ridge and the Los Alamos A-bomb test site—whose white void of sand melted into glass becomes Wiggins's metaphoric equivalent of Ishmael's meditation on the terror of whiteness as absence.

Over the decades, too, popular literature—in particular work that takes a fantastical bent—has deployed Melvillean resonances to raise ecological concerns. The daunting problems facing our planet are the subject of Daniel Quinn's cult novel *Ishmael* (1991), in which an unnamed narrator answers a personal ad ("Teacher seeks pupil") that leads to his tutelage by the title character, a telepathic silverback gorilla named Ishmael, who, drilling his pupil with philosophical dialogues modeled on Plato's *The Republic*, condemns humankind's obsession with conquering nature as leading to the earth's pending doom. Likewise, the human protagonists in the fantasy novel-within-a-novel format of Brett Ashley Kaplan's *Rare Stuff* (2022) must learn to communicate with whales, who have been warning them (in clicks coded in Yiddish) of imminent destruction, a new holocaust, if the two species don't work together to save the planet from its crazed drive for energy. And in Kate Hartman's riotous stage play *Wild Kate: A Tale of Revenge at Sea* (2000), saving the ocean—in the aftermath of the Deepwater Oil Rig disaster—becomes the mission of a teenage girl ("Call me Isabel"), who has signed up for a semester at sea on a boat helmed by "Wild Kate," an Ahab-like monomaniac (that one of Isabel's cohorts among the ragtag crew is named Quinn may not only be a nod to Queequeg but also to Daniel *Quinn*, author of *Ishmael*). Concerns about ocean pollution also permeate David Malloy's musical version of *Moby-Dick* (2019), whose set design incorporated ocean trash such as plastic bottles to serve "as a visible reminder of what we have done to our world" and waste products to depict the processing of whale blubber.[9]

In the three following sections, I focus on a series of contemporary creative ruminations on Melville and ecology that push the boundaries of form and genre to deliver their messages. First, I take up three environmentally self-conscious visual-art projects: Esteban Ruiz's *The Dream of Captain Ahab* (2018), Jos Sances's *Or, The Whale* (2019), and Christopher Volpe's *Loomings* (2015–2019). The next section is dedicated to Donovan Hohn's extraordinary travel memoir *Moby-Duck* (2011), in which the author's quest to chart the migration of plastic waste (in the form of yellow rubber ducks) across the world's oceans profoundly riffs on Melville's narrative. Finally, I take up a series of experimental film projects whose environmental themes evoke Melville. They include *Leviathan* (2012) by the sensory ethnographers Véréna Paravel and Lucien Castaing-Taylor, an extreme form of documentary that captures night sea fishing off Cape Cod in immersive, hallucinatory visuals; mayfield brooks's *Whale Fall* (2021), a dance film linking environmental degradation and Black impossibility; and Wu Tsang's multipronged project inspired by *Moby-Dick* that includes the game-generated video installation *Of Whales*, the queer-environmentalist silent feature *Moby Dick; or, The Whale*, and the collaborative exhibition *Extracts* (2022–2023).[10] In all these endeavors, the interlinking ecosystems intimated in *Moby-Dick*'s webs of imagination and information become the stimulus for challenging representations of humanity's need to think *beyond* the human if the planet as we know it is to survive. The ultimate Melville effect, one ventures, is to illuminate the potential extinction of the "wonder-world" into which Ishmael launches in order to make twenty-first-century culture face what it will mean if the last whale to survive the Anthropocene exists, as the second epigraph above suggests, light-years beyond our solar system in the form of the constellation Cetus.

Painting Pasteboard Masks

In June 2018, the Museum of Art in Málaga sponsored *The Dream of Captain Ahab*, an exhibition featuring large-scale paintings by the Spanish artist Esteban Ruiz that marked World Oceans Day and the opening of an ambitious collaborative initiative, ACCOBAMS, tasked with researching environmental threats to the cetacean population of the Mediterranean and Black Seas.[11] Involving the ministries of Spain and France, along with the International Union for the Conservation of Nature Centre for Mediterranean Cooperation, its primary research vessel, *The Song of the Whale*, launched from the port of Málaga the same month, its mission to measure the remaining whale populations in the Mediterranean's waters. Ruiz's Melville-inspired art thus formed one part of a multifaceted environmental initiative.[12]

If the "dream" of the novel's Ahab is that of revenge, a different kind of dreaming—more a sense of reverie or floating suspended in space—characterizes Ruiz's repeated depictions of the wonder and beauty of whales.

Painted on canvases up to six feet tall, the abstractly applied pigment beckons the viewer to meditate on the ever-changing, hieroglyphic surfaces of whale epidermis. The powerfully serene aura enveloping Ruiz's depiction of these majestic creatures is disturbed, however, by a discordant element repeated in several paintings: the insertion of broken dash lines marking the bodily outlines of these cetacean subjects (figure 7.1). The fact that these dashes are painted in solid colors highlights their one-dimensionality, making the whales look even more three-dimensional in contrast. Why these dash lines? A miniature image of scissors placed at the end of the line in two of these paintings hints these cetaceans can be read as "cut-outs": Follow the dotted line with your scissors to "extract" the whale's image from the page, and it becomes your own possession. By means of these lines, then, Ruiz first nods to the "cutting-in" activity on nineteenth-century whalers, stripping the blubber from the whale's body, and, second, suggests the ephemerality or disposability of the whales as a fungible commodity once they have been cut or "extracted" from their native habitat.

The tension between freedom and captivity is represented in two paintings that bear the title of the exhibition, *The Dream of Captain Ahab*. In both, giant whales are surrounded by the ghostly frames of vast structures drawn with the precise, fine lines of an architectural blueprint—a barrel-vaulted structure in one, a pitch-roofed one in the second. In the first of these "dream" visions, a single whale is trapped in its barrel-vaulted prison (the lines evoke bars of a cage). In the second (figure 7.2), not one but two whales are swimming free of the structure, escaping the attempt to secure them—Ahab's "dream" turned nightmare. As part of a multifaceted project aimed at increasing public awareness of the Mediterranean's declining whale population, the exhibition also included a workshop in which museum attendees were invited to build and paint their own whales: In this case, the technological knowledge allowing scalar reproduction is turned to creative rather than destructive purposes. Many of these models—about six to ten feet in length and painted blue and red—hang suspended from the ceiling of the atrium and galleries, adding to the museumgoers' experience of encountering the cetacean species in the wonder of its floating liquid environment.

If multiple cetaceans swim through Ruiz's paintings and drawings, Jos Sances's *Or, The Whale* (2019) features a single whale—but this scratchboard work of art, measuring fifty-one feet long, the average size of a female sperm whale, is as enormous as its content is epic (figures 7.3 and 7.4).[13] A San Francisco–based artist known for his public murals and printmaking for workers' unions, Sances was inspired to reread *Moby-Dick* after a visit to New Bedford. The Rockwell Kent ink drawings in his edition served as a further inspiration for this life-size artwork, which, in Sances's rendering, is very much a story about American class, capitalism, and exploitation. Sances's scratchboard technique

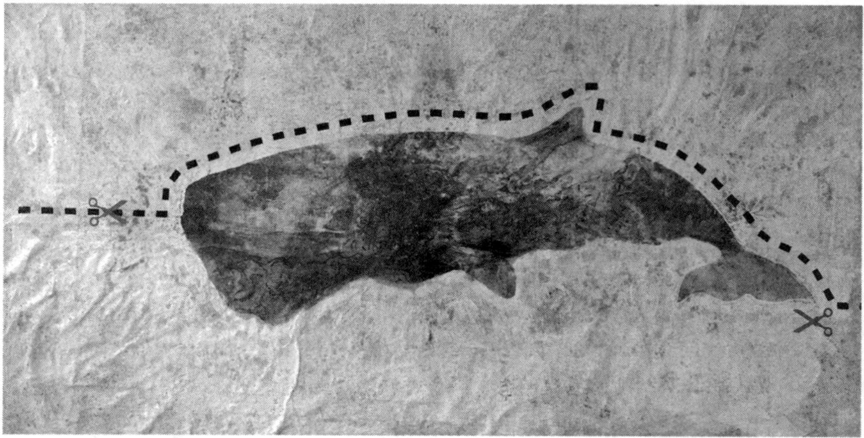

Figure 7.1. Cetacean wonder and the threat of "extraction."
Estaban Ruiz, *Tattoo from Nantucket*, 2018. Mixed media, 283 × 140 cm.

Source: Courtesy of the artist.

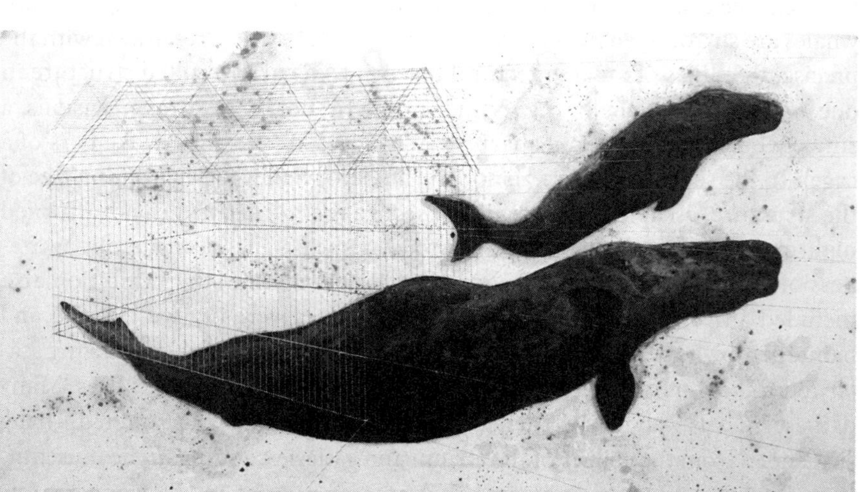

Figure 7.2. Escaping Ahab's dream.
Esteban Ruiz, *Dream of Captain Ahab #2*, 2018. Mixed media, 280 × 140 cm.

Source: Courtesy of the artist.

consists of coating the several wood panels composing the piece with a mixture of mineral substances (kale, clay, glue) that is tinted with white titanium, then painting over it with nonreflective black ink. In scratching through the black surface to "free" the subterranean images that emerge as white outlines, Sances performs his own version of Melville's deep dives,

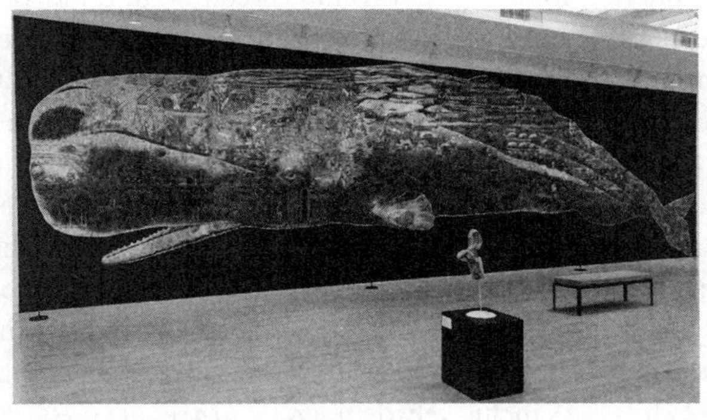

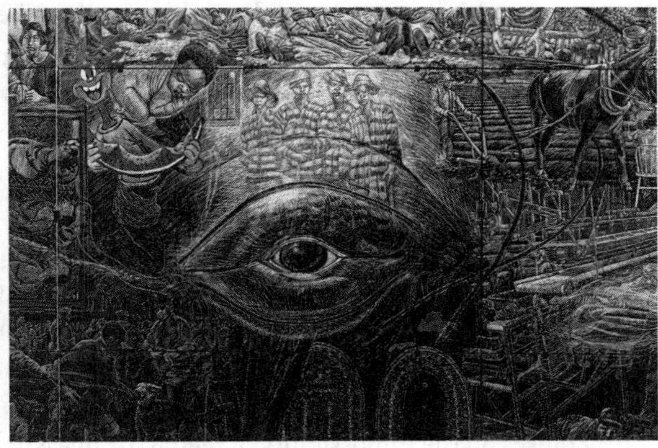

Figures 7.3 and 7.4. Scratching through to America's "understory"; detail of whale's eye. Jos Sances, *Or, The Whale*, 2019, and detail from the same image. Scratchboard and mixed media, 14' × 51'.

Source: Courtesy of the artist.

delving below the surface to bring the unspeakable or repressed into visibility. In a sense, the scratchboard is the pasteboard mask (but black instead of white), which once broken through reveals not the singular truth that Ahab seeks but the diverse inclusiveness that is, or should be, American democracy. That the color whiteness becomes the means by which this "understory" becomes visible is, Sances indicates, his version of Ishmael's meditation in "The Whiteness of the Whale" chapter.

As Sances discusses with Elizabeth Schultz in a wide-ranging interview, he takes Melville's bestowing of the name of an Indigenous tribe on Ahab's ship as the author's acknowledgment of America's historical origins in extermination.[14] Melville's representation of shipboard life on the *Pequod*, furthermore, implies that continued exploitation (both of peoples and environment) has been foundational to the nation's rise as a dominant world power, despite its premise of democracy for all. With this interpretation in mind, Sances makes the whale's epidermis both a canvas for acknowledging and celebrating the downtrodden and forgotten whose hard labor has made this triumphant story of nation possible as well as a means of paying homage to the brave activists fighting for this underclass of citizens throughout America's history. One recognizes, among the hundreds of images scratched into the black ink, Martin Luther King Jr., John Lewis, John Brown, Harvey Milk. Their faces are dispersed among tableaux featuring field hands, immigrant women seamstresses in sweat shops, Latino workers on the assembly line, the homeless and dispossessed. "Everybody is here," Schultz marvels, likening the work's panorama to Whitman's inclusively democratic *Leaves of Grass* (1855).[15]

Schultz also teases out the profoundly ecological message embedded in *Or, The Whale*. At the top center, one glimpses a polar bear in a pristine arctic environment—although the broken ice floes beneath the white creature's feet may hint at global warming. In contrast to this unspoiled topography, near the jaw at bottom center, directly under the polar bear, rodents scramble across heaps of technological waste. Sances used images of actual landfills as the basis for his representation of these disposable items, including sixty to seventy discarded flip-phones, hundreds of empty plastic bottles, and more than three hundred broken-down cars. Contemporary signs of the planet's fragility also appear in the circular shapes depicted on the tail of the whale (which represent threatened coral reefs), the corona virus symbol, and the earth as it appears from outer space. If Ishmael famously muses on the impossibility of seeing the live whale "whole"—raising this impossibility to an aesthetic principle—Sances similarly notes that because he created the artwork in sections, he never saw "the whole piece at once" until its final assembly at the Lawrence Arts Center in 2019: Attempts to impose one truth or interpretation (whether on Melville's White Whale or on Sances's whale) belie the rich diversity and ambiguity encompassed by the whole.

At the same time, the title Sances gives this monumental work may also imply the antithesis of ambiguity: choice. Most obviously, *Or, The Whale* echoes the subtitle of the American edition of Melville's novel, in which case the conjunction *or* might seem to posit limitless possibilities ("or . . . or . . . or"). But in the context of Sances's contemporary iteration, the emphatic beginning with "Or" also suggests that in some matters, such as the rights of the downtrodden, neglected, and minoritized or the wasting of our planet, there is *no* ambiguity at all; there is a clear "either/or." We can make a choice; we can take a stand. Sances's scratchboard indicates one such stance—a repoliticized definition of American democracy in which everyone's rights are honored. The closing of Melville's novel anticipates the "end of time," Sances muses, but the artist holds the hope that the environment is "still fixable," noting that in his reading of the novel there are two survivors—not just Ishmael but also the whale.[16]

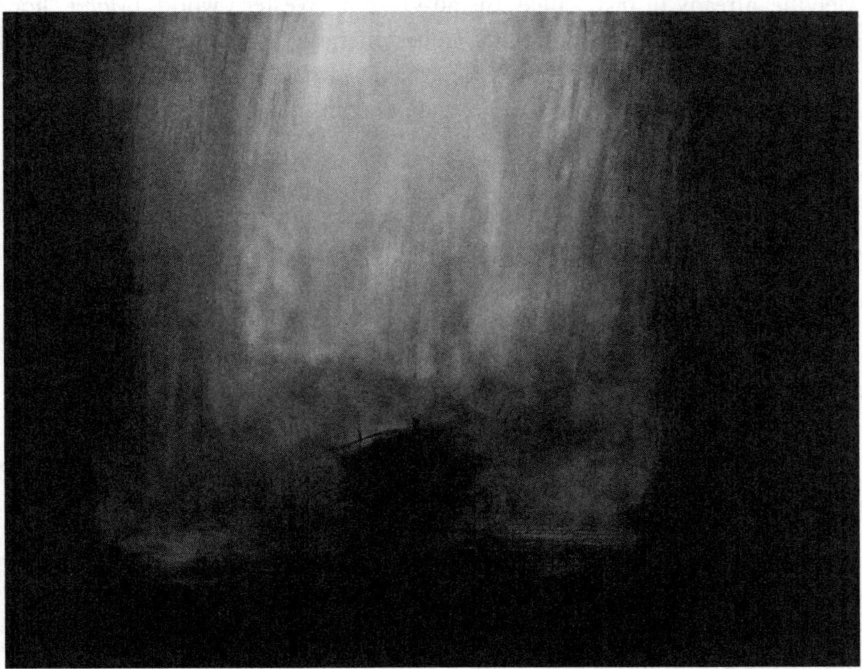

Figure 7.5. The life of tar(s) and ecological "loomings."
Christopher Volpe, *Any Human Thing ("I promise nothing complete; because any human thing supposed to be complete, must for that very reason infallibly be faulty")*, from the *Loomings* series, 2015. Tar and oil on canvas, 36" × 48".

Source: Courtesy of the artist.

Rather than representing one whale (Sances) or many (Ruiz), Christopher Volpe's series of paintings *Loomings* (2015–2019)—taking its title from chapter 1 of *Moby-Dick*—portrays murkily impressionistic oceanscapes (figure 7.5). Hauntingly dark and enigmatic, touched with melancholy, the nearly four dozen paintings that make up *Loomings* may bear titles taken from phrases in the novel, but they are emphatically, deliberately not literal illustrations of these passages. Executed in oil, tar, and gold leaf, the series combines the proto-impressionism of William Turner's brushstrokes and the moody tonality of Albert Pinkham Ryder's scenes of shore and sea with the angry black slashes of Franz Kline's abstract expressionism and the liquid-drip technique of Jackson Pollock. Volpe's online artist's statement makes clear the environmentalist intention of his work and its inspiration in Melville's prophetic vision of the dependency of America's pursuit of wealth on humans' brutal conquest of nature: "America's global industrial dominance began with the Quaker whaling ships. . . . [W]hale oil . . . greased the machinery for the rise of what

Melville, already in 1851, called 'the all-grasping Western world' [*Moby-Dick*, 296]." Instead of representing this conquest literally, Volpe intends his abstract images to confront us, as do Melville's themes, with "our own ignorance, our melancholy quest for knowledge, reality, and enlightenment in an unknowable universe."[17]

The most evocative aspect of these paintings is also their most experimental and innovative: Volpe's inspiration to use the medium of tar to create the canvases' shining black depths as well as their lighter, more liquid sepia tones (achieved by thinning the tar). In the nineteenth century, tar or pitch, made by burning pine wood, was ubiquitous on ships; the highly water-resistant substance was used to seal the wooden boards of the ship's hull and decks; it fortified the rope riggings; it was sometimes used to waterproof sails (the word *tar* derives from *tarpaulin*, the flax canvas coated with tar oil); the fibrous oakum derived from burned pitch was used to caulk leaks; sailors dipped their pigtails in tar to keep the wind from whipping their hair into their faces. Sailors were thus colloquially known as "tars" for good reason. At once primordial and manufactured, today's tar is derived from coal or petroleum, the fossil fuel that was the successor to whale oil in the second half of the nineteenth century. Thus, as Volpe notes, the very medium giving his paintings their materiality has deep "resonance for our moment in history," that of what I referred to earlier as "fossil modernity."[18] This medium, moreover, allows Volpe to grapple with what he sees to be the goal of all painting—to make the material express the immaterial. As such, his aesthetic tenets are very much in tune with Melville's own: wrestling with the possibilities and limits of the written word in expressing the inscrutable. Another sign of this affinity is Volpe's use of chiaroscuro, or plays of darkness and light, aligning his work within an American literary imagistic tradition that began with Charles Brockden Brown and Edgar Allan Poe and reached its apogee in Nathaniel Hawthorne and Melville. In confronting this century's "signs and portents of extinction," Volpe's paintings ask the conundrum facing all artists in the Anthropocene: Can humanity use art to recast its relation to nature in a way that, as Volpe puts it, "turn[s] the pain and confusion of being human into beauty that is not forgetting?"[19]

Rubber Ducks in Plastic Oceans

One might assume that a subtitle as long as the one that Donovan Hohn bestows on *Moby-Duck* (2011) tells us everything we need to know about its subject matter: *The True Story of 28,000 Bath Toys Lost at Sea & of the Beachcombers, Oceanographers, Environmentalists & Fools Including the Author Who Went in Search of Them* (figure 7.6). But, in fact, these twenty-seven words reveal only the tip of the iceberg when it comes to this book, whose debt to Melville is

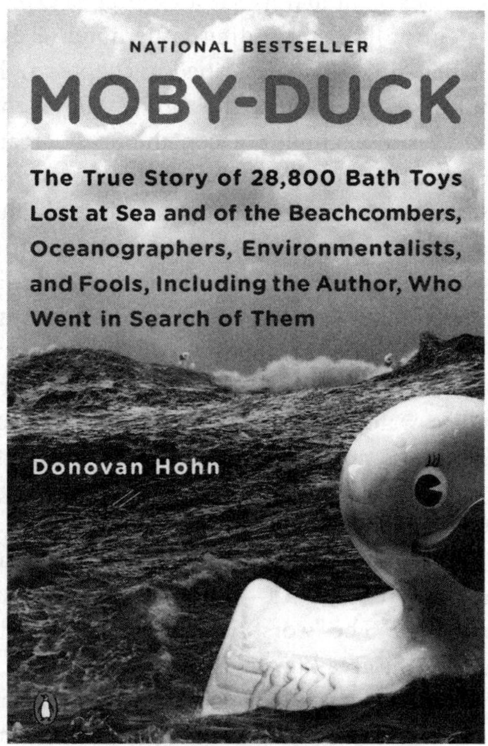

Figure 7.6. Rubber ducks and Melvillean quests.
Donavan Hohn, *Moby-Duck* (Penguin, 2011), cover.

Source: Courtesy of Penguin Publishers.

acknowledged upfront in the punning reference of its title. *Moby-D—* . . . what? That slippage from *i* to *u* in *Duck* grabs our attention, gives pause, causes us to wonder.

Wonderment is only one of the emotions summoned forth in this reenvisioning of the quest narrative for our times, a work whose mix of genres evokes Melville at his most hybrid. Like *Moby-Dick*, *Moby-Duck* exemplifies the genre of the quest narrative, of the story of a journey into the unknown (I'm "off the grid," Hohn writes), whose dimensions are both metaphysical *and* quixotic (Am I on a fool's errand? Hohn muses).[20] Second, the book forms a prose equivalent of an eighteenth-century cabinet of curiosities or wonders, crammed full of idiosyncratic observations, facts, riffs, memories, self-reflections. Third, as environmental treatise, *Moby-Duck* belongs to the genre of cautionary ecological fable. Fourth, Hohn's account of his journeys aligns him with the genre of travel writing. And, finally, *Moby-Duck* is a profoundly personal memoir, filled with Hohn's ruminations on humanity's restless urge to explore the unknown and the countervalent pull of impending fatherhood (a dynamic noted in Guy Ben-Nur's kitchen-sink video described in chapter 2). Hohn's incorporation of these multiple genres under the sign of Melville makes this work one of the most successful examples of contemporary creative nonfiction I know as well as one of the most profound meditations produced by today's Melville effect.[21] Readers who accompany Hohn on his epic journey find themselves as defamiliarized as the author as he learns to resee the globe from the perspective of its oceans. "Like its literary eponym," Bill Marvel comments, "*Moby-Duck* plunges into the depths of what it is to be land-walking mortals in a world surrounded by water," likening the result to an "encyclopaedic rummage through the mysteries of the ocean."[22] This radical reorientation of perspective from land to water echoes the call sounded by Patricia Yaeger for oceanic ecocriticisms to comprehend the magnitude of climate change and its effects.

The inspiration for Hohn's literal and metaphysical quest was the ocean spill in 1992 of 28,800 bath toys called "floaters"—including a blue turtle, a green frog, a red beaver, and a yellow duck—from a veritable "floating warehouse" (10), a subarctic freighter.[23] The "worst shipping disaster in history" (237), this accident occurred near the area known as the Great Pacific Garbage Patch or Graveyard of the Pacific (9), where the Pacific gyres have amassed a collection of waste, a viscous "plastic-plankton soup" (45), that encompasses 620,000 square miles. The spill in 1992 became the stuff of legend when in 2003 one of the toys—a yellow duck—was discovered halfway around the world in Maine's Kennebunk Harbor. Just how the little duck had made this seemingly impossible journey ignited worldwide attention, and beachcomber organizations sprang up to discover more of these lost floaters, "hatched from their plastic shells and drift[ing] free" (10) until washed ashore.

Of the four shapes, it was the yellow duck with its zany smile that captivated the public. Hohn ties this interest to the ubiquitous bath toy's association with childhood and innocence—after all, its function is to provide children with something other than their own body parts to fondle while immersed in the hygienic surrounds of the bathtub.[24] The metaphoric lesson Hohn takes from the duck, however, is definitely more existential and hazardous than this sanitized fantasy. Contemplating these "smiley refugees on an impossibly interminable road, prisoners in the labyrinth of drift" (272), Hohn determines that he too will set himself "adrift": "What if I followed the trail of toys wherever it led, from that factory in China, across the Pacific, into the Arctic? . . . The trip had gone adrift. I'd go adrift, too" (27). Later, Hohn iterates this modus operandi in terms that evoke Ishmael's narrative strategy: "I was improvising, surrendering to happenstance, riding the drift, and with every passing day the drift was leading me into wilder waters" (123). Venturing into the unknown to find his own story of these lost ducks, Hohn, like Ishmael, gives himself over to a realm existing beyond the margins of the known, a Melvillean "wonder-world" of awe that also turns out to be a reckoning with humanity's capacity for destruction and a critical revaluation of human identity.

The book is arranged around Hohn's accounts of the six journeys he makes in chasing his White Whale—the diminutive yellow duck—around the globe (chapters are titled "First Chase," "Second Chase," and so on in a nod to *Moby-Dick*'s climactic chapters). What *is* Hohn's White Whale, the mystery he seeks to penetrate? In part, Hohn's quest poses an age-old metaphysical question: What is the meaning of existence? What ultimate truths lie behind the pasteboard mask of reality? In part, the book narrates a personal quest to discover why myths of wilderness, of the untamed, attract the human imagination and ignite our restless desire to explore the unknown, then to uncover what this has to say about humankind's fraught relationship with nature. Together, the metaphysical and personal registers of these quests and questions lead to Hohn's discovery at sea of the *hitherto unimaginable*: the degree to which our oceans have become "synthetic, mass-made" (110), a reality that, Hohn argues, calls for a rethinking of the terms *nature* and *humanity* and therefore of the relation between the two.

As Hohn travels to witness the Garbage Patch up close, joins groups of beach scavengers and environmentalist cleanup crews, and tracks the floatees down to their place of manufacture in China's Pearl Delta, Hohn fills his narrative with dozens of hard facts about our "synthetic" oceans. For one, the size of the Garbage Patch, an "island" in the center of the Pacific, staggers belief. Hohn's description of the "becalmed heart" (37) of this floating mass of sea trash grimly echoes but reverses Ishmael's paean to the "insular Tahiti" (*Moby-Dick*, 255) that lies in the souls of men as well as "the enchanted calm" (302) formed by the circle of whales in "The Grand Armada" chapter. The "becalmed heart" Hohn witnesses is a mass of mostly plastic-waste materials: Ninety-five percent of marine debris is plastic, and 60 percent of plastic floats, never sinking (42). When worn down to microscopic size, these bits of indestructible polyethylene carbon are ingested by sea creatures and then enter the bodies of all those species (including humans) that eat the sea's produce (252 varieties of plastic were found in the digestive system of the carcass of a single albatross, Hohn reports [72]). To witness the wonder of the ocean—marveling at the migration of yellow ducks across the globe—is thus also to witness the threat of irrevocable oceanic change and the effects those changes are having on the planet as a whole. Human complicity in creating the tragedy of the ocean's commons is an inescapable fact, Hohn ruefully muses at the end of his journeys. "If I were Ishmael—Melville's Ishmael, not the Bible's—I'd probably at this point in my narrative say something allegorical, about how we are all precarious aloft . . . dangling above a planet too big for one mind to encompass, a planet that in large part thanks to our imaginings and desires and restlessness is changing more quickly than we can comprehend" (360).

One of the reasons that Hohn's narrative is so effective is the seamlessness and subtlety with which his prose absorbs the very text and texture of Melville's aesthetics and style. Not only does narrative indirection prove the path to insight, as Hohn frees himself to "drift" with the flow, following wherever his information leads him, but his ocean crossings also launch myriad interior voyages in which free association and verbal riffs worthy of Ishmael transform facts into metaphysical insights. Hohn's ability to channel Ishmael's language and effortlessly transform it into his own original insights via contemporary references shines on nearly every page. "What misanthrope, what damp, drizzly November of a sourpuss," he writes, winking at Melville's famous opening, doesn't feel "a Crayola of sunshine brightening his gloomy heart" upon seeing a yellow duckie with its "happy face," looking every bit like a "floating emoticon" (47). This clever wording is just the prelude to a riff on how images of animals once treated with animistic reverence in prehistoric cave art have evolved into children's "innocent" bathtub playthings (57). At the Great Garbage Patch, Hohn finds himself, again Ishmael-like, "gazing doubtfully and fearfully into the bottomless ambiguities" (175). "Hast thou seen the yellow duck?" (297), he will hail an officer on his final trip, a scientific expedition into the "latitudes of perpetual daylight" (340) of the Arctic, archly commenting, "So long as I survive to tell this tale, I want to see what the North Pacific can dish out" (247). Notably, the two books he finds aboard the craft taking him to the Pacific convergence zone where the Garbage Patch idles are a tattered paperback of *Moby-Dick* and Daniel Quinn's cult ecological novel *Ishmael.*

Riding the waves of Melville's prose, Hohn thus finds a voice for a profoundly environmentalist message that is uniquely his own. In the last pages of this remarkable account, Hohn recalls the penultimate lines of *Moby-Dick*, occurring just before the epilogue that reveals Ishmael's survival. Here Melville writes with elegiac lyricism of the "great shroud of the sea" that rolls over the sinking *Pequod* "as it rolled five thousand years ago" (427). Melville's language evokes eternal timelessness: As "all collapse[d]," we are back at the beginning of time, when all life on the planet, except that on Noah's ark, has been destroyed by the great flood. "But I now know," Hohn writes, "that the sentence is, scientifically speaking, illusory. The oceans have never been immutable, eternal. . . . I know now that it is upon Rachel Carson's ocean, not Melville's, that I've sailed" (378).

Cinematic Ecologies of the More-Than-Human

Although *Leviathan* (2012) is overtly a documentary about contemporary commercial fishing from a trawler prowling unidentified waters at night, the shadow of Melville hangs over this hauntingly surreal film—a film as brutally fascinating as it is disturbing and disorienting. One Melvillean hint lies in the title. Although this trawler hauls aboard fish and mollusks, not whales, there is something both "leviathan" and epic about the pitiless hunt the documentary records. A second hint occurs in the final credits, where viewers learn that this fishing expedition launched, like Ishmael's quest, from New Bedford. A third lies in the affinity between the filmmakers' gargantuan ambitions and Melville's aesthetics and textual complexity. Making highly experimental use of their medium, the creators' refusal to coddle viewers renders *Leviathan* as maddening to some contemporary audiences as *Moby-Dick* was to mid-nineteenth-century readers.

Founders of the Sensory Ethnography Laboratory at Harvard University, Lucien Castaing-Taylor and Véréna Paravel have pioneered a sensory mode of documentary that is entirely immersive: "The idea is not to show you a way of life, but to show you how that way of life might feel."[25] Measured by this standard, *Leviathan* succeeds with a vengeance. For the first twenty or so minutes, viewers are so immersed in stimuli and deprived of reference points that we hardly know what we are "seeing" or "hearing"—we just *feel* the mysterious experience unfolding before our eyes. The film's opening in media res is the first event that throws us off balance: There is no explanation or voice-over to guide us, only a screen so dark that we aren't certain *what* we are seeing, except that everything seems in chaotic motion and saturated with glistening black water. "All is chaos," Peter Bradshaw notes, "as if at the beginning of the world or out in space."[26] We hear the sounds of chains, of winches, the crash of what must be ocean waves against what we gradually intuit are the sides of a boat; dim white shapes flitting across darkness are, we eventually realize, hungry gulls following in the boat's wake and devouring the fish parts washed overboard. The blurriness of the water-drenched images makes it difficult to tell the difference among the wet slickers that the men are wearing, the equally glistening catch, and the sodden decks of the boat: Boundaries separating objects are in a state of dissolution. This plethora of sensory stimuli, of unreadable images, does more than destabilize our point of view and hence our ability to comprehend in a rational manner; it begins to disorient our certitude in the concept of subjectivity itself. We are being trained to essentialize neither nature nor humans.

This decentering of subjectivity is enhanced by the filmmakers' use of miniature GoPro cameras, which can be attached to clothing, passed hand to hand, mounted on a swaying pole far overhead, plunged into the sea. The visual effect is vertiginous, with the swinging motion of the cameras, rocking to the motions of the trawler, amplified by the quick succession of multiple angles of vision achieved by film editing. Gradually, we sense that we are seeing only what the eyes of the fishermen see—the quintessence of an immersive experience—but as the documentary proceeds, we also have, as Bradshaw puts it, "the freaky, hallucinatory sense that we are also seeing what the fish see, what the gulls see, even what the ship sees"—which turns out to be precisely the case.[27]

Even as images become clearer, and we begin to grasp the sequence of events unfolding on this expedition—we recognize silvery fish squirming in nets lifted from the ocean, we watch them being sorted into disarmingly familiar plastic laundry bins and lowered into the hold, we follow the motion of knives gutting the catch in the boat's interior—the men aboard the trawler are revealed primarily as bodily parts, part-objects in an assemblage. For minutes on end, the cameras linger on colored plastic boots moving through slimy waste; gloved hands arranging the fish, some still helplessly flopping in stacked layers; fingers lighting cigarettes that dangle from lips of obscured faces; arm tattoos that become one of the only means of distinguishing among these anonymous bodies going about their tasks with machinelike efficiency. Indeed, inside the boat where the fish are gutted and sorted, one gets the sense of a bloody "floating factory" equivalent to the one aboard the *Pequod* described by Ishmael.

Intermittently, the cameras follow the discarded fish parts as they are hosed overboard in sprays of bloody water that strike the black surface of the ocean like crimson waterfalls. Underwater angles capture the waste as it sinks, turning the water into eerily beautiful hues of red and orange. Amid the flotsam drift the only survivors of this slaughter, live starfish that have been caught up in the nets and are now thrown overboard. As these starfish fan out across the screen, swimming through the blood-tinged water, a metaphorically star-filled cosmos opens to our vision: Whole universes exist, unseen, beneath the surface of the ocean (figure 7.7). As the camera tilts upward, blurry shapes cross the screen: seagull scavengers flying in the air, seen through the filter of the ocean and thus blurring the elemental boundaries of air and water. Time and again, point of view radically shifts. At one point, a camera sways atop a mast or pole high above the ship; at another, it has been positioned in the front of the ship, whose prow relentlessly plows through the dark, churning waves toward . . . us. The boat may be returning to port, its task accomplished, but its movement feels aimless, without goal or purpose, in this engulfing darkness—this feels like a world without beginning or end, one in which we find ourselves as adrift as Hohn on his plastic quest.

Immersing the viewer in this world without commentary, *Leviathan* is never explicitly environmentalist or political. But the result, as Hila Peleg notes, is a profoundly non-Anthropocenic aesthetic: The "camera does not focus primarily on humans as privileged actors in the world but rather on the fabric of affective relations among the natural elements, animals, technology, and our physical lifeworlds."[28] This fabric of relations constitutes an ecosystem of activities and instrumentalities, or in Jane Bennett's terms in *Vibrant Matter*

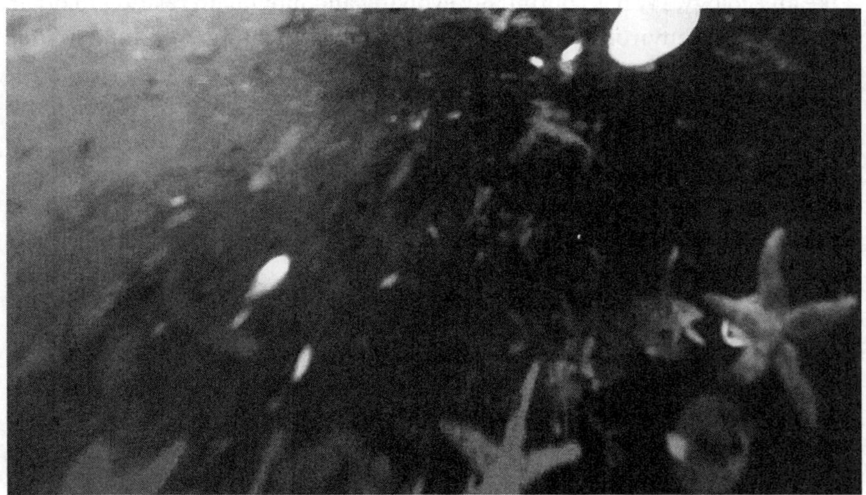

Figure 7.7. Starfish and the undersea cosmos.
Still from *Leviathan* (Véréna Paravel and Lucien Castaing-Taylor, 2012).

Source: Photograph courtesy of Lucien Castaing-Taylor.

(2010), "assemblages of agencies" that can help us think beyond the human and, from a posthumanist point of view, begin to understand the interfaces of the human and nonhuman as "a swarm of vitalities at play."[29] Such assemblages, in light of the previous chapters, call to mind Melville's hybrid aesthetics, his patchwork assemblies of bits and parts; these "swarm[s] of vitalities at play" describe the Melville effect itself, a rhizomatic event unfolding in time and space.

This interface of the human and nonhuman also characterizes the dancer mayfield brooks's *Whale Fall* (2021), a filmed movement piece in which the concerns of environmentalism, critical race theory, and posthumanist philosophy overlap. "A poetic exploration of grief," *Whale Fall* should not be mistaken for a video recording of a dance performance.[30] Foremost, it is an experimental dance *film* in which the framing of camera shots and angles, evocative use of lighting, and cutting and splicing are integral to the final product and its effects (the film was shot by Suzi Sadler).[31] mayfield brooks (they/them) is a movement-based performance artist and dancer whose interdisciplinary practice, Improvising While Black, uses movement to explore, as brooks's website explains, "the decomposed matter of Black life." Brooks's description of the philosophy underlying this method of artistic engagement resonates with the environmental issues raised by other artists participating in the Melville effect:

"Like an ecology, IWB is continually evolving and moving in relation to other organisms and environments to conjure ancestral healing with human and non-human ancestors."[32]

What brooks means by the "decomposed matter of Black life," as well as by the possibilities of renewal or "healing" hinges on the analogy between Black lives and whales at the heart of *Whale Fall.* In turn, this analogy provides the link, both implicit and explicit, between this project and Melville. The scientific term *whale fall* describes what happens when whales die and their carcasses sink to the abysmal depths of the ocean floor, their decomposition providing a concentrated food source for deep-sea organisms and creating unique ecological systems as their disintegration sustains successive marine communities. In addition, as Devin Griffith explains, whale falls function as a "carbon sink," carrying to the sea floor immense amounts of carbon dioxide that remain "locked" in this "deep sea environment." In merely two hundred years, Griffith reports, "whaling is estimated to have reduced the biomass of all marine mammals by 80%," and this vast reduction in naturally occurring whale falls due to the decimation of global whale populations has profound implications for the environment and climate change.[33] Further, brooks equates the toxicity trapped in the blubber of whales—carbon that upon sinking is transformed into a means of feeding and replenishing marine life—with the toxic effects of the traumas, historical and present-day, held in Black bodies. This analogy is furthered by the historical dovetailing of whaling and slaving as shipping industries (at times, whaling vessels were converted into slave ships, and vice versa, brooks notes). Deceased Black bodies tossed overboard during the Middle Passage underwent their own version of a "whale fall" to the depths—begging the question, What, if any, regeneration can come of such death?[34] That, as we will see, is where "ancestral spirits," an amalgam of the human and the nonhuman, enter into and form the climax of brooks's *Whale Fall.*

brooks's myth of oceanic death yet regeneration into a new mode of being or becoming has its inspiration in the myth of the underwater kingdom Drexciya, populated with the unborn children of pregnant African women thrown overboard during the Middle Passage. This story was created by the techno-pop group Drexciya in the 1990s and first printed in the sleeve notes to their compilation album *The Quest* (1997). These unborn children, having adapted to breathing underwater, have mutated into a webbed race that exists somewhere between the human and the nonhuman, defying known categories and hierarchies, including the human–animal distinction historically used to dehumanize Black people. Thus, Drexciya's creation myth not only transforms the traumatic deaths of the Middle Passage into a replenished, living potentiality but also posits—as Justine M. Bakker writes—a "submarine sociality . . . of blue black mysticism" that eschews subjectivity and humanness in favor of new forms of being that are relational and rhizomatic.[35] The "ancestral spirits" to which brooks's "whale fall" leads are akin to this mystical, new race of submarine Drexciyans.

This myth dovetails with Melville in brooks's creation. Ten minutes into the film, as brooks "sets the stage" of the empty rehearsal space by moving various objects around the room, a whispery voice-over intones Ishmael's famous line, "Whenever I find myself growing grim about the mouth. . . ." For Melville's Ishmael, going to sea is his substitute for thoughts of suicide, and, as the epilogue shows, he survives the sinking of the *Pequod* to return to land. The voyage depicted through dance in *Whale Fall*, however, is (like that of the victims of the Middle Passage) a one-way journey with no return. Rather, as the voice of Ishmael/brooks whispers, "Whale said . . . You can't reappear on earth . . . you will die [but] be born again. You will replenish the earth with yourself and your body" (ellipses added). This symbolic death and rebirth, unlike Ishmael's literal one from the black bubble of the vortex bearing the *Pequod* to its doom, is the climax of brooks's whale fall, created by the "cellular" recombinations of one's decomposing matter with one's sunken Black "ancestors."

The dancer-performer's enactment of fall and disappearance from "earth" into the ocean calls to mind not just suicidal Ishmael but also the cabin boy Pip, who, having fallen overboard during the whale chase, is left behind to face the infinite voids that he glimpses underwater. Pip survives, but only at the expense of his sanity. Tellingly, the garbled phrases that come to his tongue—"Missing. . . . Reward for Pip! . . . a little negro lad, five foot high" (*Moby-Dick*, 391–92, 400)—echo the wording of wanted posters for fugitive slaves: His return to life is not just "enslavement" in madness but also a haunting return of memories of the institution of slavery. In contrast to Pip's crazed survival, the "falling" figure of *Whale Fall* undergoes a sea change into, in Shakespeare's words, "something rich and strange"—into more-than-human matter as, at the climax of the piece, ancestral spirits merge with brooks at the bottom of the ocean.

brooks's performance begins with an empty room and words projected onto the screen: "Whale come to visit me today / Whale said, / Hey do you have a moment?" Whale continues, "I'm going to take you to the depths, to the place where my body falls after I die." The whale's interlocutor protests—as the words scroll down the screen—"I won't be able to breathe there," to which Whale responds: "You can't breathe here on earth. Your ancestors sent me here to remind you of your impossible existence. . . . It's better to know the ghosts you've given up." This prologue links three topoi: the philosophical "impossibility" of Black existence in an oppressive social system that denies minority subjects full being; the embodied example of such impossibility in brooks's repetition of George Floyd's dying words ("I can't breathe"); and the biological phenomenon of the whale fall. The overlapping of these three strands proposes a new understanding of ecological life and collective survival, for as the decomposed whale matter becomes life-giving materials that replenish other species, so too the category of the "nonhuman" ceases solely to be a pejorative deployed throughout Western history to demarcate Black lives as a subspecies separate from white humanity. Embracing the "nonhuman" now becomes a means of generating hope, healing, and a different modality of survival. As Devin Griffiths notes, in brooks's deployment of the concept of "cellular" decomposition, the word *cell* shifts from conjuring the mass incarceration of Black people to indexing the organic material that, in contrast, gives life.[36]

Following this prelude, brooks enters the performance space dressed in white, puts a record on a player that evokes the sounds of waves, begins to knit an object of blue yarn (the clicking sound of the needles perhaps implies whale communication, while the blue evokes the oceanic, and the act of knitting the creation of story, Penelope-style, a homecoming "yarn" in both the literal and the figurative senses). After rearranging objects in the space, brooks's movements involve attempts to climb over stacked folding chairs and up the bare wall, as if attempting to escape the ocean into which they have fallen. During this sequence of moves, brooks's inchoate wailing is overlaid with Billie Holiday's singing of "Bitter Fruit," a song that memorializes another kind of "fall," the hanging of Black bodies from the tree branches on which they have been lynched. These wails grow more and more painful as brooks's body falls in slow motion, then curls up fetuslike on the floor.

A new act is signaled with a loud clap, and brooks moves about the rehearsal space drawing black curtains over the windows as angry screaming sounds continue in the background; a blackout is followed by the sounds of whales, then a bare leg emerges out of the darkness of the drawn curtains: Rebirth is commencing. The camera cuts away, refocuses on two emerging feet till brooks's whole body appears. Now clad in oceanic blue rather than white, brooks rolls and crawls, infantlike, across the floor to the opposite side of the room to the accompaniment of intensifying water sounds. At this point, a side door opens in a flood of heavenly light, and three women—ancestral spirits—enter. What follows is beatific, ritualistic, as these spirits enrobe brooks in a piece of shimmery fabric attached to a braided headdress. Accompanied by a backdrop of whale wails and sounds of human breath (recalling George Floyd's gasps), the women sit in a circle and first pass around a murky liquid potion in a jar and then eat a dried substance (seaweed?), signifying the otherworldly transmogrification of the "fallen" whale/Black body into new, salvic being: All four figures break out in joyous laughter, then close their eyes as if in prayer as the screen goes dark.

Conceived and composed during the COVID quarantine and the rise of Black Lives Matter as a response to Floyd's death, *Whale Fall* gave brooks a way to work through multiple levels of grieving. "This time has been for me," brooks told Gia Kourla in a *New York Times* interview in April 2021, "a contemplative dive into what it means to just be constantly faced with death."[37] As Melville famously wrote in reference to Emerson, "I love all men who dive. Any fish can swim near the surface, but it takes a great whale to go down stairs five miles or more."[38] In metaphorically making this "dive" with the dying whale, and in learning to move "in relation to other organisms and environments" in an improvisational dance of the human and nonhuman, brooks discovers a model for holding and processing (or, in brooks's word, "decomposing") grief, allowing that grief to transform into healing celebration: "Maybe the whales are teaching us something about holding the toxicity and the pollution of the human problem of waste and climate change," brooks explained to Kourla. "When something is rotten to the core, how do we get inside it and then try and work toward a whale fall?"[39] Performing an ecology in which the environmental and the racial are inextricably intertwined and in which past and present, living and dead, human and nonhuman come together in a dance of improvised motion, *Whale Fall* provides an evocative response.

Brooks's *Whale Fall* of April 2021 morphed into an ongoing multimedia project. *Whale Fall II* (June 2021) consisted of a week-long series of encounters at the Center for Performance Research that included not only the film but displays, handwritten poems, a knitting circle, and online consultations with an oracle. *Wail-Fall-Whale-Fall* (October 2021), promoting itself as an "ACTIVATION," invited the public into its Wail Room "to wail, release, and find relief in a world where grieving is often shunned."[40] Likewise, Wu Tsang's trilogy inspired by Melville is a multipronged, multimedia event produced in 2022 and the result of large-scale collaborative efforts.[41] Its three parts include a feature-length experimental film, *Moby Dick; or, The Whale* (which premiered at the Schauspielhaus Zürich); a large-scale, computer-generated video installation, *Of Whales* (which premiered at the Venice Biennale); and a nonnarrative video installation, *Extracts*, whose archival imagery included dance sequences cut from the silent film (which premiered at the Whitney Biennale and was produced by Tsang's frequent collaborator, Moved by the Motion).

The award-winning Tsang has been lauded "for [her] ability to combine disparate genres and forms" and her "expansive but rigorous experiments in form and content"—and such facility in creating mixed artworks extends Melville's hybrid, rhizomatic aesthetics.[42] Her works consistently probe the slipperiness of language (an affinity shared with Melville), while searching for alternative modes of communication, especially in situations lacking a common language. Looking for such alternatives dovetails with Tsang's vision of art's goal: to communicate "other realities, other ways of being." It is thus fitting that Tsang, who is trans and biracial, engages in a practice that she calls "betweenness" in the hope, as she responds in an interview, of breaking through the limits that keep humanity from apprehending these "in-between" modes of being: "[Our] perception of what is human shapes so many things. In making art, I want to open up those categories."[43]

Opening up the categories "of what is human" underlies and invigorates the cinematically innovative companion pieces, *Of Whales* and *Moby Dick; or The Whale*. This expansion of what it means to be human is evinced not only in Tsang's intense engagement with Melville's open-ended text but also in her openness to trying out new technologies to expand the language of her art. Tsang admits she's "drawn to stories that have . . . messy politics," and Melville's "flamboyant, queer, and juicily layered" narrative provided further enticement for reenvisioning his classic for the twenty-first century.[44] Tsang was inspired to read *Moby-Dick* after attending a lecture on the Trinidadian historian C. L. R. James, whose Marxist, anticolonialist reading of Melville's novel in *Mariners, Renegades, and Castaways* (1953) celebrates the whaling crew's proletarian solidarity. Despite the novel's sometimes problematic politics, its "messiness" invited Tsang to plunge into its subterranean, queerer layers, which include its representations of sexuality, race, the environment, and the limits of the human. A conversation between Tsang and Sophia Al-Maria (who cowrote the screenplay) gives a sense of why Tsang was drawn to Melville as source material when Al-Maria notes that *Moby-Dick* is an open book for today's creators: "It feels very 'open-source' and collaborative as a text. There is so much room . . . for the reader/adaptor to wander [in] and riff [upon]."[45]

The resulting Melville project marks the first time Tsang explored the new elements that virtual reality (VR) technology could bring to her creative work. Using game-engine technology to create cinematic experiences, Tsang suggests, is closer to theater than traditional filmmaking. "You're creating the environment and all the parameters for things to happen," but (as in theater once the actors take to the stage) "you don't really have control so much over how [things] happen . . . you have to let them live in the [created] environment."[46] While embracing such open-endedness, Tsang simultaneously cautions that the possibilities offered by cutting-edge digital technology are not as limitless as some advocates claim: "The more we can do [with digital technology], it's still just a reflection of our human consciousness. So it's always gonna be limited in that sense. It's always going to be a reflection of the world that we can conceive. Even if we set the parameters for things to be randomly generated, there's still a human, somewhere, telling the computer what to do." Thus, when queried for her thoughts on the buzz surrounding the concept of the metaverse, she replies that "it just becomes another way to talk about what it means to be a human."[47]

For an avant-garde artist whose projects often embrace the "more-than-human," Tsang's take on technology rings an interestingly humanist note. This "between" positioning—embracing the new but not abandoning the old—shares affinities with the "post-postmodernist" turn in fiction discussed in chapter 3 as well in many other creative endeavors emanating from the Melville effect: Twenty-first-century artistic innovation need not repudiate the historical, human, or affective dimensions of creative world making. This productive tension between limits and possibilities glosses Tsang's attraction to the imaginary universe that Melville created in *Moby-Dick*. For if VR "is both infinitely full of possibility and also very limited," so, too, is this novel: "And I love that as a form for *Moby-Dick*, because in a way I think Melville's book is like a VR game. It's that coded and dense, and also limited in its construction of the world."[48] The same is true of Ahab's monomaniacal plotting of the White Whale's movements: "[His] obsessive quest feels like a mirror of what VR is. We're obsessively mapping a universe, but that universe is still just our conception of the universe."[49] In Ahab's case, the end result is solipsistic imprisonment in a singular desire. This solipsism blinds the captain to his role in the industrial ecocide of which the whale case is the portent. "We are still living in a society," Tsang says of the contemporary Ahabs of the energy industry, "that is on a mad quest to extract all the oil from the earth. To produce and fuel a modernizing, expanding society that's literally destroying the planet."[50]

Thus, environmental concerns become a major theme in Tsang's reenvisioning of Melville. What it means to be human in the larger ecology of life-forms is the subject of the fifty-seven-foot-wide immersive video installation *Of Whales*, created for the Fifty-Ninth Venice Biennale, whose focus was "humankind's precarious relationship with the nonhuman," and Tsang's response was to make her contribution a "freeform" counterpoint to her *Moby Dick* silent-film project, using VR technology to envision the world through the nonhuman perspective of the whale (figure 7.8).[51] Repeating in one-hour loops that begin with the whale's descent and end with its resurfacing for air, the video's point of view plunges us, observes Tavia Nyong'o, into "a liquid cosmos in which the possessive gaze is no longer the center."[52] In effect, the viewer "becomes" the whale, seeing, paradoxically, what humans can never know.

Displayed on a giant screen set under the stone arches of the Arsenale, its oceanic imagery uncannily reflected in the lagoon water, the video's otherworldly effects were created on a cross-platform gaming engine, Unity, which generated its sixty-minute loops of underwater simulation in real time—the average time a sperm whale spends underwater before breaching. The simulated details of this watery world—waves, schools of fish, air bubbles expelled, water currents, sea plants, changes of color, increasingly surreal visions of the oceanic depths—occur in iterative but randomized patterns such that each one-hour loop is never quite the same. One can set parameters to this created environment, but one can't control what happens or unfolds within the structure. "It's more like a window to a world where we see all of these things that are a kind of choreography and they just keep happening," Tsang explains, "which is exciting to me as a filmmaker because it's a totally different way to create images. . . . Somehow [it] feels more alive."[53] Robert Barry captures the viewer's experience of inhabiting the whale's perspective: "We plunge deep into a CGI ocean, passing from recognizable sponges, anemones and jellyfish to ever-more abstract and fantastical imagery." At times, Barry notes, what floats before our vision seems "like an outer-space starscape," akin to the "unwarped

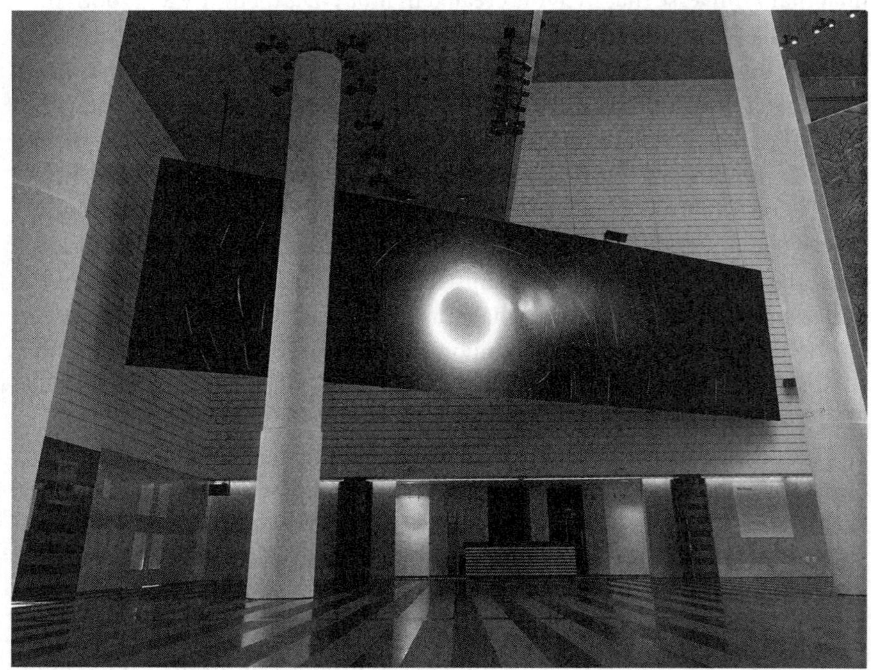

Figure 7.8. An underseas "wonder-world."
Wu Tsang, *Of Whales*, 2022. Installation view, San Francisco Museum of Modern Art (SFMOMA).

Source: Collection SFMOMA. Purchase, by exchange, through a gift of Michael D. Abrams. © Wu Tsang. Photograph by Katherine Du Tiel.

primal world," and the "wondrous . . . firmament" and "colossal orbs" (*Moby-Dick*, 321) that glide before Pip's eyes when he nearly drowns.[54] This sensation of a starry cosmos existing under the ocean's surface also recalls those uncanny moments in Castaing-Taylor and Paravel's *Leviathan* where living starfish drift through the bloody detritus hosed overboard the fishing trawler. In both works, immersion in a defamiliarizing, liquid cosmos alters the viewer's sense of scale and hence of humanity's place in a greater-than-human universe. At such moments, both examples of the Melville effect engender yearnings that are planetary.

The companion piece of the installation *Of Whales*, an innovative film that clocks in at seventy-five minutes and features twenty-five actors, *Moby Dick; or, The Whale* reenvisions the novel through queer, environmental, and decolonial lenses. It is half queer love story and half "cautionary tale warning against humanity's unrelenting exploitation of the earth's resources."[55] On the level of film technique, the project deliberately blends old and new. Harkening back to the first motion pictures, Tsang shoots her reenvisioning as a silent film with intertitles; it is filmed on a sound stage using constructed sets and background projections instead of location shots. Its actors overemote in the style of silent films, their gestures deliberately exaggerated to convey what the viewer cannot hear.[56] In keeping with the era of silent film, its showings have been accompanied by a live orchestra playing music composed by Caroline Shaw and Andrew Yee to match the film's rhythms. The result—like so many examples of the Melville effect—is a dazzling celebration of mixed media. Simultaneously with these nods to a bygone era of filmmaking, Tsang incorporates the latest in sophisticated digital technology, using the Unreal Engine 3D Creation tool to produce the film's simulated nautical environments and fill the screen with lush, lurid colors that give the action a heightened, dreamlike aura.

Tsang strategically reorders plot elements of Melville's text to foreground the capitalist underpinnings of the floating factory in which sailors serve as cogs in the machine; this foregrounding allows Tsang to emphasize (in the spirit of C. L. R. James) the democratic collectivity and queer desires of these working-class renegades and rebels. Thus, the film begins with an event that Melville doesn't narrate until chapter 94: the depiction in "A Squeeze of the Hand" of the tars squeezing whale sperm—"a petrochemical slurry of gel and glitter"—and each other's hands in tactile ecstasy.[57] The physicality and steamy eroticism of the moment allows Tsang to play on tropes of hypermasculinity by presenting more gentle models of masculinity, the men's shirtless and oiled bodies campily recalling "the silent-era Hollywood cinema of Cecil B. DeMille and the sometimes surreal erotica of Wakefield Poole," as Robert Barry aptly jests.[58] This eroticism also imbues Tsang's rendering of Ishmael and Queequeg's relationship as an *explicitly* sexual one: A one-night stand turns into full-fledged love affair when the two men awake twined in a single hammock and declare themselves married. This is the point at which Ishmael delivers his famous line, "Call me Ishmael," which in the context of the film becomes a sign of intimacy, to which Queequeg responds, "Not you and I, but us. We." The queerness of this bonding is intensified by the fact that Tosh Basco, the actor playing Queequeg (an artist formerly known as "boyfriend" and Tsang's frequent collaborator and former partner), is, like Tsang, nonbinary trans.

This trans queerness makes the plural pronoun *us* of the declaration "not you and I, but us" even more resonant. "Betweenness" is also manifested in Tsang's conversion of Melville's Sub-Sub-Librarian into an otherworldly figure—"some mixture of queer sailor and voodoo priestess"—who inhabits a cavern under the sea.[59] Bedecked in green-glitter eyeshadow and flowing robes, surrounded by teetering stacks of books, the Sub-Sub intones bits of Melville's "Extracts" (along with other texts) in a voice-over narration—the only spoken words in the otherwise silent film. One is reminded of mayfield brooks's "ancestral spirits" and the mythicized new race of Drexciyans, underwater survivors of the trauma of the Middle Passage. That the Sub-Sub is played by the Black theorist Fred Moten, whose work invokes the oceanic "undercommons" as a new form of fluid, unfixed Black sociality transcending conceptions of individuality or humanness, heightens Tsang's exploration of rhizomatic links among the oceanic, race theory, the more-than-human, queer "betweenness," and ecologies of survival.[60]

The film's environmentalist message, meanwhile, is first sounded by an onshore seer figure (the equivalent of Melville's crazed Elijah, who warns Ishmael and Queequeg not to board the *Pequod*), prophesying that soon "the sea will run red with demon algae."[61] Visual allusions to environmental decimation continue in scenes of the crew cutting the whale's glittery blubber into cubes on a factory conveyor belt. Another allusion to industrial capitalism occurs when Pip searches the horizon for whales through a spyglass. What he discerns is a modern-day oil derrick, which transforms into the White Whale spouting "rotoscoped glitter" akin to that found in the whale spermaceti and the Sub-Sub-Librarian's green eyeshadow.[62] This glitter becomes the leitmotif anticipating the ending's big reveal and Tsang's original addition to Melville's text: namely, that two, not just one, survive the sinking of the *Pequod*. As in the novel, Ishmael floats to the surface, saved by Queequeg's coffin. But, in contrast to the novel, Pip drifts downward to an underwater cavern, where he discovers a gold-embossed book that turns out to be *Moby-Dick* and a jar of the green-glitter mascara worn by the Sub-Sub-Librarian in earlier scenes. The inference is that the Sub-Sub is the grown-up Pip, now an otherworldly and more-than-human denizen of the deeps, whose underwater library is the source not only of *Moby-Dick*'s "Extracts" but of the entire film. Instead of the act of extraction marking another depletion of the earth's resources, the Sub-Sub's extracts replenish.[63] In the process, Melville (like Tsang's Pip) lives to experience another afterlife. Revivifying Melville through this queer, environmental lens thus becomes Tsang's means of reimagining the category of the human within an ecology of creatively renewable resources.

***

Throughout this chapter, we've seen how the Melville effect encompasses innovative creative work in which ecocriticism and environmental concerns combine to suggest that future hopes for the planet depend on humans learning to create productive rather than destructive alignments with the overlapping ecosystems within which our species fragilely coexists. The fact that all these artists find in a *nineteenth-century* author the genesis for *twenty-first-century* visions not only is remarkable but also underlines one of the basic intuitions underlying this book: What some dismiss as outmoded or retrograde "literary history" continues to matter to many of today's most creative artists and thinkers. Returning to and thinking across the history of literature as well as across affiliated traditional art forms not only have the potential to revivify the past for present-day concerns, but allows the past to live again in a fluid circuit that circumvents linear understandings of time, of old and new, of the outdated and the avant-garde. The afterlives of literature both inspire work in the here and now as well as anticipate directions in the future of the arts, and they do so in an ever-evolving, technologically and digitally advanced world that sometimes seems to throw the very categories of artistic creativity and imagination into question.

The conclusions to which Tsang and brooks bring their future-oriented works provide an allegory for the importance rather than the irrelevance of literary history for contemporary and future ends once literary history is understood as projective as well as retrospective and as a generative component in the larger, hybrid, rhizomatic constellation of animate and inanimate works and worlds that environmentalist criticism warns us to disregard at our own peril. If the ending of Tsang's film envisions Pip's future survival as an avatar of Melville's Sub-Sub-Librarian, an under-the-radar seer promoting the queer "betweenness" that exists outside binary understandings and forms a portal into the future, this prophet of the future is nonetheless surrounded and nourished by an overflowing library of ancient, worn, well-used volumes, traces of bygone worlds that give birth to Tsang's avant-garde, multimediated, and multipronged vision. And in the climactic moments of mayfield brooks's *Whale Fall*, the transformation of the whale's death into new life-forms depends on its encounter at the ocean's bottom with simultaneously dead-but-living ancestral spirits whose rites are as potent as the extracts drawn from the Sub-Sub's revered tomes in revivifying the dead, making something new, something "rich and strange," out of the deaths, the traumas, the extractions that have come before. The role played by the mediating spirit of Melville in this relay of past and present in order to augur new visions, new ways of being also makes itself felt in Volpe's transformation of tar—the veritable "glue" keeping nineteenth-century vessels afloat—into the medium with which he paints; it reverberates in Hohn's transformation of the name of Melville's larger-than-life whale into that of a diminutive plastic toy whose fate engenders profound insights into the ecological crisis occurring across the globe's oceans; it relives in the presence of the historical figures of protest and radicalism, from John Brown to Martin Luther King Jr., who break through the black surface of Sances's gigantic whale scratchboard painting to remind us that democracy at its best is the sum of all its peoples.

By Way of Conclusion

The Melville effect, this book has been arguing, is expressive of a collective zeitgeist specific to the end of the twentieth century and beginning decades of the twenty-first. I began my research with two simple questions: Why *Melville*? And why Melville *now*? The preceding chapters, I hope, have gone some distance in documenting and making sense of the still-expanding network of interconnected, entangled, and proliferating filaments that make up today's Melville effect. I've already had occasion to cite Daniel Hoffman-Schwartz's observation about this iconoclastic nineteenth-century writer's "permanent contemporaneity," his "way of flashing into relevance at every new cultural-political conjunction."[64] This prescience has made Melville's life and work adaptable to any number of issues and events over the past century and into our own. Likewise, this "permanent contemporaneity" continues to be galvanizing for today's artists who aim to push their chosen genres and media into new terrains, to transform our understanding of the complexities and messiness of the world that we precariously inhabit. The inspiration that Melville's work holds for such artists is the combined effect, then, of three factors: first, the degree to which his musings continue to speak to many of today's most urgent concerns; second, the dense mediality of his work, including his openness to both his own literary history and his era's rapidly evolving modes of entertainment; and, third, the attraction that the promiscuous mix of forms making up his messy, multimediated aesthetics holds for contemporary artists. The result has been an explosion of imaginative energy and risk-taking well worth noting, for this constellation of creative responses to Melville suggests an alternative genealogy of literary reception and transmission, one that is neither temporally nor spatially overdetermined. And in expressing this genealogy, this book forms an alternative critical history for measuring the literary and cultural effects of authors and their works.

What is remarkable, when all is said and done, is that Melville's writings *continue* to raise so many questions and to inspire others to follow his lead in making their own queries, which in turn lead to our own. The results are encounters that—at their richest—remain moments of contact in which the literary history of which Melville is now emblematic becomes the grounds for meditations that, in their ever-partial, never-complete open-endedness, suggest why the Melville effect occurring in art today reverberates with such energy, inventiveness, and possibility. What this interplay among Melville, his legacies, his afterlives, and contemporary culture so vividly demonstrates is the fact that literature and art are inevitably projective as well as retrospective, existing somewhere between "ephemerality" and "immortality," between "then" and "now," in a zone of significations that move back and forth in and across time and space.

Reenvisioning Melville—as all the artists included in *The Melville Effect* have in their various ways attempted—turns out to be a reenvisioning of the transtemporal potentiality of the arts and of culture itself, suggesting all the insights that twenty-first-century humanities stand to gain by engaging the past and bringing its heritages into vibrant contact with present and future horizons.

The effects are ours to ponder.

ACKNOWLEDGMENTS

Conceiving and writing this book wouldn't have been possible without the generosity of year-long fellowships provided by the Stanford Humanities Center (2014–15) and the National Endowment for the Arts (2021–22). Arriving in Palo Alto with the merest outline of a future project in hand, I began my deep dive into all things Melvillean and amassed a great share of my archive. The uplifting spirit of community and goodwill that pervaded the SHC largely derived from the example of its director, Caroline Winterer. Among the fellows who have become lifelong friends, the art historian Erika Doss stands out for her enthusiastic encouragement, her advocacy of the project's potential, and, most of all, her rapid-fire forwarding of contemporary Melville allusions, many of which blossomed into full-scale investigations. In addition to Erika, the enduring friendships forged with Stephanie Hom, Anton Matytsin, Frederic Clark, Fred M. Donner, Lucy Alford, Bruno Perreau, and others made every day at the center—to say nothing of our evening celebrations in the courtyard—a joy.

If the Stanford Humanities Center gave me the ballast for this project, the NEH grant allowed me to finish writing it. In between these fellowships, a month-long residency at the Bogliasco Foundation in Italy in spring 2018 provided the tranquility in which to begin my first chapter. This was my second time at Bogliasco, and the experience was as magical as my earlier stay; one cannot heap enough praise on Laura Harrison for transforming her grandfather's home into this foundation or on its gracious administrative staff—especially Ivana Folle and Valeria Soave—for making the villa a hub of creative inspiration. As exceptional as the multicourse dinners we shared nightly were the friendships formed with my extremely talented fellow residents, including the dancer Joanna Kotze, the artist Jonathan Allen, the poet Joanna Klink, the novelist Gioconda Bello, the translator Daniela Fargione, the photographer Oihana Marco, the filmmaker Shelly Silver, the playwright Sylvia Milo, and the musician Nathan Davis.

An unexpected joy of working on contemporary art has been contacting several of the living artists invoked in *The Melville Effect*. I have been delighted to receive insights from Eleen Lin, Marianne Wiggins, Ellen Driscoll, Tom Sleigh, Chad Harbach, Christopher Volpe, T. S. Solien, and Robert Del Tredici, and I am very grateful to everyone who happily granted permission to reproduce images of their artwork in these pages. Closer to home, my USC Americanist colleagues John Carlos Rowe and Tim Gustafson stand out for their sage advice and enthusiastic endorsement of my efforts; along with John, Emily Anderson and Barbara Smith provided incisive critiques of a laughably Leviathan-sized draft of my first attempt at an introduction. Dean of Faculty Rebecca Lemon valiantly managed, against extreme budget restrictions, to eke out appreciated subvention relief, as did my English chair Dana Johnson. The brilliant Melville scholars Samuel Otter and Robert Wallace have patiently answered my queries about Melville arcana. Gordon Hutner was particularly attentive in editing the version of chapter 4 that appeared in *American Literary History* 35, no. 4 (July 2022) as "Whalebone, Hoop Skirts, Corsets: Women and the Melville Effect in Contemporary Art." Thanks to Oxford University Press and *ALH* for permission to reprint material from this essay. Thanks as well to the Johns Hopkins University Press, © copyright, for permission to reprint, in revised form, "The Melville Effect in Contemporary Fiction: An Approach to Post-Postmodernism in the Novel," *Studies in American Fiction* 48, no. 2 (Fall 2021): 129–150, and to the journal *Leviathan* for permission to reprint "Perverse Afterlives: Leos Carax, Claire Denis, and the Melville Effect," forthcoming in a special issue, *Melville's Queer Afterlives* (2025).

I owe special thanks to Carla Kaplan, Michelle Latiolais, and Moshe Sluhovsky, who have been particularly generous boosters of this project, too often in the invaluable form of writing me letters of reference. A network of other close friends have provided the encouragement to keep going, including Dale Wall, Bill Handley, Dana Johnson, Brian Ingram, Peter Gadol, and Judith and Bill Holt. As always, I'm indebted to my brothers—Harry, John, and Ben—and their extended families for their unfailing support. The reports provided by the manuscript's anonymous readers were brilliantly detailed and have made this book much stronger. Among mentors who have "been there" since the beginning of my career, I want to give a special shout-out to Joseph Wittreich and his recently deceased partner, Stuart Curran—they formed a model couple for the ages. Last but not least, I'm grateful to my research assistant Ryan Fawwaz; to my editor, Philip Leventhal, for his championing of this work; and to the talented team at the press, including Emily Elizabeth Simon and Annie Barva, for seeing *The Melville Effect* through to the end.

But "the end," when it comes to Melville's afterlives, is never *quite* the end. On the very day I wrote these acknowledgments, I received an email from the Anita Rogers Gallery in NYC alerting me to Gary Gissler's *Transcriptions* (fall 2025). This large-scale art installation includes 136 individual drawings that condense each chapter of *Moby-Dick* into a dense graphite image composed of *every* word in the chapter, piled on each other so that no single word is legible. The result, as the notice says, is that (true to Melville) "the meaning is just beyond reach."

So, too, with the Melville effect, as it continues to proliferate in this space "just beyond reach," its meanings expanding the horizons of art.

NOTES

Preface

1. In 2005, the Riverside Opera Ensemble, directed by Stephen Pickover, performed its reading in a studio at New York University's Tisch School of Drama, made available by dramaturg Robert Vorlicky; the LA production was directed by David Schweizer under the auspices of the University of Southern California's Musical Club and Voices and Visions and featured the great actor John Fleck trying his hand at the six avatars we'd invented for our version of the Con-Man.
2. Herman Melville, *Moby-Dick: A Norton Critical Edition*, ed. Hershel Parker and Harrison Hayford (Norton, 2002), 140.
3. Jeffrey Insko notes, "When it comes to references" to Ahab's hunt for the White Whale, "the details" of *Moby-Dick* "are almost always beside the point" since "popular culture releases texts from their authors and their historical moments of production and thereby makes them available for diverse readings in unexpected contexts." See Insko, "'All of Us Ahabs': *Moby-Dick* in Contemporary Public Discourse," *Journal of the Midwest Modern Language Association* 40, no. 2 (2007): 20, 22.
4. Daniel Hoffman-Schwartz, introduction to *Handsomely Done: Aesthetics, Politics, and Media After Melville*, ed. Hoffman-Schwartz (Northwestern University Press, 2019), 5.
5. "Permanent contemporaneity" from Hoffman-Schwartz, introduction to *Handsomely Done*, 5.
6. "Melville . . . is everywhere," John Bryant comments. "Or rather, everywhere we find *Moby-Dick*." Bryant, "Wound, Beast, Revision: Versions of the Melville Meme," in *A New Companion to Herman Melville*, ed. Wyn Kelley and Christopher Ohge (Wiley/Blackwell, 2022), 202. Richard Hardack agrees that "almost all references to Melville in popular culture rely on *Moby-Dick*." Hardack, "'Or, the Whale': Unpopular

Melville in the Popular Imagination, or a Theory of Unusability," *Leviathan* 11, no. 3 (2009): 8.

7. Strong cases for the transformation of the South Sea novels into current pop-culture vehicles are made in Chip Badley, "*Moby-Dick* from Below: Fans, Fictions, and Ship Theory," and Grace King, "Ahistoricity as Queer Method in *Our Flag Means Death*," in "Melville's Queer Afterlives," ed. Adam Fales, Dana Seitler, and Jordan Alexander Stein, special issue, *Leviathan* 27, no. 3 (forthcoming).
8. I am unaware of contemporary remediations of Melville's poetry, despite the fact that this genre occupied his attention far longer than his fiction and that much current Melville scholarship focuses on the poetry. For three contemporary poems that use *Moby-Dick* rather than his verse as points of entry, see Robin Coste Lewis, "Pull, My Boys! Sperm! Sperm's the Play," *Lambda Literary Review*, June 26, 2013, https://lambdaliterary.org/2013/06/robin-coste-lewis-the-mothers/; Andie Sheridan, three poems in "Melville's Queer Afterlives," ed. Fales, Seitler, and Stein; and J. Martin Daughtry, *Call Me Not Ishmael but the Sea* (Cathexis Northwest Press, 2023). Susan Howe's experimental "Melville's Marginalia," an amalgam of prose and poetry, appeared in her collection *The Nonconformist's Memorial: Poems* (New Directions, 1993), 83–150.
9. Gilles Deleuze and Félix Guattari, *A Thousand Plateaus: Capitalism and Schizophrenia*, trans. Brian Massumi (1980; University of Minnesota Press, 1987). For "higgledy-piggledy," see Melville, *Moby-Dick*, 8.

1. Sounding the Melville Effect: Methods and Theory

1. These operas are Jake Heggie's *Moby-Dick* (2009); Eugeniusz Knapik's *Moby-Dick: Opera-Mystery in Four Acts*, Polish National Opera (2014); and Olga Neuwirth's "musicinstallation-theatre" *The Outcast* (2019).
2. Daniel Hoffman-Schwartz, introduction to *Handsomely Done: Aesthetics, Politics, and Media After Melville*, ed. Daniel Hoffman-Schwartz (Northwestern University Press, 2019), 5. On Attica and Occupy Wall Street, see Paul Downes, "From Lina to Attica: Benito Cereno, the Nixon Recordings, and the 1971 Prison Uprising," and Emily Apter, "Bartleby Politics," both in *Handsomely Done*, ed. Hoffman-Schwartz, 113–38 and 35–53, respectively.
3. Samuel Otter details associations made in the press between George W. Bush and Ahab in "Blue Proteus: Melville and the World We Live In," Melville Birthday Lecture, New Bedford Whaling Museum, 2004, cited in Robert K. Wallace, "Ben-Ner's *Moby Dick* and Melville's Mechanism of Projection," *Leviathan* 9, no. 1 (2007): 53. Claire Sparks surveys criticism linking Melville and political ideologies in *Hunting Captain Ahab: Psychological Warfare and the Melville Revival* (Kent State University Press, 2006).
4. What Sterling Stuckey says of Melville's openness to Black artistic and cultural productions applies to his porousness to cultural differences of all sorts: "A certain fluidity of cultural thought and practice occurs when Melville relates one culture to another, enabling him to imagine the flow of influences, to one layer beneath, or above, the other." Stuckley, *African Culture and Melville's Art: The Creative Process in* Benito Cereno *and* Moby-Dick (Oxford University Press, 2011), 5.
5. Hoffman-Schwartz, introduction to *Handsomely Done*, 4.
6. Henry G. Jenkins, "Four Readers 4: Reading (*Moby-Dick*) as a Media Scholar," in *Reading in a Participatory Culture: Remixing* Moby-Dick *in the English Classroom*, ed.

Henry G. Jenkins and Wyn Kelley (Teachers College Press, 2013), 75; Hoffman-Schwartz, introduction to *Handsomely Done*, 6.

7. Christopher Castiglia, "Cold War Allegories and the Politics of Criticism," in *The New Cambridge Companion to Herman Melville*, ed. Robert S. Levine (Cambridge University Press, 2014), 220.
8. Interview in Robert K. Wallace, "Avoiding Melville's Vortex: A Conversation with Performance Artist Rinde Eckert," *Leviathan* 3, no. 1 (2001): 102.
9. Herman Melville to John Murray, March 15, 1848, in Jay Leyda, *The Melville Log: A Documentary Life of Herman Melville 1819–1891*, vol. 2 (Gordian Press, 1969), 274.
10. Alex Calder, "Blubber: Melville's Bad Writing," in *Melville and Aesthetics*, ed. Samuel Otter and Geoffrey Sanborn (Palgrave Macmillan, 2011), 15.
11. Craig Bernardini, "Heavy Melville: Mastodon's *Leviathan* and the Popular Image of *Moby-Dick*," *Leviathan* 11, no. 3 (2009): 29.
12. "NO! in thunder" from Melville to Nathaniel Hawthorne, 1851, in "Reviews and Letters by Melville," in Herman Melville, *Moby-Dick: A Norton Critical Edition*, ed. Hershel Parker and Harrison Hayford (Norton, 2002), 537.
13. Claire Illouz, "*The Whiteness, an Unreadable Book*," *Leviathan* 15, no. 3 (2013): 13.
14. See Maki Sadahiro, "Melville's Twentieth-Century Revivals," in *A New Companion to Herman Melville*, ed. Wyn Kelley and Christopher Ohge (Wiley/Blackwell, 2022), 25.
15. Brian Yothers, *Melville's Mirrors: Literary Criticism and America's Most Elusive Author* (Camden House, 2011), 8, 12; Sadahiro, "Melville's Twentieth-Century Revivals," 23.
16. Sanford E. Marovitz, "The Melville Revival," in *A Companion to Herman Melville*, ed. Wyn Kelley (Blackwell, 2006), 522, 524.
17. "Seeming miraculous rebound" from Sadahiro, "Melville's Twentieth-Century Revivals," 23; Yothers, *Melville's Mirrors*, 7.
18. Adam Fales and Jordan Alexander Stein, "'Copyright, 1892, by Elizabeth S. Melville': Rethinking the Field Formation of American Studies," *Leviathan* 21, no. 1 (2019): 105.
19. Sadahiro, "Melville's Twentieth-Century Revivals," 26–28.
20. Marovitz, "The Melville Revival," 515–17; Yothers, *Melville's Mirrors*, 7; Fales and Stein, "'Copyright, 1892, by Elizabeth S. Melville,'" 106.
21. Sadahiro, "Melville's Twentieth-Century Revivals," 31–32.
22. "A kind of contemporary of 1920s modernism" from Yothers, *Melville's Mirrors*, 13.
23. Eric Aronoff, "Cultures, Canons, and Cetology: Modernist Culture and the Melville Revival," in *Composing Cultures: Modernism, American Literary Studies, and the Problem of Culture* (University of Virginia Press, 2013), 86.
24. Paul Lauter, "Melville Climbs the Canon," *American Literature* 66, no. 1 (1994): 6, 10, 14.
25. Calder, "Blubber," 13.
26. John Carlos Rowe, *Literary Culture and U.S. Imperialism: From the Revolution to World War II* (Oxford University Press, 2000); Wai Chee Dimock, *Empire for Liberty: Melville and the Poetics of Individualism* (Princeton University Press, 1989).
27. The latest spin on Britten's opera capitalizing on its homoerotic potential is a one-act reenvisioning by Ted Huffman and Oliver Leith, *The Story of Billy Budd, Sailor* (Aix-en-Provence Festival, France, July 2025). An adaptation of an adaptation, this operatic version leaves the libretto unchanged but radically revises the instrumentation. Huffman and Leith's explicit aim is to highlight the queerness of all three characters. See the review by Joshua Berone, "A New 'Billy Budd' Is a Pressure Cooker of

Gay Desire," *New York Times*, July 19, 2025, https://www.nytimes.com/2025/07/18/arts/music/billy-budd-ted-huffman-oliver-leith-aix.html.

28. Dana Seitler, "Melville, Sendak, *Pierre*, and *Pierre*," in "Melville's Queer Afterlives," ed. Adam Fales, Dana Seitler, and Jordan Alexander Stein, special issue, *Leviathan* 27, no. 3 (forthcoming). Also relevant is Dana Luciano's theory of "attachment events," whereby eroticized attachments to past events or figures reactivate that object of desire in the present, creating modes of queer affect that exist in neither the past nor the present but in the reanimation itself. See Luciano, "Nostalgia for an Age Yet to Come: *Velvet Goldmine*'s Queer Archive," in *Queer Times, Queer Belongings*, ed. E. L. McCallum and Mikko Tukhanen (SUNY Press, 2011), 129–55.
29. Linda Hutcheon, with Siobhan O'Flynn, *A Theory of Adaptation*, 2nd ed. (2006; Routledge, 2013), 9, 20.
30. Michael Wood distinguishes these adaptations as "faithful" rather than "free" in *The Wings of the Dove* (British Film Institute, 1999), 14. Catherine Grant defines transformation as a key characteristic of free adaptations, which "capitalize on difference. They are expected to *manifest* innovation and ingenuity with regard to interpreting (and not translating) the narrative systems of their 'sources.'" Successful free-adaptation auteurs, she continues, "over-writ[e]" the source text "with their own traceable signatures." Grant, "Recognizing *Billy Budd* in *Beau Travail*: Epistemology and Hermeneutics of an Auteurist 'Free Adaptation,'" *Screen* 43, no. 1 (2007): 58, Grant's emphasis.
31. Stage adaptations of *Moby-Dick* range from Carlo Adinolfi's minimalist *One-Man Moby-Dick* (2000) to Gentile Saiah's immersive staging in Atlanta (2013), where the audience follows the action through a vast, deserted factory building (which underscores whaling as a mechanized, capitalist-driven, and global industry). Adaptations into musical theater have been as campily cringy as Robert Longden's *Moby-Dick! The Musical* (1992), in which the students at a girls' boarding school save their financially ailing academy by staging the novel in the school's basement swimming pool, and as politically self-conscious as David Malloy's musical at the American Repertory in 2019, which, *Hamilton*-style, attempts to address white privilege and America's legacy of racism by casting people of color in all roles except white Ahab. Andreas Mihan's *Moby Dick (for Children)* at the Stadttheater Giessen in 2020 is set in a world of robots where the whale is the planet's last existing animal.

    A sampling of relatively straightforward recent adaptations include Paul Stebbing and Phil Smith's scored adaptation (American Drama Group Europe, 1997); Jim Burke's Walk the Plank company's staging (in the hold of a ship docked in Manchester, 2001); Joyce Adler's *Moby-Dick* (with Hawaiʻian actors in Kahului, Maui, 2003); Julian Radd's *Moby-Dick* (Ohio Theatre, 2003); Bill Peters's *Hunting for Moby Dick* (Santa Cruz Actor's Theatre, 2004); Morris Panych's mimed production (Canada Stratford Shakespeare Company, 2008); Eric Simonson's *Moby Dick* (Milwaukee Repertory, 2015); Leo Geter's one-man *Ishmael* with folk music (Minneapolis's Jungle Theater, 2018); and Holly Griffith and Cynthia Meier's adaptation (Arizona's Rogue Theatre, 2020). Original Productions Theatre of Dublin, Ohio, partnered with Abbey Theater of Dublin, Ireland, to produce Irish American playwright Sean Cooney's *Moby Dick's Gone Missing* (October 2023). Echoing Kent Stephens's reenvisioning of the making of Orson Welles's stage play *Moby-Dick—Rehearsed* (both are discussed in chapter 5), Cooney creates a stage play based on the filming of the John Huston film *Moby Dick* (1956) in Youghal, Ireland, in which Huston's dummy whale props go missing.

A standout in finding innovative ways to capture the novel's strangeness and expansiveness for the stage is David Catkin's Lookingglass Theatre adaptation (2015, 2017), in which trained acrobat-actors execute gravity-defying aerial movements to create a vertiginous experience akin to Melville's verbal riffs. Radiohole's quasi-punk aesthetic in the irreverent *Fluke* found a kindred spirit in Melville (PS 122, 2006). Featuring fifty-odd puppets ranging from miniature to gigantic, the Norwegian company Plexus Polaire's adaptation in 2024 calls into question the concepts of bounded identity and animate versus inanimate nature. Puppetry and other media animate the Dead Puppet Society's *Ishmael* (Brisbane Festival, 2021).

Stage adaptations inspired by *The Confidence-Man* include Jim Steinman and Ray Errol Fox's musical, whose songs have a country-folk feel (1977); the Woodshed Collective's immersive production in which the audience wandered the decks and rooms of a decommissioned coastguard vessel to watch skits loosely related to characters and scenes in the novel (2008); Travis S.D.'s New Vaudeville adaptation on Coney Island in 2007; and my and Benjamin Boone's *CONMAN: A Musical Apocalypse* (2010). "Bartleby" was the inspiration for Jan Powell and Ken Stone's *Bartleby the Musical* for the Antaeus Company in Los Angeles (2008).

32. J. Martin Daughtry, "The Ship," in *Call Me Not Ishmael but the Sea* (Cathexis Northwest Press, 2023), 18.
33. As ego-driven and desirous of fame as Melville could be, his acute attention to historical contexts mitigates his universalizing of conceptions of genius: "Great geniuses *are parts of the times*; they themselves are the times and possess a correspondent change." See Herman Melville, "Hawthorne and His Mosses"(1850), in *Moby-Dick: A Norton Critical Edition*, ed. Parker and Hayford, 524, emphasis added.
34. The term *concept-metaphor* is from Fales and Stein, "'Copyright, 1892, by Elizabeth S. Melville,'" 100.
35. Joseph Roach, *Cities of the Dead: Circum-Atlantic Performance* (Columbia University Press, 1996), 2–4; Emily Anderson, *Shakespeare and the Legacy of Loss* (University of Michigan Press, 2018), 8–16, 20–21.
36. Anderson, *Shakespeare and the Legacy of Loss*, 29.
37. Gilles Deleuze and Félix Guattari, *A Thousand Plateaus: Capitalism and Schizophrenia*, trans. Brian Massumi (1980; University of Minnesota Press, 1987), 21.
38. Melville, *Moby-Dick: A Norton Critical Edition*, 8; all subsequent citations to *Moby-Dick* in this book are from this edition and are given parenthetically in my text.
39. Herman Melville, *Mardi: And a Voyage Thither* (1849), ed. Harrison Hayford, Hershel Parker, and G. Thomas Tanselle (Northwestern-Newberry, 1970), 595.
40. Dan Beachy-Quick, *A Whaler's Dictionary* (Milkweed Editions, 2008), xiii.
41. Review of *The Confidence-Man*, *New York Times*, April 11, 1857, in *Herman Melville: The Contemporary Reviews*, ed. Brian Higgins and Hershel Parker (Cambridge University Press, 1995), 212.
42. Gilles Deleuze, "Bartleby; or, the Formula," in *Essays Critical and Clinical*, trans. Daniel W. Smith and Michael A. Greco (University of Minnesota Press, 1997), 55.
43. Christopher Looby, "Strange Sensations: Sex and Aesthetics in 'The Counterpane,'" in *Melville and Aesthetics*, ed. Otter and Sanborn, 65–84. On "the extravagances that flourish in the space of a not-yet-congealed sexual specificity," see Peter Coviello, *Tomorrow's Parties: Sex and the Untimely in Nineteenth-Century America* (New York University Press, 2013), 7.
44. Deleuze, "Bartleby," 54.
45. Wyn Kelley, *Herman Melville: An Introduction* (Wiley-Blackwell, 2008), xv.

46. Samuel Otter, introduction to *Melville and Aesthetics*, ed. Otter and Sanborn, 5.
47. Warner Berthoff, *The Example of Melville* (Princeton University Press, 1962), 29.
48. Nina Baym, "Melville's Quarrel with Fiction," *PMLA* 94, no. 5 (1979): 912.
49. Calder, "Blubber," 25–26, 30. Calder borrows the term *modal discontinuity* from Morse Peckham.
50. See John Bryant, "Rewriting *Moby-Dick*: Politics, Textual Identity, and the Revision Narrative," *PMLA* 125, no. 4 (2010): 1043–60; *Melville Unfolding: Sexuality, Politics, and the Versions of* Typee (University of Michigan Press, 2008); and *The Fluid Text: A Theory of Revision and Editing for Book and Screen* (University of Michigan Press, 2002).

2. Multimedia Melville, Messy Culture, Contemporary Remediations

1. Warner Berthoff, *The Example of Melville* (Princeton University Press, 1962), 29; Brian Yothers, *Melville's Mirrors: Literary Criticism and America's Most Elusive Author* (Camden House, 2011), 51, summarizing the argument in Christopher Sten, *The Weaver-God, He Weaves: Melville and the Poetics of the Novel* (Kent State University Press, 1996); Samuel Otter, introduction to *Melville and Aesthetics*, ed. Samuel Otter and Geoffrey Sanborn (Palgrave Macmillan, 2011), 5; Alex Calder, "Blubber: Melville's Bad Writing," in *Melville and Aesthetics*, ed. Otter and Sanborn, 15.
2. Sheila Post-Lauria, *Correspondent Colorings: Melville in the Marketplace* (University of Massachusetts Press, 1996), 111–12.
3. Philarète Chasles, "The Actual and Fantastical Voyages of Herman Melville," *Revue des deux mondes*, reprinted in *The Literary World*, August 4, 1849, and August 11, 1849; R. [George Ripley], review of *Mardi*, *New York Tribune*, May 10, 1849; and review of *Mardi*, *Boston Post*, April 18, 1849; all included in *Herman Melville: The Contemporary Reviews*, ed. Brian Higgins and Hershel Parker (Cambridge University Press, 1995), 244, 225, 212, respectively.
4. Review of *Moby-Dick*, *London Athenaeum* 1252 (October 25, 1851), in *Herman Melville*, ed. Higgins and Parker, 356, emphases added.
5. Brian Yothers, "Melville's Twenty-First Century Lives: Reception and Criticism," in *A New Companion to Herman Melville*, ed. Wyn Kelley and Christopher Ohge (Wiley/Blackwell, 2022), 36.
6. "Ill-confounded mixture" appears in *London Athenaeum*, October 25, 1851; "a singular medley" in *London Spectator* 24 (October 25, 1851): 1026–27; "wantonly eccentric" in *London Literary Gazette* 1820 (December 6, 1851): 841–42; "strange conglomeration" in *London Morning Chronicle*, December 20, 1851; "hermaphrodite craft" in *Boston Daily Traveller*, November 15, 1851; all in *Herman Melville*, ed. Higgins and Parker, 356, 359, 393, 406, and 374–75, respectively.
7. Michael D. Snediker, "Melville and Queerness Without Character," in *The New Cambridge Companion to Herman Melville*, ed. Robert S. Levine (Cambridge University Press, 2014), 156.
8. Charles Olson, *Call Me Ishmael* (City Light, 1947), 13.
9. Even Evert A. Duyckinck's unfavorable review in *The Literary World* 250 (November 22, 1851): 381–83, which so upset his friend Melville, acknowledged the degree to which the novel is a "remarkable" compendium of genres: "It becomes quite impossible to submit such books [as this] to a distinct classification as fact, fiction, or essay. . . . [It is like] a remarkable sea-dish—an intellectual chowder of romance, philosophy,

natural history, fine writing, good feeling, bad sayings." See Duyckinck's review in "Reviews and Letters by Melville," in Herman Melville, *Moby-Dick: A Norton Critical Edition*, ed. Hershel Parker and Harrison Hayford (Norton, 2002), 610–11.

10. R. P. Blackmur noted Melville's debt to the sermon genre in "The Craft of Herman Melville: A Putative Statement," *Virginia Quarterly Review* 14 (1938): 266–82.
11. John Evelev argues that in stagey moments such as Ahab's theatrical address to the crew, his delivery "is filled with the hortatory rhetoric of popular antebellum theatre," particularly that of American-born Shakespearean actors—Edwin Forrest, for instance. See Evelev, *Tolerable Entertainment: Herman Melville and Professionalism in Antebellum America* (University of Massachusetts Press, 2006), 81–101. In *American Renaissance: Art and Expression in the Age of Emerson and Whitman* (Oxford University Press, 1941), F. O. Matthiessen was the first to make a thorough case for the profound influence of Shakespeare's plays on Melville.
12. Herman Melville, *Omoo: A Narrative of Adventure in the South Seas* (1847), ed. Harrison Hayford, Hershel Parker, and G. Thomas Tanselle (Northwestern University Press and Newberry Library, 1968), 74. Elizabeth Schultz notes these graphic devices in "Re-Viewing Melville: The Illustrated Editions," *Melville Society Extracts* 103 (1995): 3.
13. [George Ripley], review of *Moby-Dick*, *Harper's New Monthly Magazine* 4 (December 1851): 137, in *Herman Melville*, ed. Higgins and Parker, 391.
14. The owner of engravings of Turner's art, Melville saw originals during his trip to London in 1849–1850. See Robert K. Wallace, *Melville and Turner: Spheres of Love and Fright* (University of Georgia Press, 1992).
15. Matthiessen, *American Renaissance*, 426.
16. Sterling Stuckey, *African Culture and Melville's Art: The Creative Process in* Benito Cereno *and* Moby-Dick (Oxford University Press, 2009), 6. Scholarship on race in Melville includes Carolyn L. Karcher, *Shadow Over the Promised Land: Slavery, Race, and Violence in Melville's America* (Louisiana State University Press, 1980), and extends to current race theorists who forge a link between oceanic studies and the Middle Passage. See, for example, Justine M. Baker, "Blue Black Ecstasy: Ellen Gallagher's Watery Ecstatic, Oceanic Feeling, and Mysticism in the Flesh," *Journal of the American Academy of Religion* 91 (2023): 302–25. Also see chapter 7.
17. Herman Melville, *White-Jacket, or The World in a Man-of-War* (1850), ed. Harrison Hayford, Hershel Parker, and G. Thomas Tanselle (Northwestern University Press and Newberry Library, 1970), 58.
18. Herman Melville, *Pierre; or the Ambiguities* (1852), ed. G. Thomas Tanselle, Harrison Hayford, and Hershel Parker (Northwestern University Press and Newberry Library, 1972), 126. "Where the deepest word ends," Melville says, "there music begins with its supersensuous and all-confounding intimations" (*Pierre*, 282).
19. Michael Jonik, *Herman Melville and the Politics of the Inhuman* (Cambridge University Press, 2018), 33. Jonik (32) quotes the same passage from *Pierre* as I do in the following sentence in my text.
20. Melville, *Pierre*, 125.
21. Jonik, *Herman Melville and the Politics of the Inhuman*, 33.
22. Herman Melville, *Billy Budd, Sailor (an Inside Narrative)*, ed. Harrison Haywood and Merton Sealts Jr. (University of Chicago Press, 1962), 126. See David Copenhafer's analysis of *Billy Budd* as a "tour de force of narrated sound" in "'A Sound Not Easily to Be Verbally Rendered': The Literary Acoustics of *Billy Budd*," in *Handsomely Done: Aesthetics, Politics, and Media After Melville*, ed. Daniel Hoffman-Schwartz (Northwestern University Press, 2019), 143.

23. Nina Baym, "Melville's Quarrel with Fiction," *PMLA* 94, no. 5 (1979): 909–23.
24. Mikhail Bakhtin, *The Dialogic Imagination: Four Essays*, ed. Michael Holquist, trans. Caryl Emerson and Michael Holquist (University of Texas Press, 1982), 4–7.
25. See Ilana Pardes, *Melville's Bibles* (University of California Press, 2008); and Gail H. Coffler, *Melville's Classical Allusions: A Comprehensive Index and Glossary* (Bloomsbury Academic, 1985).
26. David S. Reynolds, *Beneath the American Renaissance: Subversive Imagination in the Age of Emerson and Melville* (Knopf, 1998); for the quotation, see David S. Reynolds, " 'Its Wood Could Only Be American!': *Moby-Dick* and Antebellum Popular Culture," in *Herman Melville's* Moby-Dick: *Updated Edition*, ed. Harold Bloom (Chelsea House, 2007), 93–94.
27. Susan Zeiger, *The Mediated Mind: Affect, Ephemera, and Consumerism in the Nineteenth Century* (Fordham University Press, 2018), 6.
28. Collamer M. Abbott, "Melville and the Panoramas," *Melville Society Extracts* 101 (1995): 4–6. Abbott's sources include the *Boston Evening Transcript* , November 9, 1847, and January 3, 1849, and Jay Leyda, *The Melville Log: A Documentary Life of Herman Melville 1819–1891*, vol. 2 (Gordian Press, 1969), 286.
29. Mark Beauregard, *The Whale: A Love Story* (Viking, 2016), 13–17. Holmes's "The Last Leaf" is about Melville's heroic paternal grandfather, Thomas Melvill. Holmes's attitude to the lecture circuit was less positive than Beauregard imagines. At a dinner party Melville attended in 1857, Holmes described the lecturer in general as "a literary strumpet subject for a greater than whore's fee to prostitute himself." Quoted in Merton Sealts, *Melville as Lecturer* (Harvard University Press, 1957), 5–6.
30. Zeiger, *The Mediated Mind*, 2.
31. Reynolds, *Beneath the American Renaissance*, 99.
32. See Hans Bergmann, *God in the Street: New York Writing from the Penny Press to Melville* (Temple University Press, 1995), 3–12, 19–24, 48–50.
33. Reynolds, *Beneath the American Renaissance*, 107–9. Daniel Hoffman explores the influence of frontier and folk tales on Melville in *Form and Fable in American Fiction* (Oxford University Press, 1961), 41–42.
34. Melville, *White-Jacket*, 76.
35. Andrew Delbanco, *Melville: His World and Work* (Vintage/Random House, 2006), 163.
36. W. Jeffrey Bolster, *Black Jacks: African American Seamen in the Age of Sail* (Harvard University Press, 1998), 1.
37. Evelev, *Tolerable Entertainment*, 113.
38. Emerson and Holmes quoted respectively in Evelev, *Tolerable Entertainment*, 141, and Sealts, *Melville as Lecturer*, 5–6.
39. Evelev, *Tolerable Entertainment*, 115–25.
40. John L. Marsh, "Captain E. C. Williams and the Panoramic School of Acting," *Educational Theatre Journal* 23, no. 3 (1971): 290–91.
41. Herman Melville, *Journals*, vol.15 of *The Writings of Herman Melville*, ed. Howard C. Horsford with Lynn Horth (Northwestern University Press 1989), entry from December, 1856, p. 66. See also Abbott, "Melville and the Panoramas," 1–14.
42. Abbott, "Melville and the Panoramas," 7, drawing on the *Boston Evening Transcript*, January 24, 1849.
43. Bergmann, *God in the Street*, 45–47.
44. Abbott, "Melville and the Panoramas," 1–2.
45. Collamer M. Abbott details Melville's references to Barnum in "P. T. Barnum in *Moby-Dick*," *Melville Society Extracts* 114 (1998): 7–8. The reviewer of *The Confidence-Man*

for the *London Literary Gazette* 2099 (April 11, 1857): 348–49, speculated that Melville and his title character were acting in "emulation of Barnum" in pulling "a hoax on the public." For this review, see *Herman Melville*, ed. Higgins and Parker, 493.

46. "Barnum's American Museum," Wikipedia, n.d., https://en.wikipedia.org/wiki/Barnum%27s_American_Museum, accessed July 15, 2025.
47. If, as Janet Marstine hypothesizes, Melville attended Williams's panorama in 1858, we witness a complete circle of self-reflexivity in action: Melville witnessing Williams reflecting Melville. See Marstine, "Panoramas and the Cyclorama in Pittsburgh: The Beginning and the End of a Unique Entertainment Genre," *Western Pennsylvania Historical Magazine* 69, no. 1 (1986): 29.
48. Marsh, "Captain E. C. Williams," 292. The details of the evolution of Williams's production come from Marsh's essay.
49. E. C. Williams, *Life in the South Seas: History of the Whale Fisheries, Habits of the Whale, Perils of the Chase and Method of Capture: Startling Incidents, Graphic Delineations, Thrilling Scenes in the Life of the American Whaleman, Compiled from Various Writers and the Author's Personal Experience* (Polhemus and De Vries, 1860).
50. Marsh, "Captain E. C. Williams," 297.
51. My knowledge of this poem owes greatly to an unpublished address that Marjorie Perloff shared with me, "*Walfischesnachtgesang/Cançãonoturnadabaleia*: Augustus de Campos," Augusto de Campos Retrospective, Pompeia Museum, São Paulo, Brazil, August 2016. I use the poem as given in Perloff's essay, but it was originally published in Augusto de Campos, *Despoesia* (Editora Perspectiva, 1994).
52. Perloff, "*Walfischesnachtgesang/Cançãonoturnadabaleia*," 4.
53. John T. Hamilton, "Whaling in the Abyss Between Melville and Zeppelin: Alex Itin's *Orson Whales*," in *Handsomely Done*, ed. Hoffman-Schwartz, 181, 190, 191, 186 (quote).
54. Hamilton, "Whaling in the Abyss," 188.
55. Laurie Anderson quoted in Porter Anderson, "Laurie Anderson's 'Moby'—the Big Blubber," CNN.web, June 4, 1999, www.cnn.com/SHOWBIZ/Arts/9906/04/review.spoleto.laurie/.
56. Samuel Otter, "Leviathanic Revelations: Laurie Anderson's, Rinde Eckert's, and John Barrymore's *Moby-Dicks*," in *"Ungraspable Phantom": Essays on* Moby-Dick, ed. John Bryant, Mary K. Bercaw Edwards, and Timothy Marr (Kent State University Press, 2006), 292.
57. Scott Saul, "Mysteries of the Postmodern Deep: Laurie Anderson's Songs and Stories from *Moby Dick*," *Theatre* 30, no. 2 (2000): 161.
58. Otter, "Leviathanic Revelations," 292.
59. Otter makes a similar point in "Leviathanic Revelations," 293–94.
60. Glen Hirschberg, "Waiting for Moby: Laurie Anderson, Standing Alone," *Los Angeles Weekly*, November 17, 1999, https://www.laweekly.com/waiting-for-moby/.
61. Saul, "Mysteries of the Postmodern Deep," 161.
62. "MOMA Acquires Israeli Artist Guy Ben-Ner's Video *Moby Dick*," *Art Radar Asia*, April 20, 2009, https://artradarasia.wordpress.com/2009/04/20/moma-acquires-israeli-artist-guy-ben-ner-video-moby-dick/.
63. Ben-Ner quoted in Robert K. Wallace, "Ben-Ner's *Moby Dick* and Melville's Mechanism of Projection," *Leviathan* 9, no. 1 (2007): 44. Wallace's exegesis of the film provides invaluable details.
64. Wallace, "Ben-Ner's *Moby Dick*," 58.
65. Quoted in Wallace, "Ben-Ner's *Moby Dick*," 44.

66. Jennifer Scappettone makes this link among "housekeeping," life on a whaler, and Ishmael's comment in her article "Accommodated, Unaccommodated Man, and Daughter: Adapting Home in 'Moby-Dick' and 'Moby Dick,'" *Adaptation*, May 28, 2008, https://smartmuseum.uchicago.edu/adaptation/2008/05/28/accomodated-unaccomodated-man-and-daughter-adapting-home-in-moby-dick-and-moby-dick/.
67. Scappettone, "Accommodated, Unaccommodated Man, and Daughter."
68. Wallace makes this point in "Ben-Nur's *Moby Dick*," 51. As he also points out, there's an allusion here to Pip's begging Ahab to let him serve as his lost leg to make Ahab whole again.
69. Wallace, "Ben-Nur's *Moby Dick*," 54.
70. Claire Illouz, "*The Whiteness, an Unreadable Book*," *Leviathan* 15, no. 3 (2013): 6. Illouz discusses her project in this article.
71. Illouz, "*The Whiteness*," 13. See also Robert K. Wallace, "Word and Shapes on Paper: Art in the Melville Society Archive," *Leviathan* 22, no. 1 (2020): 57.
72. Illouz, "*The Whiteness*," 10.
73. Illouz, "*The Whiteness*," 13.
74. Justin Quinn, "Artist's Statement," n.d., https://mannekenpress.com/artists/justin-quinn-prints/, accessed July 15, 2025.
75. Alice Bailey, "Justin Quinn's Epic E's," *Abecedarian News and Events*, 2011, https://abecedariangallery.com/store/blog/justin-quinns-epic-es/.
76. Quinn likens immersing himself in this time-intensive project to a medieval monk transcribing "some great text" with "no direct understanding of the source material" yet a dedication that approaches the sublime. Quinn, "Artist's Statement."
77. Samantha Gorman, "Language as Crowdsourced: Saussure and *Emoji Dick*," unpublished paper, 2011, 1. I owe my knowledge of *Emoji Dick* to Gorman's excellent research.
78. Sally Law, "The Revolution Will Be Crowdsourced (and Cute)," interview with Fred Benenson, *The New Yorker*, September 22, 2009, https://www.newyorker.com/books/page-turner/the-revolution-will-be-crowdsourced-and-cute.
79. Quoted in Nadja Popovich, "Fred Benenson: The Man Who Translated *Moby Dick* Into Emoji," *The Guardian*, December 11, 2013, https://www.theguardian.com/culture/2013/dec/11/fred-benenson-status-update-emoji-dick.
80. Popovich, "Fred Benenson."
81. Law, "The Revolution Will Be Crowdsourced."
82. Gorman, "Language as Crowdsourced," 3.
83. Warner Berthoff notes the "grotesquely inventive vocabulary of *Pierre*, with its participial nouns and adverbs and its bizarre coinages." Berthoff, *The Example of Melville* (Princeton University Press, 1962), 50, 51, quoted in Calder, "Blubber" 23.
84. Gorman, "Language as Crowdsourced," 6.
85. Lin quoted in Elizabeth Schultz, "The New Art of *Moby-Dick*," *Leviathan* 21, no. 1 (2019): 37.
86. "Eleen Lin's Whimsical Mistranslations," interview, *Interlocutor*, April 29, 2022, https://interlocutorinterviews.com/new-blog/2022/4/29/eleen-lin-interview-c24-gallery-mythopoeia-mythodical.
87. After the Mandarin text of 1957 was published, newer editions consulting it not only repeated the original mistakes but also added new ones and simply dropped "confusing" chapters and passages at will.
88. "Eleen Lin's Whimsical Mistranslations" (quote); telephone conversation with Eleen Lin, June 7, 2023. Thanks to Lin for her insightful comments.

89. Charity Coleman, "Eleen Lin and Tammie Rubin," *Art Forum*, Summer 2022, https://www.artforum.com/print/reviews/202206/eleen-lin-and-tammie-rubin-88645.
90. Coleman, "Eleen Lin."
91. "Eleen Lin's Whimsical Mistranslations."
92. "Eleen Lin's Whimsical Mistranslations."
93. Telephone conversation with Lin, June 7, 2023.
94. Daniel Hoffman-Schwartz, introduction to *Handsomely Done*, ed. Hoffman-Schwartz, 5.

3. Whence the Novel? Measuring the Melville Effect in Post-Postmodernist Fiction

1. Mailer quoted in George Cotkin, *Dive Deeper: Journeys with* Moby-Dick (Oxford University Press, 2012), 67.
2. Novelistic reenvisionings of Melville written since 1995 range from the seriously highbrow to those intended for a more popular audience as well as from works espousing a specific cause to those written within specific subgenres. Among historical novels fictionalizing Melville's life, both Jay Parini's *The Passages of H.M.* (2011) and Mark Beauregard's *The Whale: A Love Story* (2016) focus on the married Herman's closeted homosexual desires, whereas Larry Duberstein's *The Handsome Sailor* (2014) imagines Melville's affair with his Berkshires neighbor, Sarah Morewood. Ahab survives the sinking of the *Pequod* to live on in two rambunctious adventure stories, Jeffrey Ford's *Ahab's Return, or, The Last Voyage* (2018) and Howard Rodman's *The Great Eastern* (2019). The latter is a mash-up of *Moby-Dick*, Jules Verne's *Twenty Thousand Leagues Under the Seas* (1869, 1871), and the life of inventor-engineer Isambard Brunel (1806–1859), and it features all *three* monomaniacs (Ahab, Captain Nemo, Brunel) undergoing literal and figurative afterlives.

   Stephen Melillo's *Ahab: A Love Story* (2018) imagines Ahab's pre-*Pequod* years. A writer of "Christian romance historical fiction," Louise M. Googe has produced an Ahab trilogy—*Ahab's Bride* (2004), *Hannah Rose* (2004), and *Son of Perdition* (2006)—in which themes of redemption predominate. In G. J. Lau's *Requiem for Ahab* (2012), Ahab's son grows up and searches for answers from—whom else?—Ishmael. E. B. Dawson's futuristic *Ahab* (2020) features an interstellar war in which Ahab aims to eliminate the one remaining Mechanized Intelligence Cruiser (massive and white) to assure the Commonwealth's safety.

   Other novels make Melville a point of reference rather than the template for their plots. In John Weir's *What I Did Wrong* (2006), a gay protagonist pays homage to Melville's tomb. In Sheridan Hays's *The Secret of Lost Things* (2007), bookstore employees seek to find Melville's lost manuscript *The Isle of the Cross*. The literary critic Frank Lentricchia delivers a postmodernist riff on the crippling anxieties of authorship experienced by a Melville scholar in *Lucchesi and the Whale* (2000). Don Seligson's *Moby-Dx: A Novel of Silicon Valley* (2014) makes Silicon Valley the Nantucket of our times and molecular biology diagnostics ("Moby Dx") the industry's elusive White Whale. Two recent thrillers incorporate Melvillean motifs: Richard Price's *The Whites* (2015), where cops and former cops are haunted by their personal "Whites" (criminals who have escaped prosecution), and David Poyer's eco-adventure *The Whiteness of the Whale* (2013), in which antiwhaling activists are stalked by a mysterious sperm whale. In Anne Finger's "Moby Dick, or The Leg," in *Call Me Ahab: A Short Story Collection*

(2009), Ahab's advances cause Ishmael's homosexual panic, leading him to fabricate the tale of the *Pequod*'s demise.

Part of a trilogy, Daniel Quinn's *Ishmael* (written 1976, published 1991) features a philosophical gorilla, Ishmael, who warns his human interlocutor about the devastations the human race is wreaking upon the planet (the gorilla makes a reappearance in the third volume of the trilogy, *My Ishmael* [1996]); in the second volume, *The Story of B* (1994), a young priest is "converted" to the environmentalist teachings of an enigmatic philosopher. In Abraham Verghese's *The Covenant of Water* (2023), a family saga set in southern India, the protagonist attends a village school where students read *Moby-Dick* to hone their English. Combining absurdism, fantasy, and environmentalism, Christopher Moore's *Fluke: Or I Know Why the Winged Whale Sings* (2004) features a marine biologist who comes across a whale with "Bite me" carved in its fluke. Amy K. Marshall's *The Fisher's Widow* (2013) channels both Melville's *Moby-Dick* and Jack London's *The Sea Wolf* in a horror story juxtaposing events in the contemporary Alaskan herring fisheries and the loss of a Nantucket whaler in 1835. Brett Ashley Kaplan's metatextual *Rare Stuff* (2022) and Chris Bachelder and Jennifer Habel's autofictional *Dayswork* (2023) are recent entries in this growing field of reenvisionings, as is Xiaolu Guo's *Call Me Ishmaelle* (2025). Martin Goodman's story "Billy Budd: Captain Vere's Account" in the collection *Lessons from Cruising* (2024) takes the form of a letter that Billy, facing death, has dictated to Vere, addressed to one "Malcolm"—the name of Melville's son.

3. Sena Jeter Naslund, *Ahab's Wife, or, The Star-Gazer* (1999; Harper Perennial, 2000), 1; all subsequent citations to this novel are included in parentheses in my text.
4. Frederick Busch, *The Night Inspector* (Harmony, 1999), 21–22; all subsequent citations to this novel are included in parentheses in my text.
5. Conceiving Billy as a *Yankee* sharpshooter may have been inspired by Melville's poem "Scout Toward Aldie," in *Battle Pieces* (1866), which recounts his participation in a scouting mission to capture the legendary Rebel sharpshooter Col. John Singleton Mosby.
6. "Dive deep" from Melville to Evert Duyckinck, March 3, 1849, in Herman Melville, *Correspondence*, vol. 14 of *The Writings of Herman Melville: The Northwestern-Newberry Edition*, ed. Harrison Hayford and others (Northwestern University Press and Newberry Library, 1968), 121.
7. Mark Behr, *The Smell of Apples* (Picador, 1995), 135; all subsequent citations to this novel are included in parentheses in my text.
8. Rita Barnard links Behr's Melvillean allusions to "alternative" stories that escape apartheid ideology. See Barnard, "*The Smell of Apples, Moby-Dick*, and Apartheid Ideology," *Modern Fiction Studies* 46, no. 1 (2000): 207–26.
9. Jay Rajiva analyzes the stylistic promulgation of facist-colonial ideology in "The Seduction of Narration in Mark Behr's *The Smell of Apples*," *Research in African Literatures* 11, no. 4 (2013): 82–99.
10. See Christopher S. Durer, "*Moby-Dick* and Nazi Germany," *Melville Society Extracts* 66 (1986): 8; Claire Sparks, *Hunting Captain Ahab: Psychological Warfare and the Melville Revival* (Kent State University Press, 2006), 17; and C. L. R. James, *Mariners, Renegades, and Castaways: The Story of Herman Melville and the World We Live In* (1953; University Press of New England, 2001), 54.
11. See Cheryl Stobie, "Fissures in Apartheid's 'Eden': Representations of Bisexuality in *The Smell of Apples* by Mark Behr," *Research in African Literatures* 39, no. 1 (2008): 70–86.

12. The narrating Marnus puts the term in quotation marks and in the same sentence reveals that his mother's affectionate nickname for him is "Piccanin," a racially demeaning term.
13. Richard Eder, "Let There Be Light," *New York Times Book Review*, July 27, 2003; Bob Hoover, review of *Evidence of Things Unseen*, *Pittsburgh Post-Gazette*, June 8, 2003.
14. Marianne Wiggins, *Evidence of Things Unseen* (Simon and Schuster, 2003), 380; all subsequent citations to this novel are included in parentheses in my text.
15. Howard P. Vincent links the White Whale and the atomic bomb in *The Trying-Out of* Moby-Dick (Southern Illinois University Press, 1949): "Yesterday he sank the *Pequod*; within the past two years, he has breached five times, from a New Mexico desert, over Hiroshima and Nagasaki, and most recently, at Bikini atoll." Quoted in Andrew Delbanco, *Melville: His World and Work* (Vintage/Random House, 2006), xiii.
16. Gregory Cowles, "Big League Anxiety on the Baseball Diamond," *New York Times Book Review* , September 9, 2011.
17. Leslie Fiedler, *Love and Death in the American Novel* (Stein and Day, 1960), 24–36.
18. Chad Harbach, *The Art of Fielding* (Little, Brown, 2011), 62; all subsequent citations to this novel are included in parentheses in my text. Harbach's eponymous title refers to a book of Zen-like aphorisms, *The Art of Fielding*, written by the (fictional) all-star fielder Aparicio Rodrigo; the book is Henry Skrimshander's bible, its aphorisms strategically quoted throughout.
19. Whereas pioneering gay critics—such as Robert K. Martin in *Hero, Captain, and Stranger: Male Friendship, Social Critique, and Literary Form in the Sea Novels of Herman Melville* (University of North Carolina Press, 1986)—decode Ishmael and Queequeg's relationship as literally "gay" or "homosexual," recent critics of sexuality offer more nuanced readings of the valences that eroticized relationships between men assumed in nineteenth-century American culture prior to the institution of the hetero-homo binary. See, for instance, Christopher Looby, "Strange Sensations: Sex and Aesthetics in 'The Counterpane,'" in *Melville and Aesthetics*, ed. Samuel Otter and Geoffrey Sanborn (Palgrave Macmillan, 2011), 65–84; Peter Coviello, *Tomorrow's Parties: Sex and the Untimely in Nineteenth-Century America* (New York University Press, 2013); Michael D. Snediker, "Melville and Queerness Without Character," in *The New Cambridge Companion to Herman Melville*, ed. Robert S. Levine (Cambridge University Press, 2014), 155–68; and Natasha Hurley, *Circulating Queerness: Before the Gay and Lesbian Novel* (University of Minnesota Press, 2018).
20. See Eve Kosofsky Sedgwick, *Between Men: English Literature and Male Homosocial Desire* (Columbia University Press, 1985). Explicitly gay male desires are explored in the romance between Henry's roommate, Owen, and college president Affenlight.
21. Perhaps more radically experimental as interventions in novelistic form than any of these contemporary reenvisionings are art-book projects that, like Claire Illouz's *The Whiteness* examined in chapter 2, render words from *Moby-Dick* as part of a visual "book" object whose purpose is to be *seen*. Equally visually arresting is Damion Searls's edition of *Moby-Dick* titled *; or The Whale*, published in a special fiction issue of *Review of Contemporary Fiction* 29 (Summer 2009): 16–344. Searls took the truncated Orion edition of the novel and for his edition included only the items it *omitted*, from commas to sentences to missing chapters. In another case, Mike Keith uses precise rules of word replacement to render the entire novel as anagram; see Mike Keith, posting on the website "Anagrammy," May 20, 2016, https://www.anagrammy.com/literary/mkeith/index.html.

22. Lawrence Buell, *The Dream of the Great American Novel* (Harvard University Press, 2014), 6.
23. The quotation is from Theophilus Savvas and Christopher K. Coffman, "American Fiction After Postmodernism," *Textual Practice* 33, no. 2 (2019): 201. David Foster Wallace's essay "E Unibus Pluram: Television and U.S. Fiction," *Review of Contemporary Fiction* 13, no. 2 (1993): 151–94, is widely seen as marking a new awareness of a fictional turn from postmodernism toward the "new sincerity," a re-embrace of realism and emotional authenticity. See also Jeffrey T. Nealon, *Post-Postmodernism, or, The Cultural Logic of Just-in-Time Capitalism* (Stanford University Press, 2012); Robert McLaughlin, "Post-Postmodern Discontent: Contemporary Fiction and the Social World," *Symplokē* 12, nos. 1–2 (2004): 53–68; Samuel Cohen, *After the End of History: American Fiction in the 1990s* (University of Iowa Press, 2009); Robin van den Akker, Alison Gibbons, and Timotheus Vermeulen, eds., *Metamodernism: Historicity, Affect, and Depth After Postmodernism* (Rowman and Littlefield, 2017); Nick Bentley, "Trailing Postmodernism: David Mitchell's *Cloud Atlas*, Zadie Smith's *NW*, and the Metamodern," *English Studies* 99, no. 7 (2018): 723–43; and Timotheus Vermeulen and Robin van den Akker, "Notes on Metamodernism," *Journal of Aesthetics & Culture* 2, no. 1 (2010), https://www.tandfonline.com/doi/pdf/10.3402/jac.v2i0.5677.
24. Savvas and Coffman, "American Fiction After Postmodernism," 201.

4. Whalebone, Hoop Skirts, Corsets, Pants Roles: Women and Melville in Contemporary Art

1. Richard Brodhead, "Trying All Things: An Introduction to *Moby-Dick*," in *New Essays on* Moby-Dick; or, The Whale, ed. Brodhead (Cambridge University Press, 1986), 9–10; Julian Hawthorne quoted in Jay Leyda, *The Melville Log: A Documentary Life of Herman Melville 1819–1891*, vol. 2 (Gordian Press, 1969), 810.
2. Lewis Mumford, *Herman Melville: A Study of His Life and Vision* (1929; Harcourt, Brace and World, 1963), 137.
3. Julian Hawthorne quoted in Leyda, *Melville Log*, 2:810.
4. See, for example, all the essays in Elizabeth Schultz and Haskell Springer, eds., *Melville and Women* (Kent State University Press, 2006). In *Strike Through the Mask: Herman Melville and the Scene of Writing* (Johns Hopkins University Press, 1996), Elizabeth Renker finds parallels between the violence latent in Melville's writing methods and allegations of wife abuse (53–61). On Melville and gender, see Juniper Ellis, "Engendering Melville," *Journal of Narrative Theory* 29, no. 1 (1999): 62–84; Charles Haberstroh, *Melville and Male Identity* (Farleigh Dickinson University Press, 1980); Robyn Wiegman, "Melville's Geography of Gender," *American Literary History* 1, no. 4 (1989): 735–53; and Sarah Wilson, "Melville and the Architecture of Antebellum Masculinity," *American Literature* 76, no. 1 (2004): 59–87. On Melville and (homo)sexuality, see Robert K. Martin, *Hero, Captain, and Stranger: Male Friendship, Social Critique, and Literary Form in the Sea Novels of Herman Melville* (University of North Carolina Press, 1986); Eve Kosofsky Sedgwick, *Epistemology of the Closet* (University of California Press, 1990), 91–130; David Greven, "Men and Women and Men," in *Herman Melville in Context*, ed. Kevin J. Hayes (Cambridge University Press, 2017), 75–84; and Peter Coviello, *Tomorrow's Parties: Sex and the Untimely in Nineteenth-Century America* (New York University Press, 2013).

5. Herman Melville, "After the Pleasure Party" (1891), in *Selected Poems of Herman Melville*, ed. Hennig Cohen (Southern Illinois University Press, 1964), 134.
6. In addition to the works discussed in this chapter, see Patty Lynch's play *The Wreck of the Hesperus* (1987), set in a seamy strip club named "Moby Dick," whose owner is obsessed with white women's bodies; JoAnne Spies's one-woman musical performance piece *Me and Melville* (1997); Sharon Butler's multimedia piece *Dickathon* (2003); Stefana McClure's cut-paper construction (2005) in which lines cut from the novel have been taped onto a globe; Claire Illouz's triptych *Dear Leviathan* (2015); Beth Haber's eighteen collage works (2016) of seemingly painted-over volumes of *Moby-Dick*; Ava Blitz's life-size park sculptures of the whale made of bags of hardened concrete (Franconia Sculpture Park, Shafer, Minnesota, 2000; Grounds for Sculpture, Hamilton, New Jersey, 2004); Kathleen Piercefield's paintings and collages (1989–2016); Trisha Parish's *Will He Perish?* (1998); and Aileen Callahan's paintings and charcoals focused on the whale's epidermis (1989, 2015–2016). Many of these artists participated in the exhibition *Adrift in the Wonder World: Women Make Meaning of* Moby-Dick at the Marta Hewett Gallery in Cincinnati in 2016. See Dawn Coleman, "Whales in Cincinnati," *Leviathan* 19, no. 1 (2017): 122–39.
7. Lisa Norling, *Captain Ahab Had a Wife: New England Women and the Whalefishery, 1720–1870* (University of North Carolina Press, 2000), 36.
8. In the collection *Melville and Women*, edited by Schultz and Springer, see Elizabeth Schultz and Haskell Springer, "Melville Writing Women/Women Writing Melville," 3–14; Laurie Robertson-Lorant, "Melville and the Women in His Life," 15–37; and Charlene Avallone, "Women Reading Melville/Melville Reading Women, 41–59.
9. Eleanor Melville Metcalf, *Herman Melville: Cycle and Epicycle* (Harvard University Press, 1953), 197.
10. Susan Bordo, *The Unbearable Weight: Feminism, Western Culture, and the Body* (University of California Press, 2007), 143.
11. Elizabeth Ewing, *Dress and Undress: A History of Women's Underwear* (Drama Book Specialists, 1978), 43–44. On the hoop skirt's liberating associations in the eighteenth century, see Kimberly Chrisman, "Unhoop the Fair Sex: The Campaign Against the Hoop Petticoat in Eighteenth-Century England," *Eighteenth-Century Studies* 30, no. 1 (1996): 5–23. See also Skye Makaris, "This Difficult-to-Wear Skirt Helped to Break Down Class Barriers," *Racked*, December 7, 2017, https://www.racked.com/2017/12/7/16717206/cage-crinoline-feminism-class; and Lisa Sysun, "Hoop Skirts, Corsets, and Whalebone," *Memorable Women*, December 3, 2015, https://www.memorablewomen.com/post/hoop-skirts-corsets-and-whale-bone.
12. Ewing, *Dress and Undress*, 43, 45; Chrisman, "Unhoop the Fair Sex," 7, 9–11.
13. Leigh Summers, *Bound to Pleasure: A History of the Victorian Corset* (Berg, 2001), 22, 107; Ewing, *Dress and Undress*, 46–47, 74, 80.
14. I am grateful to Sarah Frontiera for sharing her unpublished essay "Melville's Absent Women: Production, Consumption, and the Transnational Assemblage in *Moby-Dick*" (2018).
15. In interesting counterpart, Lisa Hix notes that seamen sometimes gave their betrotheds and wives scrimshawed busks inscribed "with coded sentimental images . . . and sometimes words, the idea being that these thoughts of love would stay close to [their] heart[s]." See Hix, "From Whale Jaws to Corsets: How Sailor's Love Tokens Got Into Women's Underwear," *Collector's Weekly*, April 29, 2015, https://www.collectorsweekly.com/articles/how-sailors-love-tokens-got-into-womens-underwear/.

16. See Colleen J. Sheehy, "From Sea to Shining Sea," in *T. L. Solien: Toward the Setting Sun*, exhibition catalog, ed. Colleen J. Sheehy (Plains Arts Museum, 2013), 11. According to Sheehy, Solien found this anonymous drawing in a child's drawing book that he believes dates from the 1930s.
17. Another link between whalebone and women occurs in Bill Peters's staging of a whale being stripped of its blubber in *Hunting for Moby-Dick* (2004). The unfurling of a long strip of cloth (the blubber) slowly reveals a hoop skirt as its skeletal carcass. In Lookingglass Theater's production in 2017, the whales were portrayed by women dressed in hoop skirts and wearing steampunk goggles.
18. Solien's series is documented in Sheehy, ed., *T. L. Solein*. Erika Doss characterizes the series as "an epic body of mixed media" in "Westward Perspectives: An Interview with T. L. Solien," in *T. L Solien*, ed. Sheehy, 53.
19. Elizabeth Schultz, "*Moby-Dick*, *Ahab's Wife*, and 'the All-Grasping Western World,'" in *T. L. Solien*, ed. Sheehy, 25.
20. Michael Duncan, "T. L. Solien, the Re-Enactor," in *T. L. Solien*, ed. Sheehy, 45.
21. Sheehy, "From Sea to Shining Sea," 11.
22. Schultz, "*Moby-Dick*, *Ahab's Wife*, and 'the All-Grasping Western World,'" 25–26.
23. Schultz, "*Moby-Dick*, *Ahab's Wife*, and 'the All-Grasping Western World,'" 36.
24. Intelligible at first glance, the abstract mass of colors that rise behind Ahab's prone body at crotch level represents Queequeg, vitally "erect" in his tattooed glory.
25. *Reading with Laundry* is privately owned but can be viewed online or in Sheehy, ed., *T. L. Solien*, 77.
26. *Long Branch 2006* is privately owned but can be viewed in Sheehy ed., *T. L. Solien*, 75.
27. The Nantucketer Eliza Story recorded this verse in her journal, which is quoted in Nathaniel Philbrick, "Quakers with a Vengeance," *Smithsonian Magazine*, December 2015, 27–28.
28. Driscoll and Sleigh supplied me with an unpublished script of *Ahab's Wife, or The Whale*, to which the parenthetical page numbers in my text refer. Sleigh also supplied video of an earlier version showcased at the New Bedford Whaling Museum in July 1997. The finished product, which premiered at Snug Harbor, Staten Island, in September 1998, has increased the use of the hoop skirt as prop and symbol and reorganized the overall structure while deepening the drama's marital and existential themes.
29. Robert K. Wallace, "Review of *Ahab's Wife, or The Whale*, Created by Ellen Driscoll and Tom Sleigh," *Melville Society Extracts* 116 (1999): 27–28.
30. Wallace, "Review of *Ahab's Wife, or The Whale*," 28.
31. Sigmund Freud, *Beyond the Pleasure Principle*, ed. and trans. James Strachey (1920; Norton, 1961), 8–10.
32. Jessica Benjamin, *The Bonds of Love: Psychoanalysis, Feminism, and the Problem of Domination* (Pantheon, 1988), 134–36.
33. The script appears in Rinde Eckert, *And God Created Great Whales:* Orpheus X *and Other Plays* (NoPassport Press, 2011), 85–128, quote on 97; subsequent page citations are included in parentheses in my text. I also used a DVD of the University of Southern California's Voices and Visions performance in 2010, supplied by the director David Schweizer.
34. "Shark tooth earrings" is an addition that Nora Cole made in the Voices and Visions performances (2010), nicely broadening the audience's sense of the various feminine-beauty products produced from the sea.

35. Robert K. Wallace, "Fusing with the Muse: Eckert's *Great Whales* as Homage and Prophecy," in *"Ungraspable Phantom": Essays on* Moby-Dick, ed. John Bryant, Mary K. Bercaw Edwards, and Timothy Marr (Kent State University Press, 2006), 324.
36. For a similar reading, see Samuel Otter, "Leviathanic Revelations: Laurie Anderson's, Rinde Eckert's, and John Barrymore's *Moby-Dicks*," in *"Ungraspable Phantom,"* ed. Bryant et al., 298.
37. Olivia's image of descending on a wire to pull Ishmael from the abyss is literalized in Jake Heggie's opera *Moby-Dick* (2010) when a gigantic whaling hook descends from the fly space to pull Ishmael from the sea.
38. Pip is played by a female actor in Eric Simonson's dramatization (Milwaukee Repertory, 2006); Jim Burke's *Moby-Dick* (Walk the Plank, 2000); and Bill Peters's *Hunting for Moby-Dick* (Santa Cruz Actors' Theatre, 2004).
39. Robert K. Wallace, "Prologue: Setting the Stage," in Jake Heggie, *Heggie and Scheer's* Moby-Dick, *a Grand Opera for the 21st Century* (University of North Texas Press, 2013), 2.
40. Robert Scheer's libretto for Heggie's *Moby-Dick* grants the Black cabin boy a much larger role, shifting his abandonment at sea forward to act 1 and inventing his rescue by Queequeg so that his dilemma forms a life-changing moment for Ishmael, who joins Pip and Queequeg in a three-way vocal exchange that, in Wallace's words, highlights "Melville's global multiracial vision." See Wallace, "Prologue," 9.
41. Barry Gifford's libretto, quoted here, is part of the program for the revival of *The Outcast* by the Hamburg Elbphilharmonie in 2019. Breeches parts in Melville span high culture to low. In Robert Longden's *Moby Dick: The Musical!* (Piccadilly Theatre, London, 1992), plucky students at an all-girls school stage their musical version as a fundraising event; both pants roles and cross-dressing are used to ramp up the campy humor. High school girls are also the focus in Karen Hartman's Melvillean riff *Wild Kate: A Tale of Revenge at Sea* (Twelfth Avenue Arts, Washington, DC, 2015), in which a brainy girl ("Call me Isabel") has signed up for a semester at sea, whereupon students and crew are highjacked by a mad captain (Wild Kate) bent on a mission of revenge. In July 2024, the Berkshire Historical Society produced Elisabeth Doss's *Poor Herman* with an all-female cast at Arrowhead in Pittsfield, Massachusetts.
42. Elizabeth Schultz links Schlachter's sculpture and these passages from the novel in "'The Common Continent of Men': Visualizing Race in *Moby-Dick*," *Leviathan* 3, no. 2 (2001): 27.
43. Bill Peters's play *Hunting for Moby-Dick* (2004) creates space for women by having his entire cast—four women and three men—rotate in and out of the roles. Other stage versions make room for female performers by casting them as ocean spirits or Fates: David Catlin's *Moby Dick* (Lookingglass Theatre, Chicago, 2015), Morris Panych's *Moby Dick* (Canada Stratford Festival Shakespeare Company, 2008), and Cynthia Meier and Holly Griffith's *Moby-Dick* (Rogue Theatre, Tucson, Arizona, 2020). Another strategy has been to create a new female character altogether, such as Ishmael's mother, Hagar, in Knapik's opera (2014). In the visual arts, Schultz reviews painters who have regendered the whale to make a feminist statement, including Aileen Callahan's series of forty oils, *The Birth of Moby Dick* (2002), representing Moby Dick as a fetus and birthing calf; the Mexican artist José Antonio Farrera's work from 2009 depicting the whale as a woman cowering from the men who have hunted her down; and Mark Milloff's ongoing series of narrative paintings "in which women take the position of Moby-Dick's male characters." Elizabeth Schultz, "The New Art of *Moby-Dick*," *Leviathan* 21, no. 1 (2019): 54–55, 63.

5. Size Matters

1. Claire Illouz's artist's book *The Whiteness*, examined in chapter 2, unfolds to the length of nine feet. The Uruguayan collage sculptor Marco Maggi's response to Melville, *Great White Dialogue* (2000), is an immense seven-foot-square grid created by stacking reams of white printing paper (see Elizabeth Schultz, "The New Art of *Moby-Dick*," *Leviathan* 21, no. 1 [2019]: 29). Ava Blitz's two gigantic public sculptures of the whale are constructed of hardened bags of concrete.
2. For reinventions that find an equivalent for every word of *Moby-Dick*, see the discussions of the collaboration *Emoji Dick* and Justin Quinn's *EEEE EEEE* in chapter 2.
3. Jeffrey Insko, "'All of Us Ahabs': *Moby-Dick* in Contemporary Public Discourse," *Journal of the Midwest Modern Language Association* 40, no. 2 (2007): 20.
4. Edmund Burke, *A Philosophical Enquiry Into the Sublime and Beautiful* (1757), ed. Paul Guyer (Oxford University Press, 2015), 59. This infinitude can also attach to the miniscule in Burke's taxonomy.
5. Review of *Moby-Dick*, *London Morning Advertiser*, October 24, 1851, in "Reviews and Melville's Letters," in Herman Melville, *Moby-Dick: A Norton Critical Edition*, ed. Hershel Parker and Harrison Hayford (Norton, 2002), 595.
6. Naomi Schor, *Reading in Detail: Aesthetics and the Feminine* (Methuen, 1987), 28, 20, 22.
7. D. H. Lawrence, *Studies in Classic American Literature* (Martin Secker, 1920), 161.
8. The classic examination of these references remains Robert Shulman, "The Serious Functions of Melville's Phallic Jokes," *American Literary History* 33, no. 2 (1961): 179–94.
9. Jennifer Doyle, *Sex Objects: Art and the Dialectics of Desire* (University of Minnesota Press, 2006), 9.
10. On Parker and the Newberry, see George Cotkin, *Dive Deeper: Journeys with* Moby-Dick (Oxford University Press, 2012), 139–41, 122.
11. Robert K. Wallace, *Frank Stella's* Moby-Dick: *Words and Shapes* (University of Michigan Press, 2000), 4, 42.
12. Lawrence Buell, *The Dream of the Great American Novel* (Harvard University Press, 2014), 384.
13. Virginia Woolf, "Modern Fiction" (1925), in *The Essays of Virginia Woolf*, vol. 4: *1925–1928*, ed. Andrew McNeillie (Hogarth, 1994), 161.
14. Kassia Boddy, "Making It Long: Men, Women, and the Great American Novel Now," *Textual Practice* 33, no. 2 (2019): 322.
15. Lennard J. Davis, *Obsession: A History* (University of Chicago Press, 2008), 64. The word *monomania* for this kind of obsessiveness first appeared in France in 1810 (67).
16. Marina Van Zuylen, *Monomania: The Flight from Everyday Life in Literature and Art* (Cornell University Press, 2005), 6.
17. This tension between the generalized wholeness of the perceived object and its details is similar to the tension between Burke's theory of the sublime and Hegel's attempts to make room for the part among the whole, the fragment, as potentially sublime.
18. Doyle, *Sex Objects*, 8–9.
19. Wilson quoted in Edward K. Spann, *Unfinished and Unbroken: The Life of Artist Gilbert Wilson*, ed. Robert K. Elder (Hat and Beard Press, 2019), 180, 169. Spann's biography has shaped my understanding of this neglected artist's life and oeuvre.
20. See Robert K. Elder, introduction to Spann, *Unfinished and Unbroken*, 6–8.

21. Spann, *Unfinished and Unbroken*, 11.
22. Wilson quoted in Spann, *Unfinished and Unbroken*, 166–67.
23. *Scribner's* quoted in Spann, *Unfinished and Unbroken*, 69–70.
24. See Spann, *Unfinished and Unbroken*, 71.
25. Philip L. Gerber, "Voice from the Thirties (III): An Interview with Gilbert Wilson," *Society for the Study of Midwestern Literature Newsletter* 14, no. 1 (1984): 2–3, 18–19, quoted in Elizabeth Schultz, *Unpainted to the Last:* Moby-Dick *and Twentieth-Century American Art* (University Press of Kansas, 1995), 163, 162. Anyone wishing to learn more about Wilson needs to read Schultz's account of his life and his craft in *Unpainted to the Last*, 161–85. Schultz is responsible for bringing to public notice the existence of Wilson's *Moby-Dick* work.
26. See Gilbert Wilson, "*Moby-Dick* and the Atom," *Bulletin of the Atomic Scientists* 8, no. 6 (1952): 195–97.
27. Spann, *Unfinished and Unbroken*, 16. "When I close my eyes & see God in any human form, it is a fat man with huge genitals," Wilson wrote in his journal in 1948. Quoted in Spann, *Unfinished and Unbroken*, 140.
28. By his midteens, Wilson had "amassed an extensive collection of pictures of overweight men." Spann, *Unfinished and Unbroken*, 20.
29. Spann, *Unfinished and Unbroken*, 172; Wilson to his parents, August 1949, quoted in Spann, *Unfinished and Unbroken*, 180, emphasis added.
30. Wilson quoted in Spann, *Unfinished and Unbroken*, 172, emphases added.
31. Robert K. Elder, introduction to Herman Melville, *Moby-Dick, Illustrated by Gilbert Wilson* (Hat and Beard, 2019), 7, emphasis added. This volume reproduces hundreds of Wilson's images alongside the text of *Moby-Dick* and includes other writings by Wilson.
32. Schultz, *Unpainted to the Last*, 176. Schultz's analysis of the entire *Insanity Series* in *Unpainted to the Last*, 175–77, is especially keen.
33. Schultz, *Unpainted to the Last*, 176.
34. Wilson to George Fulton, February 5, 1953, quoted in Spann, *Unfinished and Unbroken*, 188.
35. *Kansas City Star*, July 19, 1956, and *Monroe* [Louisiana] *Morning World*, n.d., quoted in Spann, *Unfinished and Unbroken*, 209.
36. The film is archived in Special Collections at the Vigo County Public Library in Terre Haute, Indiana; thanks to the staff for making a digitalized version of the 16-millimeter unprocessed film available for my viewing.
37. Wilson, journal entries, May 5, 1954, and October 23, 1958, quoted in Spann, *Unfinished and Unbroken*, 201, 227, original emphasis.
38. Tynan quoted in Simon Callow, *Orson Welles: One-Man Band*, vol. 3 (Viking, 2015) 107, 186–87. On the nickname "Monstro," see Simon Callow, *Orson Welles: The Road to Xanadu*, vol. 1 (Penguin, 1995), 517.
39. John Crosby, review, *Herald Tribune*, October 19, 1953, quoted in Callow, *Orson Welles*, 3:140.
40. The phrase is theater critic Walter Kerr's, quoted in Callow, *Orson Welles*, 3:211.
41. Welles quoted in Callow, *Orson Welles*, 3:133.
42. David Bordwell, review, *Film Comment*, Summer 1971, quoted in Callow, *Orson Welles*, 1:571.
43. Callow, *Orson Welles*, 3:168.
44. This outline, written by Welles's friend Brainerd Duffield, is quoted in Callow, *Orson Welles*, 3:167–68.

45. Callow, *Orson Welles*, 3:169.
46. Review of *Moby-Dick—Rehearsed* quoted in Callow, *Orson Welles*, 3:184, emphasis added. See the chapter "Call Me Ishmael," in Callow, *Orson Welles*, 3:171–96.
47. Callow, *Orson Welles*, 3:206, 207.
48. Callow, *Orson Welles*, 3:207.
49. Parker Tyler, "Orson Welles and the *Big* Experimental Film Cult" [emphasis added], *Film Culture* 29 (1963), quoted in Callow, *Orson Welles*, 3:340.
50. Robert K. Wallace, "Prologue: Setting the Stage," in Jake Heggie, *Heggie and Scheer's* Moby-Dick, *a Grand Opera for the 21st Century* (University of North Texas Press, 2013), 2. Opera has been an especially generative medium for Melvillean adaptations. Besides Britten's *Billy Budd* (1951), an early example is George Rochberg's *The Confidence Man* (1982, based on the China Aster episode), premiering at the Santa Fe Opera. The Brooklyn-based West Fourth New Music Collective created an oratorio, *Moby Dick: On Death and Other Curiosities* (2014), collectively written by four composers and designed to echo the multiplicity of voices within Melville's novel. The composer Richard Beaudoin staged the first part of an opera based on *Pierre* in London in 2007.
51. Gilbert Wilson, prologue to the manuscript libretto "The White Whale," ii, quoted in Schultz, *Unpainted to the Last*, 181. The manuscript is in the archives of the Indiana University Music Library.
52. Robert Wallace makes similar observations in Heggie, *Heggie and Scheer's* Moby-Dick, 123.
53. This pronouncement is librettist Gene Scheer's creation but quite worthy of Melville. See the libretto in Heggie, *Heggie and Scheer's* Moby-Dick, 63.
54. Heggie, *Heggie and Scheer's* Moby-Dick, 16.
55. Scheer quoted in Heggie, *Heggie and Scheer's* Moby-Dick, 41, emphasis added.
56. Mark Swed, "Opera Review: Jake Heggie's 'Moby-Dick' at San Diego Opera," *Los Angeles Times*, February 22, 2012, https://www.latimes.com/archives/blogs/culture-monster-blog/story/2012-02-22/opera-review-jake-heggies-moby-dick-at-san-diego-opera.
57. Spann, *Unfinished and Unbroken*, 179.
58. Kent Stephens kindly provided me with the unpublished script, to which my parenthetical page citations in the text refer.
59. "Dizzyingly reflexive loop" from Dylan Hicks, "Kent Stephens's Latest Project Is a Play About a Play About a Rehearsal of a Play About a Novel," *Minneapolis City Pages*, July 23, 2003.
60. This link between solving the mystery of "Rosebud" (Citizen Kane's dying word) and Melville's whale is articulated early on in *Orson Welles Rehearses Moby Dick* when Gordon, whose agent tells him he's been summoned for a cold reading of a play based on *Moby-Dick*, protests, "It can't be done on stage. Whoever's attempting it must be daft." To which charge the agent jokingly responds, "Could be. It's Orson Welles." This line is immediately followed by an offstage voice-over in which Welles whispers, "Rosebud" (3).
61. Also making use of the chapter format are the Greek artist Athanasius Christodoulou's *Iconographies of A. Christodoulou* (2009), which reproduces the artwork he has created for every chapter from "Etymology" through "The Ramadan" (see Elizabeth Schultz, "The Common Continent Visualization of Race," *Leviathan* 3, no. 2 [October 2001]: 28–29); Timothy Woodman's 136 painted wood panels, one per chapter (2010–); and Driss Sans-Arcidet's sixty mounted sculptures inspired by individual chapters (1968). Other projects repeatedly engaging Melville include Eleen Lin's

ongoing *Mythopoeia* series (see chapter 2); Beth Haber's eighteen "open book" pieces (2016); Aileen Callahan's forty paintings in *The Birth of Moby-Dick* and other series (2005–2016); George Klauba's eerie portraits of the novel's characters as part avian, part human; Mark Milloff's many hyperactive narrative paintings; and Kathleen Piercefield's dozens of Melville-themed works.

J. Martin Doughtry's poem cycle *Call Me Not Ishmael but the Sea* (Cathexis Northwest Press, 2023) is a fascinating variant on this obsessive repetition. His strict method of composition involves specific rules that form the parameters of what he can or cannot do in his Melville-inspired poems: (1) he will use only the words occurring in a particular chapter for a poem that will bear that chapter's name; (2) he must split up any words that occur together in the text; (3) he is free to do whatever he wants with word order, line breaks, uses of punctuation, upper or lower case. As he writes in the cycle's opening poem, "A Bower in the Arsacides,"

I am composing a poem
Using only words found
In a single chapter of
The vast world carpet
That the Leviathanic weaver
Long ago tattooed
On the page.
(7)

The results not only remind us of the poetry inherent in Melville's prose but also give rise to often original, lyrically evocative poems. See Doughtry, introduction to *Call Me Not Ishmael but the Sea*, 2–3.

62. Schultz, *Unpainted to the Last*, 149 ("monumental"); Cotkin, *Dive Deeper*, 110 ("utterly ambitious").
63. This is the number that Schultz provides in *Unpainted to the Last*, 148; Wallace reckons the number at more than 2,700 objects in *Frank Stella's* Moby-Dick, 4.
64. Frank Stella, "1989 Previews from 36 Creative Artists," *New York Times*, January 1, 1989.
65. Wallace, *Frank Stella's* Moby-Dick, 4.
66. Moreover, as "whole" as the object appears to be, once it is mounted on a gallery wall, its shadows become part of the viewer's ever-shifting perception of it, extending its boundaries beyond itself.
67. Cotkin, *Dive Deeper*, 112.
68. Philip Leider, "Shakespearean Fish," *Art in America* 10 (1990): 187.
69. Wallace, *Frank Stella's* Moby-Dick, 64.
70. Roberta Smith, "Frank Stella's 1988," *New York Times*, February 10, 1989, emphasis added.
71. William Rubin speaks to the possibility of "abstract narrative" in Stella's work: "It is, I think, more profitable . . . to conceive of the overall vocabulary of shapes . . . as a kind of cast of characters that may be used interchangeably to act upon each other, to tell a story whose events are more pictorial than literal." Rubin, *Frank Stella, 1970–1987* (Museum of Modern Art, 1987), 135.
72. For a breakdown of these shapes, see chapter 3, "A Careful Disorderliness: The Structure of the Series and the Novel," in Wallace, *Frank Stella's* Moby-Dick, 38–52.
73. Wallace, *Frank Stella's* Moby-Dick, 29.
74. Stella quoted in Wallace, *Frank Stella's* Moby-Dick, 9, 48, my ellipses.

75. Robert Del Tredici, "Postscript," in *Floodgates of the Wonderworld: A* Moby-Dick *Pictorial* (Kent State University Press, 2001), 138.
76. Del Tredici quoted in Schultz, *Unpainted to the Last*, 210. "I ended up packing around *Moby-Dick* with me like a Bible. For me, a Bible-like book is one you can open at any point, read at random, and find inspiration on every page," writes Del Tredici in "Inner Caveman," *Leviathan* 5, no. 1 (2003): 59.
77. Del Tredici, "Postscript," 141.
78. Schultz, "The New Art of *Moby-Dick*," 57.
79. Del Tredici, "Postscript," 142–44. See also Robert Del Tredici, *The People of Three Mile Island* (Sierra Club, 1980) and *At Work in the Fields of the Bomb* (Harper and Row, 1987).
80. Robert K. Wallace, "Flood Tide: Del Tredici's Return to Printmaking," in Del Tredici, *Floodgates*, 11–15.
81. Jill B. Gidmark, "Melville Cave Art, Modern Students: Robert Del Tredici's Primal Pen and Inks," in Del Tredici, *Floodgates*, 6.
82. Schultz remarks that the original eighty-five drawings, gathered unbound in a portfolio, could thus be viewed to the viewer's liking. The concept reflects Ishmael's nonchronological narrative. "My pictures may be shuffled like Tarot cards," Del Tredici explains. See Schultz, *Unpainted to the Last*, 211–12. The concept resonates with the discussion of the skewing of linear time and the use of rhizomatic formations in chapter 1.
83. Gidmark, "Melville Cave Art," 7.
84. Del Tredici has slyly inserted the faces of the Melville scholars Robert Wallace and Elizabeth Schultz into the images of the sun and moon in the background. Telephone conversation with the artist, April 2025.
85. Del Tredici, "Postscript," 146.
86. Matt Kish, foreword to Moby-Dick *in Pictures: One Drawing for Every Page* (Tin House, 2010), vi.
87. Kish, foreword to Moby-Dick *in Pictures*, v, vii, vi. In a video on YouTube, Kish recalls his childhood memory of watching the Godzilla and Peck films back-to-back. See Matt Kish, "Chapter 71. The Jeroboam's Story," posted May 8, 2013, by Remaking Moby Dick, YouTube, 11:16, https://www.youtube.com/watch?v=GKji6sUQSFs&list=PL70mKKsVm1dSb7mHY9Ik_Jq39tkQfbro1&index=52.
88. Kish, foreword to Moby-Dick *in Pictures*, viii, emphasis added. For the interview, see Matt Kish, "Chapter 54. The *Town-Ho*'s Story," posted May 8, 2013, by Remaking Moby Dick, YouTube, 14:35, https://www.youtube.com/watch?v=M6CGv9I7Q6Q&list=PL70mKKsVm1dSb7mHY9Ik_Jq39tkQfbro1&index=47.
89. Kish describes his "rules" in his foreword to Moby-Dick *in Pictures*, viii–ix; "sun-drenched" from his promotional materials, quoted in Schultz, "The New Art of *Moby-Dick*," 65.
90. Kish, foreword to Moby-Dick *in Pictures*, xii.
91. On layerings, see Kish, foreword to Moby-Dick *in Pictures*, ix.
92. Schultz, "The New Art of *Moby-Dick*," 65.
93. Echoing Wallace's painstaking obsessiveness in enumerating the primary shapes in Stella's art, Schultz precisely catalogs the "cabalistic symbol system" in Kish's 552 images: 64 versions of Queequeg, 201 versions of whales, and so on. See Schultz, "The New Art of *Moby-Dick*," 65–66.
94. Kish, foreword to Moby-Dick *in Pictures*, ix; Schultz, "The New Art of *Moby-Dick*," 69.

95. Wallace reports that Kish has created eighty-one more drawings inspired by each of *Moby-Dick*'s "Extracts." See Wallace, *Frank Stella's* Moby-Dick, 65.
96. Patrick Shea, *Call Me Ishmael: Music and Lyrics to Melville's* Moby-Dick (Lulu.com, 2012), 5, 36, 51. Shea abandoned his first plan, conceived in 2008, of writing a song *every* day when he realized that the novel's "chapter titles alone began to spark vocal melodies."

    Regarding the wide range of musical genres Shea used in writing his *Moby-Dick* songs, two clear influences are the Beatles and Morrissey. Other examples of pop, folk, or rock music inspired by Melville include Mastodon's album *Leviathan* (2004, including "I Am Ahab"); the German funeral doom metal band Ahab's albums *The Call of the Wretched Sea* (2004) and *The Divinity of Oceans* (2009); the UK Grindcore band's album *Moby Dick* (2013); and JoAnne Spies's combination of blues, jazz, and country on the album *Me & Melville* (2015), based on her one-woman show in 1997.
97. Shea, *Call Me Ishmael*, 75.
98. Shea, *Call Me Ishmael*, 29.
99. A few examples give a sense of the compilation's diverse range. The music for "The Counterpane" blends an infectious waltz beat with country-ballad vocal twang, tickling piano, and overabundance of rhyme. The result is an affectionate tribute that in its very cuteness normalizes the two men's bond. The lyrics of "The Crotch" show Shea's understanding of Ishmael's role as (disappearing) narrator:

    > I take my time . . .
    > To set the stage.
    > //And I will step aside.
    >
    > It's not the way
    > You're used to reading—
    > I'm aware of it.
    > Now let me step aside!
    > (Shea, *Call Me Ishmael*, 59–60)

    In many instances, the jaunty tenor of the music jars with the dark content for deliberately dramatic effect. Thus, Starbuck's dilemma of whether to shoot the sleeping Ahab in "The Musket" is composed as "a danceable moment of musical theatre, a moment of levity" before the first mate must make a decision. Shea, *Call Me Ishmael*, 118.
100. Shea, *Call Me Ishmael*, 124, 150.
101. Melville to Evert Duyckinck, March 3, 1849, in Herman Melville, *Correspondence*, vol. 14 of *The Writings of Herman Melville: The Northwestern-Newberry Edition*, ed. Harrison Hayford and others (Northwestern University Press and Newberry Library, 1968), 121; Cotkin, "A Note to Readers," in *Dive Deeper*, ix.
102. Cotkin, "A Note to Readers," in *Dive Deeper*, ix–x. For the full quote in which Duyckinck compared *Moby-Dick* to "intellectual chowder" in his review of the novel in *The Literary World* in November 1851, see note 9, chapter 2.

    Cotkin's essays exemplify the genre of "creative nonfiction." Other books working in this form and influenced by Melville include Nathaniel Philbrick's *In the Heart of the Sea: The Tragedy of the Whaleship* Essex (Viking, 1999); Dan Beachy-Quick's *A Whaler's Dictionary* (Milkweed Editions, 2008); Rebecca Giggs's *Fathoms: The World of the Whale* (Simon and Schuster, 2020); and Chris Bachelder and Jennifer Habel's autofiction *Dayswork* (Norton, 2023).

103. Cotkin, "A Note to Readers," in *Dive Deeper*, x.
104. Cotkin, *Dive Deeper*, 17–18. Cotkin follows this trail of linkages even further, noting that in 1856 the abolitionist publication *Frederick Douglass's Paper* cited *Moby-Dick* in an article titled "Horoscope." Here, the noted African American polymath James McCune Smith quoted the contradictory attitudes of third-mate Stubb to lament the inadequacies of white abolitionists in advancing the greater cause of "human brotherhood" (quoted in Cotkin, *Dive Deeper*, 18).
105. Cotkin, *Dive Deeper*, 51.
106. Cotkin, *Dive Deeper*, 124–26.
107. Trish Harris, "A Note from the Curator," in Tish Harris, curator, and Lissa Holloway-Attaway, dir., *Remaking* Moby-Dick (Lulu.com, 2013), 7.
108. Lissa Holloway-Attaway, "Project Director's Introduction," in Harris and Holloway-Attaway, *Remaking* Moby-Dick, 9, 11. As a digital scholar, Holloway-Attaway recognizes *Moby-Dick*'s "kinship to digital forms and media types that also defy formal generic traditions" (10).
109. Like the eighteen original video entries, most of the roughly fifty new videos are still images with accompanying soundtrack; more than two dozen chapters of *Moby-Dick* are still left unrepresented in *Remaking* Moby-Dick.
110. Jim Mezzanotte, "ishmael, new bedford, 2013," in *Remaking* Moby-Dick, cur. Harris and dir. Holloway-Attaway, 19.
111. A. J. Huffman, "I Am Classic," in *Remaking* Moby-Dick, cur. Harris and dir. Holloway-Attaway, 229.
112. Charlotte McGowan-Griffin, installation with sound by Peter Liljeqvist, cut paper, light source, looped video projection, exhibited spring 2009 at secondhome projects, Berlin. For this installation, see YouTube: https://www.youtube.com/watch?v=dZlz4-zYQPA&list=PL70mKKsVm1dSb7mHY9Ik_Jq39tkQfbr01&index=32.
113. Heather Wilson and Michael Dubrule, *Moby and Ahab Visit Toronto*; see this video on YouTube, https://www.youtube.com/watch?v=Ue-S8hRV5k8.
114. *Moby Richard: A Comical Remake*; see this video on YouTube, https://www.youtube.com/watch?v=KFM_IAz_QIs.

6. Perverse Melville and the Sub-Sub's Queer Investments

1. G[eorge] W[ashington] P[eck], review of *Omoo*, *American Whig Review* 6 (July 1847): 36–46, in "Reviews and Melville's Letters," in Herman Melville, *Moby-Dick: A Norton Critical Edition*, ed. Hershel Parker and Harrison Hayford (Norton, 2002), 489, 488.
2. Anonymous review of *Redburn*, *Blackwood's Edinburgh Magazine* 66 (November 1849): 567–80, in "Reviews and Melville's Letters," in Melville, *Moby-Dick*, ed. Parker and Hayford, 502; and John R. Thompson, review of *Pierre*, *Richmond Southern Literary Messenger*, September 1852, quoted in editors' "Historical Note" in Herman Melville, *Pierre; or the Ambiguities*, ed. G. Thomas Tanselle, Harrison Hayford, and Hershel Parker (Northwestern University Press and Newberry Library, 1971), 386.
3. See Unsigned, *Boston Post*, August 4, 1852; Evert A. Duyckinck, *New York Literary World* 290 (August 21, 1852): 118–20; Concord, *Congregational Journal*, August 25, 1852; *New York Albion* 11 (August 21, 1852): 405; and [George Washington Peck], *American*

Whig Review 16 (November 1852); all in *Herman Melville: The Contemporary Reviews*, ed. Brian Higgins and Hershel Parker (Cambridge University Press, 1995), 420, 421, 433, 437, and 446–54, respectively.

4. See unsigned review, *Graham's Magazine* 41 (October 1852): 445, and unsigned review, *Southern Literary Messenger* 18 (September 1852), in *Herman Melville*, ed. Higgins and Parker, 440–41 and 574–75.
5. The concept of the imp of the perverse has a long history in American literature, finding expression in the short fiction of Irving, Hawthorne, and Poe, with the latter writer explicitly theorizing this impulse in his short story "The Imp of the Perverse."
6. Melville, *Pierre*, ed. Tanselle et al., 181; subsequent page citations to *Pierre* are from this Newberry edition and included in parentheses in my text.
7. David Leverenz, *Manhood and the American Renaissance* (Cornell University Press, 1989), 296.
8. Modern editions further marginalize the Usher and the Sub-Sub Librarian by enclosing their histories within square brackets. More than parentheses, brackets as a typographical sign signal that the information they enclose is extraneous to the text proper.
9. Jennifer Doyle, *Sex Objects: Art and the Dialectics pf Desire* (University of Minnesota Press, 2006), 6.
10. For camp readings of Melville, see James Creech, *Closet Writing/Gay Reading in Melville's* Pierre (University of Chicago Press, 1993), 92–179; and Geoffrey Sanborn, *The Value of Herman Melville* (Cambridge University Press, 2018), 91–99.
11. Herman Melville, *Billy Budd, Sailor (An Inside Narrative)*, ed. Harrison Haywood and Merton Sealts Jr. (University of Chicago Press, 1962), 56.
12. Sigmund Freud, *The Three Essays on the Theory of Sexuality*, trans. and rev. James Strachey (1905; Basic, 1962), 2, 15, 28, 36.
13. Melville to Evert Duyckinck, February 12, 1851, in "Reviews and Melville's Letters," in Melville, *Moby-Dick*, ed. Parker and Hayford, 535; Freud, *Three Essays*, 37.
14. On Steelkit's secret, see J. F. Buckley, "Skirting the Phallus, Circumscribing the Community: Steelkit as Transvestic Rebel," *Melville Society Extracts* 104 (1996): 14–17.
15. Creech, *Closet Writing/Gay Reading in Melville's* Pierre, 59.
16. This wording appeared as copy for a first edition being sold on the AbeBooks website.
17. See Hershel Parker, introduction to Herman Melville, *Pierre or the Ambiguities, the Kraken Edition*, ed. Parker, illustrated by Maurice Sendak (HarperCollins, 1995), xi–xix, xxvii–xlii.
18. In an interview by Jacques Morice for the French cultural magazine *Télérama*, Carax reminisces about finding in Melville "un grand frère." See "Entretien avec Leo Carax, àpropos de la version télé de 'Pola X,'" *Télérama*, June 26, 2012, https://www.telerama.fr/cinema/entretien-avec-leos-carax-a-propos-de-la-version-tele-de-pola-x,83483.php. Richard Middleton-Kaplan reports Carax's feeling that *Pierre* is his "personal testament" in "Play It Again, Herman: Melville at the Movies," *Leviathan* 11, no. 3 (2009): 59–60.
19. Daniel Hoffman-Schwartz, introduction to *Handsomely Done: Aesthetics, Politics, and Media After Melville*, ed. Hoffman-Schwartz (Northwestern University Press, 2019), 3.
20. On the connection to Goddard, see Justin Vicari, "Colonial Fictions: *Le Petit Soldat* and Its Revisionist Sequel," *Jump Cut* 50 (2008), https://www.ejumpcut.org/archive/jc50.2008/PetitSoldatDenis/index.html.
21. "I always thought of Herman Melville as a brother." From the interview of Denis in Chris Darke, "'Desire Is Violence': Claire Denis on *Beau Travail*," *Sight and Sound*,

July 2000, https://www.bfi.org.uk/sight-and-sound/interviews/claire-denis-beau-travail-michel-subor-denis-lavant-gregoire-colin-french-foreign-legion-djibouti.

22. Melville to Sophia Hawthorne, January 8, 1852, in "Reviews and Melville's Letters," in Melville, *Moby-Dick*, ed. Parker and Hayford, 548.
23. Unsigned review, *Washington National Era*, August 19, 1852, in *Herman Melville*, ed. Higgins and Parker, 426.
24. The quotes are from the following reviews: Neill Matheson, "Review: Identifying (with) the Queerness of Melville's *Pierre*," *Diacritics* 27, no. 4 (1997): 30; Leland S. Person, review of *Closet Writing/Gay Reading, South Central Review* 13, no. 4 (1996): 54–55; and Thomas Dukes, review of *Closet Writing/Gay Reading, Modern Fiction Studies* 40, no. 4 (1994): 922.
25. Creech, *Closet Writing/Gay Reading in Melville's* Pierre, 185; subsequent page citations to this book are included parenthetically in my text.
26. More recent critics of sexuality tend to label the male–male eroticism rife in Melville as expressive of pre-gay-identarian modalities and affects. See Peter Coviello, *Tomorrow's Parties: Sex and the Untimely in Nineteenth-Century America* (New York University Press, 2013); Christopher Looby, "Strange Sensations: Sex and Aesthetics in 'The Counterpane,'" in *Melville and Aesthetics*, ed. Samuel Otter and Geoffrey Sanborn (Palgrave Macmillan, 2011), 65–84; and Natasha Hurley, *Circulating Queerness: Before the Gay and Lesbian Novel* (University of Minnesota Press, 2018).
27. Creech closely hews to Eve Kosofsky Sedgwick's formulation of the "epistemology of the closet," wherein such authors can "know" their nonnormative desires only as that which exists unspoken, hence "closeted"; had he been writing in the 2010s, he would probably have drawn on affect theory to support his claim for feeling as a legitimate interpretive tool. See Eve Kosofsky Sedgwick, *Epistemology of the Closet* (University of California Press, 1990).
28. Caleb Crain, review of *Closet Writing/Gay Reading, American Literature* 67, no. 3 (1995): 592.
29. Matheson, "Review," 30.
30. Crain, review of *Closet Writing/Gay Reading*, 593.
31. The actual portrait is a pastel, whereas the portrait in the novel is an oil. The "drawing room portrait" of Pierre's father that Mary Glendinning prefers echoes Ezra Ames's oil of Allan Melville (ca. 1820), housed in the Huntington Library and Art Gallery.
32. I suspect Creech overreaches here; the subject of this "gospel" is less specifically sexual than an attempt by Pierre to unveil *all* the social forces of repression creating lies and false appearances.
33. Matheson, "Review," 30, 38, 30, 33, and 34, emphases added.
34. Matheson, "Review," 40–41. The unraveling of coherent identity via characters that hardly seem characters in any realistic sense of the word is the "queerest" element of Melville's work, argues Michael D. Snediker in "Melville and Queerness Without Character," in *The New Cambridge Companion to Herman Melville*, ed. Robert S. Levine (Cambridge University Press, 2014), 155–68.
35. Matheson, "Review," 40.
36. John Bryant, "*Pierre* and *Pierre*: Editing and Illustrating Melville," *College English* 60, no. 3 (1998): 338.
37. Wendy Stallard Flory writes that Sendak's illustrations operate as "a point of departure for a powerful Melvillean . . . meditation on the artist's vulnerability in an environment of social and sexual hypocrisy—a meditation that also quietly memorializes the tragic losses of the arts community at the time of AIDS." Flory, "'The Diving and

Ducking Moralities': Sendak's Pierre, Blake, and the Vulnerabilities of the Artist," *Melville Society Extracts* 111 (1997): 17. In "Moby Dick, Creativity, and Other Wild Things," *Vassar Quarterly* 92, no. 4 (1996), Sendak expresses his "misery over the loss of gifted students and colleagues to AIDS" (12).

38. Jed Perl notes that Sendak "doesn't illustrate particular scenes so much as create a series of variations on *Pierre*'s darkening atmosphere." See Perl, "*Where the Wild Things Are*," *New Republic* (March 1996): 34.
39. Bryant, "*Pierre* and *Pierre*," 341.
40. Dana Seitler, "Melville, Sendak, *Pierre*, and *Pierre*," in "Melville's Queer Afterlives," ed. Adam Fales, Dana Seitler, and Jordan Alexander Stein, special issue, *Leviathan* 27, no. 3 (forthcoming).
41. Richard Kopley, "Sendak on Melville: An Interview," *Melville Society Extracts* 87 (1991): 1–2.
42. Kopley, "Sendak on Melville," 3.
43. Quoted in Elizabeth Schultz, "The Invisible Made Visible: Maurice Sendak's *Pierre* Illustrations," *Melville Society Extracts* 111 (1997): 5.
44. Flory, "'The Diving and Ducking Moralities,'" 9.
45. Perl, "*Where the Wild Things Are*," 30, 32.
46. Schultz, "The Invisible Made Visible," 6; Flory, "'The Diving and Ducking Moralities,'" 9–10.
47. Bryant, "*Pierre* and *Pierre*," 140.
48. Schultz, "The Invisible Made Visible," 9.
49. All the Sendak illustrations can be viewed in Maria Popova, "Maurice Sendak's Rare, Sensual Illustrations for Herman Melville's Greatest Commercial Failure and Most Personally Beloved Book," *The Marginalian*, August 21, 2014, https://www.themarginalian.org/2014/08/21/maurice-sendak-pierre-herman-melville/.
50. Flory also makes the analogy to *Romeo and Juliet* in "'The Diving and Ducking Moralities,'" 14.
51. Schultz, "The Invisible Made Visible," 19. I owe a great debt to Schultz for uncovering all these links.
52. John Taggart, "Mere Illustrations: Maurice Sendak and Melville," *Arizona Quarterly* 56, no. 2 (2000): 114.
53. "Pierre caressing Isabel's bare buttocks, with one of Pierre's fingers noticeably hidden from view. Whew," writes Daniel Zalewski in *Lingua Franca*, November–December 1995, 24, quoted in Schultz, "The Invisible Made Visible," 24.
54. Others remarking on this ambiguity include Flory, "'The Diving and Ducking Moralities,'" 15; Schultz, "The Invisible Made Visible," 19–20; Taggart, "Mere Illustrations," 124–25; and Bryant, "*Pierre* and *Pierre*," 240.
55. Schultz, "The Invisible Made Visible," 20, emphasis added.
56. Flory, "'The Diving and Ducking Moralities,'" 15–17.
57. Quote from Flory, "'The Diving and Ducking Moralities,'" 15.
58. Flory, "'The Diving and Ducking Moralities,'" 10; Schultz, "The Invisible Made Visible," 11. The narrator revealed earlier that Pierre possesses a copy of Flaxman's Dante.
59. Cramer K. Patron, review of *Pola X*, *Cramer K.*, website, December 6, 2022; no link remains online.
60. Chuck Stephens, review of *Pola X*, *Film Comment* 36, no. 5 (2000): 74, emphases added.
61. Middleton-Kaplan, "Play It Again, Herman," 59–60.
62. David Kehr, "A Poet of the Emotions Breaks His Silence," interview of Leos Carax, *New York Times*, June 27, 1999.

63. Middleton-Kaplan quotes this review, its author identified only as "Gargett," in "Play It Again, Herman," 61.
64. William L. Brown, "'Leos Carax Crazy': Postmodern Cinema Discovers *Pierre*," *Melville Society Extracts* 121 (2011): 14, 16.
65. I quote the English subtitles in the film.
66. Brown, "'Leos Carax Crazy,'" 15.
67. In Carax's retelling, at some point after Isabelle's mother dies, Isabelle's father takes the girl back to his Normandie estate. Isabelle tells Pierre that she remembers being happy at his birth. However, with her own child in the picture, Marie turns against Isabelle, falsely accusing her of attacking baby Pierre as an excuse to send her away. Learning this, Pierre comes to despise not only his father's deceit but also his mother's cruelty.
68. The relation between Isabelle and her shadowy companions is never explained; one assumes they are refugees from the same war-torn East European country. They symbolically seem younger versions of Isabelle.
69. Roger Ebert, online review of *Pola X*, October 6, 2000, http://www.rogerebert.com/reviews/pola-x-2000.
70. Stephen Holden, "Golden Boy Stalked by a Phantom," *New York Times*, October 6, 1999, https://archive.nytimes.com/www.nytimes.com/library/film/100599pola-film-review.html.
71. "I wanted to place it in an abandoned factory, to show it as a big chaotic brain. There is a moral in it; when you lie to people, you make them dangerous." Leos Carax to Morice, in "Entretien avec Leo Carax," my translation.
72. As Patron notes, "The film . . . jumps spasmodically from faerie tale to melodrama to concert documentary to Dostoevskian nightmare." Patron, review of *Pola X*.
73. Holden, "Golden Boy."
74. Scott Walker is an avant-garde composer who, like Melville and Carax, fell from commercial success to obscurity for decades but, like Carax, has maintained a strong cult following.
75. As opposed to Sendak and Creech's reading of *Pierre*, Carax's vision mutes the homoeroticism of Melville's text to only the faintest trace in the ambiguous relationship between Thibault and Pierre, who, joined with Lucie, were once "the three inseparables."
76. Doyle, *Sex Objects*, 1–3.
77. Holden, "Golden Boy."
78. Herman Melville, *Billy Budd, marin*, trans. Pierre Leyris (Gallimard, 1980).
79. Jonathan Rosenbaum, "*Beau Travail*," *Chicago Reader*, May 26, 2000, https://chicagoreader.com/arts-culture/beau-travail/.
80. Melville, *Billy Budd*, 72; subsequent page citations to *Billy Budd* are from the University of Chicago Press edition cited in note 1 and are included parenthetically in my text.
81. The title may also echo that of the Hollywood film *Beau Geste* (William A. Wellman, 1939) as a way of distinguishing itself from that film's uncritical, heroic colonialism.
82. Melville writes that Billy's ease with the other men causes Claggart's covertly watching eyes to "strangely suffus[e] . . . with feverish tears" and "a touch of soft yearning, as if Claggart could have loved Billy but for fate and ban" (88).
83. Rosenbaum, "*Beau Travail*."
84. Lawrence Ferber, "Foreign Legions: Alienation and Paranoia Drive Mesmerizing *Beau Travail*," *New York Blade* (2000).

85. The quotations are from Charles Taylor, "*Beau Travail*," *Salon.com*, March 30, 2000, https://www.salon.com/2000/03/31/beau_travail/.
86. These exercising sequences were choreographed by the professional ballet dancer Bernardo Montet. See Girish Shambu, "*Beau Travail*: A Cinema of Sensation," *Essays*, September 15, 2020, https://www.criterion.com/current/posts/7097-beau-travail-a-cinema-of-sensation.
87. "Fluid impressionism" from J. Hoberman, "A Piece of Work: 'Beau Travail' Replaces Narrative with Evocative Visuals and Narration," *Village Voice*, April 4, 2000.
88. See Vicari, "Colonial Fictions," on these links.
89. Hoberman, "A Piece of Work." In a further meta-Melvillean twist, Lavant plays Ahab in Phillippe Ramos's film *Captaine Achab* (2007), based on Melville's novel.
90. Denis draws in particular on the "O Heave! O Heave Away" chorus from the first act of Britten's opera. On the incorporation of Britten's music into the film's soundtrack, see Alex Ross, "Pushed to the Edge by 'Beau Travail,'" *The New Yorker*, October 20, 2020, https://www.newyorker.com/culture/cultural-comment/pushed-to-the-edge-by-beau-travail.
91. Translations of quotations from *Beau travail* come from the English subtitles.
92. Taylor, "*Beau Travail*."
93. Jonathan Rosenbaum notes that Denis uses these "outside" observers "as a kind of mainly mute Greek chorus," who "subtly impose an ironic frame around the story." Rosenbaum, "*Beau Travail*."
94. Taylor, "*Beau Travail*"; Rosenbaum, "*Beau Travail*."
95. See Peter Brooks, *Reading for the Plot: Design and Intention in Narrative* (Knopf, 1984).
96. Vicari, "Colonial Fictions."
97. Elena Del Rio also notes the film's use of "highly incongruous continuities [that are] . . . 'impossible' from a rational or realistic standpoint." Del Rio, "Performing the Narrative of Seduction: Claire Denis' *Beau Travail* (*Good Work*, 1999)," *Kinoeye* 3, no. 7 (June 9, 2003), http://www.kinoeye.org/03/07/delrio07.php.
98. Vicari, "Colonial Fictions."
99. Brianna Beehler, "*Beau Travail*: The Retrospective Narrator and Redemption," unpublished paper, 7. I am grateful to Beehler for these insights.
100. Rosenbaum, "*Beau Travail*"; Beehler, "*Beau Travail*," 8.
101. Beehler, "*Beau Travail*," 3–4.
102. Taylor, "*Beau Travail*." The effect is comparable to the graphic lovemaking scene in *Pola X*: Both moments "push through" or break cinematic expectations of the medium—and in Galoup's case shatter everything that has previously constituted his superego.
103. Denis explains that in an early draft the scene of Galoup contemplating suicide was placed after the nightclub scene. But in editing she decided to reverse the order "because I wanted to give the sense that Galoup could escape himself." Darke, "'Desire Is Violence.'"
104. "Fits and stops" from Del Rio, "Performing the Narrative of Seduction."
105. Vicari, "Colonial Fictions."
106. Del Rio, "Performing the Narrative of Seduction." Some viewers tend to read the scene as a moment of sexual coming-out, but this reading oversimplifies Galoup's sexual conflicts. I agree with Vicari, who notes that as a "site of fantasy" such a space cannot be the locus of a "true *public* liberation." See Vicari, "Colonial Fictions."
107. Taylor, "*Beau Travail*."
108. Del Rio, "Performing the Narrative of Seduction."
109. Taylor, "*Beau Travail*."

7. Plastic Seas, Pasteboard Masks, Planetary Futures

1. Patricia Yaeger, "Sea Trash, Dark Pools, and the Tragedy of the Commons," *PMLA* 125, no. 3 (2010): 524–30. On oceanic studies, see Hester Blum, "Melville and Oceanic Studies," in *The New Cambridge Companion to Herman Melville*, ed. Robert S. Levine (Cambridge University Press, 2014), 22–36; on Melville's transgression of the human–nonhuman binary, see Geoffrey Sanborn, "Melville and the Nonhuman World," in *The New Cambridge Companion to Herman Melville*, ed. Levine, 10–21.
2. Garrett Hardin, "The Tragedy of the Commons," *Science* 162 (December 1968): 1243–48.
3. Yaeger, "Sea Trash," 525, 527.
4. Brady Krein, "Melville's Novel Mechanisms: Charting Anthropocene Systems in *Moby-Dick*," *ISLE: Interdisciplinary Studies in Literature and Environment* 28, no. 4 (2020): 1475.
5. Krein, "Melville's Novel Mechanisms," 1462–64. Jeffrey Insko intriguingly contrasts the (depletive) extraction of energy sources from the earth and Melville's practice of literary extraction, exemplified in the "Extracts" section, which are "leaky," generative, and renewable. See Insko, "Resource Extraction and Melville's Extracts," *Leviathan* 25, no. 1 (2023): 78–87.
6. Devin Griffiths, "Or, the Whale," unpublished essay, 9; see also Krein, "Melville's Novel Mechanisms," 1468. I am grateful to Griffiths for sharing his work in progress.
7. Krein, "Melville's Novel Mechanisms," 1478; Kathleen Rooney, "No Firm Fortress No Retreat: Reading, and Mourning, 'Moby-Dick' on the Cusp of Climate Catastrophe," *Los Angeles Review of Books*, August 1, 2019, https://lareviewofbooks.org/article/no-firm-fortress-no-retreat-reading-and-mourning-moby-dick-on-the-cusp-of-climate-catastrophe/.
8. Insko, "Resource Extraction and Melville's Extracts," 78, citing Jamie L. Jones's use of the term *fossil modernity* in *Rendered Obsolete: Energy Culture and the Afterlife of U.S. Commercial Whaling in the Fossil Fuel Age* (University of North Carolina Press, 2023).
9. See Clea Simon, "Sing Me Ishmael," *Harvard Gazette*, November 27, 2019, https://news.harvard.edu/gazette/story/2019/11/dave-malloy-takes-on-melvilles-classic-novel.
10. Tsang omits the hyphen between "Moby" and "Dick" in her film's title, so I follow her lead.
11. ACCOBAMS refers to the Agreement on the Conservation of Cetaceans of the Black Sea, Mediterranean Sea, and Contiguous Atlantic Area, which was signed by twenty-nine states. For more on the agreement and its signers, see the ACCOBAMS website at https://accobams.org/about/introduction/ and https://accobams.org/about/parties-and-range-states/.
12. For this exhibition, see Ruiz's website at https://mobydicksite.com/moby-dick-the-dream-of-captain-ahab/. See also the IUCN/ACCOBAMS promotional description at https://www.iucn.org/news/mediterr%C3%A1neo/201806/m%C3%A1laga-celebrates-world-oceans-day-launch-first-large-scale-study-mediterranean-cetaceans.
13. For an image of this artwork, see Sances's website at https://josart.net/ or https://whalemural.com/.
14. "A Whale of an Art Talk: Jos Sances and Elizabeth Schultz," Lawrence Arts Center, September 25, 2000, YouTube, https://www.youtube.com/watch?v=MvdVUzKJNpA.
15. "A Whale of an Art Talk."
16. "A Whale of an Art Talk."

17. This quotation as well as the epigraph from Volpe come from email correspondence with the artist, April 3, 2023, and Volpe's website, https://www.christophervolpe.com /loomings.
18. "Loomings," Volpe website.
19. "Loomings," Volpe website.
20. Donovan Hohn, *Moby-Duck* (Penguin, 2011), 165; subsequent page citations to this work are included in parentheses in my text.
21. Miles Harvey agrees: "Hohn takes us on a journey almost as epic as *Moby-Dick*. Call me impressed." Quoted in the front-matter blurbs in *Moby-Duck*.
22. Bill Marvel, review of *Moby-Duck*, *Dallas Morning News*, quoted on the *Moby-Duck* page of Hohn's website, https://www.donovanhohn.com/moby-duck.
23. Despite the phrase *rubber duckie*, popularized by the *Sesame Street* song, the toy is plastic.
24. The *Sesame Street* hit "Rubber Duckie" (1999) illustrates the cultural fantasy equating childhood and "clean" innocence: "Rubber duckie you're the one / You make bath time lots of fun / Rubber duckie I'm awfully fond of you."
25. Nick Pinkerton, "*Leviathan* Review: A Wet and Wild Documentary Like Nothing You've Ever Seen (or Felt)," British Film Institute, 2013, updated January 30, 2020, https://www2.bfi.org.uk/news-opinion/sight-sound-magazine/reviews -recommendations/film-week-leviathan.
26. Peter Bradshaw, "*Leviathan*—Review," *The Guardian*, November 28, 2013, https://www .theguardian.com/film/2013/nov/28/leviathan-film-review.
27. Bradshaw, "*Leviathan*—Review."
28. Hila Peleg, "Véréna Paravel and Lucien Castaing-Taylor," excerpt from *documenta 14: Daybook*, n.d., posted in Public Exhibition, n.d., https://www.documenta14.de/en /artists/13709/verena-paravel-and-lucien-castaing-taylor, accessed July 15, 2025.
29. Jane Bennett, *Vibrant Matter: A Political Ecology of Things* (Duke University Press, 2010), 32. See also Yaeger, "Sea Trash," 539.
30. Gia Kourla, "A Choreographer Diving Into Grief Looks to Whales," *New York Times*, April 14, 2021, https://www.nytimes.com/2021/04/14/arts/dance/mayfield-brooks -whale-fall.html.
31. I know of only one other dance performance inspired by *Moby-Dick*, Matthew Crumbie and Tom Truss's *Rewritten* (2013), billed as "an intergenerational queer love story" that "weaves together dance, music, visual art, projection, and text." See Crumbie's website at https://matthewcumbie.com/rewritten/.
32. For this description, see "Improvising While Black," mayfield brooks, website, https:// www.improvisingwhileblack.com/about.
33. Griffiths, "Or, the Whale," 23, 22, 22–23. Griffiths also explains how the beneficial function of the "carbon sink" created by whale falls is complemented by the living whale's function as a "major nutrient 'pump' that draws minerals from deeper waters up to the photonic zone where it is released in their feces and gobbled up by photosynthetic plankton, which then multiply exponentially, photosynthetically capturing atmospheric carbon before sinking to the sea floor" (23–24). A reduction in the ocean's whale population thus directly affects atmospheric change in both directions.
34. Kourla, "A Choreographer Diving Into Grief Looks to Whales."
35. See Justine M. Bakker, "Blue Black Ecstasy: Ellen Gallagher's Watery Ecstatic, Oceanic Feeling, and Mysticism in the Flesh," *Journal of the American Academy of Religion* 91 (2023): 314. Bakker's analysis of the artist Ellen Gallagher's representation of underwater hybrids draws on the emergence of "blue humanities" (focusing on the

"ocean's alterity as a radically different space" [319–20]) and Fred Moten's conception of the oceanic "undercommons" as a mystical space where Blackness exists as a force beyond imposed categories and in relationships of sociality, resisting the "social death posited by Afro-pessimism" (312–14). The ecological imperatives driving Yaeger's analysis of the ocean as a public "commons" (Yaeger, "Sea Trash") thus parallel critical race theory's positing of an oceanic "undercommons" where blue and Black intermingle.

36. Griffiths, "Or, the Whale," 14.
37. Kourla, "A Choreographer Diving Into Grief Looks to Whales."
38. Melville to Evert Duyckinck, March 3, 1849, in Herman Melville, *The Letters of Herman Melville*, ed. Merrell R. Davis and William H. Gilman (Yale University Press, 1960), 78.
39. Kourla, "A Choreographer Diving Into Grief Looks to Whales."
40. See "mayfield brooks: *Whale Fall II*, June 12–20, 2021," Artist's Note, Center for Performance Research, n.d., https://www.cprnyc.org/mayfieldbrooksartistsnote, accessed July 16, 2025.
41. Tsang emphasizes the importance of collaboration in the creation of her installations, especially the ones with Moved by the Motion. She echoes the sentiments of many other participants in the Melville effect, for whom singular authorship or individual renown is secondary to the act of creation and community. See Ashley Tyner, "Wu Tsang on Reclaiming Moby Dick," *i-D Magazine*, January 13, 2023, https://i-d.co/article/wu-tsang-on-reclaiming-moby-dick/.
42. Thomas Rogers, "An Artist's Queer Take on 'Moby-Dick,'" *New York Times*, February 20, 2023, https://www.nytimes.com/2023/02/20/arts/wu-tsang-moby-dick.html.
43. Rogers, "An Artist's Queer Take on 'Moby-Dick.'" Cecilia Aleman, a Venice Biennale curator, comments on Tsang's definition of her practice as "betweenness" in "VIVE Arts / Behind the Scenes," July 28, 2022, YouTube, https://www.youtube.com/watch?v=BjfZ6dijFHM. Tsang explains that Moved by the Motion thrives "in th[e] nonverbal space of affect or imagery: how to create a feeling or an atmosphere that people can experience when we don't share a common language." This focus on sensory reception echoes Castaing-Taylor and Paravel's immersive approach to ethnographic filmmaking and mayfield brook's emphasis on improvisation. See Wu Tsang and Sophia Al-Maria, "*Moby Dick; or, The Whale*: The Little Lower Layers," conversation, included in the promotional materials for *Moby Dick; or, The Whale* on The Shed website, posted April 11, 2022, https://www.theshed.org/program/in-the-works/307-the-little-lower-layers.
44. Elizabeth Fullerton, "Wu Tsang—Interview: 'I'm Drawn to Stories That Have Messy Politics,'" *Studio International*, October 3, 2023, https://www.studiointernational.com/index.php/wu-tsang-video-interview-of-whales-moby-dick-or-the-whale-thyssen-bornemisza-madrid; Osman Can Yerebakan, "Artist Wu Tsang Dives Into the Depths of 'Moby Dick' with Three Simultaneous Shows About Melville's 'Flamboyant, Queer' Saga," *Artnet News*, April 28, 2022, https://news.artnet.com/art-world/wu-tsang-moby-dick-2104448.
45. Tsang and Al-Maria, "*Moby Dick*," conversation.
46. Tyner, "Wu Tsang on Reclaiming *Moby Dick*."
47. Tyner, "Wu Tsang on Reclaiming *Moby Dick*."
48. Tsang quoted in Noam Segal, "Stepping Towards Something Like an Experience: The Wu Tsang's *Moby Dick*," *Flash Art*, June 28, 2022, https://flash---art.com/article/wu-tsang/.

49. Tyner, "Wu Tsang on Reclaiming *Moby Dick*."
50. Tyner, "Wu Tsang on Reclaiming *Moby Dick*."
51. Yerebakan, "Artist Wu Tsang Dives Into the Depths of 'Moby Dick' "; Fullerton, "Wu Tsang—Interview."
52. Tavia Nyong'o, "Wu Tsang's White Whale(s)," *Them*, May 27, 2022, https://www.them.us/story/wu-tsang-moby-dick-films-interview.
53. Tyner, "Wu Tsang on Reclaiming *Moby Dick*."
54. Robert Barry, "*Moby-Dick*: A Queer Romance," *ArtReview*, April 26, 2023, https://artreview.com/wu-tsang-of-whales-thyssen-bornemisza-museo-nacional-madrid-moby-dick-review/.
55. Fullerton, "Wu Tsang—Interview."
56. "The campy overacting of the crew—which today takes on a queer valence—harks back to early American silent film, when overdoing it was a means of emoting sans sound," writes Cassie Packard in "The Terrors of Whiteness in Wu Tsang's *Moby Dick*," *Hyperallergic*, May 8, 2022, https://hyperallergic.com/728800/the-terrors-of-whiteness-in-wu-tsangs-moby-dick/.
57. Travis Diehl, "Dark Tide: Wu Tsang Trains Her Sights on *Moby Dick*," *Art Forum*, April 15, 2022, https://www.artforum.com/columns/wu-tsang-trains-her-sights-on-moby-dick-251747/.
58. Barry, "*Moby-Dick*."
59. Duncan Stuart, "On Not Reading Herman Melville; or, Wu Tsang's *The Whale*," *Exit Only*, February 5, 2023, https://exitonly.substack.com/p/on-not-reading-herman-melville-or.
60. See Fred Moten, "Blackness and Nothingness (Mysticism in the Flesh)," *South Atlantic Quarterly* 112, no. 4 (2013): 737–80; and Fred Moten and Stefano Harney, *The Undercommons: Fugitive Planning and Black Studies* (Minor Compositions, 2013).
61. Packard emphasizes the film as a portrait of ecocide "caused by the extractive ideology of whiteness." Packard, "The Terrors of Whiteness."
62. Diehl, "Dark Tide."
63. Insko, "Resource Extraction and Melville's Extracts," 86.
64. Daniel Hoffman-Schwartz, introduction to *Handsomely Done: Aesthetics, Politics, and Media After Melville*, ed. Hoffman-Schwartz (Northwestern University Press, 2019), 5.

INDEX